The Government and Politics of Ireland

BASIL CHUBB

The Government and Politics of
IRELAND

SECOND EDITION

Stanford University Press, Stanford, California 1982

Stanford University Press
Stanford, California
© 1970, 1982 by the Board of Trustees of the
Leland Stanford Junior University
Printed in the United States of America
ISBN 0-8047-1115-1
LC 81-50785

Preface to the Second Edition

I have completely rewritten this book for the second edition. There are two reasons for this. First, more than ten years have passed since the first edition was published. As I was writing that edition, big changes in Irish life and society were in train and they continued at an increasing pace. The country has altered more in the last fifteen years than it did during the whole of the previous half-century. Second, since I wrote at the end of the 1960s, a considerable volume of work on some aspects of Irish politics has been published. I cannot complain, as I did in the preface to the first edition, that there is little research work on which to draw.

On many topics, however, I have, as previously, been obliged to rely heavily on personal enquiries directed to the practitioners. I am once again indebted to far more people than I can mention here. Scores of people have answered queries with information and explanations. They include politicians, public servants, party officials, officers of many organizations, journalists, broadcasters, the executives of market research firms, and academic colleagues. If I mention a few by name, it is because I have bothered them more than most of my other contacts. I am particularly grateful to John Meagher, Chairman and Managing Director of Irish Marketing Surveys Ltd., Tony Fahey of Radio Telefís Éireann's Audience Research Department, and Seamus Gaffney, Secretary of the Department of the Public Service.

For the second time round, my colleague Dr. John Whyte of the Queen's University, Belfast, read the manuscript and offered comments and suggestions, and I thank him. I acknowledge gratefully also the assistance of Gillian McGarry, Geraldine O'Dea, and Carol O'Sullivan, all of whom worked with me at some time or another during the preparation of this edition.

The substance of some parts of Chapters 3, 9, and 10 has appeared in my *Cabinet Government in Ireland* (Dublin, 1974) and *The Constitution and Constitutional Change in Ireland* (Dublin, 1978). I thank the Institute of Public Administration for permission to reuse the material. Likewise, material in parts of Chapter 6 is derived from my contribution to *Political Parties in the European Community* (London, 1979). I thank the Policy Studies Institute and George Allen and Unwin Ltd. for agreeing to this.

B.C.

Contents

Contents

Appendixes

Tables

5. Patterns of Participation and Representation

6. Political Parties

Figures

Glossary of Irish Terms

Some, but by no means all, Irish political institutions are commonly called by their Irish names. For the convenience of non-Irish readers, a list of such terms used frequently in this book is given here.

Bunreacht na hÉireann. The Constitution of Ireland. This term is usually applied only to the Constitution enacted in 1937 and still in force.

Dáil (full title, *Dáil Éireann*). Chamber of Deputies. The popularly elected legislative assembly.

Éire. Ireland. Article 4 of Bunreacht na hÉireann says that the name of the state is "Éire, or in the English language, *Ireland.*" The name Éire is often used outside Ireland to denote the present state, which extends *de facto* over part, though the largest part, of the island of Ireland.

Fianna Fáil (literally Soldiers of Destiny). The title of the largest party, founded by Eamon de Valera in 1926.

Fine Gael (literally Tribe of the Gaels). The successor of Cumann na nGaedheal (literally League of Gaels), the pro-Treaty party. At present the second largest party.

Gaeltacht (plural, *Gaeltachtaí*). Irish-speaking areas. Most of these are situated on the Western seaboard, in Donegal, Mayo, Galway, and Kerry.

Garda Síochána. The Civic Guards, Police.

Oireachtas. Parliament.

Seanad (full title, *Seanad Éireann*). Senate.

Sinn Féin (literally We Ourselves). Originally a nationalist political movement founded by Arthur Griffith in 1905. In 1917 a number of separatist groups coalesced under the title of Sinn Féin, pledged to the achievement of an independent republic. The movement split over the terms of the Treaty with the United Kingdom (December 1921). Organizations calling themselves Sinn Féin have existed ever since.

Taoiseach (plural, *Taoisigh*). Prime Minister.

Teachta Dála (plural, *Teachtaí*). Deputy (literally messenger or delegate to the Dáil). Abbreviated to TD.

PART I

THE CONTEXT OF POLITICS

ONE

Basic Influences

The state with which this book is concerned is in the words of its Constitution called "Éire, or in the English language, *Ireland*."[1] We shall call it "Ireland" and its people "Irish." However, Ireland, the state, does not extend over the whole island of Ireland, nor does it include everyone who calls himself or herself Irish or everyone who might be reckoned to be Irish. Both inside the state and especially outside, it is often called by other names—Éire, the Republic of Ireland, the Irish Republic. In this book, whenever the use of "Ireland" would be ambiguous or confusing, the term "Republic of Ireland" will be used.

II

The Irish are a not very numerous, mainly rural people. They are, too, a peripheral people, living as they do on the fringe of the British Isles, which, in turn, is on the edge of Europe. The population of the Republic of Ireland in 1979 was 3.4 million. Almost 95 per cent were Roman Catholic and all but a tiny minority were ordinarily English speaking. After well over a century of continuous decline—in 1841, 6.5 million people lived in the area now known as the Republic—the population, then below 3 million, began slowly to increase. (For detailed demographic, social, and economic statistics, see Appendix A.)

This population, which is small for a sovereign state, is largely rural and thinly spread. With 47 people per square kilometer, Ireland is the least densely populated of the countries of the European Communities. Only in the late 1960s did the number of people living in "towns" (defined as places with a population of 1,500 or more) rise above that living in rural areas. Outside Dublin City and County and the southern region (Cork, Waterford, Limerick, and South Tipperary), the population is overwhelmingly rural. Fifty years ago, nearly 70 per cent, and as lately as thirty years ago, 60 per cent, lived in rural areas. Many people who today are counted as urban were born and reared as country people, and many more have country-bred parents. Dublin and environs, with 1 million people (about 30 per cent of the population), is the only large conurbation. Cork, the second largest city, has about 140,000 inhabitants; the other towns are mostly small regional centres serving and attuned to the farming people of their hinterlands.

The proportion of the work force engaged in agriculture, a little over 20 per cent, is the highest of the countries of the European Communities. But only thirty years ago it was 50 per cent, for Ireland has only recently begun to move quite quickly towards being an industrialized country with appropriate industrial and service sectors. Even today, half of the work force of the western region (Galway and Mayo) is in agriculture. The land reforms initiated by British governments in the late nineteenth century and completed in the first decade of independence effected a rural revolution and quickly produced a class of owner-occupiers of small farms who came to dominate Irish politics. The small family farm predominates: almost 70 per cent of farms are of less than 50 acres. Most are worked by the owner-occupier—that is, the farmer—with the help of his family. Thus, the picture presented to the traveller in the Irish countryside is overwhelmingly of scattered, small farms.

The combination of a comparatively low level of industrialization and a farming sector largely comprised of small family farms is a recipe for low material wealth, at least by the standards of the most industrialized countries, and for emigration. Gross domestic product per head in 1978 was U.S. $3,780. Although this put Ireland among the rich countries of the world with a highly literate population enjoying high standards of social services, it was, nevertheless, the lowest in the European Communities. In 1980, it was less than 40 per cent that of Germany, the richest member; one-half that of the Communities as a whole; and 58 per cent that of the neighbouring United Kingdom. Economic growth, at 3.1 per cent per year between 1968 and 1978, was fractionally above the average for the European Communities as a whole. At that rate and in the absence of positive Community policies to redress the differences between the members, Ireland's position relative to her neighbours is not likely to alter materially in the near future. Emigration, both a social safety valve and a debilitating haemorrhage, was for a century and a half a feature of Irish life. Fluctuating between 5 and 15 per 1,000 of population from independence to the mid-1960s, it was not only halted but reversed— perhaps not for all time—by the rapidly rising level of domestic prosperity of the 1960s.

III

Identification of the basic political attitudes of a community is largely a matter either of impressionistic generalization or of drawing inferences from survey data. What is perceived or adduced can often be explained only by reference to the past, for contemporary perceptions, beliefs, and attitudes are inevitably to some extent the product of the conditions and events of the past. They are moreover changing continuously, sometimes slowly as in Ireland between independence and the early 1960s; at other times more rapidly, as in the 1960s and 1970s, when the pace of social and economic change was unprecedented.

Again, these generalizations can often be little more than statements about "most people," for even in a comparatively homogeneous community like that in the Republic, there exist groups, such as the tiny Protestant minority, that have an outlook that is to some extent different from the outlook of the majority. Of more political significance, the attitudes and values of town people are likely to be different in some respects from those of rural people. If, as is the case in Ireland, there is a continuous movement from the countryside to the town, there will be urban dwellers who are but slowly becoming town people: perhaps they never will be, though their children probably will. Even to talk of an urban culture and a rural culture is misleading if doing so suggests that everyone can be placed in one or the other of two identifiable groups, for this is to ignore the stance of great numbers of people who are in-between. What is possible, though, is to identify the cultural influences that have contributed, or are contributing, to the production of the Irish citizen and to suggest their political effects in general terms.

The British influence. Geography and history combine to make the British influence the most important in determining the pattern of much of Irish political thought and practice. This is a simple matter of the geographical propinquity of a large national group and a small one, and the historical facts of political dominion, social and economic domination, and cultural blanketing. Ireland, like Scotland and Wales, became an English province, her politics and her economic and cultural life dominated by, and oriented to, England.

The process of assimilation was aided both by the settlement in Ireland of people of English and Scottish origins who were Protestants and by the emergence of an elite class whose members gave loyalty to Britain, in many cases their place of recent origin and in all cases the guarantor of their political and economic power. The "plantations"—that is, the placing of English and Scottish families as farmers in Ireland—in the sixteenth and seventeenth centuries and the Irish wars of the seventeenth century resulted in massive transfers of property. In 1641, nearly 60 per cent of Irish land was owned by Catholics; by 1703, only 14 per cent. The province, for that was what Ireland was, particularly after the Act of Union (1800), was dominated by a Protestant landowning class until the late nineteenth century. If this class and the better-off Catholics who identified with them had specific Irish interests, they were nevertheless essentially provincials, London being their metropolis as it was for the Welsh and the Scots. The nineteenth century, moreover, saw the rise of the English-dominated, London-centred "United Kingdom of Great Britain and Ireland" to the status of a world imperial power, engendering in its people and particularly its English ruling class the belief that their values and habits were in all respects excellent. Lesser breeds, among whom they included the Irish, could by espousing them hope to tread the same path of progress.

Inevitably, in these circumstances, Irish people acquired much of the culture, including much of the political culture, of the British and more particularly of the English. The substitution of the English language for Irish was especially important. During the seventeenth and eighteenth centuries the number of people speaking Irish declined very rapidly. By 1851, less than 30 per cent of the population could speak it; by 1871, less than 20 per cent. Although significant (but diminishing) numbers in the west continued to speak Irish, in Dublin and the east, which dominated social and economic life, only 5 per cent or less could speak it from the middle of the nineteenth century. The process of absorption of English ways and values was most complete in Dublin, the bigger towns, and the east of the country generally. In addition, Ireland enjoyed, and came to expect, standards of public services, including education, health, and welfare services, comparable in general with those of Great Britain.

As in the case of the white communities of the British Commonwealth, many of the currently held political traditions and values were inculcated and absorbed during a most critical and formative period: the period of the advent of mass democracy. Extensions of the franchise in Britain were followed by extensions, with modifications, in Ireland; and Irish people acquired democratic habits and values. Political ideas were almost wholly expressed in British categories, for, from Daniel O'Connell to Charles Stuart Parnell and beyond, the political experience of many Irish leaders was gained in British political life, and they practised the parliamentary ways of Westminster. However, Ireland, geographically and in other ways more peripheral than Wales or Scotland, was never integrated to the extent they were, because of the survival in greater measure of a preindustrial rural society and the centrifugal pull of national feeling and consequent nationalism made stronger by religious differences. Yet even Irish nationalism itself was "a revolution within and against a democracy and could not help using many of that system's institutions and procedures."[2]

There is no better way to illustrate Irish acceptance of democratic values and British forms than by the history of the independence movement and the formation and consolidation of the new state. Although, with the founding of Sinn Féin in 1905, Irish nationalism turned away from parliamentary methods, the parliamentary tradition and the belief in the legitimacy of a democratically elected assembly can be seen to have been strongly ingrained in both the leaders and the majority of the population. By 1916, in Brian Farrell's words, "modern Ireland already existed . . . ; most of its political values—as well as its political structures—were not merely modern but were articulated in a distinctively British way."[3] The revolutionary Dáil of 1919, legitimized by election, continued in being as a parliamentary assembly through revolution and war. If it did not in fact control the situation, nevertheless it claimed the right to do so, and those who sustained it recognized its importance in the eyes of a people, many of whom had imbibed liberal-democratic values. Farrell concluded from his study of its origins and record that it was "as intent on maintaining the framework of an established society and its associated values as with attempting to change it."[4]

The general acceptance of the most important norms of democracy is well shown by the widespread recognition of the duly elected government in 1922 despite its rejection by Eamon de Valera and his supporters, by the rapid acceptance of this group when they abandoned force (which was getting them nowhere) for constitutional and parliamentary methods, and, finally, by their transformation into a majority government at the election of 1932. Frank Munger has cogently argued that the events of that year were as fateful for democracy in Ireland as were those of a decade earlier: "The government that had defeated de Valera in the field permitted him to triumph through the ballot. From our present acquaintance with political processes in new nations, we know how strange these events are. What seemed to the Irish natural, normal, even inevitable, has occurred in few other places."[5]

Political independence did not automatically bring economic or cultural independence. The Irish economy was not a balanced and viable whole, the less so because of the retention by the United Kingdom of the northeastern part of the island, which included Belfast, the only industrial city. Agriculture, insofar as it was market oriented, was wholly geared to British needs. Banking, insurance, industry, and trade were largely British dominated and almost wholly British oriented and only slowly became centred upon Dublin. Britain was, and still is, Ireland's biggest customer and her main supplier. As recently as 1968, 70 per cent of Irish exports went there. Only in the last decade, and particularly since Ireland's accession to the European Communities, has this pattern begun to change quickly.

The boundaries of the Irish state were from the beginning highly permeable. People and ideas have always passed freely across them. The newly independent Irish Free State, as it was called, was a member of the British Commonwealth and as such its citizens were not classed as aliens in the United Kingdom or in Commonwealth countries. Even when, later, Ireland left the Commonwealth, this situation was not altered. Passports have never been necessary to travel in either direction, and citizens of each country can settle in the other without any formalities whatsoever. Much of Irish emigration was always to Great Britain; today there might be as many as 800,000 persons living in Great Britain who were born in the Republic. These and their families, together with seasonal and short-term migrants, have always moved freely between the two countries on a large scale, the larger recently as growing affluence has increased their propensity to take holidays "at home." Although Ireland has a full range of home-produced newspapers and its own radio and television services, British newspapers and magazines circulate freely; British radio transmissions can be received throughout the country; British television is available to people in the north and east of the country (nearly half of Irish television sets can receive it); and most of the books read in the country are published in Great Britain.

Britain not only influenced the Irish, it also insulated them. In the words of Jean Blanchard, "L'Irlande est une île derrière une île."[6] Little of continental European thought or experience was directly tapped or assimilated by the Irish. Knowledge of continental European languages has always been very poor by the standards of most Western European countries. Because of the irredentist obsession of political leaders with the problem of the six northern counties still in the United Kingdom and consequent neutrality in and after the Second World War, Ireland was cut off to a considerable degree from the mainstream of Western European life from independence until the 1960s. Only the prospect of membership in the European Communities, and its actuality ten years later, led to slowly widening horizons as the Irish government and Irish business and agricultural organizations began to operate in a broader context than before. An increase in foreign travel had the same effect and, reflecting all this, the media expanded their coverage.

The influence of Britain upon Irish politics has been pervasive. The British legacy to the new state was enormous, as we shall see throughout this book. The constitutional forms adopted were those of British parliamentary democracy: the governmental system was based on the Westminster model; the administrative system, on the Whitehall model. The main lines of many public services had been laid down under the aegis of the British government and parliament in the formative period of the welfare state in the late nineteenth and early twentieth centuries. These services continued barely touched by the takeover by a native government and parliament. Because of this and because the country had comparable educational standards and a full-fledged civil service on British lines, it was not only wholly equipped for statehood but could embark on it with no break at all in continuity.

That the political institutions then established and the services then taken over continued largely unaltered in basic design was due, first, to the conservatism of the community and its leaders; second, to the continued cultural impact of British contacts at almost as high a frequency as hitherto; and, third, to a long-continuing ignorance of the experience of other countries. Ireland settled down politically independent but, like the white Commonwealth countries, with institutions closely modelled upon those of the imperial power from which its freedom had been won. Only recently have the horizons of politicians and administrators been extended to other European countries.

Nationalism. Since the British influence was so great, it may well be asked: why did not Ireland settle down politically as a British province? The answer lies in the fact that it was more peripheral to England than were Wales and Scotland and, notwithstanding considerable cultural penetration, was less assimilated. The preservation of a separate identity was greater because the religion of the masses continued to be Roman Catholicism and because a preindustrial society persisted in rural areas, particularly in the west. In time, nationalist feeling evolved, asserted itself, and grew stronger: "Irish nationalism, as it took organized mass political form in the last quarter of the nineteenth century, had its core of support in that part of the Irish population which was isolated by all these divisions: the Gaelic, Catholic, agrarian, peasant community which was the largest element in Irish society outside of eastern Ulster."[7] The state itself owes its existence to the successful outcome of a typical nationalist movement for independence.

When a national movement succeeds, people are very self-conscious about their statehood, however passive many of them may have been before. If the state is small and weak, anxiety about its continued existence and integrity is inevitably reflected in a heightened self-consciousness. Until quite recently, memories of the struggle for independence and the myths of Irish nationalism were continually revived by political leaders who, having won power by evoking nationalist feeling, naturally continued to exploit it. The "revolution" that they had desired to make involved only a transfer of power and not great socioeconomic reforms.

In the Irish case, also, the emergence of the Irish Free State was not the end of the matter. Some national issues were still unresolved. Nationalist feeling remained high because the break with Great Britain was not complete. The new state had Commonwealth status, but for some people this was not sufficient. For the majority, the fact that the country was partitioned and the state did not extend over the whole island of Ireland meant that the job had not been finished. Irish nationalism continued in the form of a typical irredentist movement, doomed to sterile frustration because the true nature of the Northern Ireland problem—arising from the fact that the majority of the unredeemed did not see themselves as such—was simply not recognized, running counter as it did to one of the strongest of its myths, namely, that the people of the island are one people.

For forty years from independence the manifestations of nationalism altered very little. Constitutional issues and the problem of "the border" never ceased to obsess political leaders, who assiduously kept them alive in the public mind. Those leaders who survived the successful independence struggle, and their kinsmen, virtually monopolized political leadership positions for thirty years and dominated politics for even longer.[8] Their appeals to old and familiar national issues paid them dividends in terms of electoral support; and their differences, which concerned these same issues, were the basis of party allegiance and rivalry. Hence there was great political stability, which in time became sterility. A largely rural electorate, set in its ways and slow to change, was exposed to unvarying appeals. Ireland became a thoroughly conservative society whose leaders until the mid-1950s hardly attempted to tackle many of its social and economic problems, let alone solve them. Likewise, there was a tendency to ignore international issues other than those related to the traditional nationalist problems, a tendency increased by the insulating effect of the nearness of Britain and by Ireland's small size and limited interests. Foreign policy, except in relation to Great Britain, usually evoked little or no interest and played no part in parliamentary or electoral politics.

This situation began to change slowly from the mid-1950s. Age eventually caught up with the first generation of political leaders, the veterans of the national struggle, and they gave way to new and in many cases less obsessive men. Ireland, hitherto barred from the United Nations because it was neutral during the Second World War, was admitted in 1955, and her soldiers joined peacekeeping forces in Cyprus and the Congo. The challenge of the European Communities was slowly apprehended and its opportunities and implications recognized. By the 1960s, when the country embarked on industrial expansion and enjoyed economic growth and prosperity at an unprecedented rate, nationalism began to wither. Although the onset of civil war in Northern Ireland from 1969 brought old issues back to the centre of politics again, the reaction of people in the Republic made it quite clear that nationalist fires were almost extinct, the burning of the British Embassy in Dublin in 1972, a surrogate for real action, notwithstanding.

By the late 1960s, also, many people and most politicians were at last coming to recognize the Northern Ireland problem for what it was—a struggle between two deeply divided communities in the North itself, not soluble simply by British withdrawal. The new stance of Irish governments that evolved in the early 1970s probably reflected changing public opinion. Ireland, it is now widely accepted, can be united only if and when the Protestant majority in the North are willing to join an all-Ireland state. They ought not to be, and in any case cannot be, coerced into it; and it will at some time be necessary and right to make changes to the Constitution and law of the Republic to accommodate them. Although policies based upon these propositions are intended to realize a national ideal, they reflect attitudes that are a far cry from the nationalism of even twenty years ago.

Traditionally, Irish nationalism involved being anti-British, and that too changed little over the years. Cooperation with the powerful neighbour was emotionally unpalatable and politically unrewarding. Of course, the connections built up over time and the exigencies imposed by propinquity could not be ignored. Considerable conformity and cooperation with public authorities and other organizations in the United Kingdom were, and are, obviously necessary and beneficial. Many of the advantages now accruing to citizens of the states of the European Communities have always been enjoyed by Irish people in Great Britain. It is obviously to their considerable benefit that they should be able to enter the professions and the labour market and generally to enjoy the benefits of being treated like British citizens. Because of this, because of the continuing penetration of British ideas and standards, and because of emigration, which led to many Irish families having relatives "across the water," a curiously ambivalent attitude to Britain developed. On the one hand, there was willingness (besides often a necessity) to go there and live there, a personal friendliness for British people as individuals, and a propensity to accept British standards and values. On the other hand, there was an almost ritualistic antipathy to "the British," more recently called "the Brits," and particularly to manifestations of British military power or symbols of British monarchy—uniforms, warships, the Union Jack, members of the Royal Family, even statues, monuments, and buildings.

Although the intensity of anti-British sentiment has slowly lessened, a decade of trouble in Northern Ireland notwithstanding, this ambivalence still persists. The enquiries of Pfretzschner and Borock among Irish secondary-school pupils in 1972 showed that "they do not really trust the British and their government. Yet they like the British as people."[9] At the government level, this attitude inhibits cooperation in security measures and military defense. In the press and among the public, pleasure at any discomfiture of "the Brits" is a common reaction, as is a readiness to see slights and to ascribe hostile or sinister motives to British policies and the activities of British politicians, administrators, businessmen, farmers, and other groups.

Equally persistent has been the cultural nationalism that developed in typical fashion to support the independence movement in the late nineteenth century. The Gaelic League and the literary movements were intended to be nonpolitical though they, and particularly the first, became so.[10] The language was a highly political subject in independent Ireland. The problems of reviving it, its place in education, its use in everyday business and for official purposes, and the treatment of those dwindling communities whose mother tongue it still is have always been exacerbated because the most ardent nationalists have insisted on identifying the language with Irishness, thus making rational appraisal impossible and rational solutions politically inexpedient. Recently, however, Irish governments have been able slowly to adopt less emotionally charged and more practical policies.

The other gaelicizing force in the independence movement was very different and very effective. The Gaelic Athletic Association, founded in 1884 to promote national—that is, gaelic as opposed to "foreign"—games, "was a mass movement, unintellectual and positively grounded in militant separatism from the outset."[11] Its branches formed a countrywide network that embraced large numbers of people. Its strongly nationalist and exclusive policies did much to socialize generations of Irish people. Many of the country's political leaders came, and some still come, from its ranks.

The rapid disappearance of the ascendancy, the former ruling class, and a marked thinning of the ranks of middle-class Protestants after independence opened the way for the emergence of a bourgeois Catholic elite. Protestant domination of business, commerce, and the professions declined; and although the number of Protestants with large farms did not fall, the social and political leadership of the "West British" gentry was ended. These had been the leaders of the most significant minority community in the country. Although it could be said that a Protestant subculture still exists today, based upon religious, educational, and in some instances social, separation, this small minority of less than 5 per cent has been to a considerable extent almost everywhere absorbed into the larger community.

Because of the numbers involved, political divisions along religious lines were not to be a general feature of politics in independent Ireland as they were in Northern Ireland. Of far greater importance was the cleavage that resulted from the division in the nationalist movement over the terms of the Treaty of December 1921 with the British and led to civil war. The split in Sinn Féin and, subsequently, in the country as a whole into Treaty versus anti-Treaty factions polarized Irish politics, with tremendous consequences. There is much evidence, as Erhard Rumpf pointed out, to suggest that this division at first reflected regional and socioeconomic divisions as well as political and personal differences.[12] Certainly, it aggravated, if it did not cause, great conflict in Irish society. It was reflected in social life, in nationalist associations and ceremonials, and in politics. In politics it was the major polarizing agent and formed the basis of party division: Fianna Fáil and Fine Gael, the two biggest parties, derive from it. Even though its causes have been removed, the polarization of politics remains to this day, for the parties developed their own life and momentum. Yet it might be argued that by polarizing politics, they prevented the rise of strong left or agrarian movements. Thus, it could be said that the Treaty split inhibited or at least softened class or other divisions.

Although the major groups involved in the split of Sinn Féin eventually learned to live together, the extremists could not be assimilated. De Valera, for all his republican principles, was essentially practical and entered constitutional politics when his circumstances required it. Others were not so practical. A tradition of extreme republican movements has continually produced people who do not recognize the government or the state and who resort to force and to outrage. Such people are now very few and have become increasingly estranged from the community, but they epitomize a small element of republican radicalism to be found mainly in parts of the southwest and the border counties and among members of certain social groups, particularly urban workers and very small farmers.

The reservoir from which this tiny stream of extremists comes is today larger than is generally realized. Among the secondary-school pupils whom they surveyed, Pfretzschner and Borock discovered "a sizeable minority of students who do not . . . display a confidence in the system. . . . they do not exhibit a high regard for democracy . . . and are attracted to violence as an acceptable means to the solution of political problems. Our analysis suggests that roughly one-third of the students falls into this . . . category."[13] No less than 40 percent of their respondents favoured the use of force "if necessary" to end British rule in Northern Ireland. Such attitudes might indeed be more widely held in the community generally than is ordinarily supposed. Davis and Sinnott, in a controversial study published in 1979, concluded that "the stark fact remains that 21 percent of the population emerge as being in some degree supportive in their attitude to I.R.A. activities."[14]

The dying preindustrial society. Ireland is a fringe country: geographically on the fringes of Europe, socially and economically on the fringes of the British Isles, and, for long, a fringe province of the United Kingdom. Like West Wales, Cornwall, and the highlands and islands of Scotland, Ireland lacked the essential minerals of the industrial revolution and was geographically remote. The development of an industrial society in Great Britain touched such areas last and least; the further west, the more delayed and the smaller were its effects.

Although the dominance of Britain during the formative period of modern mass politics ensured that the values of an industrial, urbanized, liberal-democratic society would prevail, Ireland's traditional social-geographic pattern continued to survive. For hundreds of years, Ireland exhibited what Rumpf called "das allgemeine Ost-West Gefälle," an east-west gradient corresponding to the degree of anglicization that could be observed in the number of Catholics in the population, the size of farms, the number of inhabitants per square kilometer of cultivated land, and the types of farming.[15] Thus the cultural picture is one of modern urban values permeating an older peasant society inexorably but to differing degrees—more and faster in the towns than in the rural areas and more in the east than in the west. However, despite the decline of the one culture in the face of permeation by the other, one of the most critical factors in modern Irish politics has been the dominance of the countryman, more particularly the small farmer, whose characteristics and attitudes to some extent reflect an older, preindustrial society.

We can label this rural culture a "peasant" culture, but we should do so with reservations. To begin with, some Irish sociologists have in recent years challenged the whole idea of a single peasant political culture in premodern Ireland.[16] Even if one does not go that far, the very term "peasant" must be used cautiously. A "peasant society" proper, according to Teodor Shanin, consists of "small producers on land who, with the help of simple equipment and the labour of their families, produce mainly for their own consumption and/or the fulfilment of their duties to the holders of political and economic power. . . . The family farm is the basic unit of peasant ownership, production, consumption and social life." As Shanin goes on to point out, the ties of family and the land and the wide variety of tasks to be performed, which causes the peasant to operate at a relatively low level of specialization, lead to many of the distinguishing characteristics of peasant life and thought: "The peasantry is a pre-industrial social entity which carries into contemporary society specific, different and older elements of social inter-relation, economics, policy and culture."[17] The impact of a money economy, of towns, and of modernization, however, generally is relentless and makes inroads into this culture. Gradually, the peasant becomes an agricultural producer. "This pattern of development of the peasantry into a cohesive, increasingly narrowing and professionalized occupational group of farmers is seen clearly in most parts of North-Western Europe."[18]

In broad outline Irish experience was along the lines indicated by Shanin. The land reforms of the late nineteenth and early twentieth centuries produced a class of highly conservative small owner-occupier farmers. Although they were increasingly concerned with producing for the market, their type of farming and their life styles retained some peasant characteristics. To some degree this continues to be so today, though, as time goes by, to an ever smaller extent. All the same, for this class, land is by no means simply a resource to be exploited and managed.

The impact of the values of the countryman, more particularly the small farmer, on Irish politics has been considerable. The values of this class influenced the pattern of development of an independent Irish state in the 1920s and continued to do so. It was no wonder. As A. J. Humphreys observed, "the small farm families, taken collectively, hold and exercise the largest measure of power in the rural community," which, be it remembered, has been in the majority until recently.[19]

The predominant social value of the countryman is loyalty to family and neighbours. David Schmitt noted that "virtually every writer about Irish society has observed the importance of close personal connections among community and family members."[20] Country people are strongly locally oriented, and they set great store by face-to-face contact. In the past, even the recent past, Mass on Sunday, fair day, the cooperative creamery, all had significance far wider than their primary purposes for a people who were dispersed on their own small family farms and who were not very mobile until recently when car ownership rose quickly. An important characteristic of such a society is "personalism"—that is, "a pattern of social relations in which people are valued for who they are and whom they know . . . where extreme personalism exists, family and friends determine one's chances for success."[21] These features lead to a great emphasis upon the personal and local in politics. They have been clearly reflected, as we shall see, in the selection of candidates for elections, in electoral behaviour, in the role of elected representatives, and in representatives' relationships with their constituents. It was these features that caused political institutions closely modelled upon the British to work in some respects in a markedly different manner.

The dominance of the small farmer was also largely the cause of the static conservatism that marked Irish politics so strongly for the first forty years of independence. Only in the poorest areas on the periphery did poverty and discontent spawn a measure of peasant radicalism that issued in extreme republicanism. Elsewhere, smallholders with their little farms secure but undercapitalized were conservative, shrewd in the short run, but unimaginative in their attitudes both to their livelihood and to politics. In these circumstances, productivity was low and the rural population declined as emigration to the city and, until the late 1960s, overseas also drained off the young, the loss being particularly severe from the poorest areas. Although emigration obviated the development of a more radical type of rural politics, it left a sad legacy in the areas most affected. There hung over such areas a torpor that was death to initiative: it is not wholly dissipated yet.

Although Ireland experienced unprecedented economic expansion for a decade from the early 1960s, it was almost wholly in the urban, industrial sector. If the climate in rural Ireland changed in the 1970s, it was largely the result of membership in the European Communities, which benefitted farming, whether efficient or otherwise, greatly. Both the effects on rural prosperity of the Community's agricultural policy and the impact of television-set ownership in rural areas grew rapidly from the end of the 1960s. The increased prosperity of the young people was immense. By 1980, the life styles and values of the rural young, both those who stayed at home and those who worked in Dublin but could now afford to go home regularly, were closer to those of their urban counterparts than they ever had been.[22]

The persistence of a peasant culture has been the greater because it was identified by late-nineteenth-century nationalists with the gaelic tradition. In turn, the gaelic peasantry came in those same eyes to epitomize the Irish nation: "The whole national movement . . . fused with the cause of maintaining the integrity of the peasant tradition against an insidiously destructive colonial power."[23] Once established, the new state was concerned to preserve not only its political but also its cultural integrity. Irish leaders, and in particular De Valera, cherished a vision of a rural gaelic Ireland and pursued it as a political objective. Not until after he and his generation left politics—De Valera finally retired from active politics in 1959—were old myths discarded and more realistic and materialistic objectives accorded priority.

Irish Catholicism. The persistence of older traditions and conservative attitudes, which owed much to the identification of the nation with the peasantry, was still further strengthened by their identification in turn with Catholicism, more particularly the Catholic Church in Ireland. This symbiosis, accomplished by the end of the nineteenth century, was to have enormous political consequences. In Emmet Larkin's words: "What really evolved . . . in the making of the Irish state was a unique constitutional balance that became basic to the functioning of the Irish political system." More specifically, "the price Parnell paid . . . for the accommodation of the Church . . . was to make his *de facto* Irish state essentially a confessional one: it was left to de Valera to make it formally confessional."[24]

Ninety-five people out of a hundred in the Republic of Ireland are Roman Catholics. The attachment of most people, Catholic and Protestant, to their church is strong. A national survey conducted by the Irish Episcopal Commission for Research and Development in 1973 and 1974

showed a high level of religious belief and practice among Catholics in the Republic of Ireland. Nine out of ten Catholics fully believed in God, Christ's Resurrection, Our Lady's Immaculate Conception, Our Lady's Assumption, Transubstantiation and that sins are forgiven in Confession. The level of religious practice was also high with nine out of ten attending Mass at least once a week, and Communion and Confession at least once a year.[25]

Most Irish people are conscious of religious differences, and a person's religion is almost always recognized and mentally noted on first acquaintance. Education is organized to a great extent on confessional lines and so are some forms of social intercourse; for example, there are Scout and Guide associations for Catholics and Protestants. Mixed marriages are uncommon—though becoming less so—and disapproved of by many in all denominations. However, there is virtually no discrimination in employment or in economic associations. In politics, religious divisions are comparatively unimportant, largely because of the small size of the non-Catholic element in most areas. Although it exhibits some of the signs of being a distinct subculture, the Protestant community is politically absorbed except in Donegal and perhaps elsewhere in the Ulster counties of the Republic. There, and only there, does the Republic at all resemble a thoroughly segmented society such as Belgium or Holland, let alone Northern Ireland.

Traditionally, Irish Catholicism was an austere and puritanical variety, somewhat cold and authoritarian and rather cut off from continental European influences. It was a folk church geared to what it saw as the needs and limitations of a peasant people. Many of its clergy themselves came from that background: "The traditions of the Irish Church bear the marks of a settled rural based culture which changed remarkably little over centuries. The measured pace of rural life gave a tone to the Church in its liturgies and in its style of government. There did not appear to be any good reason why the old ways should not persist until recently."[26] The power and influence of the Roman Catholic Church increased considerably during the nineteenth century. Its position was further enhanced because it "managed to build itself into the very vitals of the nation by becoming almost at one with its identity."[27] The parish clergy, too, were community leaders, the more so since many of them identified themselves—sometimes despite the Hierarchy—with the agrarian and nationalist aims of the country people, and because the Church, not being a great landowner, was not a source of envy to land-hungry men.

The political effects of the dominant position of the Catholic Church have been immense. The Irish state was from the beginning self-consciously Catholic. Bunreacht na hÉireann (the Constitution of Ireland), which replaced the negotiated Irish Free State Constitution of 1922, was a self-conscious attempt to combine the liberal-democratic tradition of Great Britain with Catholic social teaching. The impact of Catholic teaching has always been evident in the content of public policy on marriage and divorce, contraception, censorship, health services, and, above all, education.

The influence on specific political issues of the Hierarchy, who, so far as most people are concerned, speak for "the Church," is hard to measure. Surveying more than half a century, from independence to 1979, John Whyte concluded that "the hierarchy is more than just one interest group among many; but it is not so powerful that Ireland must be considered a theocratic state. Some middle view has to be worked out."[28]

There can be no doubt, on the other hand, of the direction in which its weight has been cast. It has almost always been conservative. Those seeking social change would say reactionary.

What kept Irish society so unchanged for so long, however, was neither the political power of the Hierarchy nor the social control exercised by the clergy. Rather it was the wholehearted acceptance by the vast majority of the people of a seemingly immutable set of Catholic ideological and social values. Father A. J. Humphreys S.J., an American sociologist, identified these "traditional Catholic beliefs" as "a special brand of Catholicism"—namely, Augustinianism. He found them strongly inculcated in the "New Dubliners"—that is, country people recently come to the city—whom he studied. These values survived largely unaffected by urbanization. He described this ideology thus:

By comparison with other orthodox views within the general framework of Catholic doctrine, the Augustinian tradition lays relatively greater emphasis on the weakness and evil to which human nature is prone as a result of original sin. By the same token, it attributes relatively less efficacy to natural knowledge and human action and relatively more validity to God's revelation and more power to the action of God's grace. Under the impact of this particular Catholic conception of life, aided and abetted by the traditionalism characteristic of the rural areas, the Irish countryman has acquired a more than average distrust of native human reason. . . . The tradition he inherits tends towards a certain historical and theological positivism in regard to the major truths and values of life, and, together with other historical factors, has led him to an intensified reliance upon the teaching power of the Church as voiced by the clergy. . . . he inclines to a jaundiced view of sex and a generally ascetic outlook which places a high premium upon continence, penance and, in most spheres of life, on abstemiousness.[29]

It was the persistence of these attitudes and values, their inculcation in generation after generation, and their resilience in the face of individualist, rationalist, and secularist attitudes of the invading industrial, urban culture that explain the slow pace of social change and legislative reform.

Authoritarian attitudes. A society dominated by values and attitudes such as those described by Humphreys is a society that tends not to question authority. "Throughout Irish history, social institutions have been highly authoritarian" and, in David Schmitt's view in the early 1970s, "most remain substantially so today."[30] Authoritarianism has traditionally manifested itself particularly in family life, where deference to males, parents, and the elderly was a marked feature at least until recently; in the Church, which was and still is run on hierarchical lines and where deference to the clergy was in the past extreme; and in the school system, where the clergy controlled many aspects of education because the management of elementary schools was almost universally in their hands until 1975, and secondary schools were almost all owned, managed, and largely staffed by them.

In the view of Charles McCarthy, the education system was the basic cause of the authoritarian attitudes that he described in the late 1960s. He identified the national (elementary level) schoolteacher as the principal socializing agent:

> In all this the national teacher is the key figure. These young men and women were drawn from the most academically able in the country, but, certainly in the case of the men, from a remarkably limited social group. It appears to me that they came primarily from small farmers and small shopkeepers in the south and west, and in many cases had themselves left home as early as thirteen or fourteen years of age, attending first the preparatory colleges (which now fortunately have been disestablished) and also the diocesan colleges, all residential in character. From there they went to a residential training college which was conducted on remarkably authoritarian lines. No doubt the Church authorities were anxious to secure this rigorous training knowing that ninety per cent of Catholic children would receive their education from national teachers.[31]

Authoritarian attitudes, it has often been maintained, are not conducive to the successful practice of democracy. However, despite some signs of paternalism on the part of some politicians and bureaucratic attitudes on the part of some public servants, Ireland has been as successful a democracy as many other states that claim to be so. Once the state was established, democratic government was never seriously threatened. In a tense period in 1932 and 1933, when De Valera came to power, there was a threat of the development of rival paramilitary organizations. In the 1930s, also, there were a few signs of activity by individuals with fascist leanings. These manifestations are noteworthy only to illustrate how firmly democratic, rather than authoritarian, ideas have dominated politics.

Seeking to explain this apparent paradox, Schmitt suggested that deferential attitudes help maintain stability in the early days of a new state's existence. In the Irish case, people were willing to accept the authority of the government in power as legitimate despite the military action of De Valera and his colleagues against it. Thus Schmitt concluded: "Ironically, authoritarian and personalistic norms have facilitated democratic political development in Ireland."[32] As we shall see in Chapter 2, however, the existence of authoritarian attitudes side by side with democratic beliefs results in a cultural portrait of the Irish people that is curiously ambivalent.

More obvious than authoritarianism in politics, however, are other characteristics that are undoubtedly connected with the influence of the Church but also with the national and agrarian struggles of the past, and perhaps with the continuing survival of a rural society. These are loyalty and a marked anti-intellectualism in Irish life.

Loyalty. In traditional rural society "the bases of man's behaviour . . . were kinship, friendship, loyalty and obligation."[33] In the nationalist movement, loyalty to the concept of the Irish nation became identified for most with faithfulness to one's religion and to the Church. The fierce partisanship evoked by the split over the Treaty and the civil war that ushered in the new state put a further premium upon fidelity to one's leaders. Thus, loyalty became and remained an especially important feature in Irish political life. Old comrades who had become political leaders remained loyal one to another. Adherence to one's party was for most a matter of being faithful to its leaders. Throughout his political career, De Valera continued to prefer and stand by his civil war comrades—and their sons.

This loyalty was, and is, to persons and institutions rather than to ideas. It reinforces powerfully the natural tendency of people generally in the past to adopt the political affiliations of their parents and to support their chosen parties consistently. Although it is often suggested that the young today are politically more volatile than previously, parents' party preference is still by far the most reliable predictor of a young person's choice of party when he or she votes. Pfretzschner and Borock found that seven out of ten of their secondary-school respondents who declared for Fianna Fáil reported a Fianna Fáil father and/or mother, and six out of ten who declared for Fine Gael had a Fine Gael father and/or mother. It is loyalty, too, that leads members of the Oireachtas (Parliament) to vote solidly with their parties: back-bench revolts are not a feature of Irish parliamentary life. Loyalty, of course, evokes recognition, and the need and desire to reward it leads to another feature of political life, the expectation that it will be acknowledged by preferment or a reciprocal service. Such an expectation is greater in a society in which many have hardly yet abandoned the norms of traditional rural life.

Anti-intellectualism. The historical and social factors that led to authoritarian attitudes and a stress on the virtue of loyalty also produced in Irish society a marked anti-intellectualism, which has persisted to this day, though it is less marked than it was. The Church, cut off to a large extent and for a long time from continental European Catholic life and thought, maintained its traditional ways and attitudes to a considerable degree. It has never been given to speculation on the great issues that engaged continental Catholics. Maynooth College, its major intellectual centre, was described by Jean Blanchard in 1958 as "trés conservatrice" and remained so until recently.[34]

Irish writers and artists in the past have in all too many cases been driven to Britain or farther afield not only by economic necessity but by the uncongenial and unsympathetic intellectual climate, reflected in phenomena such as ubiquitous signs of tastelessness, censorship, and the cold suspicion of the Church typified in this passage from the Archbishop's 1967 *Lenten Regulations for Dublin Diocese:* "They who give themselves the title of intellectuals have grave need of being constantly warned that a common danger exists that no one may disregard, and that artistic or literary merit does not excuse indulgence in sensuality."[35]

Inevitably, the process of *aggiornamento* initiated by Pope John XXIII and the Second Vatican Council meant a particularly agonizing reappraisal for the Irish clergy, and they were reluctant to embark upon it. It failed at first to produce the intellectual ferment that was engendered in some other Catholic countries. Many of the clergy, while anxiously awaiting authoritative pronouncements giving them their marching orders to new positions that they earnestly hoped would be very little distance away, preferred to argue that nothing had changed. Although, from the late 1960s, the clergy did recognize the need for more dialogue between themselves and the laity and for open discussion of issues such as divorce and contraception, with few exceptions they have not contributed much to the creation of a more lively intellectual climate or to the formulation of social policy.

In politics, a similar anti-intellectualism was for long evident. After the emergence of the new state, a rural, nationalist, and Catholic community neither felt the need for, nor got, bold new initiatives from its leaders. At first these leaders were absorbed in establishing and consolidating the state on conservative lines. Until the late 1950s, they were more concerned with the outstanding constitutional issues than with new ones. From the 1920s to the 1960s, few enquiries of any depth were made into social and economic problems, and even those were mostly of pedestrian quality or, like the *Report of the Commission on Vocational Organization* (1943), by common consent were ignored. New social services and new legislation tended to follow *mutatis mutandis* the existing British pattern. Neither public servants (politician or professional) nor the universities provided new ideas, and there were few attempts to observe and adapt the experience of countries other than the United Kingdom.

This anti-intellectual conservatism began to change in the 1960s. The new climate was epitomized in the series of reports on economic and social matters put out by the National Industrial Economic Council and its successor the National Economic and Social Council, both influential advisory bodies appointed by governments desirous of engaging in economic planning, itself a sign of changed times. This harnessing of the social sciences to the service of the state is now generally accepted. Nevertheless, it cannot yet be said that the traditional distrust of intellectuals in politics has been wholly dissipated, as witness the innate hostility of many politicians to the mass media in general and their distrust of "pundits," or the general reactions in the 1970s to the intellectual pyrotechnics of Dr. Conor Cruise O'Brien. On the other hand, the second largest political party, Fine Gael, chose an intellectual, Dr. Garret FitzGerald, as its new leader in 1977. However, it is arguable that the debacle the party suffered at the polls in that year might have precipitated the choice, for he was one of the more radical of their top men.

IV

Throughout this chapter, it has been necessary to point out that changes from the traditional patterns have begun to occur. Generalization after generalization has had to be somewhat qualified because Irish society began to change quite quickly from the early 1960s, having remained comparatively stable throughout the entire previous history of the state. The seemingly rigid framework created by the interaction of the influences that have been identified in this chapter has begun to loosen, perhaps even to disintegrate. In particular, the rate at which traditional rural values and attitudes are being replaced by the habits and standards of a more uniform, Western European, urban, industrial culture is constantly accelerating. Such changes could be expected to have their impact upon politics. These changes are the subject of the next chapter.

TWO

The Changing Face (and Mind?) of Ireland

Rapid changes have been taking place in Irish society in recent years. The traditional values associated with nationalism and with the lingering, preindustrial society, together with the values inculcated by an austere and authoritarian church, which between them inhibited the development of liberal and individualistic attitudes, are being fast eroded as Ireland becomes more assimilated to ways of life and thought characteristic of Western European industrial countries. New influences have begun to operate to modify the old. In this chapter, we shall explore the changing face (and mind?) of Ireland. In particular, we shall enquire whether the changes now occurring have resolved apparent contradictions in the political culture of the Irish—namely, the existence, alongside democratic values, of authoritarian and personalistic attitudes that, according to some political scientists, are not usually to be found in a democratic society. Can the Irish yet be said to hold the values of a thoroughly democratic people, what Almond and Verba called "the civic culture"?[1]

II

Inexorable changes in the structure of Irish society are evident in the statistics of population and the economy. Although in 1980 Ireland remained by Western European standards a rural and agricultural country, the proportion of the population living in rural areas was declining all the time and was less than one-half. The number of people working in agriculture had decreased at a very high rate since the Second World War and was less than one-quarter. Fewer people were self-employed. The pace of economic growth since the early 1960s was in most years higher than ever before. Ireland had become, somewhat belatedly, a typical post–Second World War affluent society. Growing prosperity was hastening the spread of life styles resembling those of the richest industrial countries.

It would be dangerous to assume that structural changes of this sort automatically produce immediate changes in people's values. Yet, undeniably, changes did take place, seemingly at a more rapid pace than hitherto. The reason lies in the fact that structural changes such as those just mentioned coincided with, and indeed are connected with, a number of other changes that had the effect of widening the experience of Irish people and revealing new horizons.

The prospect of membership in the European Communities brought Ireland face to face with unpleasant economic realities and, at the same time, opened up possibilities of growth and prosperity. Britain's failure to be admitted in 1963 delayed Ireland's chances for a decade but came at a time when the economic stagnation that marked the last years of the gerontocracy of the first-generation political leaders was being tackled by new men. Ireland began to adapt to the new postwar Europe and, because conditions were favourable, the 1960s were years of rapid economic growth. Membership in the Communities (from 1972) ensured that the challenge would be permanent and that Ireland would henceforth move roughly at the same pace and in the same direction as the other countries of the Communities. As contacts increased enormously, Irish people began to notice what was happening in continental Europe, many of them almost for the first time.

The challenge posed by the European Communities coincided with a slowly growing awareness of the changes occurring in the Roman Catholic Church following the Second Vatican Council and the significant reforms that were then initiated. The Second Vatican Council touched on topics that had hitherto not been regarded by most Irish people as matters even for discussion, let alone being open to change—matters involving the liturgy, relations between the clergy and the laity, marriage, divorce, contraception, attitudes to other religions, and the role of the state. Urban middle-class people in particular began to question the existing rules of their Church and to adopt a new, more independent attitude to their clergy as they rejected rules and relationships that they thought suited only to a rural, peasant society.

In the late 1960s, too, Ireland's unfinished business, the problem of Northern Ireland, came to the fore again. Now, however, in contrast to the views held in the past, it was increasingly realized that if a united Ireland was ever to be a reality, those laws and conditions that most affronted Northerners would have to be modified. To do so would involve questioning basic Catholic attitudes and values. If the house was to be made ready for the bride, spring cleaning would not suffice; structural alterations would be required.

Above all, the coming of television in the 1960s brought all these matters right into the home together with the blandishments of the advertisers of the consumer society. Television programmes reflected to a considerable extent the urban, metropolitan values of a new generation of broadcasters and programme makers, who "tended to adopt both the style and some of the independence they detected in the neighbouring British model," with whom they were in competition.[2] Furthermore, among the broadcasters "there was a conscious iconoclasm that breached at least some of the established conventions of Irish society; the mere fact that those in authority were seen to be asked questions (no matter how deferentially) was an important advance."[3] Although people in rural areas, especially the poorer farmers, were slower than the urban population to acquire television sets, from the late 1960s set ownership increased rapidly among country people (see Table 2.1).

In addition, one might note the impact, especially upon the middle class, of foreign travel, student militancy, and women's liberation movements. The position of women, indeed, became one of the political issues of the 1970s. The Commission on the Status of Women sought in its report (1972) to have Irish women brought up to the levels generally appertaining in Western Europe. A growing corps of somewhat strident women journalists, most of them working for the *Irish Times,* kept women's issues before the public; and women newsreaders and programme presenters began to appear on the programmes of Radio Telefís Éireann (the national broadcasting authority). However, it was the impact of membership in the European Communities, bringing legal obligations in respect of equal pay, equal opportunities, and nondiscrimination, that did most to govern the pace of change in this area. At the 1977 general election, the leaders of Fianna Fáil deemed it necessary to add women candidates to the locally chosen panels in six constituencies. However "in spite of the heightened interest in the women's issue,"[4] the number of women elected rose by only two, from four to six.

The young, too, began to be accorded more consideration. In 1972 the Constitution was amended almost without debate to give the vote at age 18, each of the political parties falling over itself to claim that *it* had been the first to propose the change. Young people, being more prone than their elders to emulate what they saw upon the television screens and, with growing affluence, more able to do so, began to set the pace of change in clothes, leisure, drinking habits, and sexual *mores.* As with women at the 1977 election, so too with the young voter: "Younger can-

TABLE 2.1

Percentage of Households Owning a Television Set, 1967–79

Location of household	1967	1971	1974	1979
Total	59%	76%	79%	90%
Community:				
Urban	61	89	89	93
Rural	39	63	69	86
Region:				
Dublin	77	92	90	94
Rest of Leinster	55	78	83	92
Munster	54	71	77	89
Connacht and Ulster (part)	31	59	63	81

SOURCE: For 1967 and 1971, data made available by Irish TAM Ltd. For 1974 and 1979, data made available by Radio Telefís Éireann Audience Research.

didates were encouraged and promoted, and younger voters were wooed."[5] It is no wonder: an increasing proportion of the electorate is in the youngest age brackets. In 1977 one-quarter of the electorate was under 25 and voting for the first time. There is some evidence that the young are now beginning to support the major parties in different proportions than hitherto. The Labour Party seemed to be attracting a higher increment of new voters, and the more conservative Fine Gael Party, in the view of its leader at least, was attracting less than a proportionate increment of the younger voters at the 1977 election.[6]

III

It would be premature to assert on evidence of this sort that there have been political cultural changes, particularly in the younger generation. However, it does appear that most of the changes of the 1960s and 1970s just identified reinforced one another in their impact upon society as a whole. The general direction in which they are moving society is already evident. Although Ireland would have to change a very great deal more than it has so far before it could be labelled a "pluralistic" society, let alone a "secular" society, it is undoubtedly moving in this direction.

In *Towards a New Ireland,* Garret FitzGerald defined a pluralist society as one "within which people of different religious, cultural or linguistic traditions would be treated as equal citizens, and would be subjected to no disability because they did not share the tradition that happens to be that of a numerical majority of that population."[7] It was this sort of society that he advocated for Ireland, and he outlined the legal changes that would have to be made in the Republic to achieve it. FitzGerald was no doubt ahead of majority opinion, not least in his own party, but, as a practising politician, probably not all that much ahead. Certainly, if the book did not forward his career, his persistent advocacy of a plural society in the years that followed did not ruin it, for in 1977 he was elected to the leadership of his party, the second largest in the state.

Significantly, FitzGerald was concerned in that book with the Northern Ireland problem. T. P. O'Mahony was probably right in 1977 when he stated that "it has been the worsening situation in the North which hastened the move towards a consideration of genuine pluralism in the Republic."[8] Nevertheless, the spread of pluralistic attitudes does owe something to the liberalizing changes in the Roman Catholic Church, which issued in the ecumenical movement and drew attention to the illiberal state of the Irish Constitution and law. It was on the need for constitutional and legal reforms that the debate was mainly centred from the late 1960s onwards. As early as 1967 the Committee on the Constitution recommended that sections of Article 44.1 that accorded recognition to named religions and gave the Catholic Church a "special position" should be deleted as should the article prohibiting the passing of any law providing for dissolution of marriages. In 1969, Cardinal Conway declared that personally he "would not shed a tear" if the "special position" provision were removed.[9] In 1972, that provision was removed with the Church's agreement by constitutional amendment.

Issues such as contraception, divorce, and interdenominational education have proved to be altogether more contentious. In a genuinely pluralist society, it is claimed, the law would not require people to conform to the particular standards of one religious community, however overwhelming in numbers that community might be; nor would its young people be educated in denominational schools. Such matters might thus be regarded as indexes of the existence of a pluralist society, the more so since in respect of two of them, contraception and divorce, Protestants favour the removal of legal restrictions.

Debate about the desirability of legalizing the import and sale of contraceptives went on ceaselessly through the 1970s. Despite the fact that the Supreme Court in 1974 decided that the law forbidding the importation of contraceptives for personal use violated the constitutional rights of the citizen,[10] successive governments were slow to propose amending legislation. The reasons are clear: neither the Hierarchy nor a majority of the public favoured change. Although, by 1978, the Hierarchy had conceded that the responsibility in this matter lay with the state, it made it clear that the state should know where its duty lay. Public opinion remained very divided on the issue. As the data in Table 2.2 show, by

TABLE 2.2

Attitudes Towards a Law Legalizing the Sale of Contraceptives, 1971–77

Attitude	1971	1974	1975	1976	1977
The sale of contraceptives should be permitted by law through chemists	34%	54%	47%	45%	49%
The sale of contraceptives should be forbidden by law	63	43	37	37	40
Don't know/No opinion	3	3	16	18	11
N	1,600	1,600	1,587	1,400	410

SOURCE: Derived from data made available by Irish Marketing Surveys Ltd.

TABLE 2.3

Attitudes Towards Legislation on Contraceptives
in the Context of a United Ireland, 1980

(Responses to the proposal that contraception be made as freely available
in a united Ireland as it is now in Northern Ireland)

Category	Accept	Reject	Don't know
Total (*N*=1,000)	48%	43%	8%
Age:			
18–34	66	27	8
35–54	49	46	5
55+	26	61	13
Class:			
Middle class	61	34	5
Working class	51	41	8
Farmers	31	57	12
Region:			
Dublin	60	33	7
Rest of Leinster	53	40	7
Munster	42	50	8
Connacht and Ulster	34	52	13

SOURCE: Derived from data made available by Irish Marketing Surveys Ltd.

1977 about one-half of the adult population approved the legalization of the sale of contraceptives; one-third had done so in 1971. However, even in 1980 differences of opinion according to age, class, and region were still considerable (see Table 2.3). Legislation in 1979 providing for the sale of contraceptives on doctors' prescriptions was, perhaps inevitably, a temporary compromise, "an Irish solution to an Irish problem," as the Minister for Health and Social Welfare called it.

In respect of divorce, the Roman Catholic Church was adamant and majority opinion clear until the very end of the decade. Although there was only a small shift of opinion in the early 1970s in favour of legisla-

TABLE 2.4
Views on Divorce, 1971–80

Category	Would favour legislation to make divorce available	Against	Don't know/ No opinion
1971: Total	22%	73%	5%
1975: Total	28	62	10
1980:			
Total (*N*=1,400)	51	43	6
Age:			
18–34	56	37	7
35–54	53	42	4
55+	41	52	7
Class:			
Middle class	64	33	3
Working class	50	43	7
Farmers	38	54	8
Region:			
Dublin	60	34	6
Rest of Leinster	51	43	5
Munster	45	49	6
Connacht and Ulster	44	48	8

SOURCE: Derived from data made available by Irish Marketing Surveys Ltd.

tion permitting divorce and six out of ten still opposed it in 1975, by 1980 a majority had come around to it. As in the case of contraception, there were considerable differences according to age, class, and region (see Table 2.4). In these circumstances, there would be no proposals to change the law, except perhaps in the context of a wholly new constitution for a united Ireland, and that was not likely to arise.

Another barometer of pluralist attitudes is education. Although the clergy were in practice reluctant to cede their control, it is evident that political leaders desire change, not least because of Northern Ireland. In April 1975, Jack Lynch, leader of Fianna Fáil, asserted: "We must preserve the best traditions of the existing system while we promote the new and more exciting systems of interdenominational education and pass on their management to the laity. . . . The denominational nature of primary education north and south of the border should be gradually phased out."[11] Less than two years later, Garret FitzGerald, leader of Fine Gael, had this to say:

Because of a particular sociological view that has been widely held in the Roman Catholic Church, we have tended to view our educational system primarily as a means of transmitting inherited values. . . . Without entering into the merits of this thesis . . . one must . . . raise the question as to whether one can ultimate-

TABLE 2.5

School Denominational Preferences: Three Dublin Surveys, 1974–76

Denominational aspect of school preferred	Marley Grange (1974)	Firhouse (1975–76)	Denominational aspect of school preferred	Dalkey (1975)
Multidenominational[a]	59.5%	61.6%	Multidenominational[d]	75.0%
Interdenominational[b]	23.5	26.1	Single denominational	16.9
Denominational[c]	12.8	10.0	Other arrangements	4.8
Other/No response	5.2	2.3	Other/No response	3.3
Response rate	60.3%	60.5%	Response rate	77.0%
N	213	480	N	1,900

SOURCE: *A School for Our Children: Education Survey Report* (Marley Grange and Highfield Residents Association, Rathfarnham, Dublin, 1975); *Choice of Primary School for Our Children* (Firhouse Community Council, Dublin, 1976); *Dalkey School Project: Survey of Attitudes and Preferences Towards Multi-denominational, Coeducational, Democratically Managed National Schools* (Dublin, 1976).

[a] Multidenominational: a single school for children of all denominations with separate provision for religious education for children of each denomination.

[b] Interdenominational: a single school for children of all denominations providing religious education common to all denominations and no provision for separate religious education.

[c] Denominational: separate schools for each religious denomination.

[d] A democratically elected management committee would determine the exact form of religious instruction.

ly reconcile this view of the educational process with the fullest personal development of the individual.[12]

Politicians, however, will act only if and when they feel it opportune to do so—that is, when public opinion has shifted enough. The data reported in Table 2.5, though confined to certain middle-class areas of Dublin, seem to suggest that by the mid-1970s that shift had already taken place in metropolitan middle-class society, and perhaps this was the case in Dublin generally. In a survey conducted in 1972 and 1973, Father Micheál MacGréil and his colleagues found that 78 per cent of their respondents agreed that "interdenominational mixed free community schools are preferable," an attitude he judged to be "highly liberal . . . since the vast majority of schools are single-sex, denominational, noncommunity schools."[13] However, the majority of the clergy themselves, whether Protestant or Catholic, probably did not desire integrated education. In any case, except in Dublin, the issue did not loom very large. Certainly, the bishops who in December 1978 chose publicly to support the right of their colleague the Bishop of Cork to insist that the Protestant party in a mixed marriage sign a statement agreeing to raise any children of the marriage as Catholics, were still far from condoning a pluralist society.[14]

Not all Catholics were as rigid and unyielding. In 1978, an Irish Jesuit, Father Timothy Hamilton, writing in *Studies,* a Jesuit journal, argued that "the Church has lost by over-protectionism"; he urged the need "to maintain a critical distance from the traditional values of Irish Catholicism." Hamilton observed with approval that

> people are beginning to see that it is possible for the Irish to create a community which is not a sell-out to permissiveness, nor to modernism, nor to secularism, but which is yet something new and modern in Irish relationships . . . which will hold fast to the heritage of Christian belief and practice, yet at the same time will wish and strive to do this in a new context where a new priority of value is set on freedom, reconciliation and unity.[15]

Many Catholics, both clerical and lay, would not agree with him. In the words of T. P. O'Mahony, "the road to pluralism in Ireland is likely to prove a very rocky one,"[16] precisely because many believe that this is the road not to pluralism but to secularism.

In a secular society, many people do not practise religion and little importance is attached to religious practice. The role of the clergy is an attenuated one; religion is isolated from the social, political, and economic spheres of life. In such a society, the institutions of the state would not be used or expected to support any church. In Ireland from the 1960s, it seemed that secularist attitudes were spreading; outward and visible signs of this were becoming evident. Many commentators associated these changes with the spread of urban life styles that got people used to self-service and supermarkets, to women and young people in pubs, to instalment credit and the "Late Late Show." A related theme, the spread of materialist attitudes, was also much used by many religious and some civic leaders.

Perhaps most immediately obvious was the enormous widening in the 1960s and 1970s of the range of topics that the mass media were prepared to treat, and the change both in the views they expressed and in the language they used. In 1966, a bishop thought it necessary and worthwhile to telephone Radio Telefís Éireann to express immediately his protest at the television programme he was watching, which had just shown women in a studio audience being asked—and happily telling— what they had worn in bed on their wedding night. Today, the episode of the "Bishop and the nightie," as it is now known, is an old joke. Radio Telefís Éireann has long since crossed the rubicon of full frontal nudity and by 1977 could broadcast a programme on homosexuals in Ireland.

An obvious index of the extent of secularization is the practice of reli-

TABLE 2.6

Weekly Attendance at Mass, 1973–74

	Survey	
Category	Catholic Communications Institute, 1973	Market Research Bureau of Ireland Ltd., March 1974
Total	91%	91%
	(N = 2,499)	(N = 571)
Sex:		
Male	88	87
Female	93	94
Marital status:		
Married	93	92
Single	87	88
Age:[a]		
Young	85	87
Middle	94	92
Older	92	93
Community:		
Urban	85	85
Rural	94	96

SOURCE: *Irish Times*, September 9, 1975.

[a] For column 1, "young" is defined as ages 18–30, "middle" as ages 31–50, "older" as over 50; for column 2, the ages are respectively 18–29, 30–54, and over 54.

gion. It is significant that in the 1970s this began to be monitored by, among others, organizations connected with the Catholic Church itself. Such enquiries showed that a small number of young people lose their faith. A survey in 1976 of university students, an above-average "at risk" group, showed that "one in every seven respondents who was brought up a Roman Catholic no longer regards himself/herself as such. In fact, it is probable that he or she considers himself or herself an Agnostic or Atheist."[17] No doubt such figures do suggest a secularist trend; but, as the same survey showed, the level of religious belief and practice among those who still regarded themselves as Catholics was "quite high." In any case, as Table 2.6 indicates, nine out of ten people in Ireland still attended church regularly. A society of such people was a long way from being a secular society, even if, for some of them, attendance was a formality.

The evidence of secularization most usually cited in Ireland itself is that concerning sexual practices, notably contraception and abortion. Precise figures are not available; in the decade to 1980, however, the import and sale of contraceptives obviously increased markedly, and a few family-planning clinics began to operate, though some of them suf-

TABLE 2.7

*Number of Women Giving Republic of Ireland Addresses
Who Had Legal Abortions in Great Britain, 1969–80*

Year	No. of women	Year	No. of women
1969	122	1975	1,573
1970	261	1976	1,802
1971	578	1977	2,183
1972	974	1978	2,451
1973	1,193	1979	2,767
1974	1,421	1980 (Jan.–June)	1,695

SOURCE: *British Office of Population Censuses and Surveys: Abortion Statistics* (Her Majesty's Stationery Office, London).

NOTE: These data grossly underestimate the number of Irish women who go to Great Britain for abortions, because many give British addresses. The figures are intended to give some indication of the upward trend. (Doctors have no doubt about it.)

fered harassment. As Table 2.7 indicates, the practice of abortion, too, was increasing. Whether the growth of such practices is evidence of secularization or not, most Irish clergy believe that it is. Attacking a speech by Dr. Conor Cruise O'Brien—at that time a minister in the Fine Gael–Labour Party coalition—in which he questioned the wisdom of denying young people "effective means of limiting families and the knowledge of how to limit them," Dr. Jeremiah Newman, the Bishop of Limerick, argued that

it shows that he appears to be committed to the idea of a secular state in which the moral standards of the majority of the people, insofar as they are rooted in their religious persuasions, would be of no concern whatsoever to the state. . . . It is surely a monstrosity for anybody to imply that the moral attitudes of the generality of Irish Catholics—whether South or North—based as they are on a code that is reflective of their traditional faith, are in any way sectarian. For such a people rejection of a secular state is a basic political right. . . . It is something we will have to fight against to the end. . . . We have got to give leadership to the people to stand up against a secular state and those who represent it.[18]

Thus, some bishops, holding as they did a domino theory of change in Ireland, could still be heard demanding that due to their numerical superiority Catholics are entitled to expect the state to provide a "supportive framework."[19] A community that tolerates laws that buttress the teaching of a particular church is, of course, the antithesis of a secular society: Ireland in 1980 was still in some respects such a community.

IV

Evidence of a trend towards a more pluralist society together with some signs of secularist attitudes throws into higher relief those beliefs and values of many Irish people that might seem to be alien to a democratic ideology. Writers like David Schmitt have pointed to the paradox of the successful practice of democracy in the manner of the most advanced Western countries by a people who in some aspects of their social life display characteristics generally regarded as inappropriate to a democratic society. There was, as John Whyte observed, "a notable convergence of views among writers on Irish political culture" on this point.[20] However, until recently, these conclusions were based largely on impressions. In recent years, though, evidence from public opinion surveys has become available to confirm such impressions.

This work, and in particular that published by John Raven and others in *Political Culture in Ireland: The Views of Two Generations* (1976) has been much influenced by the work of Gabriel Almond and Sydney Verba that resulted in *The Civic Culture* (1963). By linking up with the civic culture survey, Raven and Whelan in particular "were able to make comparisons with the five countries that Almond and Verba had studied."[21] In many respects the responses of Irish people fell into the same patterns as those of the Americans, Germans, and British, but they were not wholly consistent. In Whyte's words, "to a striking degree their findings confirm what observers had suggested"—namely, that some Irish people hold attitudes that are not conducive to democracy.[22]

Citizens of democratic countries, according to Almond and Verba, can be expected to be aware of the impact of government on their daily lives and to know something about the political system. Raven and Whelan found that "the large majority of the Irish are, like Americans, British and Germans, in Almond and Verba's terms, 'cognitively oriented to governmental action.'"[23] (See Table 2.8.) Likewise, as was the case in

TABLE 2.8

Estimated Degree of Impact of National Government
on Daily Life in Ireland and Other Countries

Degree of impact	Ireland	United Kingdom	United States	Germany (F.D.R.)	Italy	Mexico
Some effect	80%	73%	85%	70%	54%	30%
No effect	19	23	11	17	19	66
Other	0	0	0	0	3	0
Don't know	1	4	4	12	24	3
Base (=100%)	1,226	963	970	955	995	1,007

SOURCE: J. Raven and C. T. Whelan, "Irish Adults' Perceptions of Their Civic Institutions and Their Own Role in Relation to Them," in J. Raven *et al., Political Culture in Ireland: The Views of Two Generations* (Dublin, 1976), p. 22. The figures for all countries except Ireland are derived from G. Almond and S. Verba, *The Civic Culture* (Princeton, 1963). In the case of Mexico, the sample was limited to cities with populations of more than 10,000.

TABLE 2.9

Political Interest and Knowledge in Dublin and Other Countries

*(Proportion able to name some party leaders when asked
to name seven from major parties)*

No. of leaders named	Dublin	United States	United Kingdom	Germany (F.D.R.)	Italy	Mexico
Four or more	64%	65%	42%	69%	36%	5%
None	5	16	20	12	40	53

SOURCE: For Dublin, Munger Survey, 1966 (details not published). For United States etc., G. Almond and S. Verba, *The Civic Culture* (Princeton, 1963), pp. 89, 96.

TABLE 2.10

Irish Adults' Ability to Identify Politicians, 1971

*(Responses on being shown cards with pictures of seven well-known
politicians and asked to name each and identify his party)*

	Response (N = 1,226)					
	Name			Party		
Politician	Right	Wrong	Don't know	Right	Wrong	Don't know
Colley	52.4%	4.1%	43.6%	53.9%	3.8%	42.3%
Haughey	73.9	2.0	24.1	73.7	2.1	24.2
FitzGerald	48.9	5.1	46.1	48.6	6.4	45.6
Lynch	87.6	0.8	11.9	86.3	0.9	12.8
Browne	30.2	7.1	62.7	31.5	6.3	62.2
Cosgrave	65.5	3.3	31.2	67.0	2.8	30.2
Corish	69.2	2.1	28.7	69.6	2.8	27.7

SOURCE: See Raven and Whelan, "Irish Adults' Perception of Their Civic Institutions," p. 31. These data, which were not published, were made available by the Economic and Social Research Institute (Dublin).

the Almond and Verba study, there were differences according to education and between town and country people.

In respect of political knowledge, both Frank Munger's survey of Dubliners made in 1966 and Raven and Whelan's national survey nearly ten years later suggested that people were well informed (see Tables 2.9 and 2.10). Likewise, Pfretzschner and Borock in their study of Irish secondary-school pupils found that "the executive in Ireland, as in so many other countries, was well-known and considered important." Ninety-seven per cent of their sample (aged between 11 and 18) selected correctly the name of the Taoiseach (Prime Minister) from a list of four possibilities.[24]

Another indicator used by Almond and Verba was citizens' expectations of the kind of treatment they would receive at the hands of public

TABLE 2.11

Expectation of Treatment by the Police in Ireland and Other Countries

Expectation	Ireland	United States	United Kingdom	Germany (F.D.R.)	Italy	Mexico
Equal treatment	87%	85%	89%	72%	56%	32%
Unequal treatment	13	8	6	5	10	57
Depends	0	5	4	15	15	5
Other	0	0	0	0	6	0
Don't know	0	2	0	8	13	5
Base (=100%)	1,226	963	970	955	995	1,007

SOURCE: Raven and Whelan, "Irish Adults' Perceptions of Their Civic Institutions," p. 46. The figures for all countries except Ireland are derived from Almond and Verba, *The Civic Culture*. In the case of Mexico, the sample was limited to cities with populations of more than 10,000.

officials. Raven and Whelan's "rough cross-national comparison" of people's expectations of treatment by their police if they had some trouble—"a traffic violation maybe, or had been accused of a minor offense"—indicated that here too "the Irish pattern is almost identical to that found in the U.K. and the U.S.A." (See Table 2.11.) Like Almond and Verba, too, Raven and Whelan found that level of education did not make all that much difference.

The foregoing suggests that the Irish resemble the peoples of the rich, industrialized, democratic nations; but there is also evidence from the same sources to suggest that the Irish do not conform in some respects to the democratic norms suggested by Almond and Verba. In fact, as the authors themselves recognize, their findings are not wholly consistent. John Whyte observed that many impressionistic writers "were struck by an autocratic strain in Irish life," which is accepted by the people as a whole.[25] Raven and Whelan confirmed this. When they measured the "subjective competence" of Irish people—that is, the extent to which they think they can exert influence over the authorities that govern them—and compared it with other countries, they found the Irish to be "less subjectively competent at all educational levels than the Americans, British and Germans."[26] (See Table 2.12.) It should be noted, however, that Pfretzschner and Borock reported quite high levels of "subjective competence" among secondary-school students. Just as Almond and Verba had found a great gap between people's perceptions of their influence and their actions, so too did Raven and Whelan: "When we look at action instead of feelings, we find that only 3 per cent at the national level and 11 per cent at the local level had in the past acted with the intention of influencing the government."[27]

On the basis of these and other responses, Raven and Whelan con-

TABLE 2.12

*Expectation of Likelihood of Effectively Opposing a
Very Unjust or Harmful Local or National
Regulation in Ireland and Other Countries*

Nation	Can do something about local regulation	Can do something about national regulation
United States	77%	75%
United Kingdom	78	62
Germany (F.D.R.)	62	38
Ireland	53	42
Italy	51	28
Mexico	52	38

SOURCE: Raven and Whelan, "Irish Adults' Perceptions of Their Civic Institutions," p. 26. The figures for all countries except Ireland are derived from Almond and Verba, *The Civic Culture*. In the case of Mexico, the sample was limited to cities with populations of more than 10,000.

TABLE 2.13

Authoritarian Attitudes in Dublin, 1972

Statement summary	Per cent agreeing ($N = 2,271–2,282$)
Prostitution is a crime	51.7%
Communism should be outlawed in Ireland	53.6
A thing is either right or wrong	48.4
Obedience to clergy is the hallmark of a good R.C.	44.7
Homosexual behaviour between consenting adults is a crime	39.9
Skinheads should be locked up	39.2
Gardaí (police) should be armed always	31.9
There should be very strict control of Radio Telefís Éireann	28.8
Student protest should be outlawed	25.2
The dole should be abolished	22.8

SOURCE: Derived from M. MacGréil, *Prejudice and Tolerance in Ireland* (Dublin, 1977), p. 413. MacGréil classifies these items as "authoritarian and 'fascist-type.'"

curred with Ian Hart, who concluded from his enquiries in 1970 that "the attitude of the citizen towards the political process and citizen participation is ambivalent to say the least."[28] They found their respondents on the one hand expressing positive attitudes to participation, on the other stressing strongly the importance of "a good strong leader" and the role of government in determining the future of the country. Again, both Raven and Whelan in respect of adults and Pfretzschner and Borock in respect of secondary-school students found considerable intolerance and a willingness to use force in certain circumstances. Raven and Whelan summed up their findings thus: "Four-fifths of our informants believe that political groups which abuse freedom of speech should be curbed; three-fifths feel that one is justified in imposing one's values on others; and one-fifth feel that the use of force is sometimes the only way to advance an ideal."[29]

There is further evidence of authoritarian attitudes in Father Micheál MacGréil's survey of Dubliners. Replies to "authoritarian and 'fascist-type' items . . . included with the main purpose of establishing the extent of authoritarianism as a personality type" indicated "a relatively high degree of authoritarianism among the respondents—when taken as a unit." (See Table 2.13.) MacGréil thought that the replies of the intolerant section of his respondents indicated "a mental disposition . . . conducive to stereotypical thinking and moralistic judgements."[30] He concluded that there was in Dublin "a relatively high degree of overall authoritarianism," though he detected a trend towards some weakening of those attitudes.[31]

V

Findings such as these ought to be viewed with caution. Whatever their intrinsic value might be, too much should not be inferred from them. Indeed, some political scientists have argued that what is essential for the successful practice of democracy is not that democratic values be universally held in the community, but that those who are politically active and influential hold them. Others would say that the proof of the pudding is in the eating and that what is really significant is how people behave. If so, the question we should concentrate upon is: do the Irish practise democracy? This book aims to present the evidence upon which an answer to this question might be based. A major artefact of such practice is a democratic constitution that provides a framework of limited government. The constitution is, therefore, the subject of the next chapter.

THREE

The Framework of Limited Government

The desire to limit the power of public authorities and to define the rights and duties of citizens is a characteristic feature of the liberal-democratic world. To effect such a limitation involves formulating and formalizing the basic and most important of these powers, rights, and duties in rules of law that have special significance and status. Thus, "the constitution, for most countries in the world, is a selection of legal rules which govern the government of that country and which have been embodied in a document."[1] A constitution is both an instrument by which public authorities can be controlled and a point of reference in disputes over rights and duties.

A constitution, however, is no more than a selection of the rules governing the more formal political procedures and relationships, together with an enunciation of the basic rights and duties of the citizens, plus declarations on other matters thought to be important by its framers. At best, it will enunciate only the general pattern of political and legal organization and relationships. The day-to-day operations of government will make necessary both the creation of a body of law dealing with matters too detailed to include in the constitution and the development of a series of working conventions to implement the constitution.

Unless a country is governed by an alien power that ignores indigenous traditions, its constitution at the time it is written is likely to reflect the political beliefs, values, and standards of the inhabitants or at least those of the dominant group. Thus it might well be an important source of information about the political beliefs, values, and standards of its makers and those for whom they spoke. Going further, one might judge the worth of a constitution by the extent to which it does reflect the political beliefs, values, and standards of the community. Insofar as it does, it is a political force of considerable influence.

However much a constitution at its inception mirrors the basic values of a community, changes in the community's values and in the pattern of its social and political life, and new ideas about the rights and duties of citizens, will cause the original wording to fit less well in places. Then, new meanings are given to the words of the constitution; they might be stretched by ingenious judges to cover situations never contemplated by its authors. Unless it is constantly changed, whether by way of judicial interpretation or by formal amendment, a constitution will increasingly contain matter that is outmoded or inappropriate. Sometimes, if a constitution was never "a good fit" or if times change radically, a new constitution altogether might be needed.

As it happens, the constitution in force in Ireland today, Bunreacht na hÉireann (the Constitution of Ireland), did, when it was enacted in 1937, and to a great extent still does, reflect the values of the great majority of the people in the state. One can easily detect in it many of the "basic influences" that we identified in Chapter 1. Equally, some of the changes made in it by the courts and by amendment reflect changes in Irish society that have occurred since 1937 and particularly in the last decade or two. By 1980, more than forty years since its enactment, changes were being increasingly canvassed.

The accession of Ireland to the European Communities in 1972 brought the state into "a new type of international organization with much greater powers over member countries than those traditionally given to international institutions."[2] A new body of law, including the Treaties of Accession themselves and the fruits of fifteen years of Community activity, had to be received into Irish law. Community institutions have continued to make laws that either apply directly in Ireland or necessitate compliance by the Irish government and parliament by the enactment of appropriate domestic legislation. Community law, to which Irish law, including Bunreacht na hÉireann, must be adapted, adds another dimension to the framework of limited government within which the Irish government operates. It can hardly fail to have an impact upon the development of the Constitution itself.

A constitution, then, though a collection of basic rules and a point of reference, should be viewed as an adaptable instrument of government. In fact, the constitution in force today—Bunreacht na hÉireann—was itself an adaptation of earlier constitutions; its enactment marked an important stage in the evolution of the state. To understand both the occasion for it and its contents, it is necessary to see it as the successor of two previous constitutions—the Constitution of Dáil Éireann (1919) and the Constitution of the Irish Free State (1922). All three were the product of the same movement, and each succeeding version reflected another stage reached in the evolution of an Irish state with constitutional symbols and an international status broadly acceptable to the majority of the population. They thus reflected evolution rather than revolution. This continuity is evident not only between the three constitutions themselves but also between Ireland as part of the United Kingdom and the Republic as an independent state.

II

The Sinn Féin candidates who were elected at the general election to the United Kingdom parliament in December 1918 and who constituted themselves Dáil Éireann (House of Commons or Chamber of Deputies) in January 1919 were members of an independence movement engaged in active struggle. The formation and operation of a "government" and the meetings of the Dáil itself were part of their campaign; so, too, was their constitution, the Constitution of Dáil Éireann.[3] In such circumstances, the Dáil Constitution was not seriously intended to meet all the needs of an effectively operating independent state; rather it was essentially part of a publicity exercise. It was short, its five sections covering the appointment of a chairman, the competence of the Dáil, the appointment of a Prime Minister and a government and their powers, the provision of funds, and the audit of expenditure. In addition, the Dáil passed a "Declaration of Independence" and a "Democratic Programme" of rights and duties that reaffirmed and elaborated what had been contained in the proclamation of the Republic on Easter Day 1916.

These enactments reflected the democratic and republican nature of the independence movement. The Dáil Constitution made no mention of a republic, and there was no provision in it for a president to represent the state. Nevertheless, it was clearly intended to be a provisional constitution for an independent republic, which the representatives hoped to make a reality. At the same time, continuity was also very evident; these enactments showed how much of the British and how little of any other foreign tradition the independence movement had absorbed. In the words of Brian Farrell, "Irish political culture was already developed into an established and sturdy parliamentary mould prior to political independence." There was, Farrell thought, "a considerable consensus in Ireland on what the process of representation and government was about. There was never any serious dispute; a familiar and acceptable model—the Westminster model—was available and was simply taken over."[4] In fact, this was a takeover, not a revolution.

The pattern of government envisaged was cabinet government in the

British style. The Prime Minister and other ministers were to be members of the Dáil, chosen by it and answerable to it. Perhaps other provisions reflected the desire of some Dáil members to lean more to parliamentary government than to cabinet government; if so, their hopes were not realized. In general, during the period of operation of the Dáil Constitution, from 1919 to 1922, "the Cabinet controlled the Dáil. It had a secure majority, no organized opposition and the advantage of a war situation to stimulate consensus."[5] The Democratic Programme covering the ownership of property and matters such as the right to education, social welfare services, and equality, and stressing international cooperation, no doubt reflected Sinn Féin principles; but it also had a strong early-twentieth-century socialist flavour, being the work of leaders of the more left-wing elements in the independence movement. It was probably not really acceptable to the majority of Dáil members and certainly not to some of the leaders, including De Valera himself. One of them afterwards doubted "whether a majority of the members would have voted for it, without amendment, had there been any immediate prospect of putting it into force."[6]

The Constitution of the Irish Free State, and linked with it the Treaty between the United Kingdom and the emerging Irish state, marked the success of the independence movement. In contrast with its predecessor, it was a constitution for an effective sovereign state, but a state that had perforce to remain in a special relationship with the United Kingdom.[7] The result of having to negotiate a treaty with the British government was that the Irish leaders had to accept both then-current British ideas of the proper arrangements for emergent colonies—that is, Commonwealth status—and also a number of safeguards for defence and for the protection of the Protestant minority left in the new state. Consequently, the Irish Free State Constitution reflected two different political theories. One was the theory of popular sovereignty, which was couched in dogmatic assertions about the rights of the people, intended by Irish leaders to mark the break with Britain. The other was British constitutional theory, for the break was not complete. The state was to be a member of the British Commonwealth and, at British insistence, the Constitution provided for the symbols and institutions of government considered at that time to be necessary and appropriate for such membership—recognition of the Crown, a Governor General, an oath of loyalty, and the constitutional fictions connected with "His Majesty's Government."

The provisions for political organization and procedures expanded the sketchy arrangements of the Dáil Constitution considerably, following quite closely the existing British patterns. However, although the British cabinet system and the Westminster model generally were the basis of the machinery of government, attempts were made to correct what some leaders of the time thought were imperfections in British government. Included in the Constitution of the Irish Free State were devices intended to increase popular and parliamentary control and to prevent the development of a strong cabinet backed by a majority party from establishing hegemony over the Oireachtas. The Constitution contained provisions for referendum, the initiative, and "Extern Ministers"—that is, ministers elected directly by the Dáil, who did not need to be members of the Dáil and were not members of the cabinet. Confidence in the power of constitutional devices to modify British-style government was quickly seen to have been unfounded. Within five years, all such devices were removed or inoperative. Indeed, modification had never been desired by some of the state's first leaders. In the circumstances of the time, strong government was needed to establish the state successfully in the face of civil war and guerilla activity both within the state and on its northern border.

The need for constitutional declarations of rights and duties was as foreign to early-twentieth-century British constitutional theory and Commonwealth practice as assertions of popular sovereignty, but the constitutions of most other countries, following American and French precedents, do include them. In any case, the independence movement had social as well as national aims to which the enactment of the Democratic Programme in 1919 had borne witness. The Irish Free State Constitution guaranteed a catalogue of rights and provided for judicial review of legislation "having regard to the provisions of the Constitution." Included were personal rights such as *habeas corpus,* freedom to practise any religion, freedom of association, the right to free elementary education, and the inviolability of the citizen's home. Notwithstanding a statement that all the natural resources of the country belonged to the state, the tone of this Constitution was less socialistic than the statements of 1919, reflecting the conservative stance of the surviving leaders and their acceptance of the British liberal-democratic tradition and British legal concepts. In its prohibition of the endowment of any religion and of discrimination on account of religious beliefs, the Constitution was secular in tone.

The Irish Free State Constitution was much amended. Until 1932, most changes were confined to the machinery of government, for the leaders of the pro-Treaty party (which became Cumann na nGaedheal), then in power, felt bound by the Treaty. With the coming to power of

Eamon de Valera, the leading opponent of the Treaty, a radical revision of the whole position in respect of the Commonwealth was certain, for this was what he had stood and fought for. If the substance of independence had been sufficient for the moment for many in 1922—and was in any case the best that could be got—the majority accepted the need for revision. Many who had helped elect De Valera had done so to enable him to carry it out. Such a revision involved, first, the removal from the Irish Free State Constitution of all signs and symbols of Commonwealth status and, then, the construction of an entirely new constitution "unquestionably indigenous in character."[8] This constitution would stress the republican and popular nature of the state, superseding the Commonwealth concept entirely.

III

Bunreacht na hÉireann was almost literally De Valera's constitution. He drafted it or supervised its drafting, clearing its principles with his government and taking advice from officials and others, including a number of Catholic clergy. He personally piloted it through Dáil Éireann and presented it to the people in a radio broadcast. Inevitably, therefore, Bunreacht na hÉireann provides for a state that is in essentials a republic.[9] The basis of all governmental authority, including the authority to enact the Constitution itself and to change it, is the people. In the words of the Preamble, "We, the people of Éire . . . do hereby adopt, enact, and give to ourselves this Constitution." It is important to notice that the people here referred to are in principle the people of the whole island. Article 2 makes clear that "the national territory consists of the whole island of Ireland, its islands and the territorial seas." However, in Article 3 the *de facto* situation is recognized, for "pending the reintegration of the national territory" the laws of the state are declared to have effect in only twenty-six counties.

In place of the symbols of British Commonwealth status, provision is made for an elected President, the symbol of republican status. Yet nowhere in the Constitution is Ireland declared to be a republic. Article 4 says only that the *name* of the state "is Éire, or in the English language, *Ireland*"; and Article 5 says that "Ireland is a sovereign, independent, democratic state." Surprising as this may seem, it was a deliberate omission, reflecting the evolutionary approach to the development of Ireland's constitutional status in general and De Valera's policy of "external association" and his hopes of acquiring the six Ulster counties in particular.

To have formally declared the state a republic in 1937 would have involved a complete break with the Commonwealth, the members of which, it was thought at the time, were linked by a common allegiance to the British Crown and could not include a republic. Such a break would be seen as deliberately removing all possibility of eventually wooing Northern Ireland into an all-Ireland state. De Valera made no bones about his motives: "If the Northern problem were not there . . . in all probability there would be a flat, downright proclamation of a republic in this Constitution."[10] He provided instead in obscure language (in Article 29.4.2°) for the continuation of arrangements devised at the abdication of King Edward VIII in 1936. At that time, opportunity had been taken to remove mention of the Crown from the Irish Free State Constitution and to reinstate it in an ordinary statute, the Executive Authority (External Relations) Act, as an organ or instrument that might be used by the Irish state for some purposes in the conduct of external affairs. These arrangements, De Valera hoped, would constitute "a bridge over which the Northern Unionists might eventually walk."[11]

It was a forlorn hope, but the arrangements made in 1937 had the advantage, as De Valera pointed out, of allowing for further evolution of Ireland's status without the need to change one word of the Constitution. Thus, when in 1948 John A. Costello's "Inter-Party" Government decided that the time had come to declare Ireland a republic, the deed was done by ordinary legislation in the Republic of Ireland Act, which declares that "the description of the State shall be the Republic of Ireland" and cancels the arrangement for the use of the British monarch provided for in the Executive Authority (External Relations) Act. On Easter Day 1949, Ireland became formally and unequivocally a republic. Ironically, at this very time, the possibility of establishing an intimate relationship between a republic and the British Commonwealth, first explored by De Valera in the 1930s and now extinguished, was being pursued with some success by other countries emerging from British control to independence.

Although Ireland's status in the world of states was now finally fixed *de jure* as it had been *de facto* in December 1921, the realities of her position in relation to the United Kingdom had still to be recognized. It was, and still is, neither convenient nor practicable for the United Kingdom to regard Ireland as a foreign state. Under the Ireland Act (1949), the Republic of Ireland, as the state was in future to be known in the United Kingdom, was not to be a foreign country, nor were its citizens to be classed as aliens. Instead, they were to continue to enjoy the exemption from that status accorded in the British Nationality Act (1948) and to have all the privileges of Commonwealth citizens. Today, they are even more privileged, for the restrictions applied to the entry of Commonwealth citizens to the United Kingdom under the Commonwealth Immigrants Act do not apply to Irish people. In this way, as in many others, the unique association of the two countries is constantly demonstrated. However, the accession of both countries to the European Communities is having the effect of making a special relationship less possible or necessary.

The dissatisfaction of De Valera and Fianna Fáil with the Irish Free State Constitution did not extend to the system by which the country was governed. On the contrary, the trend toward a system of the British type, operating in a similar manner, was confirmed after 1932. To a large extent Bunreacht na hÉireann continued what already existed formally or in practice. Some of its words and phrases were identical with, or very similar to, those used in the 1922 Constitution. The most important changes were intended to increase the status and power of the Prime Minister (now called Taoiseach), but even this was to some extent only to make formal what was in fact the practice, at least since the accession of De Valera. Otherwise changes were comparatively minor, though the occasion was taken to make yet another—not very successful—attempt to solve the difficult problem of the composition and powers of Seanad Éireann (the Senate).

In general, therefore, the machinery of government provided for in Bunreacht na hÉireann followed the British model, and the similarity is heightened because of the persistence of similar working practices. These similarities extend to government-parliament relationships, parliamentary procedure and behaviour, the forms of administrative organization at both the national and the local level, the structure and working of the civil service, and to much else besides. After more than half a century, these similarities persist. There are differences, of course. Because there is a great disparity in scale, Irish government is less complex. Because there are social and cultural differences resulting from the fact that the political traditions and culture of the Irish contain elements other than those derived from Britain, the conduct of government and the political behaviour of those involved are by no means always similar. To a great extent, what this study of Irish government is concerned with is precisely the working of British-type institutions in a cultural setting that, though it owes much to Britain, is very different.

IV

If the enactment of Bunreacht na hÉireann marked another stage in the progress of the Irish state to an international status that satisfied its inhabitants, it also heralded the formal recognition that this was a

Catholic state. The Cumann na nGaedheal governments of the first decade had passed a number of acts reflecting an austere Catholic outlook. The 1937 Constitution confirmed the acceptance of Catholic principles as guidelines for the country's political life and institutions and for its social policies. John Whyte in his *Church and State in Modern Ireland, 1923–1979,* called it "the coping stone of this development."[12] Thus, mixed with liberal and democratic elements derived from the British tradition were principles and precepts drawn from Catholic social theory and, in particular, papal encyclicals.

This mixture is mostly to be seen in Articles 40–44, the articles dealing with the rights of the citizens, and in Article 45, which is entitled "Directive Principles of Social Policy." These articles follow closely a statement of Catholic principles known as the Social Code drawn up in 1929 by the International Union of Social Studies in Malines, Belgium; but they perhaps owe something to a discarded draft of the Irish Free State Constitution, prepared in spring 1922 by Professor Alfred O'Rahilly, that De Valera seems to have consulted when he was preparing Bunreacht na hÉireann. Elsewhere the 1937 Constitution, though clearly Christian in tone, is not especially Catholic, except in Articles 15, 18, and 19. Those articles, taking up a political idea put forward by Pope Pius XI in the encyclical *Quadragesimo Anno* (1931) and much in vogue among Catholic publicists, make provision for occupational or as they called it, "vocational" representation.

This mixture of liberal-democratic and Catholic principles seems on the whole to have been successful, and certainly it satisfied the vast majority of the citizens of the Republic, at least until recently. In hindsight it is easy to see that it would not evoke the support or inspire the loyalty of the Protestant population of the six counties of the North. However, most people in the twenty-six counties were unable or unwilling to recognize that at the time or to accept that, this being the case, an all-Ireland republic was not possible because the Northern Protestant majority could not be coerced.

Article 40, entitled "Personal Rights," enunciates many of the personal and civil rights that are the product of the liberal tradition. It declares citizens to be equal before the law and to have the right of *habeas corpus.* Citizens' homes are not to be forcibly entered "save in accordance with law." It also guarantees the right of free expression "including criticisms of government policy," the right of peaceful assembly, and the right to form associations and unions—all "subject to public order and morality." It expressly forbids political, religious, or class discrimination. Elsewhere in the Constitution, notably in Articles 15.5 and 34–39 (the articles that deal with the courts), other liberal rights connected with legal processes are laid down.

Although the liberal tradition was the inspiration for Article 40, in the last ten years or so the courts have found in it, and particularly in Article 40.3, the basis for a concept of "undisclosed human rights" that, in the words of Mr. Justice Kenny, "result from the Christian and democratic nature of the state."[13] This ingenious conflation of principles has provided a fruitful source of new rights recognized by the courts. Contrariwise, the Constitution seems to have been well able to accommodate the need to provide the police and other authorities with discretionary powers and the right to act in emergencies and to protect the security of the state.[14]

If Article 40 reflects the liberal tradition, Articles 41, 42, and 43, which deal with the family, education, and property, are obviously Catholic in content and tone. Article 41 declares that "the State recognizes the Family as the natural primary and fundamental unit group of Society, and as a moral institution possessing inalienable and imprescriptible rights, antecedent and superior to all positive law." The integrity of the family is, therefore, carefully protected by constitutional safeguards. The state guarantees to guard the institution of marriage, and the enactment of laws granting a dissolution of marriage is forbidden. Further, a person who has been divorced in another country and whose marriage is "a subsisting valid marriage" in Irish law may not legally remarry in the Republic while the original spouse is alive. Similarly, even persons whose marriages have been "annulled" by Catholic Church authorities may not legally remarry in the Republic.

In Article 42 the family is recognized as "the primary and natural educator of the child." Parents have the right and the duty to provide education for their children, but they may, if they wish, provide it in their own homes; the state steps in only in default. The enunciation in Article 43 of the right to possess property and its qualifications are also unmistakably Catholic: "The State acknowledges that man, in virtue of his rational being, has the natural right, antecedent to positive law, to the private ownership of external goods." The state, therefore, will pass no law attempting to abolish the right of private ownership or the right to bequeath and inherit it. However, the exercise of property rights is to be regulated by "the principles of social justice," and the state may "delimit by law the exercise of the said rights" for "the common good."

In Article 44, which deals with religion, De Valera—for it was his solution to a difficult problem—made a brave attempt to reconcile contemporary Catholic teaching on the treatment of religions by the state with his aspirations, and those of the majority, for a united Ireland.[15] The desire to end partition, which involved allaying the fears of "Rome rule" held by the Protestant majority in Northern Ireland and the need, for the same reason, to renew the guarantees on religion given in the Irish Free State Constitution, required that contemporary Catholic principles be not strictly applied. This turned out to be the most contentious article in Bunreacht na hÉireann: it was attacked at first for not being Catholic enough and, later, after the Church at the Second Vatican Council had changed its stance and no longer sought a privileged position, for being too rigidly Catholic. It is one of the few articles to have been amended.

In Article 44 in its original form, which remained the law until 1972, the state acknowledges the duty to respect and honor religion and "recognizes the special position of the Holy Catholic Apostolic and Roman Church as the guardian of the Faith professed by the great majority of the citizens." It also recognizes the other religious denominations that existed in the community at the time of the enactment, and it guarantees "freedom of conscience and the free profession and practice of religion." Article 44 guarantees not to endow any religion, not to impose any disabilities on religious grounds, not to discriminate in providing aid for schools, and not to take over church property compulsorily except for "necessary works of public utility and on payment of compensation."

In the late 1960s, this article came under attack, largely in the context of Northern Ireland but also by those promoting ecumenism. In 1967, an all-party committee on the Constitution recommended the removal of two sections, but it was the declaration of the Primate, Cardinal Conway, in 1969 that he personally "would not shed a tear if the relevant subsections of Article 44 were to disappear" that gave a clearance for the Fifth Amendment of the Constitution Bill in 1972. This amendment removed sections 2 and 3, i.e. the "special position" section, and the section according recognition to named religions.[16]

As in Articles 41–44, so too in Article 45, entitled "Directive Principles of Social Policy," are the precepts of Catholic teaching much in evidence. The principles enunciated in this article supplement the fundamental rights in Articles 40–44, for they consist of a collection of welfare-state aims "for the general guidance of the Oireachtas." The state is bidden to seek "a social order in which justice and charity shall inform all the institutions of the national life" and so to organize affairs that all men and women "may through their occupations find the means of making reasonable provision for their domestic needs." The state should have special care for the weaker in the community. Concerning property, the Catholic position is once again stated: the public must be protected against "unjust exploitation," and "the state shall favour and, where necessary, supplement private initiative in industry and commerce."

Finally, we should notice in Article 45 an enunciation of the idealistic dream of a rural, peasant-owner society so dear to the heart of De Valera. The state is directed to secure "that there may be established on the land in economic security as many families as in the circumstances shall be practicable." The figures of the numbers engaged in farming, of population movement, and of emigration from Ireland show how far this ideal was from being realized, and perhaps from reality.

Article 45 was addressed to the Oireachtas. The application of the principles set out therein "shall not be cognisable by any Court." Notwithstanding the apparent finality of the wording of the article, the courts in recent years have not regarded themselves as completely excluded from considering its provisions. In particular, it has been held "that a court may consider those principles when considering whether a constitutional right claimed by a citizen exists."[17]

V

However well suited a constitution might seem to be when it first comes into effect, the inevitable changes that time brings will lead to a need and desire to alter or develop it. Such modifications can be made by the courts, if they have the power to review and invalidate any action of any governmental agency on constitutional grounds, as the Irish courts have. Changes can also be made by amendment, which very often requires a special procedure that in Ireland's case involves enactment by the Oireachtas followed by popular approval at a referendum. After a tidying-up period from 1938 to 1941, during which time two amendment acts were passed by ordinary legislation as provided for in "Transitory Provisions," the Constitution was hardly developed at all either by interpretation or by amendment for a quarter of a century.

The enactment of Bunreacht na hÉireann had evidently given Ireland what Karl Loewenstein has called a "normative" constitution—that is, a constitution that was "not only valid in the sense of being legal but also real in the sense of being fully activated and effective."[18] In the eyes of its author, De Valera, and of the country as a whole, the Constitution suited Ireland's traditions and expressed its aspirations. It tended, therefore, to be regarded as a finished product and not as a developing instrument of government. This was especially so both because its author dominated politics for most of the next quarter of a century and because the judiciary had for even longer a diffident attitude towards their power to review and a conservative bias when it came to interpretation.

Since neither war nor revolution afflicted the country to precipitate the kinds of social and economic change that most other Western European countries experienced after 1939, Ireland was very conservative until the 1960s. Reflecting the changes that then began to take place, there was a period of judicial creativity in interpreting the Constitution and, in the early 1970s, a short burst of amendment, which, though it seemed to presage a radical revision of at least some parts of the Constitution, was not followed up.

After a comparatively negative period that lasted until the mid-1960s, during which time Irish lawyers trained in the British tradition were slow to put their new powers of review to creative use, judicial interpretation of the Constitution became "increasingly bold."[19] From that time, judges of the High Court and the Supreme Court, on whom falls the task of interpreting the Constitution, were prone to take a broader approach towards interpretation, seeking guidance from a range of sources wider than the mandatory clauses. In their deliberations they considered the Preamble, Article 45, the nature of the Irish state, and even, in the words of Chief Justice O'Higgins, "concepts of prudence, justice and charity which may gradually change or develop as society changes and develops, and which fall to be interpreted from time to time in accordance with prevailing ideas."[20] In particular, the judges enlarged the range of personal rights. In an important judgment in the case of *Ryan* v. *Attorney General,* Mr. Justice Kenny declared that "the personal rights which may be invoked to invalidate legislation are not confined to those specified in Article 40 but include all those rights which result from the Christian and democratic nature of the State."[21] The judges have used the same approach to broaden access to the courts.

Ironically, the first use of the amending procedure served to show how important it is in preventing governments from making changes that they desire though the public does not. Both in 1959 and in 1968, attempts to replace proportional representation by the single transferable vote with the "first-past-the-post" system at elections were rejected at the referendum (see Chapter 8 and Appendix C).[22] In 1972, however, three amendments were made. The addition of a subsection to Article 29.4 made it possible for Ireland to join the European Communities. The minimum voting age specified in Article 16 was lowered to 18 years; and the excision of subsections 2 and 3 of Article 44.1 removed all mention of particular religions. Up to 1980 these were the only major changes. Two minor changes were effected by referenda held in 1979. One related to the law on adoption, the other to the representation in the Seanad of graduates of universities and other third-level educational institutions. Thus, despite the fact that from the late 1960s there was continual talk of amending and, increasingly, of replacing Bunreacht na hÉireann, there were in fact few changes.

The growing discussion in the 1970s about changing the Constitution was almost always in the context of the Northern Ireland problem and centered on the changes needed to suit a state that would embrace all Ireland. In retrospect, it might seem strange that thirty years or more elapsed before political leaders in the Republic began to canvass the need to make changes of this sort in Bunreacht na hÉireann—that is, to seek to effect yet another stage in the evolution of the Irish Constitution. For if, as we have argued, Bunreacht na hÉireann marked a step forward in the process of Irish political development, it did so only from the perspective of one of the two communities in the island. Although it laid claim to a thirty-two-county state and looked forward to a united Ireland, some of its provisions were hopelessly unsuited to Northern Ireland with its Protestant majority. Conor Cruise O'Brien put it thus:

If indeed he [De Valera] was interested in wooing "the North"—in practice, the Protestants of Northern Ireland—his Constitution of 1937 was an odd bouquet to choose.
Article 2 of the Constitution declared the national territory to be "the whole island of Ireland, its islands and the territorial seas."
Article 3 asserted—while leaving in suspense for the time being—"the right of the Parliament and Government established by this Constitution to exercise jurisdiction over the whole of that territory."
Article 44.1.2° recognized "the special position of the Holy Catholic Apostolic and Roman Church as the guardian of the Faith professed by the great majority of the citizens."
Thus, the Protestants of Northern Ireland were declared incorporated *de jure* into a State which recognized the special position of the Roman Catholic Church.
It would be hard to think of a combination of propositions more likely to sustain and stiffen the siege-mentality of Protestant Ulster.[23]

However, if, as seems to be the case, De Valera's ideals—a thirty-two-county republic that would be both Catholic and gaelic—were mutually incompatible, it should be remembered that they were not seen to be so by most people in the South, who indeed shared them. Very few at that time could or would appreciate the hard realities that flowed from the existence of two antipathetic communities in Northern Ireland divided by religious and national loyalties.

When, from the late 1960s, these realities did become widely recognized and better understood, one might have expected that changes intended to make the Constitution more acceptable to Northern Protestants would have been effected; certainly they were much canvassed. That, up to 1980, only one such change was made (the amendment to Article 44) has been largely due to the view of Fianna Fáil that "the time to discuss this is when elected representatives of North and South get around a table to discuss the future of the country."[24] In part, too, the general lack of constitutional changes agreeable to Protestants in the North reflects the reservations that the Catholic clergy had to any changes in the law relating to marriage and divorce, which they, and most lay people also, associate with the highly contentious issues of contraception and abortion. In comparison with issues such as these that arouse great feeling, the need for other reforms, not least those arising from membership in the European Communities, does not get much attention. Nevertheless, it is likely that the changes made in Bunreacht na hÉireann in the last few years have been but the first instalment of what will eventually be a radical revision by way of amendment or replacement.

VI

Today, the legal framework within which Irish public authorities operate is not confined to domestic law. At the beginning of this chapter, mention was made of Ireland's accession to the European Communities. This had the effect of superimposing on domestic constraints and treaty obligations (which are entirely matters within the competence of the government and the Oireachtas to decide) another body of law that not only governs member states but applies in part directly to individual citizens. Potentially, the constraining effect of European Community law upon the actions of public authorities is enormous. Already, in practice, Irish governments have experienced a foretaste of its vigour and power.[25]

Bunreacht na hÉireann, being a product of the interwar years when the possibility of international organizations with powers of this sort was not contemplated, could not encompass such a development without amendment. Article 29.6 states that "no international agreement shall be part of the domestic law of the State save as may be determined by the Oireachtas." The obligations of membership in the Communities require otherwise, and the Third Amendment to the Constitution—a simple addition of one subsection to Article 29.4—both permitted accession and declared: "No provision of this Constitution invalidates laws enacted, acts done or measures adopted by the State necessitated by the obligations of membership of the Communities or prevents laws enacted, acts done or measures adopted by the Communities, or institutions thereof, from having the force of law in the State."

Following this enabling amendment, the European Communities Act (1972) provided that "the Treaties governing the European Communities and the existing and future acts adopted by the institutions of those communities shall be binding on the state and shall be part of the domestic law thereof." Thus, European law has been welded on to Irish law.

The European Communities have the power under the Treaties to alter national law directly. Community *regulations* and *decisions* are directly applicable in member states and binding upon all to whom they apply, including public authorities. *Directives* oblige governments to achieve the objectives stated therein by enacting the appropriate legislation or taking the appropriate actions through their own domestic procedures.

The objectives of the Treaties, though limited, embrace a wide range of matters. The major aim, the creation of economic ties and the making of economic arrangements to generate increasing prosperity and to improve the living and working conditions of all the citizens of Community countries, involves common action and the reconciliation and harmonization of the relevant laws and practices of member countries. In addition, Community institutions have become increasingly active in the fields of social welfare and human rights, particularly those connected with economic activity such as antidiscrimination in pay and employment practices, the right to work, and freedom of establishment. The European Court, like the Irish courts, is identifying and creating new rights, and this Court is available to Irish citizens, even to proceed against their own state. When any question involving Community law arises in an Irish court, that court can and, if it is a final court of appeal must, refer the matter to the European Court.

The impact of Community law upon Irish law and the obligations upon governments to implement directives are matters of great consequence for Irish politics. In 1976, for example, an Irish government was obliged to abandon an inadequate antidiscrimination bill that it had already introduced into the Oireachtas. In 1978 its successor in office was found to have breached Community nondiscrimination rules with measures it had taken to prevent fishing near the Irish coast.

By 1980, the full implications of Ireland's accession to the Communities had not been widely recognized, though the importance of the common agricultural policy (CAP) for Irish farmers' profits was well understood from the beginning and was a matter of continuing, lively concern. From the point of view of Bunreacht na hÉireann, it is arguable that accession has made a number of articles otiose or inaccurate. Not least, membership in an international organization as powerful and as ubiquitous as the Communities seems to cast doubt upon the declaration in Article 5 that "Ireland is a sovereign . . . state." Ironically, this matter, which rival leaders regarded as so important as to contest it for nearly three decades and even to take up arms one against another, today goes largely unremarked.

FOUR

Political Communications and the Mass Media

One of the most fruitful approaches to the study of politics is to see it as a system of communications involving a network of channels of information and institutions for transmitting ideas, demands, and orders. People's political opinions and actions are to a great extent governed by information, advice, and precepts coming from many sources and in many ways, some of them not at all conventionally thought of as political. Thus, a communications network can be seen as "the nerves of government."

Some of this communication is "horizontal"—ministers of state conferring together or with community leaders, men talking in a bar, children learning to sing "Kevin Barry" or "Derry's Walls" at school. Those who, because of their elite status in the community, can communicate horizontally in a direct manner with members of a government or other political leaders or senior public servants are likely to be comparatively well informed and influential. For most people, political information, ideas, and values are communicated either horizontally at a low level within the family, school, religious group, or work place, or vertically from the top or source downward and by more formal media. Conversely, some, but regrettably much less, information about public attitudes and demands passes vertically upward to political leaders. Obviously, in a modern society, television, radio, newspapers, and to a lesser extent other printed material are powerful means of wholesale vertical communication—thus the term "mass media."

So important are the mass media that their ownership, direction, and standards are commonly and rightly regarded as matters of crucial public importance and, hence, proper for governments to control. In regimes based upon a totalitarian ideology, state regulation is inevitably directed to fostering and reinforcing the political system and the rulers who interpret the ideology. In Western democracies, views differ about the proper role of the state vis-à-vis the media. One view sees the media as being, properly, business enterprises that should be free to serve the market. A second sees them as a "fourth estate." This is the view that journalism is an autonomous activity carried on by professionals whose unfettered power to expose public authorities enables them to be held to account and allows the people to get at the truth about public affairs. A third view, that is perhaps the prevailing view in most democratic countries as the press becomes concentrated in fewer and fewer hands and broadcasting more often than not is a monopoly, is that the media have a social responsibility that it is the duty of the state to nurture and enforce.

This duty has turned out to be difficult to perform, not least because the would-be controllers, the politicians, are also clients and users of the media and are properly regarded with suspicion by journalists. In addition, the tendency in many countries toward a declining number of newspapers, with ownership concentrated in the hands of a few, coupled with the enormous development of political broadcasting, has exacerbated a problem that is in any case inherently difficult in a liberal democracy. Not surprisingly, today, in John Whale's words, "the media and the State—the whole apparatus of Government—are in two minds about each other. On the one hand, a certain tension separates them: on the other, undeniable ties bind them."[1]

It is clear, therefore, that although it is legitimate and convenient to treat the structure, functioning, and outputs of the media at any given time as an important part of the *context* of politics, it must be recognized that they are themselves influenced by political factors. In a broad and general way, their pattern is governed by the dominant ideology of the community, and the translation of that ideology into laws and public policy governing the media falls inevitably to the government of the day.

II

Although there is no denying the importance of the mass media for politics, it is essential to an understanding of how political attitudes are formed and behaviour is shaped to recognize that the mass channels—the press, radio, and television—are by no means the only suppliers of political information and ideas. Political communications in advanced countries like Ireland consist of "a fusion of high technology and special, professionalized processes of communication with informal, society-based and non-specialized processes of person-to-person communication."[2] Although this chapter is mainly concerned with the "special, professionalized processes of communication" (the mass media), these might make surprisingly little impact upon the basic political attitudes of most consumers. Face-to-face contacts and informal communications might be of much greater importance.

In any case, there can be no doubting the preeminence of basic social groups such as the family, religious groups, and the school in the political socialization of individuals and in holding them fast. Some social scientists investigating the impact of mass media claim that "opinions and attitudes which are important to an individual's image of himself, or to his picture of society, cannot easily be changed by a fusillade of communications, however persuasive. . . . Such opinions are often anchored in and shielded by a person's primary group affiliations—'ensconced in protective group cocoons.'"[3] Whatever is said about the mass media must not obscure this most important political fact.

III

A free, private enterprise press was established in Ireland parallel with its establishment in Great Britain. Mass-readership daily papers, produced in Dublin and reflecting a number of shades of opinion, were well established with strong traditions of independence before the First World War. Other newspapers and journals, including those advocating the independence of Ireland, were produced and circulated, although, as the national struggle grew sharper, some extreme publications were banned from time to time. Thus, independent Ireland emerged with an established free press, home-produced and privately owned and operated. It embraced the full range of newspaper and journal production—national morning, evening, and Sunday newspapers, local papers, weekly and monthly journals, and magazines. British newspapers, journals, and magazines continued to circulate in small but significant numbers and still do. Furthermore, many of the books read in Ireland are produced in the United Kingdom.

At the end of the 1970s, the situation was but little changed. There were then four morning daily newspapers, three of them dating back to well before independence, and the other, the *Irish Press,* to 1931. The *Irish Independent,* the *Irish Press,* and the *Irish Times* were national papers; the *Cork Examiner* was a regional paper, over 90 per cent of its readers being in the province of Munster. Three of them had associated evening papers and two had associated Sunday papers. The following tabulation shows circulation figures for January to June 1980:

Independent Group		Irish Press Group	
Irish Independent	190,000	Irish Press Group	
Evening Herald	125,000	*Irish Press*	99,000
Sunday Independent	282,000	*Evening Press*	173,000
Sunday World	348,000	*Sunday Press*	388,000
Irish Times	80,000	*Cork Examiner*	70,000

In addition, British newspapers circulate in the Republic, some of them in Irish editions. Although they increased their share of the market in the late 1970s, "they cannot be said to make a major impact on the communication network."[4] In 1979, the approximate circulations of the most important of them were as follows:

Daily		Sunday	
Daily Mirror	54,000	*News of the World*	144,000
Daily Express	10,000	*Sunday Mirror*	78,000
		Sunday People	65,000
		Sunday Express	55,000
		Sunday Times	37,000
		Observer	21,000

At the end of the 1970s, all the Irish newspaper groups were in private hands. Although they had their roots in, and in the past served, particular publics, with the exception of the Irish Press they had all moved a long way from their origins. All competed for the biggest share they could get of a small total market, but they appeared to pursue distinctive market strategies aimed at attracting particular publics identified by market research.

The Independent Group was owned by Independent Newspapers Ltd., whose chairman in 1980 was A. J. F. O'Reilly, an Irishman who was chief executive of Heinz. Formerly family owned, its bourgeois, Catholic papers gave independent support to the pro-Treaty–Cumann na nGaedheal–Fine Gael cause; but, with a change of ownership in the 1970s, it became the most frankly market oriented of the groups. Its morning paper, the *Irish Independent,* carried the biggest headlines, used the most brash layout, and gave the most "popular" treatment of all the dailies. One of its Sunday papers, the *Sunday World,* was a tabloid—a new departure in Irish journalism—with some colour, a small amount of political or any other news, and a large number of eye-catching features and titillating items.

The Irish Press Group was, as it always had been, associated with a family, the De Valeras, and a party, Fianna Fáil. It was founded by Eamon de Valera. Its daily, the *Irish Press,* was launched in 1931 as a weapon in his political crusade with funds raised in the United States and from the people of Ireland, the bulk of the latter collected in small amounts. In the late 1970s, De Valera's son, Major Vivion de Valera, was the dominant shareholder and the "controlling director" of the company, a position not subject to election. As controlling director, he had "sole and absolute control of the public and political policy of the company and of the editorial management thereof."[5] The *Irish Press* was still regarded by the party faithful as what in origin it was—the organ of the movement. Since in practice its editor and political staff had some elbowroom to pursue independent lines, the paper was sometimes attacked for disloyalty.

The *Irish Times,* formerly the unofficial organ of the Protestant and unionist minority, long ago became a politically independent, liberal, middle-class paper with a reputation in Europe as one of the great newspapers. Formerly owned and run by Protestant business and professional men, in 1974 it was transformed into a trust. Compared with the other dailies, it had in the jargon of the advertising profession "a more distinctly up-market profile."[6]

Besides the national newspapers and the Cork regional papers, there is a thriving local press, mainly weeklies. In 1979, there were fifty-three of them. Most were still independent units owned by individuals or by small companies producing a single paper. A few were grouped in chains under a common ownership; one such was owned by the Independent Group. Many of the local newspapers flourished in a modest way by concentrating on local news, including "parish pump" politics, and local advertisements and by using their presses for miscellaneous commercial printing besides the production of a newspaper. They had an extraordinary continuity based on a loyal readership, and they were of great importance in the localities they served. The following tabulation shows circulation figures for those that made them available:

Below 5,000	1	25,000–29,999	1
5,000–9,999	8	30,000–34,999	1
10,000–14,999	12	35,000–39,999	0
15,000–19,999	13	Over 40,000	1
20,000–24,999	3		

The Irish press is a free press. That does not mean that editors can print anything they choose under all circumstances. What it does mean, however, is that editors have a very wide freedom to print news, comment, and opinion that is unpalatable to the government without danger of penalties, legal or other. Of course, there are legal limitations, but these do not usually operate to restrict the publication of political news or comment on matters of current political moment. The Censorship of

Publications Act forbids the publication of matter that is "indecent or obscene" or that "advocates the unnatural prevention of conception," both prohibitions arising from a zealous regard for Catholic morality. The libel laws, which are still patterned after the comparatively severe British code, and the laws concerning contempt of court are perhaps the most important editorial inhibitors, but only very infrequently do these operate to prevent publication of matter of political significance. "Parliamentary privilege" has never been invoked to inhibit political comment.

The only legal restrictions of much potential consequence for politics are those contained in the Offences Against the State Act (1939). Under sections 2 and 10 of this act, newspapers are forbidden to refer to organizations declared illegal under the act, in other words, to the Irish Republican Army. In practice, newspapers have not been inhibited from reporting or commenting on the activities of the IRA. When, as happened once or twice in the past, the government of the day decided to enforce the law, the papers simply substituted the term "an illegal organization." The neighbouring British and Northern Ireland press, radio, and television were not so prohibited.

During the period of civil war in Northern Ireland from 1969, the press covered the activities of paramilitary organizations in much their normal manner. The organizations themselves on both sides, either directly or through their cover organizations, issued communiqués, held press conferences, and gave interviews and briefings. The record of these years serves to confirm the freedom that Irish papers enjoy. As we shall see, it contrasts markedly with the experience of broadcasters, and it also underlines the absurdity of censorship in a society that is so open to its neighbours.

Another potential external influence upon newspapers is commercial pressure. The influence that advertisers have upon editorial material is a subject of much speculation, but such pressure, when it occurs, is not likely to be directed towards modifying political material. It is increasingly obvious that the amount of space given to various types of material and their juxtaposition are influenced by the need to win and hold advertising, but this is not likely to affect the treatment of political matters. The influence of commercial advertising is rather to be seen in its effect upon the structure of the newspaper industry as a whole and in particular upon the variety of newspapers available. Advertisers are interested only in minority newspapers that have a solid middle-class, business, and professional readership. Thus radical or "alternative" views of society have less chance of being publicized. Nevertheless, there are vehicles for views of this kind in Ireland. In 1979, the most important were

Hibernia (circulation 25,000), an anti-establishment republican weekly, and *Magill* (circulation 30,000), a monthly magazine with radical views and colour advertising. Both were aimed at the intellectual, liberal section of the urban middle class.

Editors (and other newspeople) are inevitably subject to unofficial representations and appeals from ministers and other political leaders, as well as from officials, to exclude, soft-pedal, or give prominence to items. Many such requests are likely to be resented and resisted. Of course, ministers and politicians generally have contacts with the press, but these exist for mutual convenience and cannot be counted as political interference. All in all, legal and other outside restrictions on editors publishing political material are few, and newspapers are well placed to resist outside pressure and influence if they wish. Whether they are well placed to acquire information from a government and administration that are, in the British tradition, inclined to cagey secrecy is another matter. What restrictions or irresistible pressures, if any, there are on editors in political matters arise not from the law or from importuning by politicians or business interests, but from inside—from the owners and boards of the papers and, lately, from the trade unions.

If Irish newspapers enjoy considerable freedom from outside pressures, it might be thought that there is no cause for concern on democratic grounds. If that were so, Ireland would be out of step with much of the rest of the democratic world. There, the story has been of contraction in consumption and ownership, of takeover by big business, of mergers, and of devices to give financial support to newspapers by way of tax advantages, loans, and direct subsidies from public funds. Wherever these things have occurred, they have evoked public concern and, ironically, demands for state intervention. The state is increasingly expected to guarantee the operation of an independent press with an adequate number of organs.

Surveying this trend, Anthony Smith found that "throughout Western Europe, with a few important exceptions, government is, in the late 1970s, already being looked to as the primary guarantor of the press's existence." State intervention, he thought, had reached a stage where new formulations of the traditional ethic were needed, for "we are now witnessing a turning point in history which removes the media from the private to the public sector of society."[7]

There were few such developments in Ireland by 1980 and little sign of public unease. There had been no public enquiry into the state of the press and no demand for one (the United Kingdom had three royal commissions in thirty years); no public concern about concentration, for the only major takeover was that of the *Sunday World* by the Independent Group; no press council to hear complaints and protect standards; no state subsidies for newspapers; and no tax concessions. Alone of all the governments of the European Communities, the Irish government gave no tax advantages to newspapers, and the Irish newspaper industry was the only one to pay value-added tax (VAT) on its sales. Table 4.1 shows what a contrast there was between Ireland and some other European Community countries in this respect.

Evidently, the press in Ireland had not yet reached the turning point of which Anthony Smith wrote. Perhaps, however, there are some signs that it will follow the same road. Observing that newspapers are tending to become "just appendages to conglomerates and big business," T. P. Coogan, editor of the *Irish Press,* noted that "this tendency has begun in Ireland also; the whey-faced clerks are moving into the seats of power; banking and conglomerates have a markedly influential say on two of the three major Dublin newspapers."[8] With the takeover by the Independent Group of the *Sunday World*—itself a significant Johnny-come-lately onto the newspaper scene—and the Group's acquisition of a number of local papers, there are the makings of an empire—and a public problem. Developments of this kind might start Ireland down the road that others have already travelled.

TABLE 4.1

Tax Concessions, Grants, and Other Financial Aids Available to Newspapers in Ireland and Other Countries of the European Communities, 1977

Type of subsidy	Belgium	Denmark	France	Germany (F.D.R.)	Ireland	Italy	Netherlands	United Kingdom
VAT concessions	+	+	+	+		+	+	+
Other tax concessions	+	+						
Direct grants	+		+			+	+	
Low-interest loans		+		+		+	+	
Postal concessions	+	+	+	+		+	+	+
Telephone/Telegraph concessions	+	+	+	+		+	+	
Rail concessions	+		+			+	+	
Transport subsidies						+		
Government advertising	+	+				+		
Training and research grants					+			
News-agency subsidies			+			+		

SOURCE: A. Smith, "Subsidies and the Press in Europe," *Political and Economic Planning,* Vol. 43, no. 569 (June 1977), App. 1, p. 110.

In the circumstances of considerable freedom from outside pressures, what Irish newspapers choose to print presumably depends upon the commercial judgment and social and political attitudes of those who control them—their owners, managers, editors, and, of growing importance, their unions. At the national level, commercial considerations are most obviously and increasingly in evidence. In the late 1960s, there was a considerable uniformity in the amount and proportion of space given to various types of material and in the treatment of news and comment. By the late 1970s, there was more variety. Compared with the popular British papers, the Irish morning dailies were still serious papers, but their styles and images differed from one another more than they had a decade earlier.

To take the extremes: on the one hand, the *Irish Independent* had moved a long way towards being a "popular" newspaper; on the other hand, the *Irish Times* was increasingly realizing its editor's aphorism that "a newspaper is a collection of minority interests."[9] The *Irish Times* had the widest news coverage, particularly of foreign news, the largest amount of space given to parliamentary reports, and the biggest number of surveys of social, economic, and political topics. As the newspaper of record it printed major reports and documents *verbatim* or *in extenso:* on March 16, 1979, for example, it carried the full text of the encyclical letter *Redemptor Hominis* of Pope John Paul II. It was at the same time the most trendy of the dailies and was aggressively liberal. Nevertheless, these differences were probably less important than the fact that all three Dublin dailies were still comparatively serious papers. As Table 4.2 shows, their coverage of general elections in 1969 and 1977 was strikingly uniform.

The evening and the Sunday papers were very different. They carried less news, and far less political and foreign news, than the morning papers. The Sunday newspapers in particular resembled the British popular Sunday papers. One of them was a typical tabloid, and its first appearance in 1973 perhaps signalled the beginning of a new era in Irish journalism. By the late 1970s the question of a tabloid daily was a live one; advertisers were beginning to consider whether the time was right for the introduction of store-coupon advertisements; and the real estate supplements of some of the dailies were showing signs of commercial influences.

The local papers cover political events in their own districts and any national political news that has local significance—for example, the parliamentary questions and other interventions in debate offered by the local TDs (Teachtaí Dála, members of the Dáil) and senators. They

TABLE 4.2

Campaign Coverage by Morning Daily Newspapers, 1969 and 1977

Coverage	Irish Independent	Irish Press	Irish Times	Cork Examiner
Average space per day (% of total space):				
1969	19.4%	20.1%	20.0%	14.0%
1977	13.4%	18.2%	16.7%	9.6%
Number of page 1 lead stories:				
1969	3	5	4	5
1977	15	12	15	6
Number of editorials:				
1969	21	12	15	7
1977	17	11	19	10
Coverage of party manifestos in 1977 (column inches):				
Fianna Fáil	214	287	282	81
Coalition	223	217	269	81

SOURCE: Derived from B. Farrell, "The Mass Media and the 1977 Campaign," in *Ireland at the Polls: The Dáil Elections of 1977*, ed. H. R. Penniman (Washington, D.C., 1978), pp. 113–14.

feature reports of the proceedings of local authorities, health boards, and other public bodies. Such a focus might well reinforce the strong local orientation of many country people, the more so if such people do not read the national dailies.

Newspaper reading habits vary somewhat in Ireland as between regions, communities, and social groups. Because we know little about the effects upon people of consuming what the media produce, we can only point out these differences and suggest that they *might* be important in explaining people's political attitudes and behaviour.

A readership survey carried out in 1979 and 1980 showed that 57 per cent of all adults (age 15 and over) saw an Irish morning paper, 88 per cent saw a Sunday paper, and 61 per cent saw a local newspaper.[10] These figures, however, mask a number of different patterns. As Table 4.3 shows, for most people in the rural community the major sources of printed political information were the Sunday and local papers, which were read by nine out of ten of them; the evening and Sunday papers constituted the main reading fare of most Dubliners. Likewise, Table 4.4 shows considerable differences between social groups. The poorest in both town and country were the least likely to see a daily paper. Both in town and in country, though, almost as many of the poor as of the better-off saw a Sunday paper, and in rural areas as many of the smaller farmers and other poor people as of the better-off saw a local paper.

TABLE 4.3

Regional and Community Variations in Adult
Population Reading Irish Newspapers, 1979–80

Category	Any morning daily news- paper	Any evening daily news- paper	Any Sunday newspaper	Any local newspaper
All	57%	47%	88%	61%
Region:				
Dublin[a]	52	82	88	9
Rest of Leinster	56	43	90	89
Munster	69	37	88	69
Connacht and Ulster (part)[b]	47	15	87	94
Community:				
Urban	58	65	88	41
Rural	55	22	89	89

SOURCE: Derived from *Joint National Media Research, 1979–80,* Vol. 1 (Dublin, 1980), made available by Irish Marketing Surveys Ltd.

NOTE: "Adult" means age 15 and over.

[a] Dublin City, Dún Laoghaire, and County Dublin.

[b] Cavan, Donegal, and Monaghan in Ulster.

TABLE 4.4

Differences in Newspaper Reading Habits
According to Socioeconomic Status, 1979–80

Social class	Any morning daily news- paper	Any evening daily news- paper	Any Sunday newspaper	Any local newspaper
All[a]	57%	47%	88%	61%
Upper middle and middle class	86	52	90	40
Lower middle class	74	62	91	49
Skilled working class	54	63	93	55
Other working class and those at subsistence level	43	50	83	58
Farmers or farm managers on holdings of 50 acres or more	65	17	91	88
Farmers with holdings of less than 50 acres and farm workers	42	10	86	92

SOURCE: Derived from *Joint National Media Research, 1979–80,* Vol. 1.

[a] Age 15 and over.

The same readership survey also provides data on who reads the various newspapers. Tables 4.5 and 4.6 show that of the morning papers with a truly national circulation, the *Irish Independent* substantially outsold the *Irish Press* except among the least well off. The *Cork Examiner* was read by all classes in Munster. The *Irish Times* had the small-

TABLE 4.5

Adult Readership of the Principal Morning Daily, Evening,
and Sunday Newspapers by Region and Community, 1979–80

Newspaper	All	Region				Community	
		Dublin[a]	Rest of Leinster	Mun-ster	Connacht and Ulster (part)[b]	Urban	Rural
Irish Independent	30%	31%	39%	22%	28%	30%	29%
Irish Press	15	10	18	16	20	15	16
Irish Times	12	25	9	6	5	17	4
Cork Examiner	12	1	1	38	0	10	14
Evening Press	27	53	25	15	10	36	15
Evening Herald	20	43	22	4	6	29	7
Cork Evening Echo	6	0	0	21	0	9	2
Sunday Press	55	45	55	59	62	48	63
Sunday Independent	51	55	57	48	43	53	49
Sunday World	47	44	50	50	44	49	45

SOURCE: Derived from *Joint National Media Research, 1979–80*, Vol. 1.
NOTE: "Adult" means age 15 and over.
[a] Dublin City, Dún Laoghaire, and County Dublin.
[b] Cavan, Donegal, and Monaghan in Ulster.

TABLE 4.6

Adult Readership of the Principal Morning Daily Newspapers
by Socioeconomic Status, 1979–80

Social class	Irish Independent	Irish Press	Irish Times	Cork Examiner
All	30%	15%	12%	12%
Upper middle and middle class	39	15	50	12
Lower middle class	44	17	25	12
Skilled working class	31	16	7	11
Other working class and those at subsistence level	20	15	3	11
Farmers or farm managers on holdings of 50 acres or more	36	12	1	19
Farmers with holdings of less than 50 acres and farm workers	20	16	2	7

SOURCE: Derived from *Joint National Media Research, 1979–80*, Vol. 1.
NOTE: "Adult" means age 15 and over.

est circulation of the national dailies—much larger in Dublin than elsewhere, much larger in urban communities than in rural—but included a
higher proportion of the upper middle and middle class than any other
group. All the Sunday papers had a national following, and everywhere
some people saw more than one of them.

TABLE 4.7

Profile of Irish Times *Readers in 1968 and 1979–80*

Category	1979–80	1968
Region:		
Dublin	60%	59%
Rest of Leinster	16	11
Munster	15	23
Connacht and Ulster (part)	9	7
Community:		
Urban	85	84
Rural	15	16
Socioeconomic group:		
Upper middle and middle class	42	29
Lower middle class	35	30
Skilled working class	12	15
Other working class and those at subsistence level	7	15
Farmers or farm managers on holdings of 50 acres or more	1	8
Farmers with holdings of less than 50 acres and farm workers	2	3

SOURCE: For 1968, *National Readership Survey in Ireland, 1968,* prepared by the British Market Research Bureau and Social Surveys (Gallup Poll) Ltd. For 1979–80, *Joint National Media Research, 1979–80.*

The readership of the *Irish Times* is thought by many to be of particular political significance. Certainly, the majority of its readers in the late 1970s were urban, middle-class people living in and round Dublin. Compared with a decade before, it had become even more of a middle-class paper, as Table 4.7 shows. During the 1970s, it captured a bigger proportion of the upper-middle-class and middle-class groups. During the same period, the *Irish Independent*'s share dropped by 16 per cent.[11] Nevertheless, it is important to notice that this does not mean that the *Irish Times* was the most widely read paper by the middle class generally, let alone by the larger farmers of whom only 1 per cent saw it. Even if we assume that the middle class as a whole includes the vast majority of politically influential individuals, the situation was still not the same as that in Great Britain, where to a considerable extent the politically influential read one kind of newspaper (the "quality" papers) and the working class the other (the "popular" papers). There had been a clear movement in that direction, however. In any case, in Ireland, there was still not the same contrast between the content of the daily papers as there was in Britain. Readers of whatever Irish newspapers got much the same political information and comment, albeit presented in increasingly diverse styles.

IV

Whereas the press in Ireland is essentially an industry whose activities are not greatly restricted by the law and hardly if at all inhibited by political pressure, broadcasting has from the beginning been in the public sector. In Ireland, as in most other countries, "broadcasting became a prime exemplification of the social responsibility theory: too powerful, too scarce a resource to be allowed to operate completely unfettered."[12] In fact, it was from the beginning a state monopoly and remained so; until 1961, it was under direct ministerial control. As Anthony Smith has pointed out, in Ireland's case, this monopoly is operated under particularly unfavourable circumstances—a small population undergoing rapid cultural changes; a population that is too small and too poor to produce enough revenue whether by licence fees or advertising income; a population that possesses two languages, one of which is viewed with indifference by the majority and the other of which is the broadcasting language of its inconveniently close and overpoweringly large neighbour.[13]

The first broadcasting authority, Radio Éireann (1925–61), was a branch of the Department of Posts and Telegraphs. Its staff were civil servants, and its activities were open to detailed parliamentary scrutiny like all other services operated by the central administration. The effect of this was not to subject broadcasting to party political pressures but rather the reverse, to insulate it entirely from politics. The station took a strictly neutral position simply by broadcasting no political material at all. It was truly a political eunuch: in the words of Eamonn Andrews, the first chairman of its successor, Radio Telefís Éireann, "one of the worst but best-meaning radio services in the world."[14] The introduction of a television service in 1961 coincided with a rapid development of more forthright political programmes by the rival British broadcasting organizations and, inevitably, altered this state of affairs greatly.

The Broadcasting Authority Act (1960) was intended to give broadcasting a more autonomous status. It created Radio Telefís Éireann (RTE) in the form of a "state-sponsored body"—that is, a public authority with statutory functions and powers whose governing body is appointed, and can be dismissed, by its sponsor minister. (For a discussion of state-sponsored bodies, see Chapter 14.) This act and its successor, the Broadcasting Authority (Amendment) Act (1976), are the most important statutes governing broadcasting.

The act of 1960 was in some respects modelled upon British practice. It charged the Broadcasting Authority with providing both radio and television services, and gave it the right to collect licence fees and to sell commercial advertising. Although RTE was given a legal *persona* and some autonomy, the governing principle of the Broadcasting Authority Acts is the concept of social responsibility, which it is the duty of the state to ensure. Consequently, RTE operates under certain statutory constraints and is subject to certain government controls. The most important of these relate to programming and the circumstances in which the minister may intervene. Over the years these controls have been the cause of friction between governments and the Authority, leading to political debate and acrimony.

In carrying out its functions, RTE is required "in its programming" to

a. be responsive to the interests and concerns of the whole community, . . . reflect the varied elements which make up the culture of the people of the whole island of Ireland, and have special regard for the elements which distinguish that culture and in particular for the Irish language.

b. uphold the democratic values enshrined in the Constitution . . .

c. have regard to the need for the formation of public awareness and understanding of the values and traditions of countries other than the State, including in particular . . . members of the European Economic Community.[15]

News must be "reported and presented in an objective and impartial manner and without any expression of the Authority's own views." The same applies to the treatment of current affairs, which must in addition be "fair to all interests concerned."[16] The Authority is specifically prohibited from publishing in any form "anything which may reasonably be regarded as being likely to promote, or incite to, crime or as tending to undermine the Authority of the State."[17]

Besides imposing upon RTE the ordinary obligations of a state-sponsored body, such as to present an annual report and accounts to the minister and to give him information as required, the law empowers the minister "to direct the Authority in writing to allocate broadcasting time for any announcements by or on behalf of any Minister of State in connection with his functions."[18] In addition, "Where the Minister is of the opinion that the broadcasting of a particular matter or any matter of a particular class would be likely to promote, or incite to, crime or would tend to undermine the authority of the State, he may by order direct the Authority to refrain from broadcasting the matter."[19]

The story of broadcasting since the inception of television is peppered with controversy and incidents. RTE's difficulties were the greater because politicians and the public in general believed that television had

TABLE 4.8

Percentage of Television Programmes Devoted to News,
Current Affairs, and Other Information in Ireland and
Other Countries of the European Communities, 1977–78

Station	News	Information		Total news and information
		Current affairs	Other information	
BRT (Belgium)	8.4%	11.2%		19.6%
DR (Denmark)	7.9	8.9	17.4	34.2
AZF (France)	10.0	1.5	33.4	45.0
FR3 (France)	16.1	4.3	8.2	28.6
TF1 (France)	12.7	3.1	18.4	34.2
ZDF (Germany)	9.1	17.2	6.4	32.7
RTE (Ireland)	9.7	3.7	7.2	20.6
NOS (Netherlands)	6.9	4.9	20.3	32.2
IBA (United Kingdom)	10.1	11.0	1.0	22.1
BBC (United Kingdom)	7.3	17.7	10.7	35.7

SOURCE: Derived from data made available by Radio Telefís Éireann Audience Research.

tremendous power to influence, even brainwash, viewers. The evident concern shown in the legislation and in RTE's domestic procedures to ensure fair and balanced programmes reflects this belief in the enormous impact of broadcasting and the cagey suspicion that politicians have of journalist broadcasters. Programmes that might contain political messages were subjected to particular scrutiny and criticism. As Table 4.8 shows, RTE's output of television programmes that are likely to be important from the point of view of politics is among the lowest of the countries of the European Communities. Television news and current affairs programmes in 1977 and 1978 composed 13 per cent of total transmissions.

At election time, however, the Irish public gets a surfeit of political programmes. At the 1977 general election, RTE carried thirty-two "party political broadcasts" (time was allocated to parties in an agreed ratio: twelve programmes on television and twenty on radio) and presented sixteen programmes of constituency profiles totalling 127 minutes on radio and twelve constituency profiles totalling 173 minutes on television. In addition, campaign coverage was carried daily in news and feature programmes. To do this, RTE created, in Brian Farrell's words, "an elaborate machinery to plan and monitor its performance."[20] On that occasion, the station went to great lengths to fulfil its statutory obligation to be "fair to all interests concerned" and to ensure that "broadcast matter is presented in an objective and impartial matter and without any expression of the Authority's own views."[21] The need to do so and to be seen to do so is evident when one considers the audiences for programmes that have, or might have, a political content.

Almost everyone has access to a radio, and in 1979 over 75 per cent of adults listened to RTE at some time each day. The importance of radio lies mainly in its audiences for news programmes. In 1979, each of the two morning newcasts in English was heard by 25 per cent of the adult population; the lunchtime newcast, by about 40 per cent. Magazine-type programmes with a considerable political content, broadcast in the daytime when there was no television, attracted 20 per cent of the adult population. Once television was available, however, less than 5 per cent listened.

By 1979, the proportion of the population in homes with television, at 93 per cent, was approaching the saturation level (about 95 per cent) already reached by most of the countries of the European Communities. The marked discrepancies in set ownership that had been such a feature of the past were fast disappearing. Rather, there were differences in viewing habits. In 1979, 45 per cent of televisions in the Republic would receive British (including Northern Ireland) programmes, and, as Table 4.9 shows, these programs had a considerable attraction. Almost six out of ten Dubliners watched at least some British programmes each day, as did four out of ten urban families generally. Rural—that is, mainly farming—people and the people of Munster generally did not because they could not.[22]

TABLE 4.9
Television Viewing by Adults in Ireland, 1979–80

| | Viewing yesterday | | |
Category	Any TV at all	RTE	All other stations[a]
All	80%	71%	29%
Region:			
Dublin	79	62	59
Rest of Leinster	80	73	33
Munster	81	80	2
Connacht and Ulster (part)	82	70	22
Community:			
Urban	80	69	40
Rural	80	74	14

SOURCE: Derived from *Joint National Media Research, 1979–80,* Vol 1.
NOTE: "Adult" means age 15 and over.
[a] BBC and Independent Television broadcasts from both Northern Ireland and Great Britain. People who watched both RTE and some other station are included.

TABLE 4.10

Audiences for RTE's Main Television News and Current Affairs
Programmes, January–April 1979

Programme	TAM ratings[a]	
	Lowest	Highest
Main evening news		
(seven-day average)	54	60
"Newsnight"[b]		
(Monday-to-Friday average)	6	15
"Frontline"[c]		
(average for Monday and Friday editions)	35	49
"Feach"[d]	15	33

SOURCE: Derived from data made available by Radio Telefís Éireann Audience Research.

[a] Audiences are measured by Irish TAM Ltd. A TAM (Television Audience Measurement) rating of 50 for a programme means that 50 per cent of all households with a television set were viewing that programme.

[b] "Newsnight" was the late-night news programme broadcast on RTE 2.

[c] "Frontline" was the major current affairs programme.

[d] "Feach" was a current affairs programme mostly but not wholly in Irish.

TABLE 4.11

Audiences for Party Political Broadcasts at the 1977 General Election

Party	Percentage of supporters who watched the party political broadcasts on behalf of:		
	Fianna Fáil	Fine Gael	Labour
Fianna Fáil	69.1%	56.9%	40.6%
Fine Gael	65.6	67.8	42.2
Labour	69.8	64.2	49.1

SOURCE: Derived from unpublished information from the Irish Times/National Opinion Polls Election Survey, made available by Richard Sinott.

The audiences for programmes between January and April 1979 that were most likely to have an important political content are set out in Table 4.10. The major current affairs programme was regularly among those with the largest audiences. Similarly, at the 1977 general election audiences for television election programmes "each numbered among the weekly 'top ten' programmes transmitted by R.T.E."[23] An Irish Times/National Opinion Polls survey indicated that there were differences according to party. About two-thirds of the supporters of Fianna Fáil and Fine Gael and rather less than one-half of Labour supporters watched the party political broadcasts (see Table 4.11). Audiences were smaller in areas where alternative—that is, British—programmes were available.

"Undoubtedly the introduction of television marked a watershed in Irish mass communication. It was novel and adventurous in a way the older media could not be expected to emulate."[24] The most conservative elements in a very conservative community found television coverage disturbing. Surveying the troubled history of Irish broadcasting, Desmond Fisher concluded that "it was from the programming itself and from the evolution of broadcasting's new relationship to the state, to government and to the different elements in Irish society, itself going through a period of rapid and sometimes painful adjustment, that difficulties developed."[25] Powerful interest groups like the Catholic Church and language and sporting organizations—all foundation pillars of Irish society—complained frequently in the early days, and occasionally still do, at what they considered RTE's sins of omission or commission. "It was, however, in the political field that the biggest problems arose."[26]

In this respect, Ireland was not alone. On the contrary, Anthony Smith has drawn attention to "the remarkable way in which television has developed along similar lines since the 1950s in so many different countries." Ireland joined the scene in the early 1960s when, in Smith's words, "television had seemed for a moment to escape from all its bonds and become a free and international medium, operated by an almost autonomous profession *despite* its legal and constitutional background." However, to quote Smith yet again, "the most important change which appears to have taken place since then is the realisation everywhere that the practices of television will inevitably and necessarily be subjected to political scrutiny and politically imposed change. The genie has been put back in the bottle."[27] This was precisely the experience in Ireland, and it was a painful one.

In its first years, RTE worked in an optimistic atmosphere. "Its rapid expansion provided opportunities for a new generation of broadcasters ... who were not unduly constrained by the restrictions of the act; indeed in many cases they were scarcely aware of them."[28] From the mid-1960s, there were a number of clashes between the Broadcasting Authority and ministers or other politicians. They arose partly from the absence of any settled ground rules governing the relationship of broadcasting journalists and the state, such as existed in respect of the press; partly from fears and suspicions of the new medium; and partly because "occasional programmes did not adequately meet the required standards of objectivity and impartiality."[29]

It became increasingly clear, however, that "senior politicians did not share the ideal of an independent service free from government interference."[30] At its most vulgar this came down to the view of some politicians that RTE, being a state body, should treat all public representatives with respect; report their speeches, whether important or not; and never ask them awkward questions. More serious was the view that RTE was "an instrument of public policy," put forward in 1966 by the Taoiseach of the day, Seán Lemass, during a Dáil discussion on an incident involving the station and a minister:

Radio Telefís Éireann was set up by legislation as an instrument of public policy and as such is responsible to the Government. The Government have overall responsibility for its conduct and especially the obligation to ensure that its programmes do not offend against the public interest. . . . To this extent the Government reject the view that Radio Telefís Éireann should be, either generally or in regard to its current affairs and news programmes, completely independent of Government supervision.[31]

This was a strong expression of the social responsibility theory. Although Lemass' statement was made in the context of pressure by a minister to alter a news item, it was probably not intended to cover petty interference. It was, however, in respect of the treatment of events in Northern Ireland after 1969, an altogether more serious subject, that the matter was put to the test.

In its desire to report developments in Northern Ireland in a full, balanced, and rounded way, RTE considered that it should report the views of republican organizations such as the IRA as expressed by their spokesmen. Governments took the contrary view, that such reporting would give undesirable publicity and encouragement to organizations whose aim was to subvert the state and perhaps would imply that their spokesmen had some status. In 1971, the Fianna Fáil Minister for Posts and Telegraphs directed the Authority under section 31 of the Broadcasting Authority Act "to refrain from broadcasting any matter that could be calculated to promote the aims and activities of any organization which engages in, encourages or advocates the attaining of any particular objective by violent means." Disagreement arose over the interpretation of this directive; and when, in November 1972, after growing political criticism, RTE broadcast a reporter's account of an interview with a provisional IRA leader, the Authority itself was dismissed.

During the period of office of the Coalition Government that succeeded Fianna Fáil in 1973, there was further disagreement. In October 1976, Conor Cruise O'Brien, then minister, issued another directive forbidding broadcasts or reports of interviews with members of a number of republican organizations and of organizations proscribed in Northern Ireland by the British government. Cruise O'Brien himself subsequently put the matter, as he saw it, quite clearly:

Since membership of a private army is a crime, propaganda in favour of such an army is incitement to crime, and therefore is itself a crime. That much is clear. But whether given words and images constitute propaganda or incitement is endlessly debateable—or rather would be endlessly debateable if, in practice, somebody did not have to decide it. But who should that somebody be, in relation to broadcasting . . .? I could have left that decision to the Authority itself. In the circumstances . . . I thought it safer to act myself.[32]

These events—and there is a similar and continuing history of tension between British broadcasters and British governments—demonstrate clearly that when it comes to sensitive matters, broadcasters are not going to be left free to treat them according to their own standards or be permitted to interpret the requirement to be "objective and impartial" in their own way:

The meaning of impartiality as drawn from the model of the journalistic role in the fourth estate, implying divorce from attachments which might colour or prejudice reportage, [does] not fit, and in fact would inevitably clash with, the meaning as applied in political crises. . . . Given the formal status of the government vis-à-vis the broadcasting organizations it can ultimately ensure that opposed realities do not arise by defining within what context impartiality will operate.[33]

Of course, broadcasters chafe at this. They have the more reason to do so because politicians, particularly those in office, continue to be prone, on the one hand, to petulant sensitivity and, on the other, to seeking to influence or thwart broadcasters for immediate political advantage.

Radical critics of Irish broadcasting, including some in broadcasting itself, have a more general complaint. In their view, current affairs programmes, and programmes generally, reflect the values of a small but powerful minority: "When analysis does occur, most often it is presented by dominant class figures of the society and here must be included the professional broadcasters who, because of their job, have become encoders and voices of the accepted values of the achievement society in which we live."[34] Certainly, given the tendency of a conservative and homogeneous society to expect conformity and the general expectations, not least among the urban working class and the farming community, that broadcasting will not upset conventional attitudes too much, there has always been strong pressure on broadcasters to confine themselves within the framework of dominant values. Nevertheless, as a group, they have sought consistently but gently to broaden the framework, and in some matters, such as sexual morality, they have done so with some success.

In politics, however, they were locked in by the law and the attitudes of politicians in power. At the end of the 1970s, they worked within written "guidance" and "guidelines" laid down internally in an attempt to satisfy the station's political masters. They were subjected also to a system of "upward referral" to the director general, who thus functioned as an "editor-in-chief."[35] Commenting on this practice, which developed in the United Kingdom also, Anthony Smith makes the point that "the visitation upon the hapless figure of the chief executive of an obligation to make all programme decisions on a particular subject is, in Ireland as in Britain, a compromise with those politicians who believe that radio and television are infiltrated, consciously or no, by people predisposed to undermine existing authority."[36]

For their part, some journalists resented this interference with their exercise of their profession. A *Report on Censorship in R.T.E.* (that was strongly criticized by the Authority for unsubstantiated allegations) complained *inter alia* in 1977 that the statutory restrictions "had the effect of intimidating journalists in their work, and of promoting self-censorship" and that "there is growing evidence of unnecessary interference" in their work."[37]

They were not alone. As Anthony Smith, surveying Western Europe, pointed out, "There is a danger that the rethinking which has characterized the years since 1970, and which has led to reorganization of parts of broadcasting internally and externally, will slip imperceptibly into another period of self-censorship and damaging restraint."[38] Perhaps Michael Tracey was right when he observed that "broadcasting organizations as institutions within society have no actual autonomy and in that sense they have never possessed a legitimate membership of the 'fourth estate.' . . . That fundamental absence of legitimacy as autonomous entities has always defined the political reality of political broadcasting."[39]

V

The effect of the mass media upon political attitudes and behaviour is a subject that has come to be widely recognized as among the most perplexing in modern politics. In the case of Ireland, very little can be said because of the lack of data. We may suspect that the mass media actually communicate less to politicians about the feelings and desires of the public and less to the public about the whys and wherefores of ministerial action than either politicians or newspeople like to believe. As Rudolf Klein has argued, "Newspapers and politicians have an almost incestuous relationship: they tend to have closer ties with each other than the newspapers have with their readers and politicians have with their voters. The result is that they both tend to overestimate their influence on the country at large—when, in fact, their main influence is often on each other."[40] Perhaps the same might be said of broadcasters and politicians.

Certainly wide access to news, information, and comment does not guarantee close contact or mutual understanding between government and the governed, particularly since the most marked characteristic of political communications by the mass media is their asymmetry. The opportunities for leaders to address the public have vastly increased and so have potential audiences. In contrast, opportunities for the public in general and for those who disagree radically in particular to answer back have not been widened to the same extent; developments in popular access have been slow.

The problem of the remoteness of the government from the citizens is widely accepted as among the most dangerous for democracy. Given the small size and the comparative homogeneity of the people of the Republic, it ought to be easier of solution in Ireland than in larger and more diverse countries. The closer contacts between Irish ministers and rank-and-file deputies and party workers, which small scale makes possible, no doubt help them keep in touch in a way that perhaps is more difficult for the ministers of much larger countries. Even in Ireland, however, the failure of some ministers and some important sectional interests to see each other's point of view and the bewilderment and increasing frustration of a public that cannot understand what the real issues are seem to point, at the very least, to serious failures to communicate.

Today, there are fewer differences between Irish people in respect of access to political information via the mass media than there ever were. Also, as we have seen, there are no great differences in the picture with which people are presented whatever they read, see, or hear. Whereas a decade ago there were considerable differences in newspaper reading and in television viewing, today the major differences are, first, between those who read one of the comparatively serious morning dailies and those who do not and, second, between those who have access to British television and those who have not. Perhaps also the readership profile of the *Irish Times* has political significance. However, we do not know what, if any, effects these differences have. Indeed, we know so little about the impact of the political "inputs" effected by way of the mass media generally that we can hardly even begin to assess their influence upon the "outputs"—that is, people's political behaviour. Consequently, there is a formidable gap between this chapter and the rest of the book, the measure of our lack of understanding of political behaviour.

PART II

PARTICIPATION AND REPRESENTATION

FIVE

Patterns of Participation and Representation

In the two worlds of modern politics, the liberal democratic and the totalitarian, politics is mass politics. In principle at least, people are entitled, and even expected, to be involved, though the nature, quantity, and quality of that involvement vary considerably, not only between the two worlds but also inside them. Democracies might be judged by the amount of popular participation in politics, the ease with which people can become candidates for office or get access to those who hold office, and the extent of the use of the devices of competitive election and representation.

In seeking to measure the extent of participation and representation, it is necessary to pay attention not only to formal procedures and to the holders of formal offices, but also to informal activities and to people who, though they do not hold an official public position, nevertheless play some part in political decision making and perhaps have some influence on outcomes. For when it comes to making a political decision, the spokesman of a powerful group with an interest in the particular issue might well play a much larger part than an elected parliamentary representative. Nor must we forget those activities that are "outside the system," or at least outside the normal channels and perhaps even outside constitutional or legal limits. Those who engage in such activities are also participating in politics, albeit by other means.

II

Bunreacht na hÉireann in Article 6 refers to the right of the people "to designate the rulers of the state and, in final appeal, to decide all questions of national policy." This sums up people's legal rights, but it exaggerates their actual role. The only active part in governing for most people is by way of voting at elections for public offices and at referenda on questions of public policy that legally require the approval of the electorate. It is curious, therefore, when one considers the importance given to consulting the people in democratic theory, how little attention is paid to the question of the number of occasions that are in practice afforded to the people to vote. In fact, the opportunities to exercise such "sovereign" power are fewer in Ireland than they are, for example, in the United States.

The Constitution provides for referenda in two circumstances. First, if a majority of the Seanad and not less than one-third of the Dáil petition the President to decline to sign a bill on the ground that it contains "a proposal of such national importance that the will of the people thereon ought to be ascertained," the President may accede to such a request and precipitate a referendum or a dissolution of the Dáil and a general election. Because governments are able to command majorities in the Seanad, this procedure has never been invoked. Second, and of more practical importance, any proposal to amend the Constitution, having been approved by both houses of the Oireachtas, must be "submitted by referendum to the decision of the people." There were eight such instances between 1937, when the present Constitution came into force, and 1980. The importance and value of this procedure as a means by which the people are enabled to check their governments and representatives were amply demonstrated by two of them. Both in 1959 and in 1968, proposals to change the electoral system were passed by the Oireachtas but rejected by the electorate.

Irish electors have three opportunities to take part in the selection of public officials. Elections for members of Dáil Éireann are by law required to be held at least once every five years. In practice, on average, they occur about once every three to three-and-a-half years. Indirectly, this process produces a government as well as a popular assembly, for the party or group of parties that wins a majority of seats thereby acquires the right to form a government. Thus Irish electors do not directly elect their government as, for example, the American electorate choose their President. Elections for members of local authorities are provided for by law every five years, but they can be, and have in the past been, postponed by ministerial order to suit the government's convenience. The President, who, to use Walter Bagehot's terms, has a largely "dignified" rather than an "efficient" role, is also subject to election every seven years; but, here too, the politicians can connive to produce an agreed-upon candidate. This they did on four out of eight occasions between 1937 and 1980, thus depriving the people of their right to choose.

If the opportunities for Irish citizens to elect representatives to speak and act for them are few enough, the part citizens play in the selection process is greater than that played by the citizens of many democratic countries by reason of the opportunities offered by the election system that is used—the single transferable vote system. However, it is still not as great as that played by American citizens, for not only are a considerable number of congressional, administrative, and judicial offices subject to election in the United States, but the practice of having primary elections (that is, direct popular participation in nominating the party candidates to go forward for election) gives voters a bigger say than they have in Ireland.

Elections in Ireland as in many other countries give voters the opportunity to choose between the candidates who are presented to them. The choice of the great majority of these candidates as of most political officeholders is made by officials and other active members of political parties. In the same way, the choice of most leaders and spokesmen of interest groups is similarly limited. Thus, most of the more important political officeholders and the politically influential are chosen or put up for final popular choice by quite small "selectorates"—the government itself, which has enormous patronage; party executives, national and local; selection committees at all levels in parties; and bodies such as trade unions and farmers' organizations, which operate in the political arena. To a very large extent, small groups in bodies such as these choose or sponsor the personnel of politics. These active members form a middle group between the electorate and the very small number of people who hold the most important political offices.

Selection of a different kind, on criteria of merit and often by way of competition, provides another small but vital group of participants— senior public servants in the departments of state and other public authorities. Finally, there is a miscellaneous handful of people such as journalists, advisers, and consultants whose influence arises from the positions they hold or the confidence they inspire.

III

The pattern of participation has well-marked characteristics. For the vast majority, voting at elections and referenda is the limit of their active participation. Many, perhaps most, regard themselves as supporters of a political party, although they are not party members and are not much if at all involved in party politics or any kind of politics. The politically active, even on the least onerous of definitions of "active," are a small minority. The political leadership, including those who directly influence the national decision makers, is minute. In Table 5.1 an attempt is made

TABLE 5.1
Participation in Politics in the 1970s and 1980

Group	Number of participants	Per cent of electorate
Electorate (1977)	2,111,606	
Voters: 1977 general election	1,616,770	76.6%
1979 local elections	1,405,948	64.0
Have given money to help campaign or candidate in election (1976)	—	35.0[a]
Have worked on behalf of candidate at election (1976)	—	11.0[a]
Engaged in political action at local level (1971)	—	11.0[b]
Engaged in political action at national level (1971)	—	3.0[b]
Party members (1980)[c]	142,000	6.7
Party "activists" (1980)	27,500	1.3
Candidates at local elections (1974)	3,234	0.16
Members of local authorities (1974)	1,539	0.08
Oireachtas candidates (1977)	533	0.025
Oireachtas members (1977)	208	0.01
Senior public servants (1980)	2,500 approx.	0.12
Members of boards and chief executives of state-sponsored bodies[d] and leaders of major pressure groups (1980)	1,500 approx.	0.07

SOURCE: Official publications; Irish Marketing Surveys Ltd. (see note *a*); J. Raven and C. T. Whelan, "Irish Adults' Perceptions of Their Civic Institutions and Their Own Role in Relation to Them," in J. Raven *et al., Political Culture in Ireland: The Views of Two Generations* (Dublin, 1976) (see note *b*); newspapers; information supplied by parties; private enquiries.

[a] Percentage of population aged 18 and over. Source: Irish Marketing Surveys Ltd., *RTE "Survey"—Politics* (Report prepared for Radio Telefís Éireann, September 1976), Table 7.

[b] Percentage of population over 21 years of age who reported that they had in the past acted with the intention of influencing a political decision. Source: J. Raven and C. T. Whelan, "Irish Adults' Perceptions of Their Civic Institutions," pp. 29 and 30.

[c] Parties' own estimates. This is the total of individual members only. The figure does not include membership of unions affiliated to the Labour Party, which totalled nearly 173,000 in 1979.

[d] For a definition of "state-sponsored body," see p. 270.

to quantify participation. (Some of the figures can only be very approximate.) The resultant profile of participation is similar to that which has been observed elsewhere.[1]

When it comes to voting, the record of the Irish electorate is not very good when compared with that of the other countries of the European Communities. Table 5.2 offers some European comparisons. In looking at it, it is necessary to remember that there is a considerable variety of laws and practices in respect of who can vote, voting age, registration, and the obligation to vote. Voting in Ireland is not compulsory as it is in some democratic countries, and only registered voters may participate. The proportion of these who turned out to vote at the nine elections between the end of the Second World War and 1977 varied between 71

TABLE 5.2

Voting at General Elections in Ireland and Other Countries of the European Communities, 1974–79

Nation	Year	Turnout
Belgium	1978	91.6%[a]
Denmark[b]	1977	88.7
France	1978	84.7
Germany (F.D.R.)[c]	1976	90.7
Ireland	1977	76.3
Italy[d]	1976	93.2
Luxembourg	1974	90.1[a]
Netherlands	1977	87.5
United Kingdom	1979	76.0

SOURCE: *Election Fact Book* (European Broadcasting Union, Geneva, 1979).

[a] Voting is compulsory. The percentage of valid votes has been given instead of the turnout.

[b] Excluding Greenland.

[c] Excluding West Berlin.

[d] Voting in Italy is compulsory, but there is no provision for penalties.

per cent and 77 per cent; in 1977 it was 76 per cent. Turnout at Irish local elections was lower: in 1979 it was approximately 64 per cent; in 1974, 63 per cent. The referendum on joining the European Communities attracted 71 per cent; the referendum on the law governing the adoption of children, only 29 per cent.

The propensity to vote is not uniform throughout the Irish community. There are regional differences. A smaller proportion of the electorate in Dublin, the only large city, vote than elsewhere, for the urban population is more mobile and more volatile in its voting habits. Voting levels are also lower in one or two of the mountainous and least-developed western seaboard areas. Although there is not much difference between the proportion of men and women who vote, there are some differences according to age. As is commonly the case in many countries, a few per cent more of the young voters, especially those who are getting their first opportunity to vote, and of the very old abstain.

Although it is difficult to measure active participation in politics, it is quite certain that the proportion of the population who are in any way active, even by way of an occasional intervention, is very small. Raven and Whelan found that, although about half of Irish adults believe that they could do something about a harmful regulation, in fact only 11 per cent had ever acted with the intention of influencing a decision at the local level and only 3 per cent at the national level.[2] Figures for party membership in Table 5.1 were supplied by the parties themselves and, at 142,000 (nearly 7 per cent of the electorate), are perhaps optimistic:

in the late 1960s, independent enquiries suggested numbers ranging from 50,000 to 95,000.[3] Anyway, membership is in the majority of cases more an indication of commitment than a proof of activity.

In general, party branches, of which there are some fifty-five hundred, each have about five officers. It could be said that unless a branch is dormant, as some are except when elections are imminent, these officers are liable to be engaged in party work from time to time. Thus at least about 27,500 people might be said to be active at the branch level. Of course, some branches evoke considerable participation, but most do not. In any case, at election time there is a flurry of activity at the branch level, with many times this number active for a few days or a week or two.

It is not possible either to be precise about the number of those whose jobs or membership in organizations involve them in making political decisions or in seeking to influence those who do. If the chief executives and members of the boards or governing bodies of about a hundred state-sponsored bodies are included, together with the executives and chief officials of a score of organizations that engage in pressure-group activities regularly or frequently, plus a handful of others, we might reach a total of about fifteen hundred people with certainly no more than two hundred or so of these occupied full time in these posts.

When it comes to candidates for elected authorities and elected members, we are on surer ground. Candidates for seats in the Oireachtas and on local authorities number about four thousand, and at the last elections to these bodies (1979) the total number of seats was a little over seventeen hundred. Only a small proportion of the holders of these, about one-half of the Dáil,[4] and a handful of others, are full-time politicians. Certainly these number less than one hundred. Also full time are the senior civil servants, who advise ministers and manage the departments of state, and a few senior officers in other public authorities who might be said to have political duties or to exercise political influence. If we include in this group all civil servants of the rank of higher executive officer and above—and this is to cast the net quite widely—they number about twenty-five hundred. Thus, in all, perhaps less than three thousand people (0.14 per cent of the electorate) are full time at politics; about thirty thousand (less than 1.5 per cent) are "active" in politics; and another 5 per cent or so are committed enough to be associated with party politics. Politics is certainly only for the few.

So far, we have considered "system" politics. However, an examination of the incidence of "outside-the-system" activities such as demonstrations, marches, and political strikes and the numbers involved in them only confirms this picture. Crowds ranging from a few score to a few hundred and very occasionally more can be assembled by radical groups, particularly nationalist organizations evoking traditional and symbolic causes. A larger, though still small, minority support these causes in a casual way with small contributions collected in pubs and on the streets. Such support does not extend to membership, let alone to active membership in radical or extreme organizations, which is tiny. (The impact that this minute group has on politics and the community generally is out of all proportion to its numbers.)

Occasionally, a particular issue evokes a momentary flare-up of interest among larger numbers. Farmers' organizations have sometimes held mass protests, and one such, in 1980, attracted forty thousand participants; but attempts to take more militant action such as commodity strikes or the withholding of taxes or levies have not so far had much success. In recent years, conservation issues have been among those most likely to arouse interest. In August 1979, twelve thousand people went to Carnsore Point to protest about the proposal to build a nuclear power plant there. It was in 1979 too that independent Ireland experienced its first political strike, a one-day strike and marches to protest about the income-tax code. Organized by trade unions despite the discouragement of the leaders of the Irish Congress of Trade Unions, 150,000 people took part in the Dublin march. The event perhaps served to remind politicians that Irish citizens are potentially active if politicians fail them. However, if such activities are regarded as signalling the failure of "system" politics, it is evident that the "reach" of the Irish system has so far been sufficient to encompass most political aspirations. Only the numerically tiny extreme republican groups continue to operate outside the system, as they have for over half a century.

In the area of voluntary and community activity, which is not conventionally regarded as "political," there is much evidence of vastly greater participation than that evoked by "politics." There exists a surprisingly large and increasing number of voluntary and community organizations. For example, a survey made in four small towns in the early 1970s suggested that there was about one voluntary organization for every forty of the population in that type of community at least (see Table 5.3).[5] An increasing number of voluntary bodies is involved in local community welfare services, in the provision of amenities, and in protection activities. Although local authorities can and do cooperate with them, and officially recognize one community association in each area as the official

TABLE 5.3

Numbers of Voluntary Organizations in Four Rural Towns, 1971

Object of organization	Nenagh (pop. 4,500)	Westport (pop. 2,920)	Borrisokane (pop. 750)	Newport (pop. 580)
Development	11	12	2	2
Welfare	21	14	6	3
Physical recreation	25	18	4	3
Social and cultural	18	7	4	4
Educational	15	2	0	0
Trade union	21	14	2	2
TOTAL	111	67	18	14

SOURCE: Institute of Public Administration, *More Local Government: A Programme for Development* (Dublin, 1971), p. 18.

body with whom they do business, the worlds of politics and community action tend to be separate and unlinked. The problem of how to integrate them is a difficult one.[6]

IV

The extent to which people participate in politics differs according to the opportunities, institutionalized and informal, that are available, and these in turn are governed by the social norms and the political culture of the community. Everyone in the community has some "political resources"—that is, the ability to exert some influence on politics—but these vary enormously according to a person's education, occupation, wealth, status in the community, social involvement, and charisma. Whether these resources remain latent or are used depends upon an individual's interests, the stimuli he or she experiences, the organizations available, and personal psychological needs and drives.[7]

The information available hardly starts to provide an adequate answer to the question: who are the politically active in Ireland? To start with, "there is little in the way of coherent and systematic theory relating social, psychological and political variables to the act of participation in politics."[8] In particular, "it is not easy to establish clear and reliable connections between personality and political behavior," although it is certain that the influence of personality is among the most important of all the governing factors.[9] All we have for Ireland are data relating to characteristics such as sex, education, occupation, residence, and family connections.

One thing is immediately clear, however. The politically active are by no means a social microcosm of the community. The disparity between the proportion of men and women active in politics is enormous. Whereas women have had the vote in Ireland from the very foundation of the state and their propensity to use it differs little from that of men, active participation and particularly candidature is a different matter. The paucity of women in politics reflects cultural norms that are only now slowly changing; in this respect, Ireland lags behind Western Europe generally. Only in 1978 was a woman appointed a full minister and member of the government. (Countess Markievicz was "Minister for Labour" in "governments" appointed by the first Dáil, in April 1919, and the second Dáil, in August 1921, during the period of struggle for independence.)

The proportion of women candidates at local and general elections has always been tiny. At the 1977 general election, it took the intervention of party leaders and central executives in constituency nomination proceedings to bring the total of women candidates up to twenty-five (7 per cent); in 1973, it was sixteen (5 per cent). Six of the 1977 candidates were elected, but five of these were relatives of former deputies; in 1973, four women were elected. Out of the sixty senators who took office in 1977, six were women. But three of these were nominated by the Taoiseach, and two others were elected by the atypical university electorates; only one was elected by the politicians themselves who make up the electorate for the vocational panels. (For details of the system of election to the Seanad, see Chapter 11.)

In Ireland, as in other Western countries, politics is to a great extent a middle-class activity dominated by members of certain professions and occupations. Although it is not possible to say much about who is active at the rank-and-file level in the parties, there are not many labourers or very small farmers; rather it is better-off farmers, shopkeepers, publicans, and people with family businesses, together with teachers, clerical workers, and a few professional people, who predominate. Analysis of the occupations of members of local authorities (see Table 5.4) shows that at this level farmers are well represented, though usually it is the better-off farmers rather than the poorer farmers who are involved; and that "employers and managers," a group consisting mainly of shopkeepers and family business people, are greatly overrepresented, as are professional people, a large proportion of them teachers. This last category is steadily increasing as the overrepresentation of farmers is becoming less marked. Although people in the working-class groups can win seats in the smaller authorities, the working class generally is greatly underrepresented.

At the national level, the same features are to a great extent repeated in even more marked fashion. Here, it is obvious that politics is for a

TABLE 5.4

Occupations of Members of Local Authorities Elected in 1967 and 1974

Occupation[a]	County Councils		County Borough Councils		Urban District Councils		Town Commissioners	
	1967	1974	1967	1974	1967	1974	1967	1974
Farming and fishing[b]	36.7%	29.1%	0%	0%	3.0%	1.9%	4.2%	3.9%
Professional	9.8	13.7	17.6	20.4	10.4	16.9	5.8	8.3
Trade union officials	1.1	1.3	6.5	3.7	1.7	1.5	0.5	0
Employers and managers[c]	30.4	32.6	35.2	27.7	41.0	29.8	42.3	36.4
Nonmanual	10.7	8.9	24.1	13.9	18.8	14.9	15.9	15.5
Skilled manual	2.5	4.2	4.6	8.3	13.4	15.5	12.7	13.6
Semiskilled and unskilled manual	1.8	3.5	3.7	9.3	5.2	12.8	11.2	16.5
Unclassified or unknown	6.1	6.7	8.3	16.7	6.5	6.7	7.4	5.8

SOURCE: For 1967, compiled by the author from notices of poll and local newspapers. For 1974, *Administration*, 23 (1975), 465.

[a] Groupings adapted from *Census of Population, 1961*, Vol. 3.
[b] Mainly farmers and farmers' relatives.
[c] Mainly small shopkeepers, publicans, and family businesses.

very special few. The important offices are held almost exclusively by people of higher socioeconomic status with second- or third-level education and to a great extent by men in or from a small number of occupations. Table 5.5 shows that three groups dominate the scene—farmers, though in proportion to their numbers in the community they are underrepresented; employers and managers, mainly shopkeepers and owners of small businesses; and professional people, especially teachers and lawyers. The last two groups are greatly overrepresented. In contrast, the working class is greatly underrepresented, though the presence of trade union officials might be thought to mitigate this deficiency to some extent. In a population where only one-quarter complete a second-level education and well under 10 per cent get a university education or professional training, 56 per cent of the 1977 deputies had achieved second-level and another 36 per cent third-level education.

At the very top, the domination of professional men is overwhelming. Since the beginning of the state, six out of ten of all the ministers had worked in one of the professions or had trained for one before they became full-time politicians. As in many other countries, there are more lawyers than any other group at this level. The only other occupational group that has consistently provided members of the government in any numbers is "employers and managers," people who often have many

TABLE 5.5

*Occupations of Members of the Oireachtas Elected in 1977
and of Ministers Appointed from 1922 to 1979*

Occupation[a]	Population (1971)	Members of Oireachtas (1977)	Ministers (1922–79)
Farming and fishing[b]	24.7%	14.9%	7.2%
Professional	{ 6.7	31.7	59.8
Trade union officials		4.3	5.2
Industry and commerce[c]	5.1	31.3	21.6
Nonmanual	24.2	5.3	3.1
Skilled manual	16.5	2.9	3.1
Semiskilled and unskilled manual	14.5	0	0
Unclassified or unknown	8.2	9.6	0

SOURCE: For population, *Census of Population of Ireland, 1971,* Vol. 4. For occupations, compiled from data in T. Nealon, *Guide to the 21st Dáil and Seanad* (Blackrock, 1977); Flynn's *Oireachtas Companion* (various dates); newspapers; private enquiries.

[a]Groupings adapted from *Census of Population, 1961,* Vol. 3. Full-time politicians have not been classified separately. They have been classified according to their previous occupations. Many members of the Oireachtas have more than one occupation. In such cases, the job making the most demands on a member's time and energy has been counted.

[b]Mainly farmers and farmers' relatives.

[c]Mainly small shopkeepers, publicans, and family businesses.

local business interests in their area. This group has contributed another two out of ten of all ministers.

In Ireland, neither membership in a profession nor having business interests implies a middle-class origin; most such people, however, will not have come from the poorest sections of society, and their occupations will have led to their living in a middle-class life style. The same is true of the top civil servants. There is, however, no semblance of an exclusive upper-class "establishment" based on birth, school and university, and social intercourse. In the past, there was a political elite of a different sort.

The surviving leaders of the independence movement, men with what came to be known as "a national record," and their families for long dominated Irish politics. This first generation of leaders, who were "politicians by accident," and their relatives and cronies filled the top positions from the 1920s to the 1950s (most of them were very young in the early 1920s). Some of this generation were able to found political dynasties, for one of the features of Irish political life has been the family tradition. In Ted Nealon's *Guide to the 21st Dáil and Seanad* there is a section entitled "Family Seats," which begins with the following sentences: "Of the 148 deputies in the 21st Dáil, 24 are sons and one a daughter of former deputies. Of those all but three (Liam Cosgrave, Vivion de Valera and Garret FitzGerald) hold seats in areas previously represented by their fathers."[10] There were also ten other close relatives of former deputies. What Nealon could have added was that his three exceptions are exceptions because they all bear names illustrious enough in recent Irish history to make it unnecessary for them to have to confine themselves to a family seat in a particular constituency.

Apart from those who got a head start as a result of a family connection, most political leaders until recently have achieved their positions by seniority and service, perhaps allied with ability. What Cohan in 1972 called the "post-revolutionary" generation of leaders had career patterns different from those of their predecessors: "What distinguishes the contemporary elite pattern from the revolutionary pattern is the greater localism that exists today and the very clearly defined stepping stone pattern."[11] More recently, however, parties have made conscious efforts to give accelerated promotion to able young men. Even so, there are still well-marked pathways to power, and attributes such as a family name, proficiency at gaelic games, and a local political bailiwick are all well proven. Certainly, too, as we have seen, some occupations—lawyer, owner of a small business, shopkeeper, auctioneer, publican—help a political career, whereas the farm labourer, the poor farmer, and people in working-class occupations are unable to make a start, let alone get to the top.

The pattern of political participation that has emerged is by no means unusual for a Western democratic country. On the contrary, studies in many countries suggest that, as in Ireland, active participation in political affairs is not only for the few but for a special few; equality of opportunity to engage in politics does not exist. However, as Hans Daalder pointed out, we must be careful not to confuse inequality of influence with oligarchy or to fall into "the determinist fallacy which sees too direct a link between the social origins of politicians and class bias in their politics." As he says: "Politics is an autonomous process that certainly is affected by class factors but is not causally dependent on them. Theoretically a political elite (and above all competing elites) composed almost exclusively of a large number of upper class persons can still be fully responsive to pressures from below."[12] Whether they are or not must be ascertained by studying their behaviour.

SIX

Political Parties

The main political divisions in Ireland after 1921 arose out of disagreements in the independence movement on nationalist issues—Commonwealth status or republic, the extent of the state, and constitutional symbols and forms. The mass parties that developed in Great Britain from the 1860s onwards, reflecting as they did the social and political divisions of a metropolitan society, never had much relevance for the majority in Ireland. Whereas Great Britain became increasingly industrialized, urbanized, and class polarized, Ireland remained largely rural and agricultural and, as a consequence of land reform, increasingly dominated by smallholders. With the successful intervention of a nationalist movement comprising rebel political as well as military organizations, there was little continuity in the party system before and after independence, the less so because, as so often happens in the evolution of a nation to statehood, the parties of the early stages of struggle were superseded or could not take the strains of momentous change and broke up.

Consequently, the party system that emerged in the 1920s bore little resemblance to the system before independence. The Irish Parliamentary Party—the party of the middle-class, moderate nationalists—disappeared, overwhelmed by the tide of events. The split of Sinn Féin and the resulting civil war opened up a cleavage that changed that movement entirely. Only the Labour Party, founded in 1912, continued in existence; but it, too, was greatly changed, like so much else, by the events of 1916 and after.

Nevertheless, although the basis of partisanship and the party system in the new state were to a great extent new and different from what had gone before, it must not be supposed that there was no continuity. As Tom Garvin has pointed out, the "politicians by accident" who dominated the new scene did not create their movements out of nothing.[1] The two biggest parties, Cumann na nGaedheal (later Fine Gael) and Fianna Fáil, were formed and developed by rival groups of leaders of the independence movement out of the substantial remains of the existing political and politico-military organizations. In the case of Fianna Fáil, the success of its first organizers in contacting and reviving local units of the former Irish Volunteers in many parts of the country partly explains both the character of the party and its rapid rise to a dominating position in Irish politics. Cumann na nGaedheal, too, included among its founders a group of former Irish Republican Brotherhood leaders. In turn, the organizations that waged the struggles of 1916–22 were the successors of, and were built upon, a number of nationalist, populist, and agrarian mass movements and secret societies of the late nineteenth and early twentieth centuries. Thus, "the party system that emerged after 1922 was the inheritor of a long and intensive tradition of political organization."[2]

II

The split of Sinn Féin polarized Irish politics. At first, it almost prevented constitutional politics from developing at all, for it led to civil war; but quite quickly a party system emerged that was essentially bipolar. The dichotomy on which it was based was less the reflection of divisions in the community as the cause of them. Rival groups of leaders created a cleavage in Irish society based upon a division of their own making. As Garvin has pointed out, when the Irish electorate were first consulted— in the 1922 general election—they were far from unanimous that the Treaty issue was the most important one. Nor was the country split into two groups on that issue, for 40 per cent of the voters cast their first preferences for candidates other than the pro-Treaty and anti-Treaty factions of Sinn Féin.[3] However, this rapidly did become *the* issue, particularly after Fianna Fáil's entry into the Dáil in 1927, and the great majority of people were divided upon it above all else. Other parties, in particular the Labour Party, and other politicians "found their politics to be increasingly peripheral to the concerns of the vast majority of the electorate."[4]

The two major parties produced by the split helped to perpetuate it. One, Cumann na nGaedheal, was formed by supporters of the Treaty in 1923 and became Fine Gael in 1933; the other, Fianna Fáil, was founded by the opponents of the Treaty, or rather by those of them who turned to parliamentary politics in 1926 with the expectation of soon winning power.

These parties and the leaders who personified them were the poles around which the majority of the community gathered in groups large enough to allow first the one and then the other to form governments composed exclusively of their own supporters. Until 1948 at least, there was little crossing the great divide between them, though by then the issues that had split Sinn Féin were either resolved or increasingly irrelevant. Yet the parties continued—their names evoking distinctive images in the public mind, their leaders and aspirant leaders irreconcilable, their traditions (including family traditions) hardened, and their interests vested. Although since 1948, and particularly from the late 1950s, these parties have changed in respect of what they actually stand for, they have the same air of permanence as do the Conservative and Labour parties in Great Britain and the Democratic and Republican parties in the United States.

Other parties and politicians also tended to be committed one way or the other on the Treaty issue. Hence they were oriented to one or the other of the major parties. Some parties presented variations on the constitutional theme, reflecting merely the dissatisfaction of politicians at the handling of this issue. Such were the National League and Clann Éireann in the 1920s and the Centre Party in the 1930s. Others, ostensibly based on some other community interest, such as farming, were inevitably irreconcilable opponents of one major party and hence, willy-nilly, camp followers of the other. In fact, the preeminence of this issue inhibited the development of parties based on other community interests or cleavages, and at times of stress, as in the middle 1930s, those that had existed disappeared as the ranks closed and tightened. Nevertheless, because of the particular proportional representation election system that was adopted and the strength of local and personal factors in Irish politics, small parties were always likely to appear. Until the 1960s, independents were always to be found in the Dáil in numbers ranging from half a dozen to a score. Only two groups did not fit into this pattern: radical republicans, because they cared too much about the issue; and the Labour Party, because it said it cared very little.

From the earliest days of the state there have always been intransigent republicans, some of radical disposition, who have not accepted the regime. De Valera and those who joined with him in eventually founding Fianna Fáil were the first of a long line. From the mid-1920s onwards, after the major part of the anti-Treaty party entered constitutional politics, the die-hards grouped and regrouped in a succession of extreme, fissiparous, and often short-lived organizations. They and their successors have always been able to recruit a tiny minority of each succeeding generation. Some of these organizations have been on the verge of constitutional politics. Others, notably the Irish Republican Army, have been committed to force, though from time to time they had political wings or fronts. Some have sought a republic, or more accurately "the Republic," which, they have said, the leaders within the system had subverted or betrayed. Others, the heirs and successors of James Connolly or radicals of the left, have hoped for a socialist republic. The temporary success for a few years from 1948 of Clann na Poblachta, led by Seán MacBride, the radical republican and former IRA leader, was due to successful draw-offs into parliamentary politics from both these streams and their combination with radical elements of the left of both Fianna Fáil and the Labour Party, an unstable mixture that could not long survive.

In the late 1970s, those traditions still survived, perpetuated by bodies such as Provisional Sinn Féin and the Provisional IRA on the one side and Official Sinn Féin and the Irish Republican Socialist Party on the other. What they have all had in common is that they have been "anti-system" organizations—that is, they have all denied the legitimacy of the existing regime, and their members have not shared the values of the majority of the community, becoming rather almost a distinct subculture. As Pfretzschner and Borock showed in their study of secondary-school students, the reservoir from which a small but constant stream of recruits to those organizations was drawn in the 1970s was sizeable.[5] If conditions were propitious, it could yield many more than it does at present.

The Labour Party never quite fitted into the dominant pattern imposed upon Irish politics by the two major parties. Established by trade union leaders as an alliance of trade unionism and socialism, it was deprived by partition of an important source of strength—the industrialized area of Belfast and environs. It soon found itself to a great extent irrelevant in a predominantly rural country, much of whose farming was dominated by smallholders. In default, due to the refusal of anti-Treaty TDs to take their Dáil seats, it established itself as the major opposition party in the new Dáil and played an important part in the establishment of constitutional and parliamentary politics. However, the entry of Fianna Fáil to the Dáil in 1927 finally confirmed the polarization of party and electoral politics, leaving the Labour Party without a basis for mass support, the less so since it both argued—wrongly in the eyes of most people—that the Treaty was not the most important issue and advocated social and economic policies that "were essentially welfarist with a minimal attraction to the major economic sectors of the community, and were oriented towards the urban and rural proletariat, a group which, in relative terms, was electorally peripheral."[6]

Cautious in a cagey, trade union way and especially on its guard against Marxist infiltration, the Labour Party never succeeded in attracting the mass of the urban working class whom one might have expected to be its natural supporters, let alone the mass of Irish people. Neither periods in office as a member of coalition governments (1948–51, 1954–57, 1973–77) nor policy shifts to the left and back again to the centre altered its "third party" status. Rapid industrialization and urbanization in recent years with a consequential increase in the numbers of the urban or urbanized working class seem to offer the party today the opportunity to become the social democratic alternative that many European electorates have available to them.

The dominance of national and constitutional issues, as we have seen, inhibited the development of parties based on other community interests or divisions. Perhaps most surprising has been the failure of farmers' parties to emerge as permanent features of the system. Because agriculture varies considerably in Ireland—from small subsistence farming and sheep farming to dairying and the production of cattle for beef—agrarian parties, when they have appeared, have tended to be regional. The Farmers' Party of the 1920s was predominantly a party of farmers of some substance based on a Farmers' Association with headquarters in Dublin. Although it won fifteen seats and 12 per cent of the valid poll in 1923, it was absorbed within the decade, mostly into Cumann na nGaedheal, which it supported in the Dáil and with which the majority of its prominent members quite obviously belonged. Likewise, in the 1940s, Clann na Talmhan (the Party of the Land) emerged, a loose-knit organization with its electoral strength among conservative small farmers of the west (Mayo, Galway, Roscommon), who had previously supported the major parties. Its TDs were independent and locally oriented, being largely on their own when it came to fighting elections. In the late 1970s, with the increasing strength and professionalism of the main agricultural interest groups, there were signs of the development not of a farmers' party but a farmers' vote, a political phenomenon of potentially very great significance. It helped defeat the National Coalition Government at the 1977 election and had a spectacular success in the European elections in June 1979, when an independent candidate prominently associated with farming organizations won a seat in Munster.

With the single transferable vote system of proportional representation, it is perhaps easier than in most electoral systems for individual parliamentary representatives and small groups to break away from their parent body and to survive, at least for a while. Likewise, it was possible in the past for individuals who could touch some chord in their locality or espouse some popular cause or causes to win electoral support and even a seat. In most cases their support was personal, and in some cases they evoked remarkably stable personal loyalty. Occasionally there was a distinct social- or group-interest basis for an individual politician of this sort: perhaps the most obvious was the Protestant vote in the border counties. Today, with the rising cost of politics and the increasing professionalism of the parties, independents are less likely to succeed. However, already prominent deputies in rebellion against their party might still survive; three out of the four independents elected in 1977 were in this category.

III

As we have seen, party politics have always been dominated by the same three parties. Minor parties have come and gone; but, over the whole history of the state, only two of them contested elections for more than a decade, and neither of these lasted twenty years. From the late 1950s, the complete dominance of the major parties, which had been temporarily challenged for a decade or so, was reestablished and strengthened until it became overwhelming, as Table 6.1 shows.

Since the early 1930s, by which time Fianna Fáil had realized its full electoral potential as a constitutional party wedded to parliamentary and

TABLE 6.1
Combined Strength of the Major Parties, 1932–77

| Election | Fianna Fáil, Fine Gael, and Labour | | Fianna Fáil and Fine Gael | |
	First-preference votes	Seats	First-preference votes	Seats
1932	88%	89%	80%	84%
1933	86	87	80	82
1937	90	94	80	85
1938	95	95	85	88
1943	81	84	65	72
1944	78	83	70	77
1948	70	77	62	67
1951	84	85	72	74
1954	88	91	75	78
1957	84	88	75	80
1961	88	92	76	81
1965	97	98	82	83
1969	97	99	80	87
1973	95	99	81	85
1977	93	97	81	86

SOURCE: Calculated by the author from election returns.

TABLE 6.2
Strength of the Major Parties, 1932–77

Party	First-preference votes		Seats in Dáil	
	Min.	Max.	Min.	Max.
Fianna Fáil	42%	52%	44%	57%
Fine Gael	20	35	21	38
Labour	8	17	5	15

SOURCE: Calculated by the author from election returns.

electoral politics, competitive politics have been waged largely by Fianna Fáil, Fine Gael, and Labour without any one of them being able to alter the logistics of the struggle radically or for long. Table 6.2 shows the relatively small fluctuations in party support over more than forty years and how each party is in a different league from the others in respect of the size of its support and its parliamentary strength.

Lipset and Rokkan have argued that, in Western countries, "the most important of the party alternatives got set for each national citizenry during the phases of mobilisation just before or just after the final extension of the suffrage and have remained roughly the same through subsequent changes in the structural conditions of partisan choice,"[7] Irish experience conforms to this pattern. Reviewing that experience, Garvin has suggested that the stability of the Irish system is due to the fact that "the last phase of political mobilization in Irish society," which occurred between 1923 and 1932, coincided with the foundation of the state, which precipitated a split in the independence movement and led to the "national question" becoming the most important issue in politics and the basis of the major partisan division.[8]

This pattern of parties has been defined by Giovanni Sartori as "moderate pluralism," which he described as a political form in which "competition remains centripetal," which is "conducive to moderate politics" and which in its operation is essentially bipolar.[9] But Fianna Fáil held power for thirty-seven out of the forty-eight years from 1932 to 1980, including two unbroken spells of sixteen years each. With this record, the Irish party system might most accurately be described, again in Sartori's terms, as a "predominant party system"—that is, "a type of party *pluralism* in which—even though no alternation in office actually occurs—alternation is not ruled out and the political system provides ample opportunities for open and effective dissent, that is, for opposing the predominance of the governing party."[10] Such alternation did in fact occur: between 1948 and 1957 when Fianna Fáil had two spells out of office (1948–51 and 1954–57) and again between 1973 and 1977. It was brought about by a coalition of Fine Gael and Labour (with minor-party support on the first two occasions).

A combination of Fine Gael and the Labour Party as the alternative to single-party rule by Fianna Fáil has so far been the only possibility, given the electoral strength of the parties and, as the direct consequence thereof, Fianna Fáil's refusal to contemplate coalition. A party with the volume of electoral support that Fianna Fáil has is very likely to behave, in Maurice Duverger's terminology, as a *parti à vocation majoritaire,* a party that has a parliamentary majority or thinks and acts as though it is likely to be able to command one. Such a party is the less likely to favour the constraints of coalition if it sees itself as the national movement, as Fianna Fáil did and to an extent still does, and if it is led by a messianic leader, as Fianna Fáil was by De Valera, "the Chief," for over thirty years.

The fact that Fianna Fáil has always hoped to win a majority of seats at general elections and has often been able to do so has to a great extent governed Irish politics for almost half a century. Government and politics developed and retained typical features of a bipolar system, namely:

1. A "Government" and an "Opposition"—two groups in the Oireachtas, one whose members support the government consistently, the other whose members oppose it consistently.

2. Elections at which the major question directly before the electors is: who is to form the next government?

3. The possibility of an alternation of two distinct sets of party leaders in an "ins and outs" sequence.

These conditions give rise to a characteristic style of politics, and such a style has been a feature of Irish experience.

By the 1950s, the national issues that had led to the salient division in Irish politics were either resolved or had ceased to have the same importance as hitherto. New men began to come to the fore who were more concerned with urgent social and economic issues as Ireland fell even further behind Western European standards. The two major parties tended to become "catchall" parties, pragmatic in temper and given to the incremental approach often exhibited by the large established parties of relatively satisfied societies. Otto Kirchheimer wrote of catchall parties that

if the party cannot hope to catch all categories of voters, it may have a reasonable expectation of catching more voters in all those categories whose interests do not adamantly conflict. . . . Even more important is the heavy concentration on issues which are scarcely liable to meet resistance in the community. National societal goals transcending group interests offer the best sales prospect for a party intent on establishing or enlarging an appeal previously limited to specific sections of the population.[11]

Sometimes the Labour Party also seemed to move in that direction.

From the 1950s, all parties were to a great extent drained of ideology; they overlapped considerably in the policies they proposed; and they competed for the votes of a public that came increasingly to be concerned with welfare and consumer politics and less and less with national issues. By the late 1970s, the signs were that the votes of an increasing number of that public would be swayed by material issues and that the electorate would punish any government that did not "deliver the goods." Although the same three parties dominated the scene as they always had, new wine was being poured into old bottles.

IV

In recent years, studies of the social basis of party support have led to the conclusion that "Irish electoral behaviour is exceptionally unstructured."[12] It is not possible to explain Irish partisanship satisfactorily by social characteristics such as occupation, class, religion, or region, as can be done for many Western countries. One might be tempted to argue that this problem arises because the basis of the main division in politics, the quarrel over national issues, was political and the work of political leaders who succeeded in mobilizing the majority of the electorate behind them. It is necessary to be cautious here, however. Unstructured by European standards as support for the two biggest parties is today, this seems not always to have been the case. Nor can support for the Labour Party at any time (admittedly amounting to only one-sixth or less of the electorate) be said to be without any social basis.

Today, Fianna Fáil is undeniably a national party. As Table 6.3 shows, in 1977 it had more support in all classes, in all regions, and in both urban and rural areas than any other party—majority support in many categories. This was not always so. In its early days, its support came mainly from rural areas and from among the small farmers, together with many of the more recent arrivals in the cities, mostly urban working class but also middle-class people with small-farmer backgrounds. This was the "periphery," which, by dominating Fianna Fáil, Garvin has suggested, dominated political life.[13]

The moderation of Fianna Fáil's leaders when the party took up its parliamentary role, its growing conservatism in office once De Valera had made the constitutional changes that he considered of overriding importance, and its pro-business policies both attracted the support of

TABLE 6.3
Social Bases of Party Support, 1977

Category	Fianna Fáil	Fine Gael	Labour	Coalition[a]	Other	Don't know[b]
All	47%	21%	11%	8%	4%	11%
Occupational category:						
Upper middle and middle class	40	28	4	5	8	17
Lower middle class	40	27	8	7	5	15
Skilled working class	51	14	14	9	5	9
Other working class and those at subsistence level	52	12	20	5	3	10
Farmers or farm managers on holdings of 50 acres or more	40	32	2	11	4	14
Farmers with holdings of less than 50 acres and farm workers	48	31	1	11	2	7
Area type:						
Cities	42	18	16	6	6	14
Towns	44	19	15	10	2	9
Rural	51	24	6	8	3	10
Region:						
Dublin	38	18	17	6	6	15
Rest of Leinster	47	23	9	10	4	9
Munster	56	16	12	5	2	11
Connacht and Ulster	45	31	2	11	3	8

SOURCE: *Omnibus Report, Political Opinion* (June 1977), made available by Irish Marketing Surveys Ltd.

[a] Respondents who indicated support for the National Coalition without specifying which party.

[b] Includes respondents whose replies were categorized as "would not vote," "undecided," and "don't know," as well as those who refused to answer.

sections of the community hitherto hostile and, conversely, as both Michael Gallagher and Garvin have shown, lost it some of its overwhelming support in its former strongholds (see Table 6.4).[14] From the early 1940s, the composition of the party's support altered significantly, and it became, to repeat, a catchall party. Its long and continued domination of Irish politics is due to its success in effecting this transformation. It is not for nothing that Fianna Fáil is often described in Ireland as "the party of reality."

Inevitably Fianna Fáil encountered difficulties in reconciling its rural and nationalist origins with a modern catchall image. Some of its core supporters and a few of its more fundamentalist leaders began to chafe as the pace of change increased after De Valera retired from active politics in 1959. In particular, they disliked the modifications in policy towards Northern Ireland made by De Valera's successors, Seán Lemass and Jack Lynch. These disagreements came finally to a head when violence erupted in Northern Ireland in 1969, and they culminated in 1970

TABLE 6.4

*Correlations of Farm Valuation and Urbanization
with Fianna Fáil Vote, 1923–44*

Category	1923[a]	1927 (1)	1927 (2)	1932	1933
High farm valuation	−.56	−.51	−.57	−.42	−.65
High urbanization	−.41	−.41	−.49	−.60	−.48

Category	1937	1938	1943	1944
High farm valuation	−.39	−.63	−.03	−.06
High urbanization	−.31	−.42	−.08	−.04

SOURCE: T. Garvin, "Nationalist Elites, Irish Voters and the Formation of the Irish Party System: A Comparative Perspective," *Economic and Social Review*, 8 (1977), 176.

[a] Includes Sinn Féin.

with the "arms scandal" crisis, an alleged plot by some members of the government and others to import arms into the Republic for transmission to the nationalists in Northern Ireland. It led to the dismissal of two ministers and the resignation of two others and subsequently to a trial and acquittal. This long-delayed crisis of modernization was weathered with surprising ease and without losing electoral support. At the 1977 general election, the party won an absolute majority of first preferences, a feat it had achieved only once before, in 1938.

Whereas Fianna Fáil was originally the party of the countrymen and republicans, Cumann na nGaedheal (from 1933 Fine Gael) was at first the party of the Treaty, law and order, and Commonwealth status. As such, it was more attractive than Fianna Fáil to the business world, to many shopkeepers and professional people, and to the more prosperous farmers who depended on British markets. It looked and behaved like a conservative party and attracted to itself those who desired peace and stable government, those who thought that the Treaty, the Irish Free State, and the Commonwealth connection were the best guarantees of these, and those who could not abide De Valera. Former members of the Irish Parliamentary Party and former unionists supported it *faute de mieux;* in fact, most of them were politically integrated into the new independent Ireland in this way, finding in the party much that satisfied them.

In the early 1930s, when the party went through a period of metamorphosis to emerge as Fine Gael, it had on its right wing intellectuals who advocated the institution in Ireland of a vocationally organized society as suggested by Pope Pius XI in the encyclical *Quadragesimo Anno* (1931) and a few who, misunderstanding fascism, thought that it might go hand in hand with Catholicism. As Fianna Fáil established itself and showed in office that it could govern responsibly and was aiming at a conservative, Catholic republic, support for Fine Gael, which had little positive to offer, flagged. Although it continued to behave like a party that might resume office after the next election, its share of Dáil seats fell from 35 per cent in 1937 to 21 per cent in 1948, at which time it made important changes in policy and tactics. Like Fianna Fáil, it attempted over the years that followed to appear as a national catchall party. Although it had some success in retrieving its position—its first-preference votes climbed back to 35 per cent by 1973—its chances of realizing once again its *vocation majoritaire,* a hope that many in the party continued to cherish, were always poor.

Fine Gael is like Fianna Fáil a national party, though its support is much thinner in all categories and varies more. Like Fianna Fáil, it has support in every part of the country, both in urban and in rural areas, yet it remains as it always was somewhat more class based than Fianna Fáil, as Table 6.3 shows. It is stronger among the farmers, from whom it derived two-fifths of its support in 1977, and among the middle class, from which it derived one-third of its support, than it is among the working class.[15] Like Fianna Fáil also, it suffered a crisis of modernization. When some of its younger leaders launched their *Just Society* programme in the late 1960s, it did not appeal to many of the party's solid, urban middle-class supporters, much less to the conservative farmers. Garret FitzGerald, who succeeded Liam Cosgrave (son of the first leader of the party) as leader in 1977, faced the same kind of problem as did Fianna Fáil leaders—namely, how to modernize the party and make it attractive to the increasing numbers of voters who are swayed by election promises and the record, by the cost of living, by jobs, and by social welfare and tax benefits, while not alienating its core supporters.

Examining the characteristics of the supporters of these two parties in the late 1960s, John Whyte found that in respect of a number of class-related variables such as subjective social class, education, trade union membership, and home ownership, the differences between them were quite small.[16] Where they did differ was, significantly, as in the past, in the attitudes of their respective supporters to a basic national issue—the Irish language. He showed that in all social classes Fianna Fáil supporters were the most likely to advocate an Irish-speaking Ireland and Fine Gael supporters the least. (Fine Gael was the first of the parties to seek changes in the state's compulsory Irish policy in 1961.) This, Whyte considered, "fits the assumption that Fianna Fáil supporters are more nationalist in outlook than Fine Gael ones."[17] Likewise, Gallagher showed that the presence of a high proportion of Irish speakers in a constituency had always been the most significant predictor of Fianna Fáil support; the converse was sometimes true of Fine Gael.[18] Thus, although it is not possible to attribute distinctive social bases to these two parties, perhaps there are differences that have their roots far back in history—in the attitudes of Irish people to national issues more than half a century ago that have been perpetuated.

Findings of this sort suggest that partisanship is handed down from generation to generation and remains stable. There is evidence in Ireland, as in some other countries, that many people follow their parents in their party affiliation and, once oriented to a particular party, do not easily change. Pfretzschner and Borock concluded from their survey of secondary-school students that "parental influence still conditions partisan attitudes."[19] More specifically, Stein Larsen in 1971 showed that people with pro-Treaty relations or connections in the past were very likely to have voted Fine Gael in 1969; those with anti-Treaty relations or connections, Fianna Fáil. Two-thirds of his respondents who were twenty years old in 1922 and over one-half who were born in the late 1930s or after followed this pattern.[20]

The social bases of the Labour Party contrast markedly with those of the other two. Labour is a working-class party: in the late 1970s, four-fifths of its supporters came from the working class, over half of them from the semiskilled and unskilled categories.[21] It is not, however, *the* party of the working class, for Fianna Fáil has attracted far more working-class and more trade unionist votes than Labour.[22]

The most striking feature of Labour's membership in the past was that it came not so much from the urban as from the rural proletariat. It was a rural working-class party, its greatest strength lying in the south and east where large-scale, commercial farming was strongest and where, therefore, there were a bigger number of farm labourers than elsewhere in Ireland (see Table 6.5). Its original membership seems to have been garnered from a number of rural workers' organizations and remained loyal, centred more perhaps upon the deputy as an individual than on a political programme, let alone left-wing ideology. The failure of the party to take a stand on the republican issue and dissension in the trade union movement only partly explain its lack of success in Dublin. Given the size of the Dublin working class, its Catholicism, and the recent rural connections of a large proportion of it, the Labour Party could not in any case have matched Fianna Fáil or Fine Gael.

Eventually, from 1960 onwards, with the great growth of Dublin as an industrial city and with rapid cultural changes, Labour's position in the city improved by leaps and bounds. By the 1970s, it was challenging

TABLE 6.5
*Correlations of High Farm Valuation and Urbanization
with Labour Party Vote, 1923–44*

Category	1923	1927 (1)	1927 (2)	1932	1933
High farm valuation	.61	.60	.68	.60	.24
High urbanization	.09	.11	.31	.10	−.02

Category	1937	1938	1943	1944	
High farm valuation	.46	.57	.66	.26	
High urbanization	.04	.11	.35	−.22	

SOURCE: T. Garvin, "Nationalist Elites, Irish Voters and the Formation of the Irish Party System: A Comparative Perspective," *Economic and Social Review*, 8 (1977), 179.

TABLE 6.6
Pattern of Labour Party Support, 1961–77

Location of voters	1961	1965	1969	1973	1977
Dublin City	8%	20%	31%	24%	19%
Other constituencies	12	15	14	12	10
All constituencies	12	15	17	14	12

SOURCE: For 1961–73, M. Gallagher, *Electoral Support for Irish Political Parties, 1927–73* (London and Beverly Hills, 1973), p. 45. For 1977, figures supplied by M. Gallagher.

TABLE 6.7
Perceptions of Party Differences, 1969

Perception of parties	All	Supporters of:		
		Fianna Fáil	Fine Gael	Labour
Different	31%	35%	28%	33%
The same	56	53	61	54
Don't know	13	12	11	13

SOURCE: "Irish Political Attitudes," *Nusight*, December 1969, p. 26. Fieldwork carried out by Social Surveys (Gallup Poll).

Fine Gael as the second party there (see Table 6.6). Like the other parties, it had a crisis of modernization during which it moved to the left and back again. Like many labour parties, it is pulled this way and that by its leaders in their attempts to satisfy both its moderate and its socialist supporters.

How do the public see the parties? In 1969, the majority, no matter what party they supported, perceived the three major parties as much the same as one another (see Table 6.7). An enquiry by Irish Marketing Surveys Ltd. in 1976 into the use of the terms "right" and "left" in Irish politics revealed that people perceived Fianna Fáil and Fine Gael "to be positioned remarkably close to one another in the centre or slightly to the right of the centre." However, they did see a difference between the Labour Party and the other two: Labour was "generally ascribed a left wing stance."[23] (See Fig. 6.1.) Pfretzschner and Borock, too, found that among secondary-school students "Labour [was] more precisely identified than the other two parties," its appeal to the working class being specifically remarked upon.[24]

It is clear from replies that many respondents experienced difficulty in answering questions of this sort. Pfretzschner and Borock noted that many school students "failed to make sharp or clear distinctions amongst parties," and Irish Marketing Surveys reported that nearly one-third of respondents declined to reply to their question about left and right, presumably finding the concept hard to comprehend or the question difficult to answer.[25] Notice, too, that the distribution of replies in respect of Fianna Fáil and Fine Gael was very wide, which might suggest that

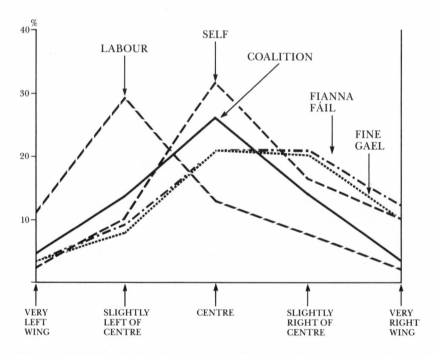

Fig. 6.1. Right, Left and Centre in Irish Politics. (Source: Irish Marketing Surveys Ltd., *RTE "Survey"—Politics* (Report prepared for Radio Telefís Eireann, September 1976), p. 6)

many found it hard to apply this criterion to these parties. This is not surprising, for the parties, including Labour, are today largely devoid of ideology, and a good many of their leaders differ little in their attitudes to many social, economic, and international issues.

V

Parties perform three main functions in the political process; from a democratic standpoint we might almost say that they render three services. First, they mobilize the electorate. Their primary aim is to win votes in order to have their nominees elected to political office. To do so involves them in communicating opinions and demands to the policy makers in their own organizations and party policies to the public. It also involves their leaders in "processing" demands by combining them into coherent courses of action or policies, which, they hope, they and their party colleagues will be able to "sell" to the public. Second, parties select candidates for political posts, especially those that are to be filled by election; they are thus important agencies for recruiting political leaders at all levels. Since the spoils system does not operate to any great extent in Ireland, there are not many nonelected public offices to which the parties nominate choices of their own. Third, party leaders, with their essential support, take on responsibility for conducting central and local government and for operating the representative and parliamentary processes of discussion, scrutiny, and criticism of government policy and administration.

The organization and procedures that parties adopt to carry out these functions differ according to the nature of the political system and the size of the party. In considering Irish party organization, a distinction must be made between the three major parties on the one hand and the smaller parties that have existed from time to time and the independents on the other. Minor parties with pretensions have usually tried to model themselves on the major parties, with a similar pattern of organization; but lack of resources, both human and material, has been against them. Inevitably they have tended to be essentially electoral alliances of deputies who closely resemble the formally independent members in that each has some sort of organization in his own area, often consisting mainly of personal contacts. To speak of party organization, therefore, is to speak of the three major parties.

Irish parties are poor compared with those of many advanced countries and especially large, rich countries. Until recently they exhibited a haphazard even amateurish approach to the tasks of building membership and getting votes. Fianna Fáil was always incomparably the best of them. In the 1970s, however, first the Labour Party and later Fine Gael began to take more interest in, and devote more resources to, central organization and services. By the end of the 1970s, each had young, active, and very professional secretaries who closely resembled one another and a growing number of paid officers.

The main institutions of the parties are the local clubs or branches (called cumainn in the case of Fianna Fáil), each linked to some sort of electoral constituency organization; an annual delegate meeting or convention (called Árd Fhéis in the case of both Fine Gael and Fianna Fáil); the National Executive Committee; the "parliamentary party," that is, the members of the party who have seats in the Oireachtas; the party leader; and the Central Office.

The Irish Parliamentary Party of preindependence days had a committee in each parish, and "it was natural that Sinn Féin should do likewise in its struggle with the party and that the two daughter parties, Fianna Fáil and Cumann na nGaedheal, carried on the practice."[26] The local branches tended therefore to be based on the ecclesiastical divisions, which were, however, the natural community divisions. In fact, the boundaries of parishes and local government electoral areas were often identical; the chapel gate was, and is, one of the most convenient places for speech making and the collection of funds. Today, branches are based on the church area or polling station area in the countryside and on the local government unit (urban area or ward) in the towns and cities. Both Fianna Fáil and Fine Gael have branches almost throughout the country. Labour is a more regional party; most of its branches are in the east and south. In 1979, Fianna Fáil had a total of about 3,000 cumainn ranging from about 50 to about 150 per constituency in the county constituencies and from 20 to 30 per constituency in the city constituencies. Fine Gael had approximately 2,000 branches and Labour over 500.

Because of the parochialism of politics and the importance attached by the local population to the role of their representatives as intermediaries, national leaders and the Central Offices have little control over the local branches. What suits an individual representative, his local henchmen, and the local party organizations in his bailiwick is not always to the advantage of the party. No matter: those at the centre can only do their best to inspire, advise, and occasionally cajole the branches into following what they consider appropriate courses of action. To the local leaders and active participants, the ideal role of the centre is essentially as an aid to their local efforts.

In the 1970s, the leaders of all parties began to be aware of the critical need to recruit their increment, or more if possible, of the burgeoning number of young people; thus, youth organizations were established. However, efforts at national and regional levels—with highly publicized youth conferences where the elders of the party spend their weekends being told what they are doing wrong by the young—have not been matched at local level. Just as local deputies and local branches find the intervention of the centre unwelcome, so, too, established elders and long-serving local workers are often less than enthusiastic about the rapid promotion in their vicinity of young people with high potential. Seniority and long service have always been, and continue to be, the major criteria for the advancement of all but the few who are favoured by their family connections.

The numbers of party members are low. Party rules require only that a person seeking to become a member must declare his or her acceptance of the party's aims and regulations, must be elected by a branch, and having been elected, must pay and maintain a subscription. The minimum number of members in a branch is small—ten in the case of Fianna Fáil—and in practice all that is required is a team of officers and the payment of a very low, minimum registration fee. Because of the likely interest of many of the active members of the branches in nominations to office, they might well not be anxious for too large a membership. In 1979, Fine Gael party headquarters was said to be engaged in purging phantom or inactive branches that existed only for purposes of influencing nominations.

The exact number of party members is hard to ascertain. The largest party, Fianna Fáil, does not know exactly how many members it has: "We leave to the constituency organisations the job of monitoring the general membership."[27] In 1979, Fianna Fáil officials claimed that they probably had about 90,000 members; Fine Gael claimed approximately 47,000; and Labour had nearly 5,300 registered individual members, making a total of 142,300 in those three parties. Almost certainly, however, this is an overestimate. In the case of Labour, following the British practice, trade unions and similar organizations may affiliate as corporate members, thus greatly increasing the nominal membership. In 1979, out of a total of over ninety unions, seventeen were so affiliated in respect of 173,000 people (46 per cent of total trade union membership).[28]

The most important functions of the branches are to nominate candidates and to fight elections. For some branches these are almost the only functions, though the officers of many serve as "contact men" and are important links in the "service" activities of public representatives for their constituents. The concomitant functions of political education and recruitment of party members, which one might think are continuing activities on which successful elections are based, are not pursued actively by most branches. In a study of a Dublin City constituency, Garvin found that "in none of the three [parties] was the explicit recruitment of new members by established members the most important source of new recruits."[29] In a few branches, mainly in the cities and to a greater extent in the Labour Party than in the others, policy is debated, particularly in preparation for the annual convention, where resolutions submitted by the branches are considered. Even fund raising tends to be confined to the annual collection and to the period immediately prior to a general election.

Evidently branches are not organs of popular participation. Rather, they conform to the "top-down" model of party organization, which sees participation "primarily in terms of services that local party members perform for party headquarters. From this perspective, the most important activity of party members on the ground is winning elections."[30] In this view, branches are not seen as centres for local popular participation or for the political education of the masses. Insofar as they act as channels of information and opinion in the other direction—that is, to the centre—it is often through the local public representatives, who are in any case very closely in touch with their constituents or at least the most important of them. Representatives might well feel that they understand and interpret local opinion better than the active members of the branches, and many would prefer to have a communications system of which they personally rather than party branches were the focal point.

It would be dangerous to view local branches purely as instruments of the party. In some, power is in the hands of a small group of the henchmen of a local representative. He and they see the branch, and indeed as many branches as they can control, as part of the representative's "machine."[31] Again, people take an active part in local party activities for a number of reasons, by no means all of them connected with the advancement of the party. A considerable number do so for what Clarke and Wilson have called "solidary" reasons—that is "for reasons of personal loyalties, for the social life, for friendship opportunities or for fun." A few, though they would not be likely to admit it, participate for material reasons like "career advancement or access to patronage."[32] Garvin found that in Dublin South Central about one-half of Fianna Fáil's and Fine Gael's local activists and one-third of Labour's remained in their branch for "solidary" reasons.[33] Even those with "purposive" motives— that is, they seek some political goals—might be more concerned with furthering another person's ambitions or policies than with promoting the people and causes favoured by the party.

It is the right and duty of branches to send delegates to the party's annual convention or Árd Fhéis. According to the rule books, the annual convention is the supreme authority in the party. In practice, despite some lip service to the proposition, it is nothing of the sort. Its very size—the Fianna Fáil Árd Fhéis in 1979 numbered about seven thousand delegates—and the nature of the gathering make it unsuitable for the effective consideration of policy and demand that it be stage-managed to some extent. It is, rather, an occasion for a demonstration of party loyalty and for the rank-and-file workers to meet their national leaders. Very occasionally, the delegates get a policy devised by their leaders reversed, but for the most part the resolutions that are passed are no more than guides to party opinion. More often the mood of the party faithful is indicated by their reactions from the body of the hall; these are no doubt noted by the leadership on the platform. The real decision makers are the party leader and his colleagues. They head the Oireachtas party together with other members of the National Executive Committee not in the Oireachtas. With these people above all rests the initiative in proposing party policy and strategy.

The National Executive Committee (in the Labour Party called the Administrative Council) is elected annually. In each case it consists of the national officers together with representatives of the Oireachtas party and of the branches. Although this body—or, in the case of Fianna Fáil, an inner executive drawn from this body—is the organ that runs the party's affairs, it is doubtful whether the policies that the party will publicly adopt are decided by it. For when it comes to policy and to parliamentary tactics and strategy, the leaders of the Oireachtas party (who in the case of the party in power are, of course, the government) are expected to take the initiative, and they are given a free hand to do so. Prominent, though not always predominant, among them will be the leader of the Oireachtas party, who is chosen by them and who is the party leader. In the case of the party in power, he will of course be Taoiseach, an office that almost inevitably puts its holder in a position above his colleagues. In practice, then, neither the rank-and-file parliamentary representatives nor the active workers in the constituencies have much to do with initiating or formulating policy. They have other tasks—the former to support their leaders in parliament and to attend to the affairs of their constituents, the latter to get out the vote when the occasion demands.

The small amount of interelection activity and the comparatively meagre services given by party headquarters to the branches are reflected in low levels of income and expenditure. Irish parties as such do not receive any public funds as do parties in some European countries where party political activity is recognized as being properly chargeable to public funds as an expense essential to democracy. The only public monies that go to the parties in Ireland are the allowances paid to the leaders of the main opposition parties in the Oireachtas to help support their parliamentary activities and a small proportion of members' salaries, which parties levy for expenses. Party finances are, therefore, the private affairs of the parties. In the case of Fianna Fáil and Fine Gael they are very private indeed; only the Labour Party publishes its (audited) accounts.

However, the broad pattern is clear enough. The most important single source of income for Fianna Fáil and Fine Gael and one of two major sources for Labour is an annual collection made by each branch, part of which must be handed over by the branch for the use of the centre, mainly to fight elections. The proceeds of the annual collection—in the case of Fianna Fáil in the late 1970s coming close to a quarter of a million pounds—though highly publicized, give little idea of the true income of any of the parties. Individual party members pay small subscriptions, which go towards financing branch activities. In the case of the Labour Party, Oireachtas party members contribute a proportion of their parliamentary salaries, and affiliated unions pay small annual subscriptions based on the number of affiliated members. In the case of Fianna Fáil and Fine Gael, the major part of their income comes from industrial and commercial firms and businessmen. In 1978, Conor Brady suggested that the annual income of Fianna Fáil "is probably somewhere in the order of half a million pounds at present, of which perhaps 40% to 45% comes through the annual collection."[34] The Labour Party's audited accounts show their income in 1978 as less than IR£45,000, hardly one-tenth of that of Fianna Fáil.[35]

Of course, at election time, parties and individual candidates for public office make special efforts to solicit financial help, and collections and appeals, both public and private, are made. It is well known that Fianna Fáil and Fine Gael accumulate election funds, though their size and how they are used are kept strictly secret. The Labour Party receives help from individual unions, but this is usually given by way of subsidies to union candidates individually.

VI

Political parties seem not to be in themselves particularly democratic organizations, though they are essential engines of democracy. Nor are they very effective channels of public participation in politics. However, they are far from being the only channels of public participation. All sorts of associations and organizations in the community engage in political activities, some of them continuously and with great effect. Many, indeed most of them, choose not to associate themselves too closely with any political party, their main political business being with ministers and civil servants, as the following chapter shows.

SEVEN

Pressure Groups

Political parties are far from being the only channels between the community and the formal institutions of government. There exists as well a very large number and wide variety of organizations that, when the occasion calls for it, press the demands of their members upon those who make public policy or other decisions that have the backing of the authorities, and upon those who might influence the decision makers. Many of these organizations, such as trade unions and farmers' associations, exist specifically to protect the interests and further the aims of their members; and, in the course of doing so, they attempt to influence public authorities.

Such organizations are usually referred to as "pressure groups," but that term will not be confined to organizations set up explicitly to represent the interests of a particular group. When they think it is necessary or useful to do so, the leaders and spokesmen of important institutions in the community such as churches or ethnic groups act in the same way; so, for example, do the managers of firms and the governing bodies of universities; so, too, in the public sector itself do the spokesmen of subordinate public authorities press their interests upon the central government. In fact, in the modern welfare state, which attempts to direct the economy and regulate the social and physical environment, almost any organization or group in the community, however remote from politics it ostensibly appears, might find occasion to press a case upon a public authority, national or local. Nor need a group have a continuous existence or a formal organization: the 700,000 people who took time off work on January 22, 1980, to march the streets of Dublin and other cities and towns demanding changes in the pay-as-you-earn tax system were participating in politics as a pressure group.

If the term "pressure group" is to be used to denote organizations that try to influence the policies or other decisions of public authorities in their favour, it is essential to differentiate them from political parties. In the words of Richard Rose: "Pressure groups do not themselves seek to win control of government by presenting a slate of candidates to the electorate. Parties differ from pressure groups particularly in the degree of their inclusiveness. . . . Furthermore, pressure groups can have extensive nonpolitical activities."[1] It has to be admitted, however, that the distinction is not entirely clear-cut. "The colonization of groups by parties and the reverse phenomenon of domination of parties by groups,"[2] which is such a feature of some countries, is not present to any great extent in Ireland today. Nevertheless, some trade unions are affiliated to the Labour Party, and, for example, in the 1920s the Farmers' Party was the political arm of a farmers' association. Also, an extreme republican organization like Sinn Féin is hard to categorize. If, as seems most appropriate, it is regarded as a political party, there has often been considerable interpenetration between it and its consort, the IRA. In general, however, the distinction between pressure groups and political parties is clear enough in the Republic of Ireland. Here, contrary to the situation in some European countries and in Northern Ireland where the Unionist Party and the Orange Order were for long closely identified one with another, pressure groups and parties are in general autonomous in respect of one another.

Also absent from the Republic is the phenomenon of "segmented pluralism"—that is, competing complexes of interrelated social, educational, occupational, and political organizations each serving distinct cultural groups or communities on the basis of religion, ideology, nationality, or some combination of these, such as occur, for example, in Switzerland, the Netherlands, and Belgium.[3] In only one or two areas of social activity are the cultural differences between Catholics and Protestants in the Republic reflected in the existence of separate organizations. Because first-level and second-level education is largely denominational, there exist a Catholic Headmasters' Association and other Catholic teachers' associations, as well as an Irish Schoolmasters' Association, which is Protestant. In scouting, too, there are the Catholic Boy Scouts of Ireland on the one hand and the Boy Scouts of Ireland (and a similar organization, the Boys Brigade) on the other. Likewise, until recently, the membership of some sports clubs has been confined to people of a particular religion.

II

For purposes of classifying Irish pressure groups, we shall use two simple sets of distinctions as proposed by Maria Maguire.[4] These are, on the one hand, between "sectional" and "attitude" groups; and on the other, between "associational" and "institutional" groups. "Sectional" groups "exist to protect and promote the sectional interest of their members, and membership is, by definition, limited to those who share that particular interest."[5] The Irish Congress of Trade Unions is an example; so, too, are the Irish Farmers' Association, the Irish Medical Association, and the Consumers' Association of Ireland Ltd. By contrast, "attitude" groups exist "to promote a cause, and membership is usually open to anyone willing to suport the issue in question."[6] Such are the Irish Association for Civil Liberties, the Irish Language Freedom Movement, and An Taisce (the National Trust for Ireland). Sectional groups far outnumber attitude groups. Their activities, particularly those of the established economic protection groups, are part and parcel of everyday political life, and they "tend to play a more consistent role in the political process than many other types of group."[7]

The most highly organized and vociferous of the sectional groups are in industry and commerce and in agriculture, despite the fact that the basic units in these sectors—firms, unions, farms—are mostly very small. In industry and commerce small firms predominate, and until a decade or so ago most of them were reluctant to finance protection services. Even yet, many individual trade associations are small and comparatively weak. However, in recent years, some umbrella organizations have grown rapidly as firms came to recognize the need to be adequately represented at the national level. A few of these organizations are well staffed and efficiently organized.

In 1979, the Confederation of Irish Industry, which is the national organization representing industry in matters of trade, economics, taxation, and development, had about two thousand member firms in a score of affiliated and sector groups. In the same year, the membership of the Federated Union of Employers, the major organization on the employers' side in all matters relating to industrial relations and labour matters, covered between 50 and 60 per cent of all economic activity in the private sector, other than the construction industry, which was catered for separately. This membership, which also included a number of public authorities, was growing at the rate of two or three hundred per year. The Federated Union of Employers had a staff of eighty and regional offices covering the whole country. The Construction Industry Federation, the representative organization of firms in the building industry, with over thirteen hundred members, also had regional offices throughout the country.

Like management, labour also is characterized by a large number of

TABLE 7.1

Membership of Trade Unions in the Republic of Ireland, 1979

Size of union	No. of unions	No. of members	Percentage of all union members
Under 1,500 members	43	23,500	4.7%
1,500–3,000	16	34,400	6.9
3,001–5,000	6	23,600	4.7
5,001–7,500	5	31,900	6.4
7,501–10,000	3	26,700	5.4
10,001–20,000	9	121,600	24.4
Over 20,000	3	237,300	47.6
Total all unions	85	498,900	100.0%
Affiliated to Irish Congress of Trade Unions	72	463,900	93.0%

SOURCE: Derived from *Trade Union Information*, Nos. 252–57 (Summer 1980), 2.

small units. In 1979 there were no less than eighty-five unions with members in the Republic, just over half of them with less than 1,500 members (see Table 7.1). However, one of them, the Irish Transport and General Workers' Union, with nearly 160,000 members, represented over one-third of total trade union membership. Together, these eighty-five unions represented almost half-a-million employees. The proportion of employees unionized in 1975—55 per cent—was the third highest of the countries of the European Communities.[8] Like the employers, trade unions, too, have their umbrella organizations, notably the Irish Congress of Trade Unions (ICTU), which comprises seventy-two of the eighty-five unions and represents 93 per cent of union membership. A handful of maverick unions are affiliated to a small but significant rival, the Irish Federation of Trade Unions, which, compared to ICTU, was very much an "outsider." In contrast with the major employers' organization, the Irish Congress of Trade Unions is poorly financed and understaffed.

Professional associations have functions similar to those of trade unions, and a few of them are affiliated to ICTU. Some of them have the added responsibility of safeguarding the standards of their profession, and they are endowed with appropriate powers to make rules governing entry and practice and to discipline or exclude members. This sector, like industry and commerce, is composed mainly of small associations because, in a country of 3 million people, the number practising in any profession is low. Professions, however, tend to be close-knit, and though only small numbers of people are engaged in particular callings, often most if not all of them are members of professional associations. In 1980, for example, 84 per cent of all national (that is, primary) teachers, lay and religious, were members of the Irish National Teachers' Organization. In a few cases, membership is a precondition of being recognized as belonging to a profession.

By Western European standards, the proportion of Ireland's labour force employed in agriculture and fishing (21 per cent in 1979) is very high. Consequently, one would expect agricultural and rural life organizations to have great political influence. Because of the diversity of interests among farmers, however, this was not the case until recently. No agrarian parties ever established themselves on any permanent basis. Nor did cooperatives develop to any great extent except in areas where milk was produced on a scale big enough to justify a collection service. Because of the diversity of agriculture, there have always been a large number of organizations representing particular interests. In 1979, the list of "client organizations" of the Department of Agriculture (that is, bodies with whom the Department did or might do business from time to time) numbered 170 (see Table 7.2); in the mid-1960s, there were about 100 names on the list.

Until recently, organizational and personal rivalries inhibited the development of a single body to speak for all agricultural interests. From the mid-1960s, the National Farmers' Association, which had been

TABLE 7.2

Department of Agriculture's "List of Agricultural etc. Organizations," 1980

Type of organization	No. of organizations
Rural life	4
General agricultural interests	21
Cattle	32
Cereals and feeding stuffs	15
Horses	21
Horticulture and bee keeping	13
Milk and dairy products	17
Pigs	5
Poultry	8
Sheep and wool	29
Other animals and products	5
TOTAL	170

SOURCE: A list made available by the Department of Agriculture giving information about all organizations except other government departments with which officers of the Department expect to do business at some time or another.

founded in 1955, emerged as the major umbrella organization. It was strengthened by an amalgamation with a number of other associations in 1972, when it became the Irish Farmers' Association. By 1979, the Irish Farmers' Association had a membership of 150,000, a staff of over eighty, and a budget of well over IR£1 million per year. It owned an influential newspaper, the *Farmers Journal* (circulation 10,000 in 1980), engaged in a number of business activities such as insurance and meat packing, and had a large headquarters and conference centre, the Irish Farm Centre. In the eyes of many, the Irish Farmers' Association was "the country's most effective lobby."[9] Despite the fact that it had often been in conflict with the other major farming organization, the Irish Creamery Milk Suppliers Association with fifty thousand, an amalgamation between the two was under discussion in 1980.

Ireland's accession to the European Communities brought farmers the considerable financial benefits of the common agricultural policy (CAP) and boosted Irish agriculture as never before. The major farming organizations, in particular the Irish Farmers' Association, seized the opportunity with both hands. In the late 1970s, Irish agricultural pressure groups were more Brussels oriented than the pressure groups of any other sector of the economy. Representation in Brussels, established well before Ireland's formal accession, soon became highly expert and efficient and more than matched the official presence.

Producers of goods and services are far better organized and equipped for self-protection than are nonindustrial and household consumers. Apart from the users of some particular goods or services such as motor cars, consumers are not organized, being at best a somewhat amorphous group. The rural nature of the Republic makes the task of organization the more difficult. Also, consumer groups are unable to tap sources of finance as producer groups can. The only general consumer organizations are the Consumers' Association of Ireland Ltd., with twenty-five hundred members, and the thousand-member Irish Housewives' Association. Membership in these, as in other more specific consumer groups, tends to be strongest among the middle class in Dublin. In rural areas, the Irish Countrywoman's Association to some extent acts as a consumer protection group.

As is the case in other Western European countries, the state has recognized the need to protect consumer interests not only by legislation and administrative action, but by providing for specific consumer representation on appropriate advisory and managerial bodies such as the National Prices Commission and the Post Office Users' Council. In 1977, a minister of state (that is, a junior minister) in the Department of

Industry and Commerce was assigned to consumer affairs. Nevertheless, consumer organizations "face an uphill battle in which they lack an influence comparable to the larger economic protection groups to which their interests are often opposed."[10]

It might be argued that the more general institutions of representation—the public representatives at the national and local levels—speak for consumers, since all people consume. There is some force in this, but at the point where many political decisions are made, policies formulated, and business decided, the spokesmen of the producers are present but the public representatives—members of the Oireachtas and the local councillors—often are not. Thus the developing practices of interest consultation have important implications for democracy.

Attitude groups, those based on a shared cause or making a particular demand, present something of a contrast with sectional groups. Many of the latter are "insider" groups and are on close and intimate terms with the public authorities with whom they do business. Many of the former are "outsider" groups, often literally: they are kept at arm's length by public officials, political and bureaucratic alike, who regard them at best as goodhearted busybodies and at worst as unreasonable and sometimes fanatical nuisances. This arises because many attitude groups advocate reforms for which there is no great public demand. They are as often concerned to mobilize public support in order to demonstrate political strength as they are to pursue the more forlorn hope of getting changes in policy agreed to directly by decision makers.

There is a contrast also in respect of numbers. There are comparatively few attitude groups, though in recent years there has been a rush of associations with names like CARE (Campaign for the Care of Deprived Children) and NITRO (National Income Tax Reform Organization). There are even fewer making major demands involving big changes. The deep division engendered by the split over the Treaty was reflected in the party system and was eventually resolved within that system. Only the small republican groups that do not recognize the regime and the tiny collections of extreme Marxists are not comprehended "within the system," but they are better thought of as political movements than as pressure groups, though they and the "front" organizations that some of them use often behave like pressure groups.

Groups devoted to the revival of Irish are of long standing and, unlike most attitude groups, have a favoured position. Since their aim is, officially, government policy (though mostly only lip service is paid to it), these groups receive public monies. Among the most important are Conradh na Gaeilge (the Gaelic League), which is the oldest of them, founded in 1893 as part of the nationalist revival, and Gael Linn, an organization that exploits the mass media to promote the language. Coordinating the activities of many of the language organizations is an umbrella body, Comhdháil Náisiúnta na Gaeilge (National Convention of the Irish Language). On the other side of the language fence is the Language Freedom Movement, devoted to the abolition of "compulsory Irish."

The largest attitude group is certainly the Pioneer Total Abstinence Association, which in 1979 claimed an estimated 200,000 to 250,000 adult members plus an unspecified number of juvenile and adolescent members. Although many of the latter were enrolled at school under the influence of clerical teachers and some will have fallen away, the Pioneer pin, worn in the lapel or on the breast, is a common dress decoration to be seen in Ireland, exceeding by far its nearest rival, the Fáinne, a circular ornament of plain metal denoting a speaker of Irish and awarded by Comhdháil Náisiúnta na Gaeilge. Both were less commonly seen in the late 1970s than they had been a decade earlier.

Reflecting the changed times also has been the recent growth in the number of, and support for, groups advocating the protection of the environment, the conservation of natural resources, and the care of the underprivileged such as itinerants, single-parent families, and the homeless. Likewise, in 1980, there were Irish branches of international pressure groups such as the Anti-Apartheid Movement, Amnesty International, and the Chile Committee for Human Rights (Ireland). The issue of family planning, which became increasingly live after the Second Vatican Council, has spawned associations on both sides. Just as such developments mirror the changing culture of the community, the comparative lack of success of associations concerned with abolishing blood sports or cruelty to animals in general reflects a more enduring characteristic of the Irish.

III

Most of the sectional attitude groups are, following Maria Maguire's typology, "associational" groups—that is, specialized structures of "interest articulation" formed for the "explicit representation of the interests of a particular group." We can draw a broad distinction between these and institutions in society, such as churches, the army, the civil service, or even large business corporations, that on occasion act as pressure groups. According to Almond and Coleman, "The distinguishing characteristic of the institutional interest group is the fact that a formally organized body made up of professionally employed officials or employees, with another function, performs an interest articulation function, or constitutes a base of operations for a clique or subgroup which does."[11] In some countries, institutional groups of this type wield overwhelming political power. This is not the case in Ireland. Just as Ireland is characteristically modern in possessing a large number of specialized associational groups, so, too, it is thoroughly civilian: the army is not a factor in politics, and the civil service is at the disposal of any properly elected government. In fact, the only great corporate institution in the community that might seem to rival the institutions of the political system is the Catholic Church. As a pressure group it has been, and to an extent continues to be, in a unique position.

In *Ireland Since the Rising,* Tim Pat Coogan observed that, "strictly speaking, the Church has no special legal status."[12] With the removal, in 1972, of the "special position" clause (itself only declaratory) from Article 44 of Bunreacht na hÉireann, Coogan's observation became literally true. The Church is legally not an "established church." It does not need to be, for the Irish are a devout people and the clergy have traditionally been community leaders, at least in rural areas. Twenty years ago, Jean Blanchard remarked on the power of the Irish clergy:

The Bishops of Ireland appear to have more power, in practice, than those of any other country in the world. As the natural outcome of a long historical tradition which has created exceptionally strong bonds between the nation and its clergy, their authority is great over the Faithful. . . . a member of the congregation listens more readily to his Bishop than he does, for instance, to his deputy (*député*). The social importance of the head of the diocese is unrivalled. Besides, the state fixes no limit to the Bishops' powers.[13]

Although the triumphalism of the period of which Blanchard wrote has disappeared and the clergy are not as influential today as they were then (particularly in the cities and among young people), considerable deference is still paid to them and to the Church, and Blanchard's judgement still has some validity.

It could hardly be otherwise, if only for the fact that most school education up to the third level is denominational and, hence, overwhelmingly Catholic. The following tabulation shows the position in the mid-1970s:

	Percentage of schools under Catholic management
National schools	92.6%
Other primary schools	89.3
Secondary schools:	
Lay	5.7
Religious	89.5
Total	95.2%

From the 1960s, the Department of Education, with the bishops' consent, began to take a more active part in developing the educational system. This "inevitably meant some reduction in their own authority,"[14] but it hardly affected the thoroughly Catholic ethos of the programme and teaching. Members of the clergy cannot, then, but have a great influence on public affairs, if and when they choose to use it. But to what extent do they use it?

Members of the clergy play no overt part and, in the case of the overwhelming majority of them, little if any part at all in party politics. This contrasts markedly with the past, when the clergy, especially parish clergy, were sometimes prominent in nationalist and agrarian agitation. Priests do not stand for political office, though no law of either Church or state prohibits them from doing so. Indeed, they do not *compete* for many offices of any sort, for in respect of appropriate social activities they like and sometimes expect to be *invited*. As local notables, they are particularly active in rural community projects, rural social organizations, and sporting associations. To the extent that such bodies act as pressure groups, the clergy plays its part like other members. A decree of the Synod of Maynooth (the Council of the Irish Hierarchy) forbids the use of the pulpit for political purposes, by which is meant *party* political controversy. For, of course, many matters that the Church considers within its sphere might be "political"—that is, matters for the attention of public authorities—notably, policy in respect of education, social welfare, health services, marriage, and contraception.

That is not to say that individual priests and bishops do not engage in political activities as advocates for some cause or interest. In 1978, for example, the Bishop of Elphin was prominent in a local campaign to save the maternity unit at Roscommon County Hospital, and in 1979 the Archbishop of Dublin intervened on a number of occasions to prevent what he regarded as undesirable changes in hospital services in Dublin.[15] In the late 1970s, also, the Rev. Professor F. X. Martin led a campaign to prevent Dublin Corporation from building civic offices on the site of a Viking settlement, a campaign that included demonstrations, sit-ins, law breaking, and legal processes. In the recent past, one or two bishops were particularly prone to comment publicly and to engage in controversy on political issues, notably Dr. Cornelius Lucey, formerly Bishop of Cork, described by Coogan as "the archetype of the commenting Irish bishop," and Dr. Michael Browne, formerly Bishop of Galway.[16] In the late 1970s, their mantle seemed to have fallen upon the Bishop of Limerick.

On major national issues it has been the Catholic bishops collectively, speaking as "the Hierarchy," who have occasionally sought to influence decisions. As a group, the bishops in the past were not notable for taking a positive position on social questions; indeed, the reverse was the case. In the postwar years, they took up a hostile and negative attitude to the extension of state services. This was a period of tension between state and Church, with a number of confrontations.[17] The most notable of these was the crisis over a proposed maternity and infant welfare service, the "mother and child scheme," in the early 1950s. From the 1960s, however, the Church's attitude to state welfare services became more positive and its reactions to challenges on politico-religious issues more supple, a change that reflected the new stance of the Church generally in the period of *aggiornamento* and after.

Many people believe that the Church is inclined to give directions to the politicians and that it often gets its way. To some extent, the view that interference is, or at least was, common arises from a widespread tendency in the past to dub every view expressed by a cleric as the view of "the Church." In a country where the clergy individually and collectively have expected to have all their statements treated as authoritative, the Church had only itself to blame if it was sometimes misunderstood. In practice, however, it is surprisingly difficult to demonstrate in any particular case that it was *clerical* pressure that had the decisive influence upon policy. John Whyte in his authoritative *Church and State in Modern Ireland, 1923–1979* explains why: "The difficulty is that the hierarchy exerts influence not on a *tabula rasa* but on a society in which all sorts of other influences are also at work."[18] In particular, since the community generally has always been strongly Catholic in its attitudes, governments are not likely to propose policies that are anti-Catholic or even unCatholic; and, in any case, because of their upbringing and education, the public would not favour them.

Surveying Church-state contacts between 1932 and 1979, Whyte came to the surprising conclusion that the bishops intervened only rarely: "It does not seem likely that contact between government and bishops at the level of policy is at all frequent. To put it in quantitative terms, one might guess that since 1923, there have been three or four dozen items of legislation or other questions of policy on which government and bishops have been in consultation."[19] As Whyte points out, this is an average of only one per year.

Moreover, even during the critical period, in the late 1940s and 1950s, when governments adopted an approach to welfare-state issues more positive than the bishops', it cannot be said that the bishops' views inevitably or even usually prevailed. Certainly, as Whyte argues, "the range of issues on which they spoke, and the vigour with which they expressed their views, meant that they were a more obvious factor than either earlier or later."[20] However, "it does not follow that, because the bishops were unusually active in this period, they were therefore usually effective in influencing government policy. On the contrary, they took some hard knocks in these years."[21] Whyte concluded that a theocratic state model—"a state in which the hierarchy has the final say on any matter on which it wishes to intervene"—had to be rejected. So also had the contrary view, that the Church was just another interest group:

The analogy between the hierarchy and other interest groups breaks down because, in a mainly Catholic country, the Catholic hierarchy has a weapon which no other interest group possesses: its authority over men's consciences. Most politicians on all sides of the house are committed Catholics, and accept the hierarchy's right to speak on matters of faith and morals. Even politicians who are personally indifferent on religious matters will recognize that the majority of the electorate are believers, and will act accordingly.[22]

How many battalions has an Irish bishop if it comes to a contest? Unusually, in 1972, it was possible to get a very rough pointer. The proposal to remove the "special position" section of Article 44 had been cleared by Cardinal Conway in 1969 and was supported by all three parties. However, Bishop Lucey of Cork and Ross opposed the change, and, a week before polling day, an editorial in the Cork diocesan magazine, *The Fold,* came out against it. In every constituency in Ireland save four, the vote in favour of the amendment was over 81 per cent, the overall national percentage in favour being 84 per cent. Of these four, three were in the See of Cork and Ross—Cork City N.W. (71 per cent), Cork City S.E. (72 per cent), and Cork City S.W. (76 per cent); the other, Limerick E. (75 per cent), was a constituency where an open campaign against the change had been waged by local clergy. Thus, on this issue, a lead from a bishop, even one handicapped as Bishop Lucey was with the Cardinal in favour and in the home territory of the Taoiseach of the day, was worth over 10 per cent of the vote.

Not surprisingly, in the 1970s, when the bishops attempted to thwart moves by politicians to make the Constitution and the law more acceptable to Northern Protestants by tackling sensitive issues such as contraception and divorce, they had some success. They made plain their view that the repeal of the "special position" clause of Article 44 was as far as they were prepared to go, and further reforms in that direction got no further. Most politicians of all parties, who in 1972 were urging the need for more wholesale changes, fell strangely silent. When a Family Planning Act was finally enacted in 1979, it was widely recognized to be an unsatisfactory compromise. The medical correspondent of the *Irish Times* wrote of it, "There can be no more sectarian, no more ambiguous, no more hypocritical piece of legislation on the Statute Book."[23] In respect also of changes in the management of schools, the bishops, though prepared to compromise, made clear the limits beyond which they would not go. In the latter half of the 1970s, the claim was still being publicly made by at least one bishop that the state should provide "a supportive framework." In 1980, the Archbishop of Dublin got his way against the Department of Health, medical organizations, and many doctors over the application of an ethical code to the terms of contract of doctors in six Dublin voluntary hospitals in which he had an interest. Truly, as Whyte observed, "the Catholic hierarchy is in a position matched by no other interest group in Ireland."[24]

IV

The strategies and tactics of those who seek to influence public authorities tend to be governed by a simple and obvious principle: apply pressure where the impact will be greatest. The choice of points of contact and methods of operation open to a group depends upon three constraints—cultural factors, the group's resources, and the political context.

In Ireland, as in other Western democracies, the legitimacy of pressure-group activity is fully accepted, and its great development is recognized as adding another dimension to representation. However, all pressure groups do not have equal access to policy makers. The tendency is for public authorities "to accept the role, place, or power, of those interest groups that have 'earned' a close relationship with government" and "to accommodate the lobby that works closely with government, because there is mutual benefit in the relationship."[25] Clearly, well-established conventions govern who is to be accorded the status of an "insider" with regular access to ministers and public servants and the right to be consulted. "Outsiders" will at most be permitted to hand in a protest to a public office, to send in a deputation of a few leaders to a minister or other politician, and to march and demonstrate. Even these activities are governed by a legitimacy scale. Some groups, for example, can approach the gates of Leinster House, the seat of the Oireachtas, even though the law forbids it; others cannot.

The institutionalization of this process has led to the development of codes of practice, well understood by the participants, and to a fairly clear agreement on what constitutes illegitimate activity. Bribery, undue entertainment, and secret bargains (clandestine operations generally) are neither accepted nor, apparently, much practised. Threats to authority are likely to be counterproductive in a society that accords legitimacy to the elected government. However, as elsewhere in the Western world, direct and even militant action is more condoned today than it used to be, though acceptability still depends upon who is involved. Verbal truculence, demonstrations, sit-ins, the withholding of local taxes, and the nonpayment of bills to public authorities are accepted. In 1979, Ireland had its first political strike, a one-day strike and march by trade unionists to protest against the pay-as-you-earn tax system. On that occasion, however, it was very obvious that the "establishment," in this case the leaders of the Irish Congress of Trade Unions, did not desire the action, though they had to accept it and join it. In the late 1960s, the action of the National Farmers' Association in blocking roads to Dublin, cutting off supplies of farm produce, and intimidation were regarded by the public, particularly the urban public, as going too far. So, too, on the other side was the action of the government in 1968 in legislating to take away from key electrical power workers the right to strike and in using the courts to send such strikers to jail; once again, it is not so certain today what public reaction would be.

Most sectional organizations are "insider" groups; the status of attitude groups, in contrast, varies enormously. In a community comparatively newly independent, in which self-conscious nationalism has remained at a high level, organizations that identify their objects with "the nation" expect, and have sometimes been accorded, special recognition, whether they are sporting organizations like the Gaelic Athletic Association, or the Irish language organizations, which, under the guidance of Comhdháil Náisiúnta na Gaeilge, dispose of public monies. On the other hand, groups advocating family planning and groups of householders attempting to preserve amenities in the face of industrial development projects offering the carrot of new jobs often find themselves operating in an unfavourable climate of opinion, hindered by public authorities, and on occasion even abused by public officials. At least one sectional group, also—namely, students—is usually treated as an "outsider" group, partly perhaps due to the tactics that student organizations choose to employ.

The resources, human and material, that a group has at its disposal necessarily govern its strategy and tactics. The principal resources are money to mount campaigns and provide the necessary intelligence and representational services, and members who are potential voters on election day. Until recently, however, neither was as effective as might have been expected; the one because it was not used, the other because, given the political climate, it was not usable.

Only in the last decade or so have even the strongest economic interests, the major agricultural and industrial employers organizations, begun to devote anything like adequate sums to their intelligence and representational services. Even today, the unions, and in particular the Irish Congress of Trade Unions, are grossly understaffed. The institution with the biggest membership of all, the Roman Catholic Church, to which 95 per cent of people belong, does not try to mobilize its members for specific political ends; as we have seen, it usually does not need to. Organizations that do try to mobilize, such as trade unions and farmers' organizations, have in the past experienced an important phenomenon of Irish politics: at elections, citizens tended to remain loyal to the party they previously supported even when they held views on individual issues that were not those being advocated by their party. It was the overwhelming salience of nationalist issues that inspired this loyalty.

Recently, there have been signs of a shift in priorities. This is most obvious in respect of farmers. It is generally accepted that the defection from Fine Gael of a significant number of traditionally loyal farmers at the 1977 general election was an important factor in the defeat of the National Coalition Government. The same "farmers' vote" moving in the other direction was identified by many observers as a major feature of the elections to the European Parliament in June 1979. No doubt most people are, and will remain, strongly oriented to the political party with which they identify. But even a modest increase in the volatility of voters as more people vote in their immediate material interest will have an important effect upon election outcomes and thus upon politics generally. Increasingly in Ireland, as in many democracies, "the making of governmental decisions is not a majestic march of great majorities united upon certain matters of basic policy. It is the steady appeasement of relatively small groups."[26]

The political context, the third constraint within which pressure groups operate, has as its major feature in Ireland the fact that, over most areas of public policy and a wide range of policy issues, the government has a virtual monopoly in proposing policy and legislation and an almost complete control of the activities and output of the Oireachtas because of the stable and assured support of its parliamentary party supporters. Until recently, this monopoly extended to all areas of public policy. Today, because of Irish membership in the European Communities, the position is different. In some areas—notably agriculture and fishing—and on some industrial, commercial, and fiscal matters, the authorities of the European Communities make the decisions, and this fact is duly reflected in the pattern of pressure-group activities, as we shall see.

In most policy areas, however, it is still Irish ministers and their professional advisers, mostly senior civil servants in the departments, who are the initiators and formulators of policy and administrative action. It is on them, therefore, that pressure groups tend to concentrate their main efforts, if they have access to them. This is not possible for some groups, particularly attitude groups that are proposing sweeping reforms or demanding major changes in sensitive areas, that defy the state itself, or that for one reason or another are not on speaking terms with ministers. These must stay out on the streets and attempt to attract the support of the public by interesting journalists in their cause, by advertising, or by attempting to lobby parliamentary representatives—courses of action that are not likely to get them any immediate satisfaction.

The range of contacts between pressure groups and ministers and their advisers is wide and their number enormous. In total, they are an important part of the ordinary, day-to-day business of all ministers and many senior civil servants. They include formal deputations to make representations to the minister or his official on behalf of their members or to exchange information on reactions to recent events, periodic reviews to fix rates or prices or to consider the progress of an industry, and routine contacts about specific cases or detailed points of administration between the professional servants of the interest groups and appropriate civil servants. In addition, there is a considerable and growing exchange of information and, as far as the more widely representative bodies are concerned, an increasing amount of positive involvement in government by members of consultative bodies such as the National Economic and Social Council and regulatory bodies such as the National Prices Commission and, more recently, by involvement in "tripartite" discussions on economic policy.

The practice of appointing advisory and consultative bodies on which interests have representation has been developed over many years; so, too, has the habit of ministers consulting major relevant interests before appointing the members of regulatory and administrative bodies such as, for example, Comhairle na nOspidéal (the Hospital Council) or quasi-judicial bodies like the Labour Court. Membership in public authorities of this sort and in advisory bodies is desired and sometimes demanded by sectional groups, for it not only signifies official recognition of the standing of an organization but affords a receptive access point to policy making and policy makers. Some umbrella associations such as the Irish

Congress of Trade Unions, the Federated Union of Employers, and the Confederation of Irish Industry have places on a large number of such bodies. In 1978, the Federated Union of Employers had representatives on 54 public bodies at the regional or national level and 9 at the international level. In 1980, the Irish Congress of Trade Unions, which is accepted by the state as representing the interests of labour generally, had representatives on, or made nominations to, at least 140 bodies in the public sector. (For detailed lists, see Appendix B.)

The fact that pressure groups centre their main efforts on ministers and senior public servants if they can by no means implies that "lobbying"—the attempt to influence the members of the Oireachtas—does not occur. Pressure groups circularize members, contact personally those whom they think might be sympathetic, and, *faute de mieux,* try to impress them by marches and demonstrations. Attempts to promote legislation directly by means of a "private member's bill"—that is, a bill introduced by a member of the Oireachtas other than a minister—are only very occasionally made and are never successful, being at most a device for securing publicity.

Some members of the Oireachtas have close connections with pressure groups. Part of the election and parliamentary expenses of some trade unionists are met from union funds, and some members of the Oireachtas can be identified to some degree with occupational interest groups. Nevertheless, except for a handful of independent senators, public representatives, however identified with specific interests in the community they might be, are primarily loyal to their parties (if not always in speech, certainly in their voting behaviour) and are insulated to some extent from group pressures by the party. When it comes to influencing policy, they are not such useful marks as ministers, though they are often included in pressure-group deputations to add weight. If the matter to be discussed is of local interest, they will themselves seek to be included in order to demonstrate their concern to their constituents.

Because of its composition, Seanad Éireann (the Senate) might appear to be a chamber of interest-group representatives. Legally and formally it has such a basis, for Bunreacht na hÉireann provides that forty-three of the sixty members be chosen from panels of candidates "having knowledge and practical experience" of certain "interests and services"—namely, the national language and culture, agriculture, labour, industry and commerce, and public administration and the social services. Furthermore, a proportion of the candidates for seats are nominated by appropriate voluntary associations. In practice, however, it is well known that because the electoral college is itself composed of elected representatives chosen on a party basis, party political rather than vocational considerations predominate. Hence, the senators so chosen are not markedly more representative of vocations or interests in the community than are members of legislative bodies elected in more orthodox fashion.

The impact of Ireland's accession to the European Communities, in particular to the EEC, has been nowhere more obvious than in agriculture, and it is the effects of this membership upon pressure-group activity in this policy area that we shall examine by way of example. Because the EEC makes agricultural policy (the CAP), the EEC policy makers, the Commission and the Council, are the focus of pressure groups. From the early 1970s, it was no longer sufficient for the Irish Farmers' Association and other groups to make representations to Irish ministers or consult with Irish civil servants: "The direct lobbying of the minister has become increasingly irrelevant, as the big battles leading to a slow-down in the rise in farm prices, or changes in commodity policies are played out at European level."[27]

The Irish Farmers' Association (IFA) was prompt to recognize the significance of accession. It had established an office in Brussels well before the event. This office, financed by a levy on turnover in certain commodities, rapidly became a highly efficient unit speaking for almost all Irish agricultural organizations and well able to exploit the considerable opportunities that arose in the 1970s to maximize the benefits to Irish farmers by way of prices and monetary grants. The Brussels office became "the right arm of the IFA."[28] The IFA also became a member of COPA (Comité des Organisations Professionelles Agricoles de la CEE), the influential umbrella body for EEC farming organizations, which is regularly and continuously consulted by the Commission before policies are proposed to the Council.

The fact that much agricultural policy is made in Brussels and is binding upon member states has added a new dimension to the relationships of the Minister for Agriculture and his Department with the agricultural pressure groups. At Brussels they are both in some respects pressure groups. It is true that the Minister has a voice in making final decisions, but it is only one voice among nine: he has not got, as he has in Dublin, the final say. His civil servants no less than the pressure-group spokesmen find themselves attempting to influence the European "minister," the Commissioner for Agriculture and his "civil servants," the senior officers of Directorate General VI of the Commission. Thus, new roles and relationships have had to be developed. As the journal *Magill* put it in October 1979, "Ministers for Agriculture have since Ireland's entry into the EEC become Ministers for Farmers." The role of the IFA also was changed. Mark Clinton, a former Minister for Agriculture, explained the change in this way:

The way in which I think the IFA's role has changed is this. . . . For a long time its whole purpose was to fight whatever Government was in power . . . for the best possible prices for farmers because all decisions on these matters were taken by Irish central government. Now it's a different ball game. Aids to agriculture come so much from Brussels . . . that they now have to be regarding themselves as in a kind of partnership with the Government.[29]

By the end of the 1970s, developments of this sort were most obvious in agriculture, but the same pattern of change was emerging in other areas of economic policy and in the fields of industrial relations and social affairs. In all of them, ministers no longer had the final say about many matters that they had formerly controlled or could have controlled if they had wished. In all of them, also, cooperation between the state and pressure groups in dealings with Brussels seemed to be desirable, even essential. On the morning flight from Dublin to Brussels, the civil servants and the pressure-group spokesmen were no longer sitting on opposite sides of a table. Such changes perhaps presage new forms of partnership. As we shall see, developments in domestic economic policy making were leading in the same direction.

V

The enormous scale of pressure-group activity, which is a feature of government and administration today, is a comparatively recent phenomenon. The pressure-group representatives who gave evidence to the Commission on Vocational Organization established by the Irish government in 1939 were full of complaints about lack of consultation. The Commission's conclusions were unequivocal: "We find that in the exercise of supervision and control over private enterprise by government departments there is relatively little consultation with vocational organizations. Such consultation as does take place is not continuous or obligatory, but is casual and haphazard. Even where bodies have been statutorily established they have been limited in function, defective in composition, and shortlived in operation."[30] Today, many interest organizations are regularly consulted, and some do almost daily business with public servants. The most representative of them have more positive governmental functions in the crucial field of economic planning. Yet it is important not to create an impression of uniformly cozy relationships. In the past, two major interest organizations—the National Farmers' Association and the Irish Medical Association—had for long

periods the worst possible relationships with the ministers and departments most closely concerned with them, bad relations that resulted in
the ministers' refusal to meet representatives and in the associations'
boycott of the ministers. In 1979, the Irish Congress of Trade Unions,
one of what had come to be called "the social partners," decided to boycott the Commission on Industrial Relations until the government would
introduce certain legislation that it was demanding.

In spite of the great increase in the volume of consultation, some of
those who come into contact with civil servants get the impression that
not all of them want genuine consultation, let alone negotiation. They
think that some civil servants tend to regard those contacts as a way of
getting information and compliance or as a public relations device and
do not see policy making as a genuinely cooperative activity.

There could be a number of reasons for such civil service reservations.
In the view of many senior officers: "Government is a mediating all-
inclusive agency holding the interests of various potential and actual,
strong and weak, implicit and explicit, organized and unorganized
groups in balance. And this of course has implications for the role of the
public service as the particular group, within this network of groups,
which has the strongest advisory role in the decision-making of government."[31] It is notorious also that some senior civil servants would prefer
their ministers to get advice only from them or through them. In the
past, at least, some civil servants had a paternalistic attitude towards
citizens and felt that, being professionals (of a sort), they knew best.
Today, these are outmoded attitudes in a world in which not only is
regular and genuine consultation an essential feature of successful government and administration but, increasingly, the peak interest organizations come to understandings with governments that involve commitments on both sides.

The occurrence of phenomena of this sort in advanced, industrial,
Western countries has led some writers to speculate about whether a
much more formalized group-centered political system is in process of
development to replace pluralism.[32] A few are using the term "corporatism." Philippe Schmitter defined and contrasted pluralism and corporatism:

Pluralism is a system of interest representation in which the constituent units
are organized into an unspecified number of multiple, voluntary, competitive,
non-hierarchically ordered and self-determined . . . categories not specially licenced, subsidized, created or otherwise controlled by the state and not exercising a monopoly of representational activity within their respective categories.

Corporatism can be defined as a system of interest representation in which the constituent units are organized into a limited number of singular, compulsory, non-competitive, hierarchically ordered and functionally differentiated categories, recognized or licenced (if not created) by the state and granted a deliberate representational monopoly within their respective categories in exchange for observing certain controls on their selection of leaders and articulation of demands and supports.[33]

Most writers, however, are reluctant to use the term "corporatism" to describe the emerging new patterns of decision making, preferring to label such developments as "tripartism," a system defined by Wyn Grant as one in which major economic decisions are discussed and agreed upon between the state and the major employers and trade union bodies.[34] In any case, the salient feature is that governments give up their position as unique national policy makers and seek "social partners" or "social contracts." When and where this occurs, in Ghıţa Ionescu's words, "the centre of decision making is no longer to be found in the centre of national representation. . . . it has been displaced to somewhere between the world of political representation and the world of the corporate forces."[35]

During the 1960s, and 1970s, there were developments of this sort in Ireland as elsewhere. The practice of associating pressure groups, especially sectional groups, with policy making and administration by way of membership in advisory and consultative bodies or by appointing leaders of such groups as individuals to membership on the boards of state-sponsored bodies is of long standing; but during the 1960s and after there were significant new developments, at first connected with the attempts to engage in formal economic planning and later as part of successive efforts to make and extend the scope of the National Wages Agreements. Characteristically, it was Seán Lemass who "presided over the establishment of new procedures for economic and social decision making"; in the words of J. J. Lee, "Under his aegis, Ireland began to shuffle towards a version of the corporate state."[36] The National Industrial Economic Council, first appointed in 1963 and "charged with the task of preparing reports from time to time on the principles which should be applied for the development of the national economy,"[37] was essentially an advisory body, as was its enlarged successor, the National Economic and Social Council. Their reports, however, influenced policy makers and therefore policy.

With the work of these bodies there began "a subtle shift in the nature of public decision making. They began the integration of management and trade unions into the formulation of public policy."[38] Nowhere was this more obvious than in the work of the Employer Labour Conference.

Although it was a voluntary body with no statutory basis composed of the nominees of employer organizations (including the state as an employer) and the Irish Congress of Trade Unions, the Employer Labour Conference was able throughout the 1970s to make successive National Wages Agreements that were subscribed to by employers and unions and adopted as state policy and therefore were binding on the public sector. Indeed, though voluntary, these agreements came to "have something of the character of public law."[39]

By 1973, the Federated Union of Employers was looking for more integrated policy making. In 1976, its director general told an OECD conference that "the role, interest and influence of Government has been growing, but not to the extent nor in the form frequently thought necessary by employers. . . . In recent years employers have argued the case for effective tripartite negotiations."[40] As the Federated Union of Employers continually pointed out, wages policy could not be considered in isolation from decisions affecting taxation or social welfare benefits and contributions and, thus, budgetary and economic policy generally. Understandings on these matters between the government, unions, and employers began to be sought and obtained. In 1976, a "tripartite conference" considered a government proposal for "a package" of tax and other measures in return for a wages agreement permitting more modest pay rises than would otherwise have had to be granted. From 1977, annual budgets contained such "packages" in return for moderate pay settlements. By 1979, the national wages agreement was incorporated as part of a formal "National Understanding for Economic and Social Development" negotiated directly between the government, the Irish Congress of Trade Unions, and employer organizations, each of which undertook commitments.

With the "National Understanding," the government had formally acknowledged a new positive role for the major pressure groups in an important sector of economic policy making and had incurred commitments to them; they in turn had incurred reciprocal obligations involving the conduct of their members. This agreement obliged employer organizations and the Irish Congress of Trade Unions to do their best to "deliver" (the term colloquially used) what they had agreed to and, this, as Leo Panitch put it, resulted in "their consequent employment as agencies of mobilization and social control for the state vis-à-vis their members."[41] The social partners had evidently travelled some distance down the road towards the corporate state.

It is necessary to be cautious here, however. Tripartism as we have defined it—the doctrine that major economic decisions should be discussed and agreed upon by the state and the major employers and trade union bodies—can operate only if two conditions are satisfied. First, relationships between the social partners must be good enough and their immediate objectives close enough to get agreements. So far as leaders were concerned, the record of the 1970s increasingly suggested that this was the case. Second, however, leader-follower relationships must be good enough to enable the accommodations that the leaders reach to be sold to the membership and, if agreed to, subsequently honoured and enforced as necessary. At the end of the 1970s, there were considerable doubts on this score, particularly in respect of the trade union movement. There was no doubt either that none of the three parties felt irretrievably committed to the new procedures; indeed, they were engaging in them with some hesitations and reservations. In any case, the prevailing view was still that, at the end of the day, it was for the government to govern. Ireland was still recognizably a pluralist and not a corporate state.

VI

From a democratic point of view, the importance of widespread and systematic exchange of information, consultation, and accommodation between the government and specific interests, particularly representative associations, is clear. S. E. Finer summarizes it admirably in his *Anonymous Empire*. The process, he says,

embodies two basic democratic procedures: the right to participate in policy-making and the right to demand redress of grievances. They are best appreciated by considering . . . government without them. Suppose parties and civil servants simply refused to have any contact with the Lobby [pressure groups]? Suppose the party simply claimed that it was "the will of the people" with a mandate for doing all it had proposed? Its rule would be a rigid and ignorant tyranny. And if civil servants likewise claimed to be merely the servants of the government in power, with no mandate to cooperate with the Lobby, its rule, in its turn, would be a rigid and stupid bureaucracy. In the age of bigness and technology, the Lobby tempers the system.[42]

On the other hand, as Finer points out, although this process adds a further dimension to democracy, it is "a very 'lumpy' kind of self-government." Close relationships between government and pressure groups are handy and are becoming more and more essential; but, "to put the matter crudely, a close relationship tends to become a *closed* one." Moreover, many of the processes and persons traditionally and commonly associated in the public mind with democratic government and the representation of public opinion—elections, parties, the Oireachtas itself—in truth play a comparatively small part in shaping policy. Much of the activity of policy making and administration is carried on far from electoral politics and the Oireachtas. Because this is so, much interest-group activity, including that which is most effective, is concentrated where the Oireachtas and the public do not and cannot see it. The increase in the volume and importance of such activity and the development of tripartism contribute to a growing isolation of electoral and parliamentary politics from public policy decision making. In Finer's words, "By the same process as it brings the 'interested' publics into consultation, it shuts the general public out of it."[43]

EIGHT

Elections

A democracy might be—perhaps ought to be—judged by, *inter alia*, the extent of popular participation in the making of political decisions. Elections, and in Ireland referenda also, are the opportunities for participation offered by the system to the mass of citizens. One may appropriately ask how much use is made of them, how extensive are the opportunities offered by the electoral arrangements, and how are they used in practice.

In Ireland, citizens have the opportunity to take part by casting a vote in four decision-making procedures: (1) the election of the President every seven years; (2) referenda on proposed constitutional amendments (up to the end of 1980 there had been seven such referenda); (3) elections to local authorities (at which people who are not citizens may also vote), supposedly every five years, but in the past sometimes postponed; (4) elections to Dáil Éireann, one of the two houses of the Oireachtas. The term of office of a Dáil is not fixed, though by law the maximum length is five years. The Taoiseach, however, may at any time advise the President to dissolve the Dáil and thus precipitate a general election. The President must normally comply. Only if the Taoiseach no longer commands the confidence of the Dáil has the President himself discretion to grant a dissolution, but in those circumstances it is almost certain that he would. Only one of the eighteen Dála between September 1922 and June 1977 lasted the maximum period of five years; five others lasted more than four years. The average length of life was a little over three years.[1]

The extent to which the popular vote is used in Ireland is much the same as in most other democratic countries, though the opportunities for Irish voters might seem to be rather few compared with those of United States voters, who participate in the selection of many more officials and in some cases have far more chances to record their views on policy proposals. However, in fact though not in form, Irish voters like Americans do have the opportunity to choose their government, for that is what, above all, a Dáil election, called a "general election," is for.

In *Political Oppositions in Western Democracies,* Robert Dahl identifies a number of "sites" where political encounters take place and categorizes states according to the relative importance of these sites.[2] In Ireland, general elections are the most important sites on which party encounters take place. It is there that the battle is fought over who shall rule the country; victory or defeat on this site is decisive. Formally, Bunreacht na hÉireann assigns to the Dáil the function of choosing a Taoiseach and approving a government. In practice, general elections—that is, elections to membership in the Dáil—usually determine which party or group of parties shall form the government; the Dáil merely ratifies a decision already made. For a party or coalition of parties to win a majority of seats in the Dáil is in practice to be able to form a government and, as we shall see, acquire an almost exclusive power to change state policies. It is "a condition that is ordinarily both necessary and sufficient."[3] In this chapter, we are concerned with these decisive political battle sites—general elections.

II

The electoral system used in general elections to the Dáil is, in the words of Bunreacht na hÉireann, "the system of proportional representation by means of the single transferable vote" in multimember constituencies. In Ireland the system is almost universally known simply as PR, as though there were no other proportional representation systems. It is used also for the election of the President; forty-nine of the sixty senators, who are elected by electoral colleges; and members of local authorities. It is also the most frequently used system for elections to membership in public bodies of all sorts and by private associations and clubs.

It might seem strange that a state whose political institutions and procedures derived largely from British practice should have adopted any proportional representation system, let alone one that, for all its theoretical and academic interest, has never been much used. As it happened, however, when the Treaty was being made, the leaders of both the independence movement and the British government were committed to it. Owing to the activities of the Proportional Representation Society (now called the Electoral Reform Society), the single transferable vote system was well known in political circles in the United Kingdom in the early part of this century. On the Irish side, it was espoused by Arthur Grif-

fith, who was a founder member of the Proportional Representation Society of Ireland, and was adopted as Sinn Féin policy. On the British
side, it was included in the Home Rule Bill of 1914 and in subsequent
legislation applying to Ireland, as a device to secure full representation
for the Protestant and unionist minority in future parliaments. In the
negotiations leading up to the Treaty of December 1921, Arthur Griffith, then leader of the Irish plenipotentiaries, promised that the single
transferable vote system would be used in the future independent state as
one of the safeguards sought by the British for the southern unionists.
The Irish Free State Constitution made provision for it. The system then
established has been retained virtually unchanged. Attempts by Fianna
Fáil governments in 1959 and 1968 to have it replaced by the "first-
past-the-post" system were rejected by the electorate at referenda.

Under the single transferable vote system, the elector has the opportunity to indicate a range of preferences by placing numbers opposite candidates' names on the ballot paper. If the voter so indicates, a vote can be
transferred from one candidate to another if it is not required by the
prior choice to make up that candidate's "quota" (the number of votes
necessary to secure election) or if, owing to the poor support given to the
prior choice, that candidate is eliminated from the contest. Voters need
not vote for all the candidates, but those who do vote for more than one
must number their preferences continuously—1, 2, 3, and so on. To
ascertain who has been elected, votes are initially sorted according to
first preferences, and any candidate who obtains a quota or more is
declared elected. The quota used in Irish elections is the Droop quota, so
called because it was proposed by H. R. Droop in 1869. It is the smallest number of votes that suffices to elect enough candidates to fill all the
seats being contested while being just big enough to prevent any more
from being elected.

If the number elected at the first count is less than the number of
places to be filled, as it usually is, a process of transferring votes takes
place in subsequent counts until all the seats are filled. First, the "excess" votes of any (winning) candidate—that is, votes in excess of the
quota—are distributed proportionally to the second or next available
choice of the winner's supporters. If, when no surpluses remain to be
distributed, there are still seats to be filled, the candidate with the fewest
votes is eliminated and his or her votes are redistributed according to the
next available preferences indicated. The transfer of the excess votes of
elected candidates and of the votes of eliminated candidates continues
until all the seats are filled. (A fuller description of the system and procedures is given in Appendix C.)

TABLE 8.1
Dáil Constituencies and Members, 1923–80

Year of Electoral Act	No. of constitu- encies	No. of members per constituency							Total no. of members	Average no. of constituents per member
		9	8	7	6	5	4	3		
1923	30	1	3	5	—	9	4	8	153	21,358
1935	34	—	—	3	—	8	8	15	138	21,536
1947	40	—	—	—	—	9	9	22	147	20,103
1959[a]	39	—	—	—	—	9	9	21	144	20,127
1961	38	—	—	—	—	9	12	17	144	20,127
1969	42	—	—	—	—	2	14	26	144	20,028
1974	42	—	—	—	—	6	10	26	148	20,123
1980	41	—	—	—	—	15	13	13	166	20,290

SOURCE: Compiled by the author.

[a] Some sections of this act were held to be repugnant to the Constitution (*O'Donovan* v. *Attorney General*, [1961] I.R. 114), and it never operated. The scheme it envisaged was replaced by that provided for in the 1961 act.

This system operates in general elections in multimember constituencies; it is also used in by-elections, where it is in effect an absolute majority system. Bunreacht na hÉireann provides that "no law shall be enacted whereby the number of members to be returned for any constituency shall be less than three." It also provides that "the total number of members of Dáil Éireann shall not be fixed at less than one for each 30,000 of the population, or at more than one member for each 20,000 of the population," and that the ratio between the number of members for each constituency and its population "shall so far as it is practicable, be the same throughout the country." The Oireachtas is required to revise constituencies "at least once in every twelve years," and it is now generally accepted that this process—"redistricting," as Americans call it—ought to be carried out after each national census. Accordingly, successive Electoral Amendment Acts have altered the number of members and constituencies (see Table 8.1). Consequent upon an important High Court decision (*O'Donovan* v. *Attorney General*, [1961] I.R. 114), the tolerance permitted in a redistricting scheme—that is, the difference between the maximum and minimum number of persons who are to be represented by one member—is very small, but because of rapid population changes it is not possible to maintain anything like an equality of ratios.

III

Legally and formally, a general election consists of a number of constituency contests to elect deputies to Dáil Éireann. In practice, it is also and indeed primarily a competition between political parties for the right to form a government and govern the country. This being so, it might be argued that the electoral system should be judged by its propensity to offer the elector a clear choice of governments and to produce governments with enough consistent parliamentary support to enable them to govern, which in the eyes of Irish politicians means, as nearly as possible, a majority of their own supporters.

Governments with stable majorities are not, of course, the product of elections alone, still less of electoral systems, but it is a fact that the application of one set of electoral laws might create a majority where another would not. In practice, as Douglas Rae points out in *The Political Consequences of Electoral Laws,* "in most cases, electoral systems function to the advantage of large established parties and to the disadvantage of small established parties and insurgents [i.e., parties new into the field]." Although, as Rae says, "it is clearly silly to conclude that P.R. causes the multiplication of parties,"[4] it is often argued that it does contribute to such an outcome. Irish experience in this respect is of particular importance because Ireland offers one of the very few examples of the use of the single transferable vote system (in 1979, it was in use in Malta, in Australia and South Africa for their senates, and in the state of Tasmania).

The major issue of Irish general elections is for most of those involved, whether actively or otherwise, who is to form the next government. Clear alternatives, however, have not been offered to the electorate on every occasion. In two-thirds of the elections from 1923, it can be said that the voters were presented with a clear enough choice of governments; but, for a decade or so from the late 1930s and again in the late 1950s and 1960s, no viable alternative to Fianna Fáil was unequivocally on offer by the opposition parties. For such an alternative to exist, electoral alliances would have been required, but these were not made. Once, in 1948, a coalition was mooted and effected *after* the election, when the results were seen to offer the possibility of ousting Fianna Fáil.

From the early 1930s, one alternative has regularly been on offer—a Fianna Fáil government. A combination of two circumstances has caused this. The first is the consistent pattern of electoral support for Fianna Fáil. Once its initial buildup was completed, a process that took from 1927 to 1932, it has always been able to win the first-preference votes of almost a majority—and on two occasions of an actual majority—of the electorate. The second circumstance favorable to Fianna Fáil is the electoral system's translating of votes into seats. This has boosted support by providing a "bonus" sufficient to enable the party to win a majority of

TABLE 8.2
Percentage of First-Preference Votes and Seats
Won by Fianna Fáil, 1932–77

Election	First-preference votes	Seats won	Position after election
1932	44.5%	47.1%	Government
1933	49.7	50.3	Government
1937	45.2	50.0	Government
1938	51.9	55.8	Government
1943	41.9	48.6	Government
1944	48.9	55.1	Government
1948	41.9	46.3	Opposition
1951	46.3	46.9	Government
1954	43.4	44.2	Opposition
1957	48.3	53.1	Government
1961	43.8	48.9	Government
1965	47.8	50.0	Government
1969	45.7	52.0	Government
1973	46.2	47.9	Opposition
1977	50.6	56.8	Government

SOURCE: For 1932–44, compiled by the author from unofficial figures published in Flynn's Parliamentary Handbooks and elsewhere. For 1948–77, compiled by the author from *Election Results and Transfer of Votes* (Stationery Office, Dublin), published after each election.

seats or sometimes, when it did not win a majority, to come close enough to enable it to assume power as though it had (see Table 8.2 for details). In these circumstances, Fianna Fáil has naturally tended to adopt strictly competitive electoral and parliamentary strategies and to eschew coalition. Consequently, Irish politics for more than half a century has been locked into a rigid framework of strict competition between Fianna Fáil and the rest. This has resulted in an "ins-and-outs" pattern of parliamentary government.

If coalition strategies have usually been inappropriate for Fianna Fáil, they might seem to be natural, even necessary, for the other permanent parties, Fine Gael and the Labour Party. In view of the pattern of popular support, electoral pacts involving the transfer of lower preference votes between the two would have led to a one-party versus two-party type of bipolarism and the possibility of more frequent alternation in office than actually occurred.

In the 1930s and 1940s, the ideological differences between Fine Gael and Labour were too great to make coalition palatable. In 1948, however, after a sixteen-year unbroken spell of Fianna Fáil government, an agreement between the leaders of all parties except Fianna Fáil, hastily arranged after the election results were known, brought about the defeat of that party and the formation of a coalition. After two three-year peri-

TABLE 8.3
Irish Governments, September 1922–June 1977

Date of appointment	Government party	Nature and duration of government		
		One-party majority government	One-party minority government	Coalition
September 1922	Pro-Treaty[a]	1 yr., 0 mos.[b]		
September 1923	Cumann na nGaedheal	3 yrs., 9 mos.[b]		
June 1927	Cumann na nGaedheal		4 mos.	
October 1927	Cumann na nGaedheal		4 yrs., 5 mos.[c]	
March 1932	Fianna Fáil		11 mos.	
February 1933	Fianna Fáil	4 yrs., 5 mos.		
July 1937	Fianna Fáil	5 yrs., 0 mos.		
June 1938	Fianna Fáil		11 mos.	
July 1943	Fianna Fáil		11 mos.	
June 1944	Fianna Fáil	3 yrs., 8 mos.		
February 1948	Inter-Party[d]			3 yrs., 4 mos.
June 1951	Fianna Fáil		3 yrs., 0 mos.	
June 1954	Inter-Party[e]			2 yrs., 10 mos.
March 1957	Fianna Fáil	4 yrs., 7 mos.		
October 1961	Fianna Fáil		3 yrs., 6 mos.	
April 1965	Fianna Fáil[f]	4 yrs., 3 mos.		
July 1969	Fianna Fáil	3 yrs., 8 mos.		
March 1973	National Coalition[g]			4 yrs., 3 mos.
TOTAL		30 yrs., 4 mos.	14 yrs., 0 mos.	10 yrs., 5 mos.
June 1977	Fianna Fáil	(still in office in December 1980)		

[a] From Spring 1923 called Cumann na nGaedheal.
[b] Government majority due to the fact that the members of Fianna Fáil, the biggest opposition party, did not take their seats.
[c] The government had the support of the Farmers' Party, which, however, ceased to operate as a party, and its members for all intents and purposes became members of Cumann na nGaedheal.
[d] A coalition of all parties except Fianna Fáil. It also included independents.
[e] A coalition of Fine Gael, the Labour Party, and Clann na Talmhan.
[f] Fianna Fáil won exactly half of the seats.
[g] A coalition of Fine Gael and the Labour Party.

ods of coalition, the major partners, disillusioned with their experience, resumed strict competition. Another sixteen-year period of Fianna Fáil government ensued.

By 1973, ideological differences between Fine Gael and Labour had almost disappeared, programmes overlapped, and some of the leaders were power-hungry. In any case, they were faced with the need to present a viable alternative to Fianna Fáil in order to retain credibility with the electorate. A coalition platform was agreed to, and a cooperative campaign was waged successfully. Disciplined transfer of lower preferences played a large part in effecting a coalition victory. The defeat of that coalition in 1977, however, led once again to the Labour Party in particular voicing doubts about coalition. There can be little doubt that Irish political leaders regard adversary politics and competitive strategies as the norm and consensus politics and coalition as at best a tiresome necessity in order to get power. For the leaders of Fianna Fáil, consensus politics and coalition have always been, and remain, unthinkable.

Although Irish politics has exhibited some of the typical features of a bipolar system, electoral support for the various parties as translated into parliamentary seats has led to almost as many governments without a parliamentary majority as with. Table 8.3 shows that, from independence to the end of the 1970s, there were nine single-party majority governments, three coalitions with a parliamentary majority of their own party supporters, and seven single-party governments without such a majority, being dependent on others. Although the table indicates also that four of the seven minority governments were short-lived, it must be pointed out that three of them—the three eleven-month Fianna Fáil governments—were brought to an end by De Valera for tactical reasons. In fact, almost all dissolutions of Dáil Éireann have been brought about by leaders who hoped to secure an electoral advantage as the government came towards the end of its term of office or hoped to improve its parliamentary support.

No Irish government has ever been forced out of office by defeat, and on only three occasions has a government gone to the country rather than risk a defeat in the Dáil. (One of these was the result of the decision of the elected members of Fianna Fáil who had boycotted the Dáil to take their seats in 1927.) Even though, as has usually been the case, parliamentary majorities have been small and usually to be counted on the fingers of one hand, the history of almost sixty years up to 1980 included two unbroken periods of office of sixteen years each (1932–48 and 1957–73) and one of ten years (1922–32). Between 1922 and 1977, governments with majorities of their own party supporters were in office for almost forty-one years, minority governments for only fourteen. This is a record of great stability. To what extent it can be attributed to the electoral system or be said to be in spite of it is another matter. Clearly, the salient factor has been, to repeat, the critical size and great stability of Fianna Fáil support for nearly half a century.

Just as Irish experience lends no support to the view that the single transferable vote system leads to instability, so too it does not contribute much evidence to support the view that PR encourages the multiplication of parties. The same three parties have always dominated the scene. Although minor parties have come and gone, none established itself for much more than a decade or so. The number of parties contesting elections and gaining representation in the Dáil has gone through two cycles, rising to seven (in the 1920s and again in the 1940s and 1950s) and falling to three (in the 1930s, 1960s and 1970s) in a way that might best be explained by the ability of the major parties to hold their supporters or to attract radicals. Often, new parties have originated out of discontent with the permanent three. In these circumstances, independents and small groups have been able to win considerable support and even seats. Nevertheless, throughout the 1970s, more parties contested elections and won seats in British general elections under the "first-past-the-post" system than in Irish general elections under the single transferable vote system.

In exploring the impact of election systems upon the number of parties in a political system, Rae devised an "index of fractionalization"—a measure for comparing the number and comparative sizes of a party's share of the vote and of parliamentary representation. He calculated averages for two groups of election systems, PR systems, on the one hand, and plurality and majority systems, on the other. Comparing Irish

TABLE 8.4

*Index of Fractionalization of Party Systems in Ireland, 1922–73,
and in Countries with PR Systems and Countries with
Plurality or Majority Systems, 1945–65*

Type of fractionalization	PR systems	Ireland	Plurality and majority systems
Electoral	0.73	0.68	0.54
Parliamentary	0.70	0.65	0.51

SOURCE: For PR systems and plurality and majority systems, D. W. Rae, *The Political Consequences of Electoral Laws* (New Haven and London, 1971), p. 98. For Ireland, M. Gallagher, "Disproportionality in a Proportional Representation System: The Irish System," *Political Studies*, 23 (1975), 503.

NOTE: The index is that devised and used by Rae.

experience with Rae's averages, Michael Gallagher found that "the level of fractionalization ... is close to that in PR systems."[5] (See Table 8.4.) However, he concluded from his investigation of the effect of "district magnitude" (the number of seats in each constituency) that this factor had only a "limited influence ... upon Irish election results."[6]

The situation in Ireland is no doubt one of "fractionalized multiparty competition," as Rae said,[7] but it is a very modest degree of fractionalization. Irish experience, as Cornelius O'Leary concluded from his survey of general elections, has, or should have, "helped to modify dogmatism" about the effect of the system on the number of parties and on the chances of stable government. It certainly suggests, in O'Leary's words, that "the PR → multiplication of parties → government instability syndrome is no longer regarded as necessary."[8]

IV

Since elections are occasions of mass involvement in politics, the quantity and quality of participation can rightly be deemed to be important criteria for judging electoral systems. The opportunities for Irish citizens to select representatives to speak and act for them, though as numerous as in most democratic countries, are few enough. Under the single transferable vote system, however, the part the citizen can play in the process is greater than in most systems. This arises because of the opportunities the system offers, opportunities that are used.

Opportunities at the nomination stage are not very great. Nomination is largely in the hands of party activists in the constituency who are sometimes guided or influenced by party headquarters; most candidates are party nominees. Candidates of the three permanent parties are all selected at constituency conventions, which are attended by a few representatives of each branch in the constituency. These conventions, which in the case of Fianna Fáil rural constituencies might number up to four or five hundred people, are presided over by one of the party's national leaders. The job of the presiding leader is to persuade or cajole the locals to nominate an appropriate number of suitable candidates selected to cover the whole constituency.

To a great extent, candidate selection is a local matter. Nominations have to be ratified by the National Executive Committees of the parties, and occasionally names are added to the slate by party headquarters. Interference, however, is usually resented at local level. For example, in 1977, the Administrative Council of the Labour Party refused to endorse a number of controversial candidates selected locally, and this led to breakaway movements and independent labour candidates and to the party losing votes and even seats. At the same election, however, the Fianna Fáil leader, Jack Lynch, with the backing of the party executive successfully exercised his right to add candidates to constituency slates— in particular, half-a-dozen women. In fact, the national leaders and professionals at party headquarters openly admit the need to influence candidate selection more than they do at present in order to get sufficient candidates of good quality into the field. In the case of minor parties, nomination is a wholly local and often personal matter, and independents are almost by definition self-propelled.

Voting in Ireland is not compulsory, but only registered voters may cast a vote. The percentage of electors who vote (the turnout) has varied from the low 60s at the first elections (1922 and 1923), when unsettled conditions obtained, to 81 per cent at the 1933 election, when there was great excitement and tension. The turnout at the nine elections from the end of the Second World War up to 1977 varied between 71 per cent and 77 per cent. (See Table 5.2, p. 87, for European comparisons.) Turnout is not uniform over the country. It is lowest in the Dublin area, where the urban population is more mobile and more volatile in its propensity to vote, and in one or two of the mountainous and least-developed western seaboard constituencies. Evidently, electors do not find it difficult to do what the law requires of them, for invalid votes are usually less than 1 per cent (0.85 per cent in 1977). The positive response of many voters to their party's exhortations about how to allot lower preference votes or to refrain from allotting them suggests that most people understand the significance of indicating preferences and how the counting system works.

In considering the use made of the information given by voters concerning their wishes, it is important to remember that voters have the opportunity to indicate support for more than one candidate if they rank candidates in order of preference. In Rae's terminology, the Irish voter has an "ordinal" choice, as opposed to the "categorical" choice facing the electors under the single nontransferable vote system—the so-called "straight vote" of the "first-past-the post" system—and some of the party-list systems.[9] When it comes to counting, more information is available about most Irish voters' wishes than about the wishes of voters under categorical ballot systems, and the rules are designed to give effect to voters' intentions.

Irish electors may vote for candidates not only on account of their party affiliations but also as individuals. The candidates are listed alphabetically on the ballot paper, and until the 1965 election their party affiliations were not even given. The proportion of electors who see their first choices elected is about 70 per cent; in 1977, it was 70.2 per cent. As important, between 75 and 80 per cent of votes cast help elect someone. Compared with party-list systems, the proportion of noneffective votes in Irish elections (between 20 and 25 per cent) is high, though not all of these are "wasted" votes, since from 3 to 5 per cent of them become nontransferable during the count by the deliberate choice of voters to abstain if their first choices are not used. The results achieved under party-list systems are due to narrowing the voters' choice to parties and having constituencies return very large numbers of members. The contrast that Irish people themselves are more likely to make is with British voters with their categorical choice and the possibility overall of considerable disproportionality between votes and seats.

Almost all Irish voters vote for more than one candidate, ranking at least some of the candidates in an order of preference. There is much evidence to suggest that in doing so they are above all party oriented and take notice of their party's advice to "vote X, Y and Z in the order of [their] choice." Between eight and nine out of ten of all electors who give their first preferences to candidates of Fianna Fáil and Fine Gael elected at the first count, give second preferences to other candidates of the same party; and almost as many do the same with their third preferences. This pattern seems to hold good to a considerable extent for all supporters of the permanent parties. In an analysis covering all elections from 1922 to 1977, Michael Gallagher investigated the proportion of transfers from each party that went to other candidates of the same party where at least one candidate of the party was available to receive transfers. He found an average of 81 per cent for Fianna Fáil, 74 per cent for Fine Gael, and 64 per cent for Labour. As Gallagher concedes, for technical reasons his findings are subject to a number of qualifications, but they are, as he claims, "a reasonably accurate indication of the attitudes of supporters of each party."[10]

Further evidence of the party orientation of many Irish voters can be seen in their propensity to comply with their party's suggestions about what to do with lower preferences when no more candidates of the party are available. The National Coalition victory in 1973 was largely due to the disciplined preferential voting of the supporters of the two parties involved, which was critical in a number of marginal constituencies.[11] Again, there is evidence that when party campaign workers urge their supporters to "plump"—that is, not to pass on transfers to candidates of other parties—many are likely to comply. Gallagher's analysis suggests that almost half of the comparatively well-disciplined supporters of Fianna Fáil between 1922 and 1977 plumped.[12]

Party preference, however, is not of itself sufficient to enable at least eight out of ten voters to cast a vote, for in all constituencies Fianna Fáil and Fine Gael, and in a few constituencies Labour also, offer more than one candidate. Although there is nothing in the law to prevent parties from attempting to influence their supporters' choice between party candidates, they do not in fact do so; in Irish conditions it might be counterproductive were they to try. Many voters and most local activists have local and personal loyalties to particular candidates and would resent direction. Many candidates, particularly in rural constituencies, are identified with particular areas in their constituency where they hope to win the greater part of their first-preference support. Each has carefully nurtured the party supporters of a particular area and hopes to garner the first preferences of enough of them to get elected or, if not, to remain in the contest in the hope of receiving lower preference votes later in the count. Each is as much in competition with fellow party candidates as with candidates of other parties for the relatively fixed number of votes the party expects to get.

In rank-ordering their party's candidates, voters might be influenced by any of a number of factors. Most people give their first preference to the senior and best-known member of their party's team or to the candidate from their own district, whom, in rural areas at least, they are likely to know. The strong localism of rural voters finds full expression through the election system. Because of this, what is formally a multi-member constituency system is in places something rather different. In John Whyte's view some constituencies are no more than "a federation of single member seats," and some writers have used terms like "fiefs" and "bailiwicks" to describe them.[13]

Personality and personal factors also influence rank ordering. Increasingly over the years, prominence in gaelic football and hurling replaced "a national record"—that is, active participation in the struggle for independence—as a prime qualification for candidature and office. Well known in Irish politics, too, is the sympathy vote, which serves to put a widow or a son into a dead man's seat, which can be retained at subsequent elections if son or widow works hard. Indeed, the dynastic element generally is strong. Ted Nealon's *Guide to the 21st Dáil and Seanad* records that of the 148 deputies elected at the 1977 general election, 24 were sons and one a daughter of former deputies; in addition, there were 3 widows, 1 brother, 4 nephews, 1 son-in-law, and 1 granddaughter (a Miss de Valera!). In many cases, they won seats in areas previously represented by their kinsmen.

Perhaps most important of all for most candidates is their record of

TABLE 8.5

Voters' Perception of the Most Important Criterion
Determining Their Vote, May–June 1977

Criterion	Percentage
Quality of Taoiseach	8%
Quality of the ministers who will form the government	18
Party policies	21
Confidence that the candidate will look after the needs of the constituency	46
Don't know	7

SOURCE: Irish Times/National Opinion Polls Election Surveys, May–June 1977, quoted by R. Sinnott, "The Electorate," in *Ireland at the Polls: The Dáil Elections of 1977,* ed. H. R. Penniman (Washington, D.C., 1978), p. 62.

"service" to their local constituents and to their area—the attention paid by them to requests for help over applications to, or difficulties with, public authorities, local and national, in connection with matters such as housing, social welfare, health benefits and facilities, land redistribution and drainage grants, and the siting of factories. A survey carried out in 1977 found that almost half of the respondents thought "service" to be the most important criterion determining their vote (see Table 8.5). Because many of these matters are handled at the local government level, most TDs think it is essential for them to be members of their local authorities. Candidates who are the most preferred of their party at one election might easily slip at the next if they have not assiduously attended to their constituents' requests for help. Such changes in popularity can and do lead to defeat.

The considerations mentioned in preceding paragraphs not only influence the order of choice of party-oriented voters, who are the vast majority, but also lead some voters to give lower preferences to candidates of other parties after they have exhausted their own party's choices. A few voters might also cross party lines in ordering their preferences, perhaps even to the extent of placing a candidate of a party other than their own first on the ballot paper. At the 1973 general election, for example, "the first preference votes for candidates such as Jack Lynch, Liam Cosgrave, Garret FitzGerald, John O'Connell [were] obvious examples of 'personal' first preference votes. In all these cases, and there [were] others, a substantial proportion of subsequent preferences [went] to candidates of other parties."[14]

The practice of voters ranking candidates and in doing so taking into account any factors that they regard as important has considerable consequences for the whole political system. It has an important effect upon the composition of the Dáil, and it greatly influences the behaviour of deputies. To a great extent, it governs TDs' relationships with their constituents and their perceptions of their role as parliamentarians. By making it possible for electors to combine in groups that do not coincide with party divisions and to support candidates who are not party choices, the system has permitted the existence of independents and the survival of party rebels and outcasts. An outstanding example in the 1970s was Neil Blaney. A deputy and former minister representing a rural northwestern constituency where he had a virtual fiefdom, he was expelled from Fianna Fáil in 1971 but retained his seat in subsequent general elections, being elected on the first count in both 1973 and 1977.

The effects of the way the electoral system is exploited by the electors upon the conduct of elections themselves are very obvious. The selection of candidates is particularly affected. Although the law does not require it, candidates are predominantly local people in the sense that they live and belong in their constituencies. Except in Dublin, almost all live in or are identified with a particular part of the constituency they are contesting, where they have a following and which they regard as their area. Consequently, most candidates for rural constituencies are countrymen; there are very few urban "carpetbaggers." This virtual requirement of local residence has a marked effect upon the composition of the Dáil.

The campaigns waged by these locally selected and usually local candidates tend to be self-contained and self-sufficient; the central organizations of the parties play only a supporting role. National issues, activities, and materials designed to influence electors at large—television and radio programmes, party manifestos and pledges, campaign tours by party leaders, T-shirts, and party songs—are, though of growing importance, still a backdrop against which a candidate seeks the support of his or her locality.

As we have seen, the candidate's best asset by far is a record of service in the home district. Here, naturally, sitting deputies have a great advantage, for they can offer—and in many cases have already given— service as a contact and advocate at the central government level as well as at city or county hall. Although a good record of service is an asset to anyone and is the foundation of the position of deputies of small parties and independents, the candidates of the main parties use it chiefly not against political opponents of other parties, but against their fellow candidates of the same party. Candidates cannot fight their fellow party candidates on policy or party record; they try, instead, to present an image of more assiduous and more successful service to constituents. Politicians know this well and act accordingly.

Concentration on the personal and local is more evident in the rural areas than in the big cities. This can be seen particularly in canvassing activities. All candidates and all party officials believe that canvassing is the most effective method of electioneering. In the city it does not matter much who the canvassers are, but in the villages and in the countryside the candidate must personally approach all supporters of consequence in his or her area and as many others as possible. In turn, prominent supporters seek the votes of their neighbours. Thus links in a chain of personal approach are forged, a matter of necessity in dealing with a rural population that values face-to-face contacts, regards personal influence as an important factor in the conduct of any business of importance, and likes to feel that a potentially influential person has asked a favour and incurred an obligation.

No doubt the increasing tendency in the television age for the parties to present elections as gladiatorial contests between national leaders and to offer tax and other inducements to an electorate that is becoming more volatile and susceptible to material offers is changing Irish elections. By the late 1970s, TV politics, the razzamatazz generated by the party professionals, and material blandishments offered at the national level were transforming the character of elections.

V

When a country has an election system that is said to be a proportional representation system, much attention is naturally paid to the degree of correspondence in practice between votes cast and seats won. It is customary to measure proportionality in terms of first-preference votes cast for each party and seats won by the party. Since, however, the Irish system is a *transferable* vote system, it might be argued that to pay attention only to first preferences is inappropriate. Taking four general elections (1922, 1937, 1954, 1977), Michael Gallagher calculated that 23 per cent of voters had their votes transferred at least once. Such transfers affected the eventual outcome in 29 per cent of three-seat constituencies, 43 per cent of four-seat constituencies, and 54 per cent of five-seat constituencies. Nevertheless, "only about one TD in nine owes his election to the transfers he has received . . . the remaining eight-ninths would have been elected even had no transfers taken place," their positions at the end of the count being the same as after the first count.[15]

Again, since the voter is not confined to choosing between parties, there is no reason to argue that the counting system is to be judged only by whether it produces a result that provides proportional representation of parties. In fact, in Irish circumstances, it *is* appropriate so to judge it because political attitudes are largely party oriented and most voters se-

TABLE 8.6

Performances of Political Groupings at General Elections, June 1927–73

Party	Average per cent votes	Average per cent seats	Average index of proportionality[a]	Maximum index of proportionality[a]	Minimum index of proportionality[a]
Fianna Fáil	44.17%	47.75%	1.08	1.15	1.01
Fine Gael	30.17	31.37	1.04	1.12	0.96
Labour	11.17	10.02	0.89	1.19	0.62
Independents	7.04	5.25	0.73	1.08	0.22
Minor parties	7.46	5.62	0.75	1.42	0

SOURCE: M. Gallagher, "Disproportionality in a Proportional Representation System: The Irish Experience," *Political Studies*, 23 (1975), 502.

[a] The index of proportionality used by Gallagher is calculated by dividing a party's share of the seats by its share of the votes. A base of 1.00 is used.

lect *first* between parties and *then* within the party they have chosen. In fact, proportionality measured in terms of first preferences for each party and seats won by each party is comparatively high. Rae concluded that, although the Irish system did not in many respects fit his categories— and he dubbed it a deviant case—"in general [it] behaves like any other sort of proportional representation. It operates quite proportionally."[16]

Gallagher has analyzed Irish experience and compared his findings with Rae's findings for his two categories of electoral systems—proportional representation systems and plurality and majority systems. Rae found that the average deviation of votes and seats for every party in all elections in twenty countries using a majority or plurality system was 3.96, and in PR countries it was 1.63. For Irish elections between 1927 and 1973, Gallagher calculated an average deviation of 1.90, which places Ireland much nearer to the PR end of the spectrum.[17] Gallagher's average figures for each party, given in Table 8.6, show that, as generally happens elsewhere, the largest parties have tended to win a more than proportionate share of seats and, in particular, Fianna Fáil has always won a bonus. Because of the size of its electoral support, that bonus has often been critical for its chances of winning power, as shown by Table 8.2 (p. 147).[18]

The number of deputies per constituency—what Rae called "district magnitude"—is often considered to have a critical impact upon proportionality, but studies by Gallagher and O'Leary cast doubt upon the importance of this factor. Certainly, variations in proportionality cannot be attributed solely to constituency size.[19] Nevertheless, politicians have always thought it important and have tried to adjust constituencies accordingly when they could. Constituency revision was carried out by the government until 1979, when a constituency commission was appointed to make recommendations. Revision schemes were, until then, prepared by the Minister for Local Government (renamed Environment in 1977) directly and frankly with an eye to maximizing party advantage within the rules.

In the 1930s and 1940s, spokesmen for governments revising constituencies openly justified their proposals to break up big constituencies and to increase the number of three-seat and four-seat constituencies on the grounds that "it is made easier for a party which may be called upon to shoulder the responsibility of government to get sufficient seats to enable them to undertake that task with adequate parliamentary support."[20] As Table 8.1 shows, district magnitude was successively decreased until the 1974 revision. Consequently, the average number of deputies per constituency also fell (see Table 8.7). Convenience of another sort, this time the convenience of deputies "servicing" their constituents (together with a strong rural bias among the deputies), led successive governments on the occasion of constituency revisions to sacrifice mathematical accuracy in order to favour rural areas—especially the western seaboard areas whose populations were scattered and declining. However, the findings of the High Court in *O'Donovan* v. *Attorney General* put an end to this.

Within the legal rules governing constituency revision, "it is remarkable what can be done by a ruling party anxious to maximize its strength," as John Whyte observed.[21] Both he and Gallagher were able to suggest guidelines for a party wishing to maximize its support. Both stressed that a party's decision to have three-, four-, or five-seat constituencies in an area depended on the size of the party's expected support.[22]

TABLE 8.7
*Average Number of Deputies per
Constituency, 1923–79*

Year of electoral act	No. of deputies per constituency
1923	5.25
1935	4.03
1947	3.65
1961	3.76
1969	3.40
1974	3.50
1979	4.02

SOURCE: For 1923–69, derived from M. Gallagher, "Disproportionality in a Proportional Representation System: The Irish Experience," *Political Studies*, 23 (1975), 504. For 1974 and 1979, data supplied by the author.

NOTE: The Ceann Comhairle (chairman) has been omitted from the count.

Surprisingly, Gallagher's analysis of constituency revisions suggested that "any attempted gerrymandering in the first three revisions [1935, 1947, 1961] was fairly unsuccessful," at least as far as constituency size was concerned. However "at the 1969 election . . . practically two-thirds of the constituencies were of optimal size."[23]

Following the alleged practice of Fianna Fáil, the 1974 revision carried out by the National Coalition was generally reckoned to have been a wholehearted attempt on the part of that government to favour itself as much as possible. The "Tullymander," as it became known—Mr. James Tully was the Minister for Local Government responsible for the scheme—might well have given an advantage of half-a-dozen or so seats to the National Coalition had the pattern of electoral support in 1977 remained relatively unchanged from the 1973 general election. However, it did not, and consequently the arrangement of constituencies, particularly in the Dublin area, seems to have favoured Fianna Fáil.[24]

Clearly, attempts by parties to manipulate district magnitude in their own interests are fraught with risk, especially if, as might be the case, more people than hitherto are likely to switch their support from one party to another on bread-and-butter issues. Perhaps neither ideologies nor traditional loyalties have the hold that they once had, and governments will be judged increasingly by their ability to "deliver the goods." Survey evidence in the period leading up to the 1977 general election and analysis of the results of that election suggest that the major issues as perceived by the electorate were prices, inflation, and unemployment.[25] As Richard Sinnott said, "from the outset and right through the campaign, the battle was apparently fought on the economic front."[26] With such issues uppermost in people's minds, the supposed failure of the government to deal with them played a decisive part in the defeat of the National Coalition.

Likewise, the heavy losses sustained by Fine Gael, particularly in the rich farming areas, were largely due to "the overall swing of a significant bloc of traditionally loyal larger farmers away from Fine Gael. . . . [This] determined the results."[27] In 1979, the elections for the European Parliament seemed to confirm the existence of a "farmers' vote" that was likely to be swayed back and forth by their reaction to government agricultural policy and performance. Again, some argue that there is a "youth vote" that is equally volatile and similarly motivated. In Irish conditions, these changes in electoral support for the parties will be rather precisely reflected in the composition of the Dáil and will have important consequences for government formation and party strategy. Such changes would clearly also make boundary manipulation a hazardous business.

If proportionality is the aim of an electoral system, chance or extraneous elements that might distort the picture of the electors' wishes ought to be eliminated so far as possible. Two such elements in the Irish system should be noted. The first arises during the count when surpluses are transferred. The proportion of ballot papers of an elected candidate that is to go to each continuing candidate is calculated as a ratio of the surplus to the number of transferable papers. Each candidate receives this proportion of the appropriate bundle of votes that show next preferences for him or her. It is when this transfer is actually made that an element of chance arises, for a physical transfer of votes is made, the appropriate number from the top of the elected candidate's pile being taken and placed with the other votes of the transferee. In a tight marginal situation at the end of a count where very few votes divide the last two candidates, it is possible that if different sets of papers had been taken earlier in the count, the pattern of next preference shown on these papers might be different and the difference might alter the end result.[28]

More important, perhaps, is the influence of printing candidates' names on the ballot paper in alphabetical order. Irish politicians have for long recognized that a candidate whose name is high up on the printed list has an advantage. Robson and Walsh, using statistical techniques, have demonstrated not only "the distinct advantage enjoyed by candidates, and non-incumbent candidates in particular, if they are alphabetically first among their party's candidates" (see Table 8.8), but also the cumulative impact this has had on the outcome of elections. They found that "TDs' surnames are now markedly different in alphabetical distribution from the Irish population as a whole."[29]

TABLE 8.8

Alphabetical Distribution of Candidates' and Deputies' Surnames in the General Election of 1973

| Group | First letter of surname | | | | | Total no. (= 100 per cent) |
	A–C	D–G	H–L	M–O	P–Z	
Random sample of Irish population	20.3%	17.9%	17.2%	25.3%	19.4%	2,100
All candidates	27.1	18.8	17.6	22.5	14.0	335[a]
TDs elected	32.6	22.2	16.0	15.3	13.9	144[a]
Incumbent candidates	33.6	20.9	16.4	17.2	11.9	134[a]

SOURCE: Derived from C. Robson and B. Walsh, "The Importance of Positional Voting Bias in the Irish General Election of 1973," *Political Studies,* 22 (1974), 191, Table 1.

[a] Includes the outgoing Ceann Comhairle (chairman), who is returned unopposed.

The single transferable vote system has been retained without any major changes throughout the whole life of the state. When, in the mid-1930s, De Valera was preparing a new constitution for the country, the system was not called in question, and Bunreacht na hÉireann provided for its continuation. It was, perhaps, too soon after the events and circumstances that had dictated its inclusion in the first place to be looking for a change. Nevertheless, faced with the tantalizing situation of permanently being the largest party and of regularly winning very nearly a majority of the votes cast, it is not surprising that De Valera and Fianna Fáil should have contemplated changing the system.

Not until the late 1950s, however, at the very end of De Valera's long reign, did he broach the question of electoral reform. In 1959, the Fianna Fáil government initiated a constitutional referendum providing for the replacement of the 40 multiseat constituencies with between 100 and 150 single-seat constituencies and the substitution of the single nontransferable vote for the transferable vote. If the reform was approved, the candidate getting the most votes would win the seat, as in the system used in the United Kingdom. This was to be De Valera's legacy to Fianna Fáil, for he was to be a candidate at the presidential election held on the same day as the referendum, and his prestige, it was thought, would ensure the passage of the constitutional amendment.

De Valera's main arguments and those of his colleagues centered on the malignant effects of the single transferable vote system. De Valera himself put it thus:

P.R. has not, in my opinion, in recent times worked out well. . . . it worked very well for a time because there were issues so large in the public eye that they dominated all other issues, and, therefore, the people voted on one side or the other. . . . Some of this stability was acquired rather in spite of the system. . . . The whole effect of the present system of P.R. has been to cause multiplicity of parties. . . . Under the system of straight voting they will have to unite beforehand, not after. . . . Those countries which have most successfully built up democratic institutions are the countries in which there is a single nontransferable vote.[30]

In the event, the proposal was narrowly defeated by 33,667 votes out of just under a million. With a 58 per cent turnout, 52 per cent voted against.

Nine years later, when Fianna Fáil for the second time attempted to get approval for the "straight vote" system, they were once again beaten, this time decisively. With a 66 per cent turnout, 61 per cent voted against. On this occasion, too, Fianna Fáil leaders used the same arguments. The *Irish Times* reported that Mr. C. J. Haughey, then Minister for Finance, warned his audience in Sligo that

proportional representation was a divisive force. Unlike the straight vote which compelled electors to make a direct choice between candidates and policies, proportional representation relieved the voters of the task of political decision. In our case because of special circumstances it had not yet—and he emphasised the word yet—brought the multitude of small parties and the instability of government that had followed in its wake as inevitably as night follows day in every other country where it existed. . . . He hoped that they would bear in mind also that in modern times democracy had never died in a country which had the straight vote, but the instances were many where it died under proportional representation and gave way to totalitarianism of one kind or another.[31]

Reviewing these two referenda, two points might reasonably be made. First, one cannot help but notice, and perhaps deplore, the continued currency of well-worn and inaccurate observations about the effects of proportional representation upon the operation of political systems, or at least their continued utterance by politicians who might even have believed them. Second, it looks as though there exists a considerable and settled public opinion in favour of the single transferable vote. This positive view is probably based upon experience with the system and the contrast offered by British experience with the "straight vote," which, because of press and broadcasting coverage, is the only other system known to most people in Ireland. Compared with the results produced by the "straight vote" in British circumstances, the outcome of elections under the single transferable vote system is perceived by most to be far more fair and not to have produced the dire consequences forecast by Fianna Fáil leaders. Perhaps as important for the chances of changing the system, whatever Fianna Fáil leaders might have said, has been the unwillingness of many party backbenchers to favour the change because it might upset their own local positions, which have been based upon the exploitation of the existing arrangements. It is unlikely that Irish politicians will put the matter to the test again for a while.

PART III

THE FORMATION OF
PUBLIC POLICY

NINE

The Policy Makers

General elections in Ireland produce governments and parliaments, the two institutions that are at the very centre of government, whether making or applying policy and laws. In Chapters 9, 10, and 11, we shall be concerned with policy making and legislation; in Chapters 12–16, we shall deal with the administration of policy.

Legal authority to make policy and law gives the government and the Oireachtas their central role. They are surrounded, however, by other persons and groups who also have a part to play in policy and law making because they too have power or influence of one sort or another. In *The Policy-Making Process,* Charles E. Lindblom explained policy making in terms of power: "Power is always held by a number of persons rather than by one; hence policy is made through the complex processes by which those persons exert power or influence over each other." He characterized these processes as a "play of power."[1]

To quote Lindblom again: "The play of power proceeds, for the most part, according to rule; it is gamelike."[2] However, all the rules of the game are stated neither in Bunreacht na hÉireann nor in law. To begin with, the Constitution gives an incomplete enunciation of the functions performed by governments and the Oireachtas, and it spells out a division of governmental powers that is incomplete and does not obtain in reality. Furthermore, it does not even mention, though by implication it allows for, the existence and activities of parties and pressure groups.

That is not to say that the Irish Constitution is a fraud or that it is flouted in the practice of politics. Rather, being a legal document, it expresses legal relationships and is written in conventional, even traditional, legal language. Conventionally, also, it embodies the *concepts* of Western, liberal constitutional theory largely in the form in which it developed in late-nineteenth-century Britain. The *practice* of cabinet government as it evolved in the United Kingdom up to the First World War was different in important respects, and it was this model that was adopted by Irish governments and is still in use.

The main features of this early-twentieth-century Westminster model, as it might appropriately be called, are as follows:

1. Governments usually emerge as a direct result of general elections. The electorate chooses leaders to govern them from rival groups of politicians, each consisting of a party leader and his or her most important colleagues. Almost all candidates are identified with one of these groups. The winners in this electoral contest acquire the right to assume government office and power. The leader, or, in the case of a coalition, the leaders of the constituent parties, form a cabinet—in Ireland called "the Government." The cabinet meets as a committee to decide the major issues of public policy and the measures they intend to present to the Oireachtas for approval, to coordinate the work of the departments they control, and generally to manage central government business.

2. The cabinet governs the country. It makes, or at least endorses, all the decisions that have to be made at the very highest political level. Its members in their various roles—as party and Oireachtas leaders and as ministers—are expected by their supporters and by the country generally to identify issues and problems of public importance, to propound effective solutions, to gain acceptance for their solutions in the Oireachtas and the country insofar as this may be necessary, and to put them into operation. In performing these functions, they have the aid and advice of senior civil servants, and they take account not only of parliamentary and party opinion but of the views of the spokesmen of relevant pressure groups (with whom they may deal directly) and of electoral opinion generally.

3. The Taoiseach is, as the Constitution puts it, the "head of the Government." He is preeminent among his colleagues. He is the leader of the party or coalition that has won the election and, as such, personifies the government. He chooses his colleagues and can dismiss them, though his freedom to choose and to dismiss in some circumstances (notably in a coalition situation) might be restricted. When he resigns, they go out of office too; and he it is who decides when to call a general election. The precise degree of his preeminence, however, might well vary from Taoiseach to Taoiseach. Personalities and political situations make for differences between one and another.

4. The government leads and is maintained by its supporters in the Dáil (they being a majority of that body) and in the Seanad. The Dáil majority is, normally, a stable one, held together by party loyalty. Al-

though the members of the majority group look to their leaders to take the initiative in formulating measures to be adopted, to manage the business of the houses of the Oireachtas, and generally to govern, they expect the leaders to consult with them and pay attention to their wishes and comments. Their views, however, are only some of the opinions that a government takes into account.

5. The government is opposed in the Oireachtas by one or more rival groups of leaders and their parliamentary supporters. These form "the Opposition," and "the leading idea upon which it is organised is that it offers itself before the country as an alternative government."[3]

6. The members of the government are politically responsible, both collectively and individually, to the Dáil. The principles of collective and individual responsibility are major features of the system but are not precise. In general, it might be said that, although each minister has special responsibility for a given area of state activity and conducts the affairs of his own department (speaking and answering for it in the government, in the Oireachtas, and in the community), the government as a whole is held liable for policy and in a general way for the manner in which public affairs are conducted. Constitutionally, the Dáil has the power to effect the removal of the Taoiseach and his government if a majority of TDs so desires. In practice, given the party composition of the Dáil and the stable support for leaders, neither individual ministers nor governments are likely to be dismissed by the actions of the Dáil. Nevertheless, expressions of dissatisfaction or signs of unrest in the majority group will have some effect, perhaps even leading to a dissolution.

7. The houses of the Oireachtas have two major functions. First, they discuss in public the proposals put before them by the government. Because the government commands the support of the majority in the Dáil and because the Seanad has only a subsidiary role in the parliamentary process, the government controls the timetable and the conduct of business and can expect to get almost all its proposals passed, though concessions to parliamentary opinion might be deemed expedient for reasons of party or election strategy. Second, the Oireachtas appraises and comments on the conduct of administration by the government and elicits information on matters big and small. In performing these functions, both sides, government and opposition, have an eye to the electorate. In this public forum they make bids for electoral support.

Within the context of this model, it is possible to characterize the policy-making process in a general way and to identify the roles of various participants. A system such as this tends to produce rather strong government and a pattern of relationships a long way removed from the traditional liberal model with its notion of a representative assembly reflecting the will of the people in legislation and policy declarations that are put into effect by "the executive" and the public service.

II

The term "public policy" had been defined by William Jenkins as "a set of interrelated decisions taken by a political actor or group of actors concerning the selection of goals and the means of achieving them within a specified situation where these decisions should, in principle, be within the power of these actors to achieve."[4] Making public policy includes deciding what matters are to be taken up and considered by authorities (in this case at national level); what is to be done about the problems, issues, or opportunities that are involved in these matters; what steps are to be taken to achieve the objectives that are decided upon; how motions or draft legislation to be put before the Oireachtas are to be formulated; and how motions and bills are to be processed through the Dáil and the Seanad. "Public policy" suggests broad rather than narrow, and general rather than detailed, decisions. It is nevertheless necessary to notice that governments and parliaments also make decisions that are very specific, simply because some issues are of great political importance. Such issues, like those of wider scope, are equally subject to the play of power.

It is important to realize that the processes we are about to analyze are not the only ones by which policy is made. General courses of action sometimes emerge from many individual and specific decisions that in their totality can be seen to fall into patterns, which might appropriately be called "policies." The courts, too, sometimes make decisions, the contents and consequences of which lead public authorities to modify state action; thus, courts make policy. For example, when the Irish courts in a series of judgements in the 1960s whittled away some of the privileges the state had enjoyed in its dealings with the citizen (privileges that had been inherited as part of the British constitutional legacy), they only did what the Oireachtas might have done and what the British parliament had actually done in the Crown Proceedings Act (1947). It is not appropriate, however, to deal with this particular form of policy making here, for it is carefully and deliberately insulated from politics and from the pressure of participants in the political process, which is to be analyzed here. (On judges as policy makers, see pp. 320–23.)

Finally, we must notice that the word "policy" is also used to describe the general decisions and conduct of subordinate public authorities. Law and parliamentary resolutions embody the policies made by governments and the Oireachtas, but other authorities have power delegated to them by the government and the Oireachtas to make rules that have the force of law. Some of these rules can appropriately be called "policies." It is quite legitimate to speak of the Electricity Supply Board's rural electrification policy or Comhairle na nOspidéal's policy on the staffing of hospital maternity units. However, the policy-making activities of these bodies and those like them are not included in this analysis, since these bodies are essentially subordinate authorities. They derive their functions and powers from government and parliament, and to some degree their policy making is constrained within the policies of the superior bodies.

III

In classifying the contributors to public policy making, Lindblom identified a core group of what he called "proximate policy makers." He defined them as "those who share immediate legal authority to decide on specific policies, together with other immediate participants in policy decisions."[5] He distinguished these from other participants who significantly influence them. In this analysis of public policy making, we shall adopt Lindblom's useful categories.

The *proximate policy makers* in Ireland are (1) the members of the government (cabinet) and ministers of state, (2) the members of the Dáil and Seanad, and (3) some senior civil servants, including temporary "advisers" and, possibly, a few other public servants. The main *influences* upon them are political parties, pressure groups, the public service (that is, the civil service, the local government service, and the executives of the state-sponsored bodies), the mass media, and public opinion (see Fig. 9.1). In addition, there is a growing external influence, the European Communities or, more precisely, the obligations imposed upon the Irish government by reason of Ireland's membership in the Communities. These influences interact upon one another. In particular, the mass media are important in informing, and perhaps influencing, those who in turn influence policy as well as those who make it.

Although ministers and the other members of the Oireachtas together with a few senior public servants can appropriately be designated proximate policy makers, their parts in the process of policy making differ one from another. As the group of leaders that won the general election, they assume the major role in governing the country. Having an overall responsibility for the welfare of the community, they are expected by their supporters, by the members of the Oireachtas, and by the community generally to take the initiative in identifying problems to be tackled and opportunities to be exploited and in preparing solutions and lines of

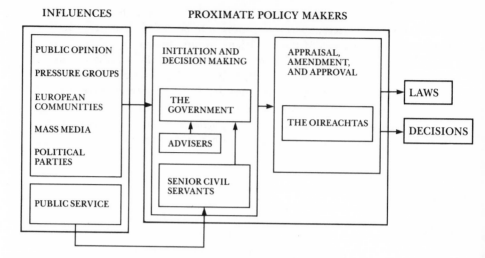

F ig. 9.1. Public Policy Making in Ireland

action. It is they who make, or at least approve of, the most important and most critical decisions in the making of policy; and it is they who decide what to adopt as government policy to be placed before the Oireachtas for approval. Moreover, they have a virtual monopoly of initiating legislation and other policy proposals in the Dáil and Seanad; except for a very occasional "private member's bill," it is their proposals that the Dáil and Seanad consider.

In carrying out their initiation and critical decision-making functions, ministers are powerfully aided by a small number of senior public servants. Almost all of these are in the top ranks of the civil service. They are the professional managers of the state's business and advisers to their ministers with whom they have contacts of a kind that might give them the opportunity to influence ministerial decisions. Besides the senior administrators, ministers might also consult professional officers in their departments—scientists, medical doctors, veterinarians, economists—but there are few of these. Even fewer from outside the ranks of the civil service are consulted to the extent that they could be called proximate policy makers. The views of a few public servants such as chairmen or chief executives of state-sponsored bodies might be sought from time to time on matters within their own areas.

Besides these career public servants, there are now a few "advisers." From the late 1960s, some ministers began to appoint one or two aides—either civil servants transferred from other duties and perhaps other departments or outsiders employed as temporary civil servants. The aides are people whose counsel ministers wish to have because they are politically in tune with them or knowledgeable or both. In the words of a former secretary of the Labour Party, Brendan Halligan, such aides "are nothing more than the political extension of the minister—they are the extension of his political personality. Their role ends when his political life ends."[6] At the end of 1979, there were only ten of them, and it could not by any means yet be said that the continental European system of the *cabinet du ministre* was a feature of Irish government. If the permanent civil servants have their way, it never will be, for on the whole they resent these outsiders. However, an increasing number of ministers are coming to recognize the need for the kind of advice and support that they cannot get from career civil servants.

It is difficult to describe in general terms the part that public servants play in policy making or to distinguish the respective contributions of ministers and public servants. In making such an attempt in the British context, Peter Self has drawn a distinction between what he called "climate setting" and the identification of major objectives, priorities, and sometimes perhaps the main objectives of a program on the one hand, and decisions on specific policies (such as what steps are to be taken to achieve major objectives) on the other. The first are without doubt jobs for politicians: "The most obvious and universal contribution of politicians to policy-making occurs through the formulation of general attitudes, opinions and ideologies. 'Climate setting' influences the way in which particular issues are approached and the kind of measures which are favourably regarded, but is too generalised an activity to produce specific policies."[7]

The accession to office of a new government is particularly an occasion for climate setting. At such a time civil servants wait for ministers to indicate what policies they will be pursuing and what their priorities will be. They have also to "size up" their new ministers and to assess their "form" and "style." Who can doubt that there was a distinct change in the climate in, for example, March 1932, when Fianna Fáil first took office; or in February 1948, when, after sixteen years of unbroken Fianna Fáil rule, the Inter-Party Government succeeded to office; or in March 1973, when the National Coalition took over after another sixteen years of Fianna Fáil government; or even in December 1979, when Charles Haughey succeeded Jack Lynch as leader of Fianna Fáil after a bitter struggle for the succession?[8]

Although climate setting and the identification of major objectives are clearly ministerial functions, in some circumstances civil servants might contribute very positively. The part played in the late 1950s by T. K. Whitaker, then Secretary of the Department of Finance, and his colleagues in launching the Irish government into the era of state planning has long been recognized. So, too, from time to time, there has been known to exist among officers of some departments fixed views about their departments' roles and general lines of policy. When this is the case, it might be hard for all but the most interested and determined minister to strike out along other lines. Again, incoming governments with election pledges to be redeemed have sometimes to be faced with harsh financial realities.

Setting the climate, identifying major objectives, and indicating priorities provide the framework within which policy is made. Measures still have to be formulated and choices made to produce an operational policy that a department or other public authority can implement. There are two distinct phases in producing such a policy. The first entails collecting and appraising data, analyzing problems, defining issues, and identifying and evaluating possible courses of action. Much of this is work for civil servants, who also do some of the negotiating with the spokesmen of the interests whose views have to be taken into account and with the other departments of state that must be consulted.

The second phase involves making policy decisions. The minister makes the critical rulings. It could not be otherwise, for the process is governed by the fact that under Bunreacht na hÉireann the minister is responsible. In making his decisions, he must satisfy his ministerial colleagues, the Oireachtas, and the public; it is his career that is at risk. For his part, the official "knows that the policies he proposes will have political consequences for Ministers. He accepts, therefore, that decisions on significant issues of policy should be taken by Ministers: they must in some sense be able to say that the policies they defend are 'their own.'"[9] The same applies also to matters below the level of policy that are nevertheless politically important because they are, or might be, contentious.

Ministers have the last and authoritative say, but how far are the decisions they make "their own"? Those who prepare the memoranda, put up the papers, and explain the issues to the minister might in some circumstances have an important, even decisive, influence upon the outcome. In some cases, a minister reading a file will see only one possible course of action, but this might be due to the way in which the matter is presented. In other cases, ministers, by temperament or habit, might be disposed to accept what is put before them. Nevertheless, interventions by the ministers are decisive, as Ronan Fanning was able to show again and again in his study of Irish administrative history, *The Irish Department of Finance, 1922–58.* In this book he demonstrates clearly that the ability of the Department of Finance to get its way and do its job as it conceived it, waxed and waned as a result of political changes.

The constitutional authority to legislate, which is to invest proposals with the force of law, resides with the houses of the Oireachtas. The Oireachtas is, therefore, by definition a proximate policy maker. However, the part it plays as an institution in formulating or influencing the content of the measures it considers and passes is meagre. A Fine Gael policy document on the reform of the Dáil published early in 1980 put it thus: "Under the Constitution the Oireachtas has the 'sole and exclusive power of making laws for the state.' Nonetheless in practice it plays practically no effective part in either making the laws or even the expert criticism of them."[10] The contrast between the Oireachtas and the parliaments of some other democracies is striking. Members of the United States Congress, for example, initiate bills; and Congress, through its powerful committees, really makes law. Bills, whatever their source, are not only subject to scrutiny and criticism but are freely altered and added to in committee by members who regard themselves literally as legislators with an actual power to make the laws.

In Ireland, by contrast, to quote the Fine Gael document again, "one of the most disciplined party systems in Europe has ensured that it is the Government, not the Oireachtas, that exercises the power."[11] The government has an almost exclusive initiative in proposing measures. With the assured, stable support of the party majority in the Dáil, and almost always in the Seanad too, the government controls the passage of business through the two houses. Its proposals are usually endorsed by the Oireachtas with few changes. As a result of criticism in debate or criticism expressed privately by government supporters after a bill is published, some revisions in wording might be made, but these rarely involve matters of principle or major policy changes. Very occasionally, a government misjudges the temper of its own parliamentary supporters and has to withdraw or extensively revise a bill. Examples in the 1960s were the Succession Bill (which dealt with the bequeathing of property) and the Criminal Justice Bill. In the 1970s, budget proposals of both Fianna Fáil and the National Coalition affecting the taxation of farmers were notable casualties, and in May 1980, the Fianna Fáil government changed its decision about the school transport system as a result of parliamentary party pressure.

The Irish system, therefore, like the British is, in K. C. Wheare's words, "a system where you can say that the Government makes the laws with the advice and consent of the representative assembly."[12] Nevertheless, the role of the Oireachtas must not be underestimated. In addition to the fact that it is the forum for *public* debate, its advice is authoritative and its consent essential. To get that consent, governments are obliged to pay attention to the opinions of the members, particularly their own supporters, when they formulate policy. The process of doing so takes place at the preparliamentary stage and largely in private.

This examination of the proximate policy makers has shown, first, that the three groups involved play different parts in the process. The necessary coordination of their activities is effected by the government, which manages the other two groups. The rules and conditions that govern its relationships with the one are of course very different from those governing the other. Civil servants are servants of the government of the day. The Dáil and Seanad are managed by the government while it retains the support of a majority, which means in effect that it must satisfy its own parliamentary supporters, who *are* the majority. The complex nature of the relationships between governments and their parliamentary supporters result in governments' enjoying stable and assured support (these relationships will be discussed in the next chapter).

This examination has also shown that the proximate policy makers are by no means all elected politicians. On the contrary, policy is formulated and made by the interaction of a few top-level politicians and a few top-level public servants. In *Administrative Theories and Politics,* Peter Self wrote of a "political-administrative arch." He described it in this way:

The junction at the top represents the critical point at which political will flows into and energises the administrative system: and it is also the point at which influences that have been generated *within* the administrative process flow back into the higher levels of the political process. There is thus, at the apex of the arch, a fusion of political and administrative influences which have been generated lower down the two arcs.[13]

Fig. 9.2 perhaps illustrates Self's concept in respect of policy making.

A third—and striking—feature about the proximate policy makers is how few they are, a fact already revealed in a general way in the profile of political participation in Chapter 5. At the apex of national government, the number of people with immediate legal or actual power or both is tiny, as the following tabulation shows:

Members of the government, ministers of state, and the Attorney General	31
Civil servants including "advisers" and other public servants	100–150
Members of the houses of the Oireachtas other than members of the government and ministers of state (omitting the Ceann Comhairle)	226
TOTAL	357–407

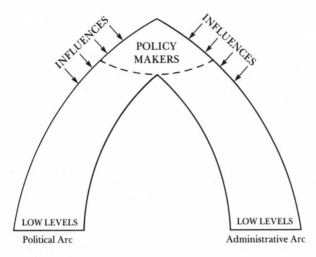

FIG. 9.2. The Political-Administrative Arch

These few do not operate in isolation, however. They are surrounded by other persons and bodies seeking to influence their decisions and the process of interaction between them and, thus, to make an impact upon the content of policy.

V

The proximate policy makers are subject to a number of constraints arising from both the cultural and the political contexts within which they work. First, public policy makers accept in a general way the political traditions of the country, which include quite well defined concepts of the roles and responsibilities of ministers, the Oireachtas, and the public service. Public policy makers respect the rules of the game. The behaviour of politicians and administrators alike is governed by their perceptions of how people like themselves ought to behave in a "civic culture"—more particularly, in a British-style liberal-democratic system.

Proximate policy makers are also constrained by the limitations both of their decision-making procedures and of the human resources available to them. To a considerable extent, politicians take these limitations for granted. They pay little attention to improving the decision-making processes or to ensuring that they have access to the kinds of professional expertise that almost certainly would improve their performance of their jobs. Without political backing for such reforms, public servants cannot get very far, even if they wholeheartedly desire to, which most do not.

Yet there can be little doubt that there is considerable scope for legislative and administrative reform.

The constraints that the proximate policy makers themselves are likely to be most conscious of are external, arising from the demands and pressures of persons and groups in the community who seek to influence the making and content of policy and, in recent years, from the obligations of membership in the European Communities. Some of these—political parties, pressure groups, and the European Communities—are very positive influences; another—public opinion—is more negative; yet another—the media—is more problematical as an influence.

As our analysis both in Part 2 of this book and in this chapter has shown, a continuous concern with policy is limited to a few in the political parties—namely, the party leaders and to a lesser extent the rank-and-file members of the parliamentary parties. However, others in the parties—some of the activists in the branches and at the annual conventions—press their leaders to adopt new policies or modify existing ones. They also act as channels of information and opinion between leaders and the "grassroots" of the parties and as sounding boxes of public opinion.

Pressure-group spokesmen, too, deal directly with proximate policy makers, particularly with ministers and senior civil servants, if they can gain access to them. If they cannot, they will try to make their voices heard from outside. Their activities were the subject of Chapter 7, where it became evident that the part played by some pressure-group spokesmen, particularly those of the major producer organizations, is such that one might almost—but, it was argued, not quite—regard them as proximate policy makers.

The 100 or 150 or so public servants, almost all senior civil servants, who have been identified as among the proximate policy makers might not be as sensitive to party and public opinion as their politician masters, but they are certainly aware of it. They will also know very well the views of at least the major pressure groups with whom they deal. Almost inevitably they will be greatly (perhaps overwhelmingly) influenced by the traditions and attitudes of their own small and intimate professional world, especially the departments they work in and perhaps have always worked in. They will also know the views of the state-sponsored bodies for which their ministers are responsible. It is they who use the resources of the departments to gather, process, and present the material that they think is relevant to the problem under review. In the course of this information gathering and appraisal, the civil servants involved will, as they must, frame generalizations and draw conclusions, many of which their senior colleagues and politician masters are not likely to question. Critical centres of what March and Simon called "uncertainty absorption" are inevitably deep inside departments, and some are way down in the departmental hierarchy. They are almost certainly coloured by service and department perceptions and attitudes.[14] The civil-servant advisers of ministers are at the confluence of a great flow of information and conclusions from which they distill the essence for transmission to their masters. All of it is expert, but some of it may well be service—and department—flavoured. In any case, most of it will have to be accepted.

Although party activists and interest-group spokesmen represent important bodies of *minority* opinion, political leaders are well aware that they do not necessarily reflect "public opinion"—that is to say popular opinions widely held. By using the press, radio, and television, political leaders are easily able to communicate with the general public directly, and to some extent these media aid the reverse flow of information and demands. In addition, political leaders increasingly resort to the use of surveys to measure public reactions to persons, situations, and policies as an aid to political decision making. Nevertheless, the flow of information from the public to political leaders is as yet imperfect.

In general, public opinion is a negative influence. To pay attention to it is "a way of estimating what the public will stand for rather than an expression of what the public wants."[15] Governments often see public opinion as placing limits upon what they can do and how they can do it. Between general elections they pay some attention to it, though the clamour from minority interests, including their own party activists, to some extent blots it out. The nearer to a general election, however, the more leaders seek to gauge public opinion.

All involved, whether proximate policy makers or those who influence them, are consumers of the products of the mass media. For all in the community, including the comparatively few who participate in policy making, the media are important sources of information; for some, almost their only sources. For some, too, the media might well be important sources of opinion, not least for the proximate policy makers and those who influence them directly, for many of these communicate with one another not only in person but by means of the media. These form a small elite where information and ideas are concerned, and horizontal political communication at this high level might constitute more of a closed system than the parties concerned realize. However, the exact effect of consuming the products of the media, particularly upon the formation and changing of opinions and attitudes, is problematical.

Besides the domestic influences upon the proximate policy makers, there is an external influence of increasing importance—the law and policies of the European Communities. Of course, this is not the only external influence upon Irish policy makers. They have always had to bear in mind the state's treaty obligations, the policies of neighbouring states, and all sorts of pressures and opportunities whose origins lie outside the state. The influence exerted by the European Communities, however, is of a different kind (see pp. 54–56). The legal instruments of the Communities in one way or another have a binding effect upon either governments or citizens of member states.

Community *regulations* and *decisions* are directly applicable in the member countries and become in effect part of the law of the member states. The Irish government and parliament have no part at all to play in the creation of the rights conferred or duties imposed by them. Community *directives,* on the other hand, which are the normal instruments used by the Communities to harmonize the laws of the members, do not themselves become part of national law. They do, however, place upon states an obligation "to bring about a specified result, but the choice of form and methods of carrying out directives is left to the national authorities."[16] Thus they oblige national policy makers to formulate policies and legislation and can appropriately be regarded as influences, albeit influences that cannot be ignored, for the elbowroom for negotiation with the European Commission over what exactly would satisfy Community requirements is small.

The influence of the law of the European Communities upon the Irish government is very great in policy areas covered by the Treaties, in particular in agricultural, fiscal, industrial, and commercial policy and, increasingly, in social policy. For example, many of the dramatic improvements in workers' rights that were introduced by statute in Ireland in the middle and late 1970s were in effect imposed upon the government by the obligation to implement Community directives. The Anti-Discrimination (Pay) Act (1974) was made necessary by a directive providing for the approximation of legislation of member states concerning the application of the principle of equal pay for men and women. The Protection of Employment Act (1977) was made necessary by a directive of 1975 concerning collective dismissals; the Employment Equality Act (1977), by a directive to ensure equality of treatment between men and women as regards access to employment, promotion, training, and conditions.

VI

Public policy making in Ireland emerges as a complex process, but it involves comparatively few people who operate against a background of comment, criticism, and advice in the media, and within the parameters of public opinion. Although the most authoritative decision makers—the government and the Oireachtas—are elected officials and the process involves consultation and negotiation with spokesmen who are in some sense representative of the groups for whom they speak, the process is far from being very open or democratic. On the contrary, the critical phases are conducted largely in private. What goes on between ministers and their civil service advisers is confidential, no doubt of necessity; so, too, is much of what passes between pressure-group spokesmen and the civil servants and ministers to whom they make representations; so, too, are the meetings of the Oireachtas parties and other contacts between party leaders and their parliamentary followers. The *public* procedures—that is, the parliamentary stages—usually begin only *after* the government has evolved a policy that it hopes is a finished product. For all the virtues of the parliamentary process in ensuring a public statement and restatement of the pros and cons of proposed measures, "what the procedure does not permit," as J. P. Mackintosh pointed out, "is an exploration of alternative approaches, an understanding of the views of outside groups (unless they think it work briefing MPs) and there is no scope for public opinion to form and react before the government has committed itself to a definite approach to the problem."[17] Mackintosh was here talking of Westminster, but what he said is true also of Leinster House. In this respect, public policy making is not even as open a process as it is in some other democratic countries whose parliaments have a more positive role.

TEN

The Government and the Dáil

The analysis of public policy making in Chapter 9 demonstrated the dominant role of the government and the modest part played by the Oireachtas. Even so, confined as it was to policy making, that analysis did not reveal the full extent of the part ministers play in politics. They have a number of positions. In their corporate capacity as a cabinet, as heads of departments of state, and as party leaders both within the Oireachtas and outside, they dominate a large part of the whole process of government. They do so while they have the support of a majority in Dáil Éireann. Such support is the necessary and sufficient condition for them to carry out their extensive functions, subject to the statutory maximum term of the Dáil, which is five years.

In Irish conditions, this all-important support is accorded to ministers regularly and continuously, for the parliamentary parties are unified and their members vote consistently as they are bidden by their leaders. The members of the government who are the leaders of the majority party or group of parties thus have an almost assured majority on any issue. Sometimes in the past a government assumed office without an actual majority behind it, its support boosted by the votes of Deputies who, though they called themselves "independents," were rather camp followers (see Table 8.3, p. 148). Although the Seanad has a part to play in the performance of parliamentary functions, the support of a majority of that house is usually not vital to governments, for they can override Seanad decisions with their Dáil majority; and, in any case, they usually command majority support in the Seanad too, and for the same reasons.

To understand cabinet government in Ireland necessitates investigating the nature and terms of this consistent parliamentary support. It involves examining not only the formal rules governing the appointment, functions, and tenure of office of the government but, more important, who and what the ministers are, the pathways to ministerial office, the ministers' pluralist role in the political system, and their relations with their parties and, in particular, with their parliamentary supporters. These relationships account for what Walter Bagehot in 1867 termed the "singular approximation" of cabinet and parliament, which he rightly identified as the "efficient secret" of British-style cabinet government.[1]

II

Rules governing the government are to be found in the constitutions of all countries. In countries with a constitutionalist tradition, these basic rules provide a framework within which the organs of government do in practice function. This is the case in Ireland, although the provisions of Bunreacht na hÉireann relating to the government reflect reality inadequately. Nevertheless, these provisions, together with a number of constitutional conventions and practices, define the tenure of office and operations of the government and provide a framework within which the politicians operate.

Article 13 provides that the President of Ireland, the formal head of the state, shall appoint the Taoiseach on the nomination of the Dáil and that he shall appoint the other members of the government "on the nomination of the Taoiseach with the previous approval" of the Dáil. Up to the legal limit of the life of the Oireachtas, the Taoiseach holds office either until he chooses to resign, in which case the other members of the government are deemed also to have resigned, or until he "has ceased to retain the support of a majority in Dáil Éireann." In this case, he must resign unless on his advice the President chooses to dissolve the Dáil and thus precipitate a general election. Also, except in the case of loss of majority support, the Taoiseach may secure a dissolution of the Dáil—and thus a general election—on request to the President, a request with which the President must comply.

The Dáil's constitutional job of appointing the Taoiseach and the government has in practice usually been purely formal, the preceding general election having settled the issue. Once, however, in 1948, a parliamentary coalition of all parties other than Fianna Fáil, with the support of a number of independents, was formed by the leaders of the newly elected representatives after the results were known and before the Dáil met. Thus the role of the Dáil is not inevitably a formal one.

The nomination of the members of the government is made by the Taoiseach. The new Dáil, having nominated the leader of the majority party or group to be Taoiseach after a short and usually ritualistic debate, adjourns for a few hours while the leader calls upon the President and is formally appointed to that office. He then returns to the Dáil and puts forward the names of the members of his government. These are approved *en bloc* by the Dáil, though in the early days of the state there was some attempt to have them discussed and approved individually. They are then appointed by the President and assigned their departments by the Taoiseach. Appointment to the government and appointment as head of a department are quite distinct. The Taoiseach has the right to assign departments to the members of his government. He informs the Dáil, but the Dáil is not required specifically to approve the assignment.

If, as has been the case for all but ten years, the government consists of members of a single party, the incoming Taoiseach as party leader will probably have had considerable freedom of choice, though powerful colleagues and the expectations of the party have no doubt imposed constraints on some prime ministers. W. T. Cosgrave in the early days of the state led a loose party and was surrounded by strong personalities; consequently, he might have had less freedom to dispose than De Valera, who from the earliest days of Fianna Fáil dominated his colleagues. Likewise, De Valera's successors in Fianna Fáil seem to have had considerable elbowroom in forming governments. It has been the greater because there are no ethnic, religious, or other divisions in the country to be taken account of, although the Minister for the Gaeltacht (the Irish-speaking areas) needs to have fluent Irish, which many TDs do not have. Nor, until the 1970s at least, was Fianna Fáil divided into factions requiring accommodation when nominations to office were being made. Some attention seems to have been paid to the need to have a balance between the number of Dublin-based and rural appointees, but the availability of posts as ministers of state—that is, as junior ministers—helps considerably to overcome this problem.

The situation of leaders of coalition governments was different. The first coalition, in 1948, was composed of five parties and a group of independents. The leader under whom they agreed to serve, John A. Costello, was not at the time the leader of his party, who was unacceptable. Costello had no say in the initial choice of his ministers, except perhaps in the case of some of his Fine Gael colleagues. The number of posts for each party was arranged by agreement, as was the allocation of certain posts to certain parties. In the case of the Labour Party, the parliamentary party filled the allocated posts from among themselves by ballot.

In 1954, the procedure was similar: each party filled the posts allocated to it, the Labour Party again by ballot. In 1973, an agreement was made between the two party leaders, Liam Cosgrave of Fine Gael and Brendan Corish of Labour, on the number of places to be filled by each party and which ministerial and junior ministerial posts each had at his disposal. Each leader made his own nominations, the Labour Party forsaking election on this occasion. It was understood that in the case of resignation, dismissal, or other change, the party holding the post or posts involved would be able to fill the vacancy, and this did in fact occur in 1976.

Article 28 of Bunreacht na hÉireann requires that the government shall consist of no fewer than seven and no more than fifteen members. The Taoiseach, the Tánaiste (Deputy Prime Minister), and the Minister for Finance must be members of the Dáil. The other members must be members of the Dáil or the Seanad, but not more than two may be members of the Seanad. (In practice, in the history of the state up to 1980 there were only two senator ministers.)[2] Every member of the government has the right to attend and speak in each house of the Oireachtas. Although there is a legal distinction between being a member of the government and head of a department, the positions are in fact virtually identical. There is, it is true, provision in the Ministers and Secretaries (Amendment) Act (1939) for the appointment of members of the government without departmental responsibilities: such a person "shall be known as a Minister without Portfolio." The government, however, may "assign to any particular minister without portfolio a specific style or title." One such equivocal "minister without portfolio" was appointed— a Minister for the Coordination of Defensive Measures, who held office from 1939 to 1945.

Until recently, the general practice was for each minister to head a single department, although occasionally as a matter of convenience a minister was put in charge of more than one. However, as the number of departments increased after the Second World War—in 1924, there were eleven; by 1950, there were fifteen; by 1977, there were eighteen— it became necessary for all governments to have some ministers managing more than one. The Department of Health and the Department of Social Welfare have usually been regarded as natural twins; so, too, from 1973 to 1980 were the Department of Finance and the Department of Public Service, which had previously been one.

Since all ministers are members of the government and the government is composed exclusively of ministers, the structure is simple. In fact, in the past there was only a handful of other politician office holders of any sort in the administration. By 1980, however, the number of under-ministers, called parliamentary secretaries until 1977, when they were renamed ministers of state, had grown from ten to fifteen. The increase was said to be in order to cope with the larger number of departments and to relieve the strain on ministers occasioned by the need to travel on European Community business. No doubt also there were party political reasons. The change marked a significant addition to the patronage of the Taoiseach, which is now considerable, for the proportion of officeholders in the parliamentary party in power is around 40 per cent.

In addition, there is a law officer, the Attorney General, with a small department. The Attorney General is the government's adviser in matters of law and represents the state in important legal proceedings. According to Bunreacht na hÉireann, he is precluded from being a member of the government, but he does attend cabinet meetings. He is not required to be a member of the Oireachtas, though Declan Costello, who held the office between 1973 and 1977, was a deputy. If the Attorney General is a TD or a senator, he may be heard in either house. He may engage in private practice in addition to his state duties, and some have done so.

III

A state that emerges as a result of a war of independence is usually governed in its first years by the surviving leaders of that struggle, people who have come to the top by routes that are not necessarily the ordinary paths to democratic office. An examination of the personnel of Irish governments shows that the independence struggle and the subsequent civil war cast long shadows.

The first government of the independent state, the Provisional Government, was composed entirely of leading figures, military and civilian, of the independence movement. Six out of seven of them had held ministerial office in Dáil governments between 1919 and 1922. That the Provisional Government did not include all the leaders was due, of course, to the split over the Treaty. In 1932, when Fianna Fáil took office, most of its ministers were leading veterans of the same struggle. Because many of the leaders were young at the time of independence, because Ireland was a conservative society with a respect for seniority, and because one party had ten consecutive years of office and its successor sixteen, the original groups on both sides remained exceptionally stable. Hence, the pattern was one of low turnover of ministers, long service, and ageing cabinets. In the case of Fianna Fáil, even after breaks from holding office (between 1948 and 1951 and 1954 and 1957), the same people and the same pattern recurred. De Valera felt great loyalty to his old comrades; many of his ministers continued in office until eventually old age overtook them. During the twenty-seven years that Fianna Fáil was in office between 1932 and 1965, only thirty people manned an administration that grew in size from ten departments to fifteen. De Valera's last government in 1957 contained four of the nine whom he had first chosen to work with him a quarter of a century before. Even after De Valera retired, those four remained in office, three until 1965 and the last of them, Frank Aiken, until 1969.

Cumann na nGaedheal exhibited the same conservative tendencies. Only seventeen persons in all manned the government in the first ten years of the state's existence. Although the Inter-Party Governments (1948–51 and 1954–57) saw more changes than had occurred in the Fianna Fáil era, the main features up to the late 1950s continued to be a small turnover, ministers with long service, and ageing cabinets. The average age of members of the January 1922 government was 33 years: members of Cosgrave's 1927 government averaged 41 years of age, and so did De Valera's government of 1932. De Valera's 1951 government, however, had an average age of 57 years.

It is clear that governments for many years were recruited on the basis of service in the independence movement and for a long time remained dominated by those so chosen. Veterans and heroes of an independence struggle evoke a very special kind of veneration and loyalty and themselves symbolize and perpetuate old causes and aspirations. This type of constancy and fidelity became marked features of Irish political life. To this day the very mention of one of the hallowed names at a party Árd Fhéis, no matter what the context, is a signal for a round of applause. The conservatism and at times near stagnation of Irish politics and society from the 1920s until the early 1960s is to an extent attributable to the long reign of the venerated "revolutionary generation," as A. S. Cohan called them.[3]

By the late 1950s, however, a process of regeneration had begun; quite quickly, a veritable generational change took place. The average age of cabinets dropped to below 50 by 1965. Members of Charles Haughey's 1979 government averaged a little over 47 years of age. The change was generational in another way also. Even thirty years after independence, Irish governments (and party leaderships generally) were composed to a large extent of people with a record of service in the independence movement, the "revolutionary generation," with a well-marked career pattern. Cohan, writing in 1973, distinguished that generation from a "post-revolutionary group":

A primary characteristic of the members of the revolutionary elite was their youthfulness at the time they came together at the onset of the revolution. . . With regard to organisational affiliation, members of the revolutionary elite displayed a different background from that of the post-revolutionary group. Among members of the revolutionary elite, the most significant organisation was the Gaelic League. . . . a significant feature of the revolutionary elite is the lack of local orientation among its members when compared to the post-revolutionary group.[4]

The "post-revolutionary group" first began to appear on the scene at the end of De Valera's period of office. Seán Lemass, De Valera's successor, tended to replace the fading older generation with comparatively young professional men picked for their potential ability, and all leaders since then have tried to raise the quality of their teams by quickly advancing people of this sort to office. Six of the fifteen members of the 1973 National Coalition had first entered the Dáil in 1969 or after, and three of Charles Haughey's 1979 government had entered the Dáil after 1975. Thus, once the original criteria for office were no longer applicable, able professional men had a good chance of quick preferment because of the paucity of ministerial talent and leadership ability in the ranks of the parliamentary parties. Nevertheless, able newcomers had to be mixed in with men of seniority and long service in order to satisfy the expectations of the party faithful. It is significant also that in the 1973 National Coalition, which included half-a-dozen comparative newcomers, there occurred names like Cosgrave, Corish, and Fitzgerald, all sons of former deputies, one of them a former Taoiseach, another a former Minister for Foreign Affairs. Likewise, Haughey's team in 1979 included three sons, one daughter (the first woman minister in the state's history),[5] and a nephew of former deputies. For all the change from the conservatism of earlier days, political leadership in Ireland remains to some extent in the hands of the sons and other near relatives of former politicians.

Although there is continuing evidence of unbroken traditions and conservatism, the post-revolutionary group differed markedly from their predecessors as Cohan pointed out. This group also "demonstrated a decidedly pragmatic and economics-oriented style."[6] The advent of a new breed of leaders occasioned strain in all the parties. The dissension in Fianna Fáil that led Jack Lynch to sack two ministers and accept the resignation of two others in May 1970 was the direct outcome of a clash between those who clung to old values and continued to pursue old objectives and those who espoused new ones. The same division manifested itself again a decade later on Lynch's retirement, when Haughey, one of

TABLE 10.1

*Occupations of the Ministers Who Held Office
Between January 1922 and December 1979*

Occupational group	Percentage (N = 97)
Farming and fishing	7.2%
Professional	59.8
Trade union officials	5.2
Industry and commerce[a]	21.6
Nonmanual	3.1
Skilled manual	3.1
Semiskilled and unskilled manual	—

SOURCE: Flynn's *Oireachtas Companions;* T. Nealon, *Ireland: A Parliamentary Directory, 1973–74* (Dublin, 1974); T. Nealon, *Guide to the 21st Dail and Seanad* (Blackrock, 1977); newspapers and other published sources and private enquiries.

NOTE: Ministers are classified according to the occupation they followed or for which they were trained before they became full-time politicians.

[a] Mostly self-employed and in family businesses, especially retail trade (shopkeepers and publicans), contractors, and auctioneers.

the dismissed ministers of 1970, won power after an internecine struggle in the party.

The first leaders of the state were "politicians by accident," active nationalists who survived the independence struggle and the subsequent civil war. They included a number of journalists, teachers, and lawyers; from the beginning, Irish governments were dominated by professional men. As Table 10.1 shows, six out of ten of all ministers from January 1922 to December 1979 were professional men or had been trained for a profession before they became full-time politicians. Further, as Table 10.2 seems to suggest, most governments in the past have contained a majority of such. As is the case in most Western countries, this tiny occupational group—perhaps less than 5 per cent of the working population—dominates the top levels of politics. Likewise as in the West, lawyers have always figured largely: about one-third of all ministers have been in the law. A recent phenomenon is the increase in the number of teachers, a category that includes all levels from primary to university professor. The other occupational group consistently to have featured largely comprises men in business and commerce: not industrialists, big corporation men, or business executives, by any means, but overwhelmingly owners of small family businesses—shopkeepers, publicans, auctioneers, contractors, often men with a number of local business interests. Almost one-fifth of all ministers have belonged to this category, which constitutes no more than 3 per cent of the working population.

TABLE 10.2

Professional People in Government, 1922–79

Profession	Aug. 1922	March 1932	Feb. 1948	March 1957	April 1965	July 1977	Dec. 1979	Ministers, 1922–79
	Certain governments, 1922–79							
Accountant	—	—	—	—	1	1	1	1
Barrister	1	1	3	1	2	3	2	14
Solicitor	1	1	—	—	2	2	2	13
Engineer	—	1	—	2	2	—	—	3
Journalist	2	1	—	—	—	—	—	3
Medical doctor	—	1	2	1	1	—	—	4
Teacher	2	2	—	1	—	5	5	18
Other professions	—	—	—	—	—	—	1	2
TOTAL	6	7	5	5	8	11	11	58
Total membership of government	10	10	13	11	14	15	15	97

SOURCE: As for Table 10.1.

NOTE: Ministers are classified according to the profession they followed or for which they were trained before they became full-time politicians.

Just as some occupations have always been strongly represented in government, others have not and yet others have been strikingly absent. Although Ireland has a large agricultural sector and up to twenty years ago a quarter of all TDs were farmers, the proportion of farmers who have attained cabinet rank has been tiny. Almost no working-class people, whether urban or rural, have reached the top in politics. Evidently they have lacked the resources that create the potential for office—time, money, "centrality" (occupations such as shopkeeper and auctioneer are very "central"), social prestige, useful relations, a record.

In more than half a century, this occupational profile has changed little. Although, as Cohan suggested, there was a marked generational change in the holders of ministerial office, the important differences were in respect of nationalist background and active service in war and revolution. If there has been a contrast between the two "generations" in their approach to political issues and in their policies, as the tensions in the parties in the late 1960s and 1970s seem to suggest, it might well have been due to the difference in nationalistic background and experiences resulting in different sets of values.

IV

The domination of the political scene by ministers arises as much or more from the roles they fill in office as from who they are or what they have done in the past. Whatever they were before, on being appointed members of the government, they become leading figures in their party, more particularly in the Oireachtas party and, therefore, in the Oireachtas itself, and heads of departments of state—all positions of considerable power and influence. In their persons they combine leadership of the majority party, management of the Oireachtas, and the control of the central administration. It is this combination of positions that gives members of the government their preeminence, whatever their antecedents, and this applies even to those few who become members of the government on their first day in the Dáil.[7] Such preeminence in turn gives them social prestige, for they are at the very centre of affairs, "in the know," and better able than most to do a favour.

Their position is the stronger since they, together with their rivals—the leaders of the opposition parties, who are a potential alternative government—have a virtual monopoly of political leadership. There are few if any other party leaders outside the Oireachtas, though it is possible that one or two trade union leaders might sometimes exercise political power and the National Executive Committees of the parties might as bodies exert some influence. There is no one to challenge party leaders in the Oireachtas, for the only officials there besides themselves are the ministers of state, the whips (party managers), and the party leaders in the Seanad, none of whom have the status, power, or influence of ministers on the government side or party spokesmen ("shadow ministers") on the opposition side. The Oireachtas does not have a strong committee system that might spawn powerful chairmen and influential *rapporteurs* in positions to challenge ministers, nor do the parliamentary parties as such make much use of committees. Furthermore, the members as a whole lack any strong sense of the dignity of the Oireachtas as the national parliament; they have a modest view of its functions and powers. Finally, there are no rival leaders in the departments, for the members of the government are themselves heads of departments and, as such, are both constitutionally and politically responsible for the actions of civil servants and conventionally the sole source of decisions and information.

The picture that emerges—of ministers with a triple role that gives them a virtual monopoly of the centre of the political stage—is by no means reflected in Bunreacht na hÉireann. That document states that the *executive* power of the state is to be exercised by or on behalf of the government. It makes the government responsible for the work of the departments. It requires the government to prepare estimates of expenditure and present them to the Dáil, and it gives the government exclusive initiative to make proposals for public expenditure. This is clearly an inadequate statement of the essentials of cabinet government in the British style, the more so because it is couched in terms of the separation-of-powers theory. Also, necessarily perhaps, Bunreacht na hÉireann makes no mention of the party role of the members of the government, though their position in the party is bound up with their other roles. Nor, finally, does it convey the overall responsibility of this group for the general welfare of the community and, consequently, the initiative that the community expects them to take in identifying and solving public problems.

V

Members of the government depend for their continuance in office on maintaining an adequate level of satisfaction in their party and also, if they are to win the next election, in the community. They hold their positions on certain conditions. To understand the government of the country, it is necessary to ascertain what those conditions are.

There are, first, some constitutional requirements to be observed, but these do not take us very far. Once appointed, the government is "responsible to Dáil Éireann," and its leader, the Taoiseach, must retain the support of a majority in the Dáil. If he does not, he must resign unless the President grants him a dissolution and, thus, an appeal to the electorate. When the Taoiseach resigns, all the members of the government are deemed to have resigned also, as are the ministers of state and the Attorney General. By mentioning the Dáil specifically, the Constitution emphasizes the minor role and importance of the Seanad.

The government's responsibility to the Dáil is collective, for the government is required "to meet and act as a collective authority." Collective responsibility is, however, an elusive concept. It suggests that ministers are a team—but how united a team? It suggests that they must answer for their performance and might be removed from office—but in what circumstances will they be obliged to go?

In *The Government of Great Britain,* Graeme Moodie describes collective responsibility in terms that are probably generally acceptable as a statement of Irish constitutional theory:

All members of the administration are expected publicly to support its policies and its actions, regardless of their private feelings on the matter. Should they for any reason no longer be prepared to do so, they must resign their office (although not, usually, their seats in Parliament). Constitutionally, they cannot acquiesce in a decision and then, at some later stage when for example, it becomes unpopular, claim that they were opposed to it and thus seek personally to escape the political penalties. . . . By the same token, it is impossible for the House of Commons to vote for the removal of a particular member of the Government, unless it is clear that the Government is prepared to sacrifice that individual either as a scapegoat or because no collective responsibility is involved.[8]

The rules do not require each member of the government personally to favour a particular proposal. What they do require, as Moodie goes on to point out, is "that the argument be conducted in private" (hence the necessary corollary of cabinet secrecy, which is quite strictly observed in Ireland), resolved in private, and the decision treated as the decision of each and every member.

Constitutional theory, however, is one thing; practice might be, and occasionally has been, quite another. Irish practice up to 1980 can conveniently be examined in three phases—the Cumann na nGaedheal governments, the Fianna Fáil governments, and the coalitions.

The Cumann na nGaedheal governments from the beginning had reliable followers in the Dáil and were able to assume functions and powers comparable with those of British cabinets. They were, it is true, broadbased governments containing "men who ranged all the way from the extreme protectionist views of Mr. Walsh, the Minister for Posts and Telegraphs, to the free trade views of Mr. Hogan, the Minister for Agriculture."[9] But economic policy choices were not the major issues for the first governments, and the essential binding element in the party was the pro-Treaty stance of its members. The three resignations that occurred between 1922 and 1932 were all the result of disagreements over important items of policy (security and the border), and it is clear that the principles outlined by Moodie were accepted by both the government and its parliamentary supporters.

With the advent of Fianna Fáil to power, De Valera's dominating position and preference for firm cabinet government and definite leadership resulted in governments with more monolithic public faces. In his time, there were no resignations over policy and no overt disagreements. His successor, Seán Lemass, inherited a party long schooled in this tradition, and being so clearly an unrivalled master of the economic policy issues that had come to dominate politics, Lemass seemed also to dominate his government. The resignation in 1964 of Patrick Smith, Minister for Agriculture, a senior and respected member of the party, indicates that in the Lemass era, too, the principle that ministers must resign if they cannot publicly support government policy continued to be accepted.[10]

Both in the early years and at the end of Jack Lynch's periods of office (1966–73 and 1977–79), there were, however, signs of a loosening of the conventions to accommodate dissensions among the party leaders. In the late 1960s, there was rivalry within the government, partly per-

sonal and partly stemming from differences over Northern Ireland policy. The eruption of civil strife there led to basic aims of the party being
called into question and long-established party shibboleths challenged.
Cabinet dissensions led to some erosion of the principle of collective responsibility, which was finally breached by the "arms scandal" in which
it was alleged that some ministers, unbeknownst to their colleagues and
their leader, were acting contrary to government policy. It could be argued, however, that on this occasion the breach was repaired, if only
belatedly, when the Opposition raised the matter formally. The dismissals and resignations of May 1970 seemed to show that collective responsibility was still at least the norm.[11] Whether it would be adhered to
would depend on the Taoiseach's ability and willingness to insist on it.
In some circumstances, that norm would be breached; and, when it was,
the Fianna Fáil Oireachtas party would not demur if the future of the
government and their own seats were in jeopardy.

A decade later, the divisions over policy towards Northern Ireland,
never far below the surface during the intervening years and occasionally
moving above it, erupted again as Lynch came towards retirement. On
this occasion, they were compounded by the struggle for the succession.
During Lynch's last months in office, Haughey, who was one of those
dismissed in 1970 but who had worked his passage back to ministerial
office, signalled his dissent from some aspects of government policy.[12]
After he had won the contest for leader, he dissociated himself even more
clearly from some policies of Lynch's government and was at pains to
suggest that his takeover heralded more than just a change in leadership.
As *Magill* (a monthly journal of current affairs) put it, "He will be
perceived as having started with a clean slate." Neither he nor his colleagues, nor indeed the members of the Oireachtas party, gave any indication that they thought this behaviour deviated from what the Constitution envisages, if it does not require.

During the periods of coalition government, necessity sometimes demanded similar practices. The first Inter-Party Government (1948–51)
was a coalition not only of all the other parties but also of some independents, who, for the sake of convenience, were regarded as a coherent
group with the right to a ministerial post in the parcelling out of offices.
The basic coalition agreement was confined to specified points: "Any
points on which we have not agreed have been left in abeyance," John
Costello, its leader, told the Dáil.[13] It was very much a government of
parties, and although it and its successor (1954–57) were comparatively
effective, their members could not always avoid explicit disagreement in
public. Sometimes ministerial statements, both in the Dáil and outside,

revealed differences of view on policy matters. The government maintained in public, and some of its members perhaps even believed, that a minister could properly speak "as an individual" on current policy issues. Referring to differences between himself and the Minister for External Affairs, Deputy Patrick McGilligan, then Minister for Finance, said in the Dáil:

Deputies on the other side of the House have anguished themselves with talk about the public embarrassment which there is over the fact that the Minister for External Affairs does not talk the same financial language as myself. I have yet to meet anybody outside the ranks of the professional politicians who is worried about that. Nobody is worried. Have we got to the stage in this country when, on a matter which may be an important point of policy when it is decided, we cannot have freedom of speech? Have we got to the stage when men, just because they join the Government circle, must all, as one Deputy said, when they go out of the council chambers speak the same language?[14]

In the latter stages of the first Inter-Party Government, disagreement and poor communications between members led in some cases to a state of uncoordinated independence. In the Dáil itself, it was necessary on a few occasions to resort to a "free vote" when the Inter-Party group was divided, and even some members of the government itself voted against the government.

These modifications of the previous practice, however, did not alter the style of cabinet government in any fundamental or permanent way. The Inter-Party Governments' area of explicit agreement was small, but within it the members operated broadly in the customary manner. Their Dáil supporters generally spoke and voted as a stable coalition until the governments were brought down by extreme elements and the defection of independents.

The National Coalition Government (1973–77) was much less a government of parties than the Inter-Party Governments had been. Some members of each of the constituent parties were conservative, others more like the social democrats of contemporary Western Europe. During its term of office, basic conventions of cabinet government were called into question less often than they had been during the Inter-Party Governments or even Fianna Fáil governments in recent years. This period, however, did witness the spectacle of the Taoiseach himself, Liam Cosgrave (together with one of his Fine Gael ministerial colleagues), voting with the Opposition against the Control of Importation, Sale, and Manufacture of Contraceptives Bill—a government measure that the cabinet had agreed to introduce. Because of unease in the parliamentary parties, the government had agreed to a free vote in the Dáil, but Cosgrave voted against the government measure without even giving his cabinet any indication of his intention so to do.[15]

Experience shows that the constitutional principles as enunciated by Moodie are in fact regarded as norms; deviations from them are only of necessity and are regarded as such. Nevertheless, the flexibility that political leaders think they have under Bunreacht na hÉireann, or at least are prepared to take or tolerate in order to retain office, is considerable.

Collective responsibility requires the government to present a united front to the public and to be accountable to the Dáil, which might remove it *en bloc*. In fact, Irish governments are rarely defeated. Since 1922, this has happened on only six occasions, the last time being in 1949. Even among these six defeats, at least one was an accident, and in no case at all was it obvious that the Taoiseach had in any general way "ceased" to retain the support of a majority in Dáil Éireann. On no occasion has defeat led to a change of government (see Table 10.3). In only two cases was it followed by a dissolution, and in both of these the defeat was welcomed by the governments concerned as an opportunity to improve their position at the general election that followed. It is rather the threat of defeat that has more often led to a dissolution, but even this has occurred on only three occasions. It may be said, then, that the Dáil can and does force governments to submit to the electorate, though this is only likely to occur in periods of coalition government. The Dáil, however, does not dismiss governments.

This record is due to the all-important fact of parliamentary party solidarity, a phenomenon that is by no means universal in Western democracies. It is the more surprising when one considers that in the end a government depends on its parliamentary supporters and cannot rely upon sanctions to enforce obedience. This is clear when one asks how a government can be defeated between general elections. It can happen only if a critical number of its own supporters defect. In Ireland, because of the volume of electoral support for the various parties and the use of the single transferable vote system, that number is usually small. What

TABLE 10.3
Reasons for the Dissolution of Dáil Éireann, 1923–77

Reason	No. of occasions
Government approaching the end of its term of office	11
Tactical reasons:	
Government chooses to dissolve	2
Government welcomes defeat to get a new election	2
Danger of Dáil defeat	3

is more, it is quite possible for individual deputies to defy their party, break with it, or even be excluded from it, and still retain their seats. Yet this seldom occurs and the record suggests, as we have seen, that Irish governments are unlikely to suffer defeat. This is because for historical reasons—the experience of the home rule movement, the independence struggle, and the civil war and their aftermath—loyalty became and remained the great political virtue. A strong tradition of allegiance to leaders was established and persisted. Changing sides, like "going over" (that is, changing one's religion), was unthinkable in oneself and treacherous in others.

Loyalty inhibits deputies from endangering their leaders' and their party's position, but they need not accept all that their leaders propose or confine themselves to passive support, though in the past they did so to a considerable extent and most still do. There has always been a considerable willingness on the part of ordinary TDs to leave policy to party leaders and to expect them to get on with it. For many deputies, the formulation of policy and its articulation and, when their party is in power, the conduct of administration have been seen as the leaders' business. Deputies' business is to tend to the personal and local problems of their constituents and, by paying attention to their home base, nurture this all-important source of electoral support. However, TDs do expect that any misgivings they express—often at the local impact of general policy—will be heeded.

This traditional willingness to give the government considerable initiative and control over policy and administration is partly attributable also to the fact that Ireland adopted the British system at a period of parliamentary decline. By the early years of the twentieth century, the British parliament had signally failed to develop effective procedures to counter the emergence of strong rule by party leaders brought about by the advent of mass parties in the late nineteenth century. British efforts since then to build a parliamentary committee system, hesitant though they have been, have not been parallelled to any extent in Ireland. Only lately has a minority of on-the-whole younger deputies, often professional people, shown a more lively interest in policy issues and in monitoring the government's performance. In 1980, it was still the fact that Irish leaders had more elbowroom for manoeuvre in many policy matters than politicians in most democracies. Governments were more likely to be halted in their tracks by pressure-group activities than by parliamentary dissent.

Constitutionally, ministers are not only collectively responsible; they are also individually responsible for their own activities and those of the departments they control. Both in the Oireachtas and outside, the minister speaks for his department, explaining and defending government policy on matters within its purview, his own decisions, and those of his officials. Because he has the right to the last say, he is held to have had that say and all departmental decisions are regarded as his. However, although he will be held responsible in law for matters within his competence, on the political front it is he who in practice decides what he will and will not answer for. That this is the case arises from a considerable failure on the part of the Oireachtas to devise and operate efficient machinery for eliciting information, assessing it, and holding ministers accountable.

It is very unlikely that the Dáil will force a minister to resign. Up to 1980, there were only ten cases of resignation, and these and the two dismissals already referred to were mostly caused by disagreements over policy. Perhaps three or four were for health or technical reasons.[16] There have been no cases of ministers being forced to resign because of foolish or unacceptable decisions, incompetence, or personal misbehaviour.[17] Have there, then, been no such decisions, no incompetence, no misbehaviour in nearly sixty years? It would be remarkable if there had not.

The truth is that a minister can be forced to resign by the Dáil only if the government or the Taoiseach with government support decides to abandon him. This is a question of their deciding which course of action would harm the government more—a forced resignation with its attendant publicity or casting the mantle of collective responsibility over a colleague in trouble and making the matter one of confidence in the government as a whole and brazening it out. It is the latter course of action that Taosigh and governments have always adopted. Thus, the enforcement of individual responsibility by the Dáil has been largely thwarted by the practice of collective responsibility. It cannot be said that a minister will be punished by loss of office for his shortcomings or those of his civil servants. In practice, in the past, the failures and the liabilities survived until the next general reshuffle; and such has been the pull of loyalty that some survived even beyond that.

VI

So far, we have talked of the government as a collective body. However, the head of the government has a special position. It is necessary, therefore, to give separate consideration to the functions and role of the Taoiseach; but, first, we must distinguish the head of the government from the head of state.

The President of Ireland is the formal head of state. He is both the symbol of the state and the centre of ceremonial. He performs many acts of government at the request of those who have the real power—namely, the Taoiseach and the government. The British constitutional myth that the government is the government of the head of state—His Majesty's or Her Majesty's Government—which had been embodied in the Irish Free State Constitution, was not perpetuated in the republican Bunreacht na hÉireann. On the contrary, the Taoiseach was specifically designated as "the head of the government." He is required only to keep the President "generally informed on matters of domestic and international policy." The President does not see cabinet papers. In the past, he was kept "generally informed" by means of a regular visit from the Taoiseach. By the mid-1970s, however, the visits were far from regular: Liam Cosgrave visited President Ó Dálaigh on only four occasions during his two years as President. In 1980, Charles Haughey refused to answer a parliamentary question asking for details of visits.[18]

The office of President as conceived by De Valera, however, was something more than a purely formal head of state. He is linked with the people by virtue of being directly elected; in the words of his creator, "he is there to guard the people's rights and mainly to guard the Constitution."[19] The President is endowed with certain real powers to this end. Bunreacht na hÉireann gives him power to act in four circumstances. In the exercise of the first three, he is obliged to consult, though not necessarily to follow the advice of, the Council of State, a body consisting of named officeholders (such as the Chief Justice and the chairmen of the Dáil and Seanad), former officeholders (such as President and Taoiseach), and not more than seven others appointed by the President himself. First, he may refer any bill to the Supreme Court to be tested for unconstitutionality (up to 1980, five bills had been so referred).[20] Second, if a majority of the Seanad and not less than one-third of the Dáil request him to decline to sign a bill on the ground that it "contains a proposal of such national importance that the will of the people thereon ought to be ascertained," the President may, if he so decides, accede to the request and precipitate a referendum on the measure. Third, he may at any time convene a meeting of either or both houses of the Oireachtas, a power obviously intended to be used in an emergency. The second and third provisions have never been used. Finally, the President has it "in his absolute discretion" to refuse a dissolution to a Taoiseach who has ceased to retain the support of a majority in the Dáil or who, having been defeated, chooses to interpret the defeat as loss of confidence. In fact, on the only two occasions (1938 and 1944) when this has occurred, a dissolution was granted; except in case of emergency, it is difficult to see a President doing anything else.

Without doubt the exercise of these powers might involve the President in political controversy, the more so since they are intended to be used precisely at moments of political disagreement or crisis by a President who will have been chosen at an election fought on party lines. It was largely the continuous existence of stable majorities in Dáil Éireann and the absence of crises that prevented the office from becoming a focus of controversy for nearly forty years. The first Presidents helped too: they were elderly, inert, and scrupulous in keeping themselves outside and above political argument. The reaction of most politicians, not least those in his own party, to the concept of a more active President put forward by Erskine Childers on taking office in 1973, was unfavourable. They were uneasy at Childers' suggestion that the President should publicly back good causes that were undeniably in the public interest and on which the parties were agreed.[21] Fortunately, perhaps, Childers did not go far in practising what he had advocated.

His successor, Cearbhall Ó Dálaigh, a former President of the Supreme Court and subsequently member of the European Court of Justice, was subjected to public criticism that led directly to a constitutional crisis and his resignation when he showed signs of active interest in another aspect of the office. In September 1976, Ó Dálaigh referred the Emergency Powers Bill (1976) to the Supreme Court to test its constitutionality. In doing so, he was clearly acting within his constitutional powers, but the National Coalition Government, or at least some members of it, were privately critical of his action. One member, Patrick Donegan, Minister for Defence, attacked him publicly and in a clearly improper manner.[22] The failure of the Taoiseach to disown Donegan unequivocally for his *bêtise* led to Ó Dálaigh's resignation.

The affair, farcical though the Donegan episode was in some respects, showed that it is not possible in Irish circumstances for the President, who is regarded primarily as an apolitical symbol of the state, exercising mostly formal powers and criticism, to act with unquestionable authority in the name of the people in an emergency or crisis. There are bound to be some who will question any discretionary action in that category and thus expose the President to criticism, very likely of a partisan nature. Rightly so, too: as John Kelly put it, the President "must be prepared for the wind of criticism to which everybody else in public life who makes a decision is also subject."[23] Perhaps, as has been suggested, "the Office of President as envisaged by Mr. de Valera and laid down by the Constitution is an inherently unsatisfactory one."[24]

VII

The model for the office of Taoiseach (the earlier title, used in the Irish Free State Constitution, was President of the Executive Council) was the British prime minister. However, to compare the Taoiseach with the prime minister is not to say very much. It does suggest that he is the central figure, to a great extent the centerpiece and symbol of the government in a way in which an Italian prime minister, for example, is not. His preeminence among his colleagues stems from four facts. First, he is usually the party leader. Second, elections have often taken the form of gladiatorial contests between two designated party leaders, thus emphasizing the personal leadership of the victor, and television and modern campaign practices have increased the propensity to focus on the leader. Third, except in the case of coalition governments, he chooses his colleagues. Fourth, by the nature of his position he has a special responsibility to take the lead or speak when an authoritative intervention is needed.

The functions of the Taoiseach have been described in this way:

He is the central coordinating figure, who takes an interest in the work of all Departments, the figure to whom ministers naturally turn for advice and guidance when faced with problems involving large questions of policy or otherwise of special difficulty and whose leadership is essential to the successful working of the Government as a collective authority, collectively responsible to Dáil Éireann, but acting through members each of whom is charged with specific Departmental tasks. He may often have to inform himself in considerable detail of particular matters with which other members of the Government are primarily concerned. He may have to make public statements on such matters, as well as on general matters of broad policy, internal and external. He answers Dáil questions where the attitude of the Government towards important matters of policy is involved. He may occasionally sponsor Bills which represent important new developments of policy, even when the legislation, when enacted, will be the particular concern of the Minister in charge of some other Department of State. Through his Parliamentary Secretary . . . he secures the coordination, in a comprehensive Parliamentary programme, of the proposals of the various Ministers for legislative and other measures in the Houses of the Oireachtas.[25]

Seán Lemass, a former Taoiseach, also put the emphasis on the coordinating role that was becoming more necessary and important in his day:

The Taoiseach's primary task, apart from acting as spokesman for the Government on major issues of policy, is to ensure that governmental plans are fully coordinated, that the inevitable conflicts between Departments are resolved, that

Cabinet decisions are facilitated and that the implications of Government policy are fully understood by all his Cabinet colleagues and influence the shaping of their departmental plans.[26]

Beyond this, as Byrum E. Carter wrote of the British prime minister, "the Office cannot be defined, it can only be described in terms of the use to which it was put by different individuals of varying abilities, who faced different problems and dealt with different colleagues."[27]

Perhaps one general trend can be discerned: both constitutionally and in practice the role and power of the Taoiseach have increased since 1922. Some provisions and wording of the Irish Free State Constitution revealed the intention to reduce the status and role of the President of the Executive Council below those of a British prime minister. W. T. Cosgrave, who held the office from 1922 to 1932, sometimes went out of his way to belittle his own position and stress that of the Council as a whole. In 1937, speaking of the dismissal and resignation of ministers in his time, he said he had not had the power to compel the resignation of his ministers, and he thought this a good thing: "Ministers in my view ought to possess security and a measure of independence."[28] In fact, he seems to have acted more like a British prime minister than either the words of the Constitution or his own utterances suggest.

Under the same constitutional rules, De Valera from the beginning had much greater status and power because he led a much more united party accustomed to his strong style of leadership. From 1932, he was able not only to exploit the possibilities that lay open to him under the Irish Free State Constitution, but also to embody his view of the proper position and powers of a prime minister in his own Constitution. The very title he chose, Taoiseach, though it is far from connoting an absolute ruler, suggests that the Irish prime minister is the essential pivot on which the government rests. Whereas the Irish Free State Constitution gave powers and duties to the Executive Council as a whole, Bunreacht na hÉireann gives them to the Taoiseach in most vital and many purely formal matters. In practice, too, De Valera towered above his colleagues as Cosgrave never did. Revered as "the Chief" by ministerial colleagues and party followers alike, he could and did dominate when he cared to, and in cases of difficulty he dealt individually with his ministers and not through cabinet procedures. His range of interests was narrow, but in matters about which he cared he usually got his own way; in others, he left ministers alone to run their own departments. He moved ministers from department to department and dismissed them as he chose, though he was far from ruthless with ageing comrades. As Brian Farrell put it:

"Undoubtedly, de Valera dominated his team. It is going too far to say he dictated."[29]

Although Seán Lemass (1959–66) had not the charisma of De Valera, he was of the "revolutionary generation" and had long been the heir apparent and the most active and able of all De Valera's ministers. After he took over, the role of Taoiseach increased. Certainly Lemass' style of leadership was more managerial. This was the beginning of a new era in Irish politics: the first of the new post-revolutionary generation of ministers had lately been appointed, and the state's role in planning the development of the economy was coming to be recognized. The extension of state activity and the need for more coordinated policy making and administration that this entailed called for stronger management than hitherto.

Lemass was by temperament a manager; he believed in crisp decision making and in following up progress after decisions were made. Unlike De Valera, he got decisions by putting matters to a vote in cabinet if necessary. He seems to have exerted more control over his ministers than De Valera, even to the extent of interfering with colleagues in matters in which he was interested. He held firmly that when a minister disagreed on a policy issue, the minister had to go: the resignation of Patrick Smith made that crystal clear. Furthermore, he told an interviewer that in the event of being unable to carry a majority of his colleagues on a major issue, he would say to them, "Do as I do or get another Taoiseach."[30]

Jack Lynch (1966–73 and 1977–79) was the first Taoiseach from the "post-revolutionary" group. He was also the first Fianna Fáil leader to attain office as the result of a contested election in the parliamentary party. In his first years he was surrounded by a number of powerful and ambitious colleagues, each of whom pursued his own ministerial and political interests in the hope that he would be the next leader. To the outsider at least, Lynch appeared to adopt a quiet, even passive, approach to leadership. After the 1969 general election, in which he proved conclusively that he was the party's greatest electoral asset, his position vis-à-vis his ambitious cabinet colleagues was stronger. His style always remained "low key," and he was prepared, if there was disagreement in the cabinet, to talk matters out or put them back for reconsideration rather than take a vote. Nevertheless, he could and did act decisively, even ruthlessly, as in spring 1970. When he needed to, he capitalized on the loyalty that Fianna Fáil had customarily accorded its leaders and, if that was not forthcoming, on the self-interested support that deputies always mindful of the next election will give a proven winner.

Lynch's experience showed that, once in office, a Taoiseach who heads a single-party government and is an election winner is probably impregnable and can, if he wishes, get his way, at least until he is near retirement. What Lynch's experience also shows is how easily an outgoing leader can be pushed aside and how inexorably power drains away from him. The controversies surrounding Lynch's retirement and the succession stakes showed, too, that the age of revered godfathers was over and that although loyalty to the party is still the supreme virtue, loyalty to leaders is likely to be conditioned by nice calculations about winning elections and being rewarded with office.

The leaders of the coalition governments were very differently placed from those of Fianna Fáil. To begin with, they were bound by coalition pacts and understandings. They had not the power of appointment, allocation to departments, or dismissal in the case of those posts allotted to parties other than their own. Even if they had wanted to, they could not have exerted the kind of forceful leadership and management open to the leader of a single-party government. If necessary, they had to be prepared to tolerate public expression of disagreement with government policy by cabinet colleagues, and they were more likely to have to use cabinet committees or similar devices to resolve policy differences. They were, then, inevitably, in Farrell's terminology, chairmen rather than chiefs. They did have some leverage by reason of the fact that their cabinet colleagues knew that the government not only had to survive intact as a group but needed to appear united if they were to win a second consecutive term of office. Up to 1980, no coalition had achieved this, despite the fact that it was not at all apparent that multiparty cabinets produced worse government than those composed of a single party.

The variations in the power, performance, and style of the successive holders of the post of Taoiseach have arisen from differences of character and from the circumstances in which they have found themselves. Perhaps the increase in the volume of state business and the greater need to coordinate social and economic policies arising from state planning have given them greater scope for strong leadership. Nevertheless, the office is indeed, to repeat, "what its holder chooses and is able to make of it."

VIII

In this chapter and in Chapter 9 we have attempted to show that the government and the Oireachtas are at the centre of the political system and that the relationships between them are perhaps the key linkages in the system. The main features of these relationships are, first, the domination of the government over the Oireachtas (which is made possible by the loyal support of backbenchers, support that is consistent and dependable but is not wholly without conditions), and, second, the view that politicians have of the respective roles of ministers and deputies. In the chapter that follows, it will be seen that the corollary of a powerful government with a monopoly of initiative and great powers to manage is a puny parliament peopled by members who have a modest view of their functions and a poor capacity to carry them out.

ELEVEN

The Oireachtas

In Chapter 9, we identified the members of the Oireachtas as "proximate policy makers," for they are among "those who have immediate legal authority to decide on specific policies." Paradoxically, however, analysis in that chapter and in Chapter 10 of the role of the Oireachtas showed that it is comparatively minor and passive. The Oireachtas as an institution is not an important, positive contributor to policy. This is due to the domination that the government has over it, a domination that is both accepted by all those involved and made the more effective by the habit of party loyalty and strict adherence to the party line in the voting lobbies.

Such a division of functions and powers is by no means universal in democratic countries. In some, parliaments won and have jealously maintained an important role in policy making and considerable powers to check and restrain governments. Where this has occurred, they tend to be very self-conscious about their autonomy and their ability to control their own business and procedures. The members of such parliaments have a high opinion of their position and carefully guard it. Such representatives contribute positively to policy and are genuine "legislators"; at the same time, they exert considerable control over the administration of policy.

In Ireland, following the United Kingdom tradition, constitutional development has been very different, although a widespread acceptance of the legal fictions of the constitutional lawyers has tended to obscure the facts of the situation. Or rather, the generally accepted propositions about the functions and role of parliament do not reflect the facts, although the behaviour of those actually engaged in politics shows that they recognize them at the level of action, if not of abstraction. Recently, however, there has been a growing recognition by Irish politicians of the weakness of the Oireachtas vis-à-vis the government, and demands have been made—as always by those out of power—for reform.

In this chapter, we shall examine the functions the Oireachtas actually performs, paying particular attention to its part in making policy, to the procedures it adopts and the resources that members have available to them, and to the members themselves, especially to how they see themselves. Before doing so, it is necessary to define exactly what the Oireachtas is. Strictly, following the British conception that parliament consists of the monarch, the House of Lords, and the House of Commons, the Oireachtas must be defined, as it is in the Constitution, as consisting not only of two houses, Dáil Éireann and Seanad Éireann, but of the President also. In practice, however, the term is used to refer to the two houses alone. Ireland has, then, a bicameral legislature, though the Seanad, like many senates, plays a minor and subordinate role.

II

In his study of parliaments, K. C. Wheare discusses their functions under the following headings: (1) making (and breaking) the government, (2) making the government behave, (3) making the laws, and (4) making peace and war (that is, the conduct of foreign relations and defence.)[1] Although the Oireachtas constitutionally and formally has an authoritative say about all these matters, the part it plays in practice is very much less than one might suppose from reading the rules.

In the choice of government, the function of the Dáil (for in this case the Seanad has no part at all to play) has been examined in Chapter 10. Usually the Dáil registers a result—that of the general election by which it was itself elected. However, this need not necessarily be so. Given the presence of more than two parties and independents, it is possible in some circumstances that post-election bargains might be struck and coalitions put together or narrow minorities turned into majorities; this did in fact happen in 1948. In Chapter 10 we saw, too, that the choice of the members of a government is made by the incoming Taoiseach and approved *en bloc* by the Dáil, though the freedom of choice a Taoiseach has and the extent of the influence upon him of members of the parliamentary party may vary considerably with the party and the circumstances. All in all, this hardly adds up to a picture of the Dáil as the maker of governments, and there is an obvious contrast here with countries where, after election results are known, consultations usually *must* take place between the parties before a government can be constructed.

It cannot be said either that the Dáil dismisses the government, if by this is meant that it is likely to pass an adverse vote that would necessitate either the government's resignation and replacement by another or a general election. The data in Table 10.3 (see p. 196) suggest quite a different picture. What can happen—and has happened—is that rising discontent on the part of even a few erstwhile supporters of the government, or their threatened defection, has forced the government to dissolve the Dáil and hold an election. Important as this is, nevertheless a contrast can be drawn once again with countries whose parliaments might and do remove governments. On the other hand, some governments do not depend at all for their existence on parliament, having a fixed term of office, as, for example, in the case of the President of the United States. An arrangement such as this, which is usually accompanied by a provision for a fixed-term parliament, makes for a very different type of government altogether.

"Making the government behave" is recognized as a major function of parliament in all democratic countries. John Stuart Mill in his classic *Representative Government* (1861) maintained that this rather than legislating is its "proper office"; some would regard the adequate performance of this function as an important test of democracy. Ministers are constitutionally responsible for their conduct of affairs but, as we have seen, cabinet responsibility is a very blunt instrument. It is a notorious fact that Ireland's model, the British parliament, failed to develop adequate procedures to make effective its scrutiny of the growing range of state activity since it fell under government domination in the late nineteenth century. That situation, transposed to Ireland at independence, has not been remedied in over half a century. Indeed, the Irish position has worsened in comparison with that in the United Kingdom, where some attempts have been made recently to strengthen parliament.

Many of the weaknesses from which the Oireachtas suffers in attempting to scrutinize the conduct of the government are equally evident when it comes to "making the laws" and even more so in "making peace and war." Here, too, contrasts may be made with some other democratic countries. To begin with, as we have seen, the government has a virtual monopoly of new legislation and policy changes; and, by its control (by means of its majority) of the timetable and of divisions, it governs the processing of bills into law in large measure unaltered, at least in essentials. This perhaps more than any other is the distinguishing characteristic of the Oireachtas and parliaments like it. They are not "legislatures" in the sense in which the United States Congress is a legislature, nor do the members consider themselves "legislators" as congressional representatives do. These facts are reflected in turn in the legislative procedure, the leadership, and the general conduct of business both in the Dáil and in the Seanad.

Almost all bills are proposed by the government; the legislative programme is decided at government meetings. Each bill is prepared by the appropriate department and is subject to overall cabinet approval after such consultation as it deems necessary. It is at this stage that the effective pressures are brought to bear and the important interests are considered. The minister thus introduces a bill, a government measure, that the government considers has already taken major interests and views sufficiently into account and that the parliamentary party will be expected to support. Nearly all bills are introduced and passed in the Dáil first and then are submitted to the Seanad; occasionally, noncontroversial bills have been introduced and processed by the Seanad before going to the Dáil.

There is provision in each house for "private member's bills" (bills introduced by members who are not ministers), but in practice these are not a significant source of law. In the twentieth Dáil (1973–77), three such bills were introduced in the Dáil and five in the Seanad; none was passed. In John Smyth's words, "the chances of a private member's bill reaching the statute book are remote, for even when the government accepts the principle of the bill, the member is normally requested to withdraw it on the assurance that the government will introduce a measure officially drafted to meet his case."[2] The private member's bill is in fact often used as a device to get publicity and evoke debate or, as in the case of Senator Mary Robinson's bills on contraception in the 1970s, to try to force the government itself to take action.

The procedure for dealing with proposals for legislation follows the characteristic pattern of the Westminster model. After a formal introduction (first stage), there is a general debate on the principles of the measure proposed (second stage), after which the bill is regarded as having been approved in principle and not subject to serious alteration. This is followed by an examination of the bill section by section, at which time amendments may be proposed that do not negate the bill as a whole (third stage). This stage is usually conducted by the whole Dáil. Although the rules of procedure permit the use of a "special committee" consisting largely of members with an interest or knowledge, this procedure is rarely used: between 1965 and 1973 only one bill was handled in this way; between 1973 and 1977, six. The bill as amended is then considered once again before being passed on to the other house, usually the Seanad.

The principles governing legislative procedure seem to be four. First, the house considers proposals in an advanced stage of preparation. The idea that governs the legislative procedures of many parliaments—namely, that a bill is only a proposal to be investigated by a committee that will interrogate its authors and hear interested parties before preparing its own version to present to the full house—is alien to Irish parliamentary tradition. Second, the principles of a bill are debated first and in full house and, having been agreed upon, are not thereafter open to amendment. Third, it is ordinarily the job of ministers to bring in bills and to sponsor them; the Oireachtas expects this and is organized accordingly. Fourth, business is so arranged and rules so framed that the government can get its bills passed without too much delay, while at the same time the Opposition has opportunities to deploy its case against them. In doing so, the Opposition will sometimes be as much concerned to persuade the public outside the house that the running of the country would be better placed in their hands at the next election as to influence the government to alter its proposals (though at the third stage particularly, much hard, detailed work is done—albeit by a small minority of members—to amend details of bills and to improve them technically). The orderly and timely passage of business is assured by the government's majority and by the activities of the party whips, who manage their respective parties, arrange the timetable in consultation with each other, and make sure that members are present to vote. As the system operates in practice, it is hard to resist A. J. Ward's conclusion that "the parliamentary procedures of the Dáil are designed to maximize the power of the government and to minimize the power of the deputies and the Dáil itself as an institution."[3]

The same principles and similar procedures obtain when the Oireachtas is considering policy proposals in the form of motions and proposals for spending public monies. In the case of expenditure, the government is required by Article 28 of Bunreacht na hÉireann to prepare and present annually to the Dáil estimates of receipts and expenditure. Annual estimates for public services are formulated into motions that are introduced in the Dáil, but only some of them ever get debated. Proposals for raising funds are also introduced as motions and when passed are incorporated in the annual Finance Bill. Financial resolutions in connection with legislation that would necessitate the expenditure of public funds are introduced and dealt with when the relevant bill is under consideration in the Dáil. The importance of finance and of the need to control it are reflected in the fact that, in dealing with money matters, power is formally allocated somewhat differently than it is in the case of policy generally. First, the authority of the Dáil as the popularly elected house is greater vis-à-vis the Seanad than it is in respect of other matters; second, the government has the exclusive power under the Constitution to propose the expenditure of public money.

III

In considering the functions and role of the Oireachtas, attention tends to focus upon the Dáil rather than the Seanad. The Seanad plays a smaller part than the Dáil and has a subordinate position. The relative inferiority of the second house is a common, though not universal, phenomenon of modern democratic states. In the case of Seanad Éireann, it is the sequel to a troubled past.

The first Irish parliament in 1919 consisted of a single house, for the independence movement neither needed nor wanted more. When the Treaty was being negotiated, however, promises were sought and given that the new state would have a senate in which the unionist minority would be strongly represented, and provision was made for this in the Irish Free State Constitution. That senate had a checkered career. No satisfactory formula for its composition could be found. When it exercised its right to hold up legislation that had been passed in the Dáil, it was immediately open to the charge not only of thwarting the real representatives of the people but of being un-Irish as well. It was especially anathema to De Valera and Fianna Fáil, and it did not long survive their accession to office, being abolished in 1936 after acrimonious debates during which De Valera declared himself unconvinced of the value of any senate but open to persuasion. However, a general belief in the usefulness of second houses prevailed, and the 1937 Constitution made provision for a new senate, Seanad Éireann.

Seanad Éireann is both singular in its composition and circumscribed in its powers. In considering a new senate, De Valera was attracted by one of the proposals of a commission set up to advise on the composition of a new house, a proposal for a body selected on a vocational basis and obviously inspired by the principles enunciated in the encyclical *Quadragesimo Anno* of Pope Pius XI. However, he recognized that the country was not in fact sufficiently organized on vocational lines to allow direct choice by vocational bodies, and he was also concerned not to have a body that would be likely to oppose the government of the day. The scheme he evolved, which has survived with only minor changes, provided for a body comprising three groups.

Six senators are elected by the Irish graduates of the two universities, three from each.[4] Forty-three are elected by an electoral college of nearly nine hundred, which is composed of the members of the Oireachtas and the county and county borough councillors. The forty-three are chosen from five panels of candidates nominated in part by bodies representing five groups of interests (education and culture, agriculture, industry and commerce, labor, and public administration and social services) and in part by members of the Oireachtas. The remaining eleven senators are nominated by the Taoiseach himself after all the others have been chosen. Thus the Taoiseach has an opportunity to give representation to any group that he thinks needs it, to bring in persons of eminence, and—De Valera frankly admitted when proposing it—to ensure a government majority.

The scheme for the election of the forty-three was admitted to be only a step toward vocational representation. Yet in itself it was defective, for not only did the structure of the community not correspond to vocational principles, but the composition of the panels, with labor separated from management, seemed actually to go contrary to those very principles. More serious for genuine vocational representation, the dilution of direct representation of vocational organizations in order to make the system more democratic permitted party domination, which has in fact been complete. The parties have controlled the elections to the exclusion of almost all the truly vocational elements. Since the Taoiseach's nominees tend also to be party men, the Seanad is composed largely of party politicians not very different from their colleagues in the Dáil and, in the case of many of them, with only tenuous connections with the interests they affect to represent. Usually between one-quarter and one-third of them have been TDs, defeated or retired, and many of the rest are party men who have earned a reward or consolation prize. In recent years, a few have been aspirant deputies, younger people using the Seanad as a steppingstone to the Dáil.

Because so many of them are rising, falling, or resting politicians, it is not surprising that many senators (unlike deputies) are not front-rank party men. A few are not real politicians at all. Only the university representatives, included to compensate the universities for having lost their representation in the Dáil in 1936, tended in the past to approximate the vocational type, representing professions such as law and medicine and the professional classes generally. Naturally, the prestige of the Seanad suffers from the fact that, by and large, it is merely another selection of party politicians chosen in an unnecessarily complicated and not particularly democratic manner.

The Seanad suffers also from its evident inferiority and subordination to the Dáil. In Bunreacht na hÉireann, it is deliberately placed to one side of the political stage. The Dáil nominates the Taoiseach and approves his government. The government is constitutionally responsible to the Dáil and must maintain a majority there. The Dáil is required by the Constitution to consider the estimates of public expenditure, to ratify international agreements, and to approve any declaration of war. Almost all legislation is introduced in the Dáil, and all major policy statements are made there. The Seanad's meagre powers to amend or delay emphasize the point that it is primarily a revising body with the power to draw public attention to a proposal by compelling the Dáil to reconsider it. Even this it has done on only a couple of occasions.

The subordinate status of the Seanad in law and in practice and its lack of prestige are emphasized by three facts. First, there are usually no senator ministers. The Constitution permits up to two members of the government to be senators, but from 1938 to 1980 only one minister was in the senate—and only because he was defeated at a Dáil election. The majority side of the house is led and business is controlled by a majority leader, who, though he is always senior, does not have ministerial rank. Second, the Seanad's business is subordinated to that of the Dáil. In the ten-year period between 1969 and 1978, according to Smyth, "approximately 90–95 per cent of the work consisted of the consideration of legislation sent to the second chamber by the Dáil." What is more, "the sittings of the Seanad are largely dependent on the volume of business sent to the House from the Dáil. While the Dáil is discussing the estimates, very little legislation is passed by it and the Seanad has no occasion to meet."[5] Later in the year, it has sometimes been forced into an unseemly rush, processing without proper consideration a number of bills that the government wishes to have passed before the recess. Third, sometimes its consideration of items on its agenda has been delayed, interrupted, or impaired by the failure of ministers to attend as arranged.

There is a vicious circle here. Lacking prestige and being government controlled, the Seanad cannot insist on a more active role or on more consideration for its dignity or convenience. Because it does not do so, it is condemned to hold an undignified position and to underuse what potential it does have. It does some useful work, however. Its debates on current issues are sometimes important; bills are improved, some considerably, as a result of its efforts; a few of its members serve on Oireachtas joint committees (and much more use could be made of them in this way). However, the air of leisure that pervades its debates, its light programme (in the decade 1969 to 1978, it met on average thirty-five times for 228 hours in each year), the absence of any feeling of urgency or of momentous political cut and thrust, and the comparatively poor publicity it gets all emphasize its lack of importance and contribute to its low prestige. If it were more important, its composition would undoubtedly evoke more than the halfhearted criticism that is now heard from time to time, but to government and to community alike, this does not seem to be a matter of much moment.

IV

In carrying out its functions of making the laws, as also in making the government behave, the Oireachtas is sadly ineffective, a fact that is now increasingly acknowledged by politicians themselves. Barry Desmond, Labour Party whip, has written: "Our present parliamentary malaise is that we have allowed our parliamentary institutions to atrophy so much that many deputies and senators are, in the parliamentary sense, politically uninvolved."[6] According to Fine Gael's policy document entitled *Reform of the Dáil,* "In practice it [the Dáil] plays practically no effective part in either making the laws or even the expert criticism of them."[7]

The Oireachtas is deficient on three counts. First, its procedures and techniques are archaic and ineffective. Second, the staff and facilities available to members are meagre. Third, the education and experience of many members and the view that they have of their job ill equip them to make the kinds of enquiries that are necessary or to appreciate the kinds of data that ought to be made available in order to judge performance. Neither the methods employed nor the personnel involved, whether representative or professional, are adequate to appraise large programmes of public expenditure for an ever increasing range of economic and social objectives, including long-term capital programmes and extensive subsidies. Even if they were, the style and demeanour of opposition—and it is the Opposition on which the performance of this function to a great extent depends—and the conception members generally have of their functions do not favour really effective or hard-hitting criticism.

The methods used by the Oireachtas to deal with the policy proposals of governments are those evolved by the British parliament in the nineteenth century. Parliaments are basically debating assemblies. In the Dáil and Seanad, as in the houses of the British parliament, ministers explain and make the case for their proposals, the Opposition opposes, and members generally comment, using a wide variety of debating-body techniques as procedural pegs on which to hang their discussions. These same pegs are used for the surveillance of the conduct of public business—that is, making the government behave. They are of three kinds—debates, questions, and committees.

Both houses of the Oireachtas debate the proposals that the government puts before them, often more than once, within the framework of procedures for dealing with various types of business—at the five stages laid down by the rules for the consideration of bills; in debates on estimates; and in debates on motions of various kinds, including motions of censure and "no confidence" and "adjournment motions." In both quantity and quality, the performance of both houses leaves much to be desired. Between 1969 and 1978, the Dáil met on average only eighty-seven days per year; the Seanad, thirty-five. It is hard to measure the quality of debate in any objective fashion. Debates are no doubt valuable as a device to deploy the pros and cons of a proposed course of action and are important for the publicity they give to it and to the case for and against. However, in Ireland—no doubt as elsewhere—debates are often discursive, uninformed, and sometimes, except perhaps to the speaker concerned, irrelevant to the major issues of the topic under discussion. In any case, the quality of debate depends inevitably upon the quality of the information available. Too often, ministers briefed by their civil servants are the only well-informed participants. The Opposition and ordinary members generally have no comparable resources for acquiring and appraising information.

Parliamentary debates are the less efficient as a method for dealing with policy proposals because of the fact that they are usually gladiatorial set pieces conducted on party lines by politicians who are wedded to the concept of strictly competitive or "adversary" politics. Counterproposals and amendments, even good ones, made by the Opposition are liable to be rejected by the government because of their source rather than their intrinsic value, except perhaps on minor matters when there is little or no publicity.

It is often said that debates in the Seanad are of higher quality than debates in the Dáil. If that is so, it is because, first, being less in the public eye, the party battle lines in the Seanad are not so rigorously drawn and, second, some senators have no need to concern themselves with local matters or to have an eye to constituents. In the Dáil, on the other hand, it is obvious that some participants in debates are using the opportunity to raise matters of local interest in order to get publicity in their local newspapers in their home territories. This is entirely rational behaviour on their part, given their constituents' and their own concept of their functions and role, the localism of Irish politics, and the operation of the electoral system. Such contributions, however, do not usually illuminate the major principles and aspects of public policy initiatives.

The main burden of debating government proposals falls upon a fraction of Oireachtas members—the members of the government and the ministers of state, the Opposition shadow ministers called "spokesmen," and a few others who by temperament or training or for reasons of ambition have a greater interest than most in general policy issues. Recently, the number of such people seems to have grown with the election of more young and ambitious professional and business people and also, in the case of Fine Gael, by reason of the conscious efforts of the party leader to involve the parliamentary party members in these aspects of business. When the party went into opposition in 1977, most Fine Gael front-bench spokesmen (there were fifteen of them) appointed "back-up" committees, not confined to members of the Oireachtas or even to registered party members, to prepare policy documents and to draft material for use by parliamentarians. Each member of the parliamentary party was asked to indicate two subject areas of special interest with the intention that he would support official spokesmen in those areas by speaking or by committee work.

By reason of its numerical weakness in the Dáil, most deputies of the Labour Party are spokesmen on some subject or other; the parliamentary party also has a handful of specialized committees. Fianna Fáil too have party committees but, because the party is usually in office, their leaders as ministers rely mostly on the civil service. The party's back-bench committees tend to languish. In 1980, when they were reorganized to facilitate, as the press release put it, "maximum involvement in the formation and implementation of government policy," there were a dozen of them.

All three parliamentary parties have regular meetings, usually weekly, when the houses are sitting. None of them make much positive contribution to legislation or policy: the Opposition committees because they are in a minority situation in a process of strictly adversary politics; the government party deputies because the government, already committed to its proposals, regards its backbenchers as at best a negative sounding board that will occasionally force ministers to think again.

Parliamentary questions are not of much importance in policy making. The Dáil has a question time on the well-known Westminster model and, as in the United Kingdom also, parliamentary questions are "a simple, convenient and speedy routine ... available to deputies for getting information from the Government."[8] The principal use of question time, however, is to seek information about, and to question, administrative action or inaction; it is thus mostly concerned with "making the government behave," to use Wheare's terminology.

In many parliaments, the most important work on policy is done in committees. For each area of policy and administration there will be a powerful committee with its own staff to process both government-sponsored and other proposals for new legislation on policy and to make its own proposals. In addition, such committees supervise the administration of policy in a particular subject area. With experience, their members and staff acquire considerable knowledge and expertise and, to some extent at least, can challenge ministers and civil servants on not-too-unequal terms.

The United Kingdom parliament, however, never developed a strong committee system of this sort, contenting itself until recently with "select committees" to enquire into the conduct of administration; rather restricted terms of reference usually precluded the questioning of government policy. That approach and that type of committee was adopted by the Oireachtas, and, until recently, there was no development beyond that point. Even in the mid-1970s, a new committee necessitated by Ireland's accession to the European Communities, the Joint Committee [that is, of the Dáil and Seanad] on the Secondary Legislation of the European Communities, was clearly hampered in its work by inadequate staffing and services.

More recently, with the appointment in 1978 of a Joint Committee on State-Sponsored Bodies to "examine the Reports and Accounts and over-all operational results of State-Sponsored Bodies engaged in trading or commercial activities," the Oireachtas achieved something of a breakthrough against the reluctance of governments and civil servants to countenance an efficient parliamentary committee. Not only was professional staff appointed to assist the Joint Committee, but the Committee itself soon found that judging the performance of public enterprises involved enquiring into their policy briefs. This it proceeded to do. It was but a short step thence to commenting on policy issues, and by 1980 the Joint Committee was doing so. Its reports were providing information on the bodies it investigated in quantity and quality never before achieved by parliamentarians. In this area at least, deputies and senators could debate with ministers on more nearly equal terms than in any other.

The potentialities of even the present committees are not likely to be realized until members of the Oireachtas show more interest in committee reports than they do at present. Reviewing the work of the Joint Committee on the Secondary Legislation of the European Communities, Patrick Keatinge pointed out that "neither house has arranged a regular procedure to discuss its reports."[9] The same is true generally of most committee reports, and also, for example, of the six monthly reports on developments in the European Communities that the government is by law required to present to the Oireachtas. Only in the Seanad have arrangements recently been made to have regular debates on the reports of the joint committees.

Most of the small but growing number of politicians who recognize the inadequacy of the Oireachtas have tended to argue that a more extensive committee system is the key to improving parliament's performance. Both Barry Desmond, the Labour Party whip, in his *Houses of the Oireachtas: A Plea for Reform,* and John Bruton, who prepared Fine Gael's policy document entitled *Reform of the Dáil,* argued this. In Fine Gael's view, "The greater and more effective use of committees is a key element in strengthening the Dáil."[10] Desmond was more specific: "A more open committee system should be introduced. Permanent joint committees of the Dáil and Senate with a qualified expert staff should have power to examine specific areas of government such as agriculture, education, energy, the environment, consumer protection, or the activities of the state-sponsored bodies."[11]

There would be difficulties in manning such an extensive system, and Desmond is undoubtedly right to seek joint committees along the lines of the two most recent additions to the system. At present, most members of the Oireachtas are not assiduous committee men. Their performance in a well-established committee system in which all were expected to work might be very much better, particularly if committees were well serviced and their reports were regularly debated and publicized. As the Fine Gael document rightly observes, "Politicians can only survive if they receive public recognition for their work."[12]

Perhaps there is a more fundamental problem, however. As Ward has pointed out, "A committee has the effect of creating within the same legislature an alternative centre of information, expertise, prestige and power which necessarily inhibits the government's freedom of action."[13] The fear of such an "alternative centre" causes governments to be slow to countenance the development of powerful committees. Without doubt, "well-developed committee systems are not easily blended with parliamentary democracy on the Westminster model."[14]

The ineffectiveness of Oireachtas procedures and the low level of performance of most members are the greater on account of the paucity of facilities available to members. To begin with, deputies' salaries (called "allowances") are barely adequate to expect them to be full-time parliamentary representatives, and many do not rely wholly on these salaries. Certainly, they are insufficient to finance anything like adequate secretarial, let alone research or professional, help. The level at which senatorial salaries are fixed makes it quite clear that being a senator is part-time work.

In many parliaments, official provision is made for secretarial and research services and for assistance generally. The Oireachtas, however, is served by thirty "clerks" plus a small ancillary staff. Most of their time is taken up with servicing the meetings of the two houses and its few committees. No committee except that on state-sponsored bodies gets the help of more than one or two clerks and that often part-time. There is an Oireachtas library with a staff of five librarians who give members some assistance, but information and research services are not available on any scale. Deputies do not even have private offices, only party rooms. The secretarial facilities officially made available to them are pathetic. In 1980, there was one secretary for every nine members, and there were delays in getting letters typed. The political parties cannot help members much either; the funds made available to them from public monies permit little in the way of intelligence or research services.

The major part of examining and criticizing the government's proposals falls to the members of the party or parties in opposition. The concept of "the Opposition" as an essential complement to "the Government" is basic to the Irish system. It is symbolized by the special, albeit inadequate, allowance paid to the leader of the opposition party or, if there is more than one opposition party, to the leaders of the two biggest, to enable them and their colleagues to carry out their function of opposing the government. The style of the Opposition resembles that which Wheare described as typical of the British system: "The leading idea upon which it is organized is that it offers itself before the country as an alternative government. It criticizes upon the understanding that, given the opportunity, it could do better itself."[15] The Oireachtas and particularly the Dáil is a platform upon which the Opposition makes a continuous appeal to the electorate.

The application of this principle has two consequences. First, the style of opposition tends to be responsible and criticism, particularly from the front benches, is often muted, for dog does not eat dog. Only a few individual TDs have occasionally conducted a different kind of opposition, more outspoken, more wholesale, more truculent, but effective; and one or two independent-minded senators have also behaved in somewhat similar fashion.

Second, this style of opposition further intensifies the strict competition that is the consequence of bipolar politics and governments with a monopoly of initiative, particularly since there are few opportunities for constructive committee work. The Opposition either does not want to play a constructive role or, if it does, it is not permitted to do so. Proposals emanating from opposition sources are all too often not considered on their merits, for no public credit can be allowed to accrue to them; equally, the job of the Opposition is to criticize the government and all its works.

Thus, locally oriented and preoccupied with servicing their constituents as most members are, they almost without exception vote consistently for the party line and are expected to do so by those who vote for them. At most, a dissident will abstain unless, being on the government side, his or her vote is critical. Even former ministers dismissed in ignominious circumstances in 1970 continued to vote for their party on critical and, for them, sensitive issues. Since genuine independents, as opposed to camp-follower "independents," have been few and far between, the Dáil has been almost completely a chamber of party blocs. In the Seanad, where a vote is usually not of critical importance, a few genuine independents are to be found, but there have never been more than four or five of these out of the sixty in the last quarter of a century. Occasionally, a party member will vote against the party line when it does not matter much.

Together, the government's monopoly of policy initiatives and the views of members on the roles of the government and the Opposition and of the appropriate style of conducting them have combined to inhibit the development of the Oireachtas as a legislature and to prevent the members from seeing themselves as legislators. For the same reasons, deputies and senators do not see themselves as constituting a corporate institution with powers to check the government on behalf of the people.

The positive contribution of the Oireachtas to policy formation on any subject is small; on some subjects, it is smaller than on others. In matters of health, social welfare, and agriculture, many members are interested and concerned, but often from the point of view of local consumers and producers. In other matters, notably public expenditure, not only have ordinary members no power of initiative, but their consideration of the government's proposals (the annual estimates and requests to approve capital expenditure) often verges on the cursory. The Fine Gael document on Dáil reform was explicit on the subject:

The present procedure for the consideration of estimates in the Dáil is very unsatisfactory. The bulk of the estimates are not considered at all by the Dáil. This is because of insufficient time. Those that are considered are considered during the year to which they apply and after a substantial portion of the money provided in them has already been spent. They are considered in debates which have a format which does not allow for detailed scrutiny of individual items in the estimates, nor for real dialogue between ministers and Members of the House. The estimates may not be amended in any way and must be accepted or rejected in toto. In fact all the Dáil does is give a retrospective rubber stamp to the Government's spending plans.[16]

Much the same can be said about foreign affairs and defence, where there is very little interest or participation at all. These are, of course, notoriously areas where, by the very nature of the subject and of the procedures involved, parliaments are in the hands of governments. The Irish Constitution requires that war shall not be declared nor shall the state participate in any war without the assent of the Dáil, but if it comes to war, this requirement is likely to be only a formality. More important, Article 29.5 requires that international agreements "shall be laid before the Dáil"—that is, published—and therefore subject to parliamentary questions. But the texts of agreements represent things already done and commitments entered into, and although Dáil Éireann does in fact have to approve, for example, the sending of soldiers to serve in UN forces, its grip on the state's foreign commitments is palpably weak. Some matters, no doubt, cannot be the subject of debate while they are in course of being negotiated, but the result is that important commitments have often been undertaken with little or no prior parliamentary discussion and presented virtually as *faits accomplis*. Ireland's accession to the European Communities stood out as an exception because it necessitated a constitutional amendment and, thus, a reference to the electorate at a referendum.

The position of the Dáil is no different in respect of the development of foreign policies in general. Matters such as the interpretation of neutrality, relations with power blocs, indeed Ireland's UN and European Community policies as a whole, are developed without the government seeking approval for them. White papers on foreign policy are rarely published. The state's attitude and actions are explained only later at some convenient parliamentary opportunity. The situation is epitomized but by no means caricatured in the notorious reply of the Minister for External Affairs in 1967 when deputies complained that the Dáil had not been consulted about what attitude the state should take to the Arab-Israeli war of that year: "Dáil Éireann was consulted on this matter ten years ago. If they wanted to be consulted and to voice any opinion, they had ten years in which to do it."[17]

More recently, Ireland's accession to the European Communities has had the effect of removing some aspects of agricultural, industrial, commercial, and social policy from Dublin to Brussels and of transferring the parliamentary consideration of these matters to Strasbourg and Luxembourg, the seats of the European Parliament. At the end of the 1970s, the Oireachtas had not come to terms with this shift of power. In particular, members did not seem to recognize the need to integrate the work of the Irish members of the European Parliament with their own efforts or to tap their knowledge, resources, and opportunities as members of that Parliament. Some deputies seemed more concerned with the problem of the "dual mandate"—whether individuals should hold seats in both parliaments, thus earning very large salaries while occupying Dáil seats that might be filled by someone else, to the parties' electoral advantage.

V

The poor performance of the Oireachtas arises partly because it is badly organized and equipped and poorly informed. But, more fundamentally, poor performance results from, first, a general acceptance by members of the dominant role of the government as policy maker, and, second, the preoccupation of many members with their own local positions. These considerations have led them to see themselves as having another function to perform, the function of "servicing" their constituents. In so doing, members of the Oireachtas generally, and TDs in particular, constitute themselves more a factor in the *administration* of state policy—particularly in detailed administration—than as *legislators*. They adopt this role both by inclination and by force of circumstances, a fact best explained by considering who and what they are and how they attain and hold office.

The generational changes in Irish political leadership to which attention has already been drawn can be seen mirrored in the composition of the Oireachtas. But, here, the most important effect has been to intensify rather than alter a characteristic that was a marked feature from the beginning—localism. As Tom Garvin pointed out, "With the passing of the revolutionary generation, the natural tendency of the system toward extreme localism asserted itself even more thoroughly than hitherto."[18]

In the past, prominent leaders, especially if they were national heroes or members of a dynasty founded on one such, could live outside their constituencies, and "their electorates exempted them from the classic duty of a parliamentary representative in a rural society with a widely-dispersed population—that is, to be a local man, well entrenched in the local social system, resident in or near the constituency and concerned more with being an ambassador for his community to the central government than with the task of making national policy or law."[19] Others had to conform to this pattern. With time, virtually all have had to.

In 1922, 72 per cent of deputies were resident in the constituencies they represented; by 1973, 92 per cent lived in or in close proximity to their constituencies. Perhaps three-quarters of these were also born there. In fact, identification with an area has always been even more specific. Many, perhaps most, TDs, except those living in Dublin, have been identified with the particular part of the constituency in which they live or are reckoned specially to represent. Multimember constituencies notwithstanding, there is a marked tendency for deputies to have "bailiwicks."[20] Senators, except those representing the universities, do not have constituencies. Nevertheless, in recent years most of the two-thirds of them who live outside Dublin are identified with their home areas in much the same way as deputies, and in practice they perform the same services for their localities as deputies.

The localism of parliamentary representatives is the greater since, for most of them, the route to membership in the Oireachtas is by way of local government and the basis of their electoral support lies in the help they can give their constituents in respect of local services such as housing and health. Most deputies and senators are members of the principal local authorities, the county and county borough councils: 77 per cent of the deputies elected to the 1977 Dáil and 53 per cent of senators were or had been local councillors. Almost all of them were also serving on one or more of a variety of other local public bodies such as county committees of agriculture, vocational educational committees, harbour boards, health boards, and regional development authorities. All these offer opportunities for influence and service that enhance a politician's local reputation and help secure a quota of first-preference votes. Nor is this to be thought of as a phenomenon of the countryside: twenty-six of the forty-three Dublin-area deputies elected in 1977 were or had been councillors as were all five of the Cork City deputies. As Ted Nealon put it: "The number of deputies who continue to serve on local authorities or seek election to them after entering the Dáil, confirms the importance of membership in consolidating a deputy's position in a constituency. It can also prove a useful position for heading off potential rivals within a deputy's own party."[21]

In addition, members of the Oireachtas are to be found in all kinds of voluntary bodies, particularly trade unions, trade associations, farmers' organizations, and other occupational bodies. Yet, strangely, they are not to be found in social, cultural, or religious organizations, with the notable exception of the Gaelic Athletic Association, membership in which is generally reckoned to be particularly useful.

As the luminaries of the revolutionary generation disappeared, they were usually not replaced by others of their kind. Their personal followings evaporated and the parties took over. By the late 1970s, only Neil Blaney exemplified something of the *personalismo* of the earlier generation of semi-independent deputies; but, significantly, he is an example of another marked feature of the composition of the Oireachtas and of Irish politics generally to which attention has already been drawn—namely, the dynastic element. The Blaneys, father and son, have represented their part of Donegal for over half a century since Neal Blaney entered the Dáil with De Valera and Fianna Fáil in 1927.

"Family seats" soon became and have remained quite numerous. Among the 144 members of the 1965 Dáil, there were 4 widows and 28 sons or daughters of former members and 9 nephews or other close relatives. The position in 1977 was much the same: 24 were sons, three were widows, and 1 a daughter of former deputies, and there were also 4 nephews and 1 granddaughter.[22] To inherit a "family seat" was almost without exception the only way a woman could become a parliamentary representative. Of the 12 women who sat in the Dáil between 1922 and 1948, 3 were widows and 3 sisters of prominent leaders of the independence movement, and 5 others were widows of former deputies. Thirty years later the position had not changed: of the 6 women deputies elected in 1977, only 1 was not in this category. In the Seanad, where the party leadership has more control over nominations and the electors, there are signs of the beginning of an effort to reduce the imbalance between men and women. Nevertheless, the 1977 Seanad contained only 6 women.

Since almost all deputies belong in their localities and since Ireland is overwhelmingly a Catholic country, there are few Protestants in the Oireachtas. In the past, Protestants have represented constituencies where the people of their faith could muster a quota of votes—for example, in Donegal until the late 1960s or in some Dublin constituencies. Where there are pockets of Protestants, the major parties sometimes find it politic to have a senator of that faith. But the Protestant population has declined in numbers and has become more assimilated into the mainstream of politics. Accordingly, where, as in the Dála of the 1920s, there were a dozen or so, in 1965 there were four, and in 1977 there was one Protestant (and a Jew) in the Dáil, plus five Protestants in the Seanad.

Generational changes are also evident in the age distribution of parliamentary representatives. The revolutionary Dáil of 1919 contained a large proportion of young men, and over half of the 1922 Dáil were under 40. Once elected, members were able to retain their seats comparatively easily and the turnover was low. Moreover, new entrants tended to be over 40, reflecting the conservatism and respect for seniority that marked Irish politics. Consequently, as Table 11.1 shows, the Dáil was a steadily ageing body until the 1950s, when, inevitably, the first generation began to be replaced quite quickly. More recently, the pro-

TABLE 11.1
Age Distribution of Members of Certain Dála Between 1919 and 1977

	Dáil					
Age group	1919	1922	1932	1944	1965	1977[a]
20–29	21%	14%	1%	2%	6%	4%
30–39	37	38	27	12	20	24
40–49	25	24	39	31	31	36
50–59	13	18	26	37	24	24
60–69	3	4	5	17	14	9
70 and over	0	2	2	1	5	1

SOURCE: For 1919–44, derived from J. L. McCracken, *Representative Government in Ireland* (London, 1957), pp. 31–91. For 1965, derived from J. Whyte, *Dáil Deputies*, Tuairim Pamphlet No. 15 (Dublin, 1966), p. 33. For 1977, T. Nealon, *Guide to the 21st Dáil and Seanad* (Blackrock, 1977), p. 135.
[a] For the 1977 Dáil, the age groupings are shifted up one year: 21–30, 31–40, etc.

TABLE 11.2
Education of Members of Certain Dála Between 1922 and 1977

	Level attained		
Year	First	Second	Third
1922	40%	34%	26%
1932	44	32	24
1944	48	29	22
1965	20	50	30
1977	7	56	37

SOURCE: As for Table 11.1.

portion of young people has begun to increase again, reflecting a belief in the parties that young candidates will appeal to an electorate one-quarter of whom in 1977 were under 25. Analyzing the composition of the Seanad in 1969, Garvin found a similar general pattern of age distribution.[23]

Likewise, changes brought about by the eventual disappearance of the old guard no doubt go some way to explain the big changes in the educational qualifications of deputies and senators; they also reflect improved educational opportunities and the growing belief of party leaders that a better educated population wants better qualified candidates. Until well after the Second World War, four or five out of ten deputies had only a primary-school education and only a quarter had third-level education or professional training. The picture has changed markedly since then. As Table 11.2 shows, over one-half have secondary education and over

TABLE 11.3

Main Occupations of the 1977 Dáil and Seanad

Main occupation	Dáil	Seanad	Oireachtas
Farming	15%	15%	15%
Professional	29	38	32
Trade union official	5	3	4
Industry and commerce	30	33	31
Nonmanual	6	3	5
Skilled manual	4	0	3
Semiskilled and unskilled manual	0	0	0
Others (including housewives and unclassified)	16	7	10

SOURCE: Compiled from data in T. Nealon, *Guide to the 21st Dáil and Seanad* (Blackrock, 1977).

NOTE: Full-time politicians have not been classified separately. They have been classified according to their previous main occupation or the occupation for which they were trained before they became full-time politicians.

one-third have third level. Garvin found the same changes in the Seanad.[24]

Higher educational standards have been reflected in a changing occupational structure. Writing in 1972, Garvin concluded that "studies of biographical information on Dáil Deputies have established clear-cut trends towards professionalisation of the House in recent decades."[25] These trends have continued as Table 11.3 indicates. In 1977, nearly 30 per cent of TDs and nearly 40 per cent of senators were professional people, mostly teachers and lawyers; thirty years before and as recently as the mid-1960s, less than 20 per cent had been professional people. Much the same proportion of the 1977 representatives were in industry and commerce, which, as we have already noted, is a group largely composed of self-employed people in family businesses, especially individuals in the retail trade, contractors, auctioneers (no less than fifteen of these were elected to the Dáil in 1977) and publicans (nine elected to the Dáil in 1977). Farmers, the only other sizeable occupational group, who in the past have usually constituted one-quarter or more of the Dáil, have been declining in numbers; in 1977 they made up only 15 per cent of the membership of both Dáil and Seanad. However, a much bigger proportion than that have an immediate interest in farming because it is quite common for men to combine their principal profession or business with farming.

This pattern of occupations means that the membership of the Oireachtas, like political office holders generally, by no means reflects the occupational structure of Irish society. Working-class deputies and senators are, and always have been, few and far between. Likewise, there are very few small farmers. Evidently, here as elsewhere in politics, the occupations that are "central" or permit time for politics tend to be overrepresented and, conversely, others are underrepresented.

These data provide a clear enough picture of the membership of the Oireachtas as measured by objective data. But how do the members see themselves? Although there are no systematic data on this, there can be little doubt of what the answer is. For most of them, a public representative is, as Léo Hamon said of the French deputy, "a man at the beck and call of his electors,"[26] though the deputies and senators themselves would prefer to use words such as "service" and "available" instead. As we shall see, the service given by representatives covers a wide range of minor administrative matters at both the local and the central government levels. The public expect this: "There is a fixed notion that cannot be got out of people's heads that Deputies can get you something that you cannot get from anybody else."[27] The election system puts a premium on it: "Of course you must canvass in another form from the day on which the election is over till the date of the next election."[28]

For a good many, the *cursus honorum* may well be through service at the local government level, and the maintenance of one's position certainly requires continuing to provide it. Service of this kind is thus an integral part of the web of personal contact and influence that is the foundation of the position of the public person, certainly in rural areas and to some extent in urban areas also. Moreover, this type of activity is not declining. On the contrary, it is if anything increasing; members certainly work at it as assiduously as in the past and perhaps more ruthlessly. The younger members who are more "policy-oriented" than the average older member are no less attentive to this aspect of their job than the rest: they dare not neglect it.

What proportion of the time of a member of the Oireachtas does this kind of work take? Valuable evidence on this subject was given in the case of *O'Donovan* v. *Attorney General*, [1961] I.R. 114, heard in the High Court in 1961, and the impression to be gained from observing and talking to members makes it clear that the position has not changed since then.[29] For most deputies and senators, whether from city or rural areas, service work on behalf of constituents is a heavy burden; for many it is their most time-consuming activity. In a single month in 1980, one Dublin deputy received 244 communications, of which more than 60 made personal requests, almost the same number raised constituency problems, and 40 were from pressure groups.[30] Yet most accept such work without resentment: on the contrary, there is evidence that many give it priority and some exploit it. Some members of the European

Parliament pursue parochial matters there too. On October 11, 1979, Seán Flanagan asked the Commission to state "whether it has agreed to grant aid to the Spaddagh-Ballyhaunis water scheme and, if so, when payment will occur."[31] There are officials who will say that some deputies deliberately create the impression among their constituents that their intervention is necessary or helpful. Even representatives who resent this type of activity recognize that they must engage in it to survive.

This preoccupation with minor administrative matters and personal cases on behalf of constituents makes the representative a factor in administration and might be seen as the obverse of his or her comparative torpor in other parliamentary roles. The result, in the view of Barry Desmond, Labour Party whip, is that "Dáil Éireann is ... to many observers a sleepy middle class, quasi-professional, male dominated, conservatively deliberative, poorly attended debating assembly. Deputies play less and less a role in the formulation and enactment of legislation and more and more occupy their time as political favour peddlars, consumer representatives, and clerical messenger boys on behalf of constituents."[32]

VI

The Irish parliamentary representative, we have argued, is more a factor in administration and a "consumer representative" than a legislator. However, it is important to note that the Constitution as interpreted by those brought up upon traditional constitutional theory does not recognize this. Mr. Justice Budd in the *O'Donovan* case declared: "Most important duties are positively assigned to Deputies by the Constitution, the paramount duty being that of making laws for the country. ... It will be found again, however, that the Constitution does not anywhere in the Articles relating to the functions of Deputies recognize or sanction their intervention in administrative affairs."[33] The welfare state creates the opportunities and the need for this type of activity. What might be doubted is whether the parliamentary representative should perform it, or at least the more routine elements in it. Yet, rightly or wrongly, it might well be that, as the citizen sees it, the representative engaged in these activities is performing "an indispensable function which no other political unit or device can perform so well."[34] Nor does it follow that representatives would give it up if they were no longer forced by the election system to do it. This kind of activity by public persons and this kind of relationship between them and their clients are deeply rooted in Irish experience. For generations, Irish people saw that to get the benefits that public authorities bestow, the help of a man with connections and influence was necessary. All that democracy has meant is that such a person has been laid on officially, as it were, and is now no longer a master but a servant.

What does not follow is that to perform service functions for constituents necessarily precludes representatives from playing a more active part in the formation and scrutiny of policy. Adequately paid representatives with access to appropriate facilities in a properly organized Oireachtas ought to be able to do both, as many parliamentary representatives in other democratic countries do. The three factors that most inhibit the development of the potential of the Oireachtas are, as we have argued, the view of all political leaders when in government that they must have a monopoly of initiative, the practice of strictly competitive politics in dealing with parliamentary business, and the acceptance by most members of the present meagre role of the Oireachtas in the political system.

PART IV

THE ADMINISTRATION OF
PUBLIC POLICY

TWELVE

The Pattern of Public Administration

By the end of the nineteenth century, the United Kingdom of Great Britain and Ireland had an up-to-date and integrated public administration. The process of constructing it had been one not only of modernization but of democratization as well. It was based upon the principle that there should be two systems of government—central government and local government. The former would be responsible to parliament by means of ministers controlling departments manned by a professional career civil service. The latter would be a subordinate system, ultimately controlled by parliament, which governed its structure and gave it its tasks, but administered by locally elected councils. Almost all public business was, in principle, to be subsumed within one or the other of these two systems. The only exceptions were functions of a quasi-judicial nature or activities, such as the recruitment of civil servants, deemed to need insulating from political nepotism. Functions such as these—and they were thought to be quite few—were allocated to independent boards or commissions.

Irish administration as part of the United Kingdom system was as far as possible moulded into this pattern, although it was always recognized that in some respects the island had perforce to be treated differently. Until the beginning of the nineteenth century, Ireland had been a separate kingdom with its own political, administrative, and judicial institutions. Because of this, because of the security needs of imperial rule, and because British governments tended to be more paternalistic towards Ireland than towards other regions of the United Kingdom, the country was treated to some extent as a special case, in terms of both the allocation of government functions and administrative structure and judiciary: a measure of decentralization was deemed both necessary and convenient.

After the Union, when Ireland became an integral part of the United

Kingdom, some Irish departments were merged with their British equivalents, but others were not. In the course of the century, some British departments acquired new duties in respect of Ireland; in other cases, purely Irish departments or offices were set up, some headed by ministers, others by appointed boards or commissions. R. B. McDowell summed up the situation:

It is apparent from a cursory glance at Irish administrative history in the nineteenth century that there was a strong tendency to tackle newly-appreciated problems on simple *ad hoc* lines, which often meant the creation of a new department with little regard for the general structure. Though functions were from time to time transferred between departments, no attempt was made to plan systematically the distribution of duties between all the departments, British and Irish, functioning in Ireland, nor were the arrangements for controlling and [coordinating] their activities adequate.[1]

Indeed, by the end of the century, when the state began to intervene on a more massive scale and when, because of the Home Rule movement, there was a desire to associate Irish people more closely with the administration of their own public services, there was a marked increase in the number and variety of organizations administering them. Ireland, it was said at the end of the century, had as many boards as would make her coffin.

The control of the Chief Secretary (a sort of Minister for Irish Affairs) over the various offices varied considerably. In respect of at least one department, the Department of Agriculture and Technical Instruction, it was very tenuous indeed, since the Chief Secretary was intended to be but a figurehead and that department had its own junior minister. Tidy-minded colonial administrators with experience in India, like J. W. Ridgeway, under-secretary from 1887 to 1893, and Lord McDonnell, who held the same office from 1902 to 1908, fretted at the lack of overall control they were able to exercise, owing to the institution of semi-independent boards, on the one hand, and the interference of the British Treasury, on the other. It should be noted, however, that although the emerging development and welfare services were in a variety of hands, the basic essentials of law and order were very firmly and directly controlled by "the Castle," which, by and large, was the center of influence and patronage.* Moreover, the scale of the administration was so modest, Dublin so small and compact, and the senior officials so homogeneous and used to meeting one another at their clubs that, as

* Dublin Castle was the centre of the Irish administration. The office of the Chief Secretary was there, and it was the headquarters of the police and of offices dealing with justice and home affairs.

McDowell recalls, George Wyndham, Chief Secretary from 1900 to 1905, found that the government of Ireland was "conducted only by continuous conversation."[2]

Even if Ireland, being an "underdeveloped" region, qualified for paternal treatment, the local government system was in most respects the same as that evolved in Great Britain itself and was democratized by the same stages. The structure of authorities and the allocation of functions between the central and local governments were almost identical to the British. The basic local government services in Ireland, as in Great Britain, were roads, the environmental health services ("public health" and the "sanitary services," as they were called), and the relief of the poor, including the provision of medical services. But in Ireland, unlike Great Britain, a combination of paternalistic attitudes and a desire to ensure military security resulted in the police being nationalized and education largely so. Furthermore, in Ireland at the end of the nineteenth century, the development of agriculture and the resuscitation of the poorest rural areas were both central services, though administered by or with the advice of boards on which Irishmen sat rather than by standard departments headed by civil servants answering directly to the Chief Secretary or some other minister.[3]

Although Ireland was something of a special case in regard to both administrative structure and functions, the same could not be said of the public service, at least from the time of the civil service reforms of the third quarter of the nineteenth century onwards. The development of a civil service divided into distinct classes common to all departments, mostly appointed by a competitive examination set on ordinary school or university subjects and advanced by bureaucratic promotion procedures, occurred in both Ireland and Great Britain. Since Irish educational standards were approximately the same as British, Irishmen could and did join the civil service in large numbers and served both in Ireland and in Great Britain. Nor were they barred from the higher posts. True, it was a standing complaint that the Treasury was niggardly in the number of "first division" (that is, top administrative cadre) posts they authorized for Irish departments, but those that did exist, together with other senior posts, were likely to be occupied by Irishmen. In an analysis of the forty-eight most senior civil servants in 1914, McDowell points out that they were "overwhelmingly Irish," only ten of them having come from across the Channel. On the other hand, twenty-eight of them were Protestants and twenty were Catholics, a manifestation of the favourable social and economic position of the Protestant community and yet at the same time evidence of the fact that it was far from a monopoly.[4]

It will readily be seen from all this that political independence for

Ireland did not precipitate the problems that later beset many of the states of Asia and Africa as they emerged to independence: "Ireland inherited a complete apparatus of government, both central and local,"[5] with its own public service, which had a sure source of recruits from well-established secondary schools and universities. In the formative period of these institutions, during the Union, they were inevitably closely assimilated into the emerging British system and in essentials were similar to the British pattern. Independence, though important politically, did not much affect the well-established and powerful departments such as those dealing with local government, agriculture, and the collection of taxes; much administration continued to be conducted as previously. At independence only the messy pattern of central authorities contrasted sharply with the position in Great Britain, but the new government saw to that at once.

II

In a notice dated January 19, 1922, the Provisional Government announced that the business of the new state would for the moment be carried on by nine departments, which would incorporate the various existing departments, boards, and other offices of the previous regime. "It will be obvious," the notice stated, "that under the altered circumstances certain of the [existing] departments . . . will be no longer required." This presaged a drastic reduction of the jungle to uniformity, which was accomplished to a large extent by the Ministers and Secretaries Act (1924), section 1 of which decreed:

There shall be established in Saorstát Éireann the several Departments of State specified and named in the eleven following sub-paragraphs, amongst which the administration and business of the public services in Saorstát Éireann shall be distributed as in the said sub-paragraphs . . . and each of which said Departments and the powers, duties and functions thereof shall be assigned to and administered by the Minister hereinafter named as head thereof.

All at once, it seemed, Irish administration was forced into a neat dichotomy. On the one hand was a central administration subdivided into ministerial departments. On the other was a system of local authorities subordinate and answerable to the Oireachtas through the Minister for Local Government and Public Health and other ministers but administering their services under the direction and control of locally elected representatives. This was not to last for long, however. Within five years, the first of a collection of boards and commissions had emerged, the prolific growth of which has been a feature of modern Irish government. A Civil Service Commission to examine candidates and recruits to the service, insulated from direct ministerial control on the British pattern, was perhaps to be expected: the senior civil servants, themselves products of the British system, certainly thought so. In 1927, four "state-sponsored bodies," as they later came to be called, were created. As T. J. Barrington pointed out, these four illustrate the "diverse origins" of this type of public authority.[6]

The assigning of the ownership and control of the generation of electricity to a public corporation, the Electricity Supply Board, was not at all strange, for it was universally agreed in the British Isles that "the Civil Service was not recruited for the purpose of running business undertakings like this."[7] The Agricultural Credit Corporation was set up to supply capital to farmers who could not get it from the banks. The Dairy Disposal Company was a rescue operation to save a number of creameries. The formation of the Medical Registration Council to control entry to the profession followed a well-established practice in the United Kingdom. These were the first of many such bodies set up to carry out an ever widening range of activities embracing not only so-called business undertakings but also increasingly diverse regulatory, social service, and developmental functions. The generic name "state-sponsored bodies" gradually became common usage (replacing the earlier "semi-state bodies"), but there is no precise definition of this term. By the early 1950s, their staffs outnumbered the civil service; by the early 1960s, they were more numerous than the staffs of local authorities as well.

The staffs of the civil service, local authorities, and the state-sponsored bodies constitute what is often called the "public service." Table 12.1 illustrates the growth of this service and its constituent parts. These three types of public authority, however, do not exhaust the variety of public bodies, nor do their staffs include all who are or might be considered to be public servants. Substantial judicial and quasi-judicial functions are carried out by persons appointed by, and perhaps connected with, the central administration. Likewise, many advisory bodies are attached both to central and to local government, and some of these might in practice acquire *de facto* administrative functions by reason of the fact that, their advice being regularly followed, they come to be the decision-making bodies in their areas of competence. Sizeable bodies of people ordinarily and rightly thought of as public servants but not as part of the "public service" as previously defined include the defence forces, numbering about sixteen thousand; the Gardaí (police), of whom there were about nine thousand in the late 1970s; and some thirty-eight thousand national schoolteachers.

The political role of the defence forces and the Gardaí and their rela-

TABLE 12.1

Employment in the Public Service, 1940–79

Category	1940	1947	1953	1969	1979
Public service employment:					
Civil service	25,387	28,832	33,299	34,400	52,000
Local authorities	57,300	49,365	55,739	50,600	35,000[a,b]
State-sponsored bodies[a]	7,803	11,988	39,534	60,000	{37,000[b] Health Boards 63,000 State-sponsored bodies
TOTAL	90,490	90,185	128,572	145,000	187,000
Total labour force	1,307,000[a]	1,298,000	1,231,000	1,122,000	1,156,000
Public service employment as percentage of total labour force	6.9%	6.9%	10.4%	12.9%	16.2%

SOURCE: For 1940–53, T. P. Linehan, "Growth of the Civil Service," *Administration*, Vol. 2, No. 2 (Summer 1954), facing p. 72; National Industrial Economic Council, *Report on Full Employment*, Table 2; reports and information supplied by the Department of Local Government; and information supplied by the Central Statistics Office, the Department of Finance, and individual organizations. For 1969, *Report of the Public Services Organization Review Group, 1966–69*, pp. 17 and 18. For 1979, Institute of Public Administration, *Administration Year Book and Diary, 1980*.

[a] Estimated.

[b] Health services conducted by local authorities were transferred to Health Boards in 1970. Health Boards are statutory authorities that most closely resemble noncommercial state-sponsored bodies, but they include in their membership representatives of local authorities. They are often classified separately.

tionship with the government and civil servants were critical matters in the first days of the state (their subordination to the government of the day is now taken completely for granted). Despite the great continuity that was the major feature of the change of regime consequent upon the Treaty, the emerging leaders of the early 1920s faced tremendous tasks of state building in the midst of guerilla and terrorist activity. Security was their most urgent priority, and here they confronted typical problems of controlling the security forces and determining their role in the state and of their relationship with government and parliament.

The personnel of both the new army and the new police force (the Garda Síochána) were drawn largely from among the members of the Irish Republican Army who had followed Michael Collins into the pro-Treaty faction against De Valera and the anti-Treatyites. After initial dissatisfaction and difficulties leading to indiscipline in the newly recruited Gardaí in spring 1922 and a halfhearted officers' plot in the army in March 1924 that was easily dealt with, both forces settled down as loyal servants of the civilian government. Of course, their leaders were comrades of the ministers in the government, and their officers were not members of either a traditional or a natural ruling class or of a modernizing elite and so were not prey to the temptations that have since beset officers in so many new states in the second half of this century.

The Cumann na nGaedheal governments and their security forces, however, were not universally accepted in the country; nor, conversely, was De Valera, the former rebel turned constitutional politician. The critical test for and of the army and the Gardaí came in 1932, when De Valera took over. If there were tremors in the army at that time, they were very minor and there was no purge. Because of its composition and because of terrorist activity, members of the Garda Síochána in some areas had all too often found themselves combatting subversives, and the "Special Branch," the unit concerned with state security, was certainly pushed into the role of a political police by IRA activity. With De Valera's accession there were a few dismissals at the top and a few additions. The "Special Branch" became "a definite Fianna Fáil presence" in the Gardaí.[8] However, after a period of indecisiveness, the force settled down to serve the new government as efficiently as it had the old. The rubicon had been crossed.

Thus, neither army nor police became independent forces outside the control of the civil authorities or got involved in the struggle for political power. In the British tradition, their officers did not even conceive of themselves as having a right or duty, should the circumstances arise, to protect the state against the politicians. On the contrary, both accepted the legitimacy and were the servants of elected governments. The Garda Síochána, in contrast to its predecessor, the Royal Irish Constabulary, which had "combined the functions of a rural gendarmerie, a civil police and—outside of the larger towns—a rudimentary civil service,"[9] was an unarmed force whose role was very like that of the British police in Britain, though it was a unified national force. By the late 1930s, when the Fianna Fáil government had demonstrated that it was impartial in its administration of services and had shown that it, too, would not tolerate subversives (even former comrades), "the lot of the gardaí in rural areas became an infinitely more pleasant one,"[10] resembling at last that of the British "bobby." The role of the defence forces, apart from acting as a reserve force for internal security, was much less clear, for the state obviously could not go to war against its powerful neighbour and at the same time was protected against external third parties by the British military and naval shield.

Over the years, both forces tended to be ground down by civil service parsimony and ministerial indifference, which held up their acquisition of equipment and their ability to make use of new technology. The defence forces enjoyed some expansion during "the Emergency" (the term used in Ireland to describe the period of the Second World War in which Ireland was neutral) and were rejuvenated by service in UN peacekeeping forces from the mid-1950s onwards. The role of the Garda Síochána from the mid-1940s was so placid and uneventful that few noticed how little the force was permitted to develop and keep abreast of modern police methods. The Northern Ireland troubles from the late 1960s, with their spill-over effects in the Republic and the eventual appearance in Ireland of signs of the urban industrial society syndrome of drugs, violence, and hostility to the forces of law and order, found the Gardaí less well equipped to handle the problems posed than they might have been. For half a century at least, however, there has been no doubt about the position of either force as servants of the elected government of the day, no matter who composes that government.

III

The administrative machinery of the new state did not have to be created: what existed was taken over by nationalist rebels, most of whom were by no means revolutionaries looking to effect great social and political reforms. In any case, they had other, more urgent problems on their minds, and they worked in a pragmatic, common-sense way to construct the machinery of government as quickly and economically as they could. Their senior civil service advisers, steeped in the British tradition, saw no need for changes in administrative structures or practices. They looked for and got much friendly cooperation and avuncular advice from the Treasury, the very centre of British bureaucratic traditions.[11]

The administrative system established by these busy young national leaders and their conservative civil service advisers was not systematically reviewed for almost half a century, and even today it is not very different in essentials from what it was in the 1920s. It is hard to discern what, if any, were the principles on which new functions as they were assumed were allocated among departments and between departments, local authorities, and state-sponsored bodies. Growth and change were handled in a decidedly pragmatic way, at least until the 1970s. Many apparent inconsistencies and discrepancies can be explained only by history, contemporary reasons of political or administrative convenience, and an *ad hoc* approach by ministers whose manner was as pragmatic as that of Irish administrators in the nineteenth century. Until the late 1950s at least, there seemed to be no need to review the administration systematically. A Commission of Enquiry into the Civil Service in the 1930s heard little or no complaint and found no major faults. Certainly senior civil servants, from whom any initiative for change would necessarily have had to come, saw no need to pay much if any attention to organization. Over a century ago, Walter Bagehot observed that public servants as a profession tended to see the organization as "a grand and achieved result, not a working and changeable instrument." So, too, in 1969, the Public Services Organisation Review Group remarked that "resistance to change is found in all organisations" and noted that proposals in the late 1950s to reform the civil service had been successfully resisted by senior officers in various departments. The Review Group warned, "This could happen again but it must not."[12]

This is not to say that there were no changes or that general tendencies are not, in hindsight, discernible. It is true that the central administration grew only modestly, by the subdivision of existing departments for immediate political or administrative convenience when developments in health, welfare, and environmental services on the one hand, and in state planning and control of the economy on the other, seemed to call for it (see Fig. 13.1, p. 252). The local government system, however, underwent purposeful change in the first twenty years of the regime. It was modified from the late-Victorian tiered system of authorities whose activities were conducted by committees of elected councillors to a system that was predominantly county (including county borough) government, administered bureaucratically and subject to strong central surveillance and control. Increasing pressure on local authorities because of the inexorable demand for expensive services and higher standards that many had not the resources (either funds or skills) to meet, hastened this process and led also to the removal of some services from local government.

Just as the traditional local government system was found wanting, so too, eventually, was the central administration, though there was little if any overt criticism of it until the late 1950s. Evidently, the two systems, central and local, which in mid-Victorian times were expected to be able to subsume virtually all public administration, could not cope with some of the activities and services being undertaken by the state in the middle of the twentieth century. The result was a proliferation of state-sponsored bodies, a far more supple and adaptable administrative form, to cope with an ever growing variety of quasi-commercial, regulatory, social service, and developmental activities. Their creation was a haphazard business carried out with little systematic attention to the need to provide them with clear mandates or to spell out the exact extent of ministerial and parliamentary control.

Thus it is possible to see in the first half century of Irish administrative development both centralizing and decentralizing tendencies—the former in local government, the latter in the creation of state-sponsored bodies. However, in the decade from 1970, the propensity to centralize was without doubt the major feature of Irish public administration. There were two reasons for this: first, the exigencies of state planning and control of the economy and, second, the influence of the report of the Public Services Organisation Review Group, a major enquiry into public administration carried out between 1966 and 1969. The recommendations in that report and, perhaps as important, the principles on which the Review Group's recommendations were based, have had and continue to have a considerable impact on Irish public administration.

IV

The origins of the Public Services Organisation Review Group lay in a growing volume of dissatisfaction expressed in the early 1960s about the structure of the administration and the quality of administrators, especially those at the centre. The volumes of *Administration* (the journal of the Institute of Public Administration, first published in 1953) testify to an increasing awareness by at least a minority of public servants of a new and more positive role for departments and of the need for thoroughgoing reforms to enable them to fill this new role. A serious economic recession in the late 1950s brought home the size of the gap that had opened up between Ireland and the rest of Western Europe and precipitated change.

Following the publication in 1958 of *Economic Development* (a study of national development problems and opportunities) and the first five-year development programme, the 1960s in Ireland were a decade of unparalleled growth and rapid change. Events rapidly overtook an administration that was hardly adapted to cope with the tasks now suddenly demanded of it. The assumption by the government of responsibility for developing and directing the economy necessitated efficient policy-making units in departments, and these were evidently lacking.

More was needed than a reform of the civil service, however. A planned economy necessitated coordinated action between the various public authorities involved, yet not only did some central departments operate without much regard for others, but some of the bigger and more powerful state-sponsored bodies pursued very independent policies. The National Industrial Economic Council in its *Report on Economic Planning* in 1965 said that one of the main obstacles to effective planning lay in the public sector itself:

The need for steps to ensure that all departments of the public service and state enterprises play their full part in implementing the programme is reinforced by the priority given to the attainment of economic growth in the second programme. The implication of this development and the need for a realignment of policies and administrative machinery may not be completely realized as yet in some parts of the public service and in all the state enterprises.[13]

In 1966, the Minister for Finance appointed the Public Services Organisation Review Group. The Group's mandate was a wide one: "Having regard to the growing responsibilities of Government, to examine and report on the organisation of the Departments of State at the higher levels, including the appropriate distribution of functions as between both Departments themselves and Departments and other bodies." More than a decade after the Group reported, many of its recommendations had not been implemented and successive reports of the Public Service Advisory Council expressed "a sense of disappointment that so little interest, backed up by sustained commitment, is being expressed in public service reform."[14] Nevertheless, the impact of that report and particularly the great stress it laid upon the concept of a single public service strongly controlled from the centre has, for better or worse, been considerable.

The Devlin Group, as it came to be called after its chairman, Liam St. John Devlin, did not take long to diagnose two major faults in the administration—inadequate emphasis on policy making and lack of coordination within the public service as a whole. The bases of its proposals for wholesale change are summed up in the following passages from its report:

It is of the essence of government to act developmentally . . .

The first role of the public service is to serve the Government in a policy-advisory capacity, by sifting and recommending major policy alternatives, by collecting the public input, through appellate, consultative and research systems, and by assisting in the preparation of new legislation and in advice to Ministers. The second role of the public service is executive. Its task is to assist the Government in the running of the country under the rules laid down by the Oireachtas and to implement its policies. The question of what the Government should do itself and what it should delegate to others to do under a comprehensive code of instructions is central to our enquiry and has been one of the most intractable problems in the organisation of the public service. . . . The degree of discretion in executive action delegated to public servants varies widely. . . .

The evolutionary process which can be discerned is towards the loss of executive functions by local authorities and towards an increase in the executive functions of state-sponsored bodies. This is not, however, being done in a consciously planned manner. As a result of our investigation, we have been constrained to attempt a fundamental reappraisal and definition of roles and relationships.[15]

Among the many reforms proposed, three were fundamental. First, in each department a policy-making "Aireacht" comprising the Minister and top civil servants was to be hived off from "executive offices" administering the various services for which the department was responsible and controlled by "directors." The Aireacht would be the policy-making and review body for all executive units coming within the department's bailiwick, whether executive offices under their directors or "executive agencies" (that is, the noncommercial state-sponsored bodies) under their boards, and for the commercial state-sponsored bodies, which "must be effectively integrated in the public sector."[16] Second, the executive offices, though still part of their parent departments, were to have considerable legal authority devolved upon them. Ministers would no longer have direct responsibility for all executive action (or inaction); that responsibility would fall upon the directors. Third, all executive bodies would be controlled in a general way by their responsible ministers by means of four "coordinating systems"—finance, planning, organization, and personnel. At the departmental level, each Aireacht would include the heads of these "staff" units. At the level of the central administration as a whole, the Department of Finance would have overall control of finance and planning, and a projected new department, the Department of the Public Service, would be responsible for organization and personnel. "Through these functions, essential communications can be maintained throughout the public service and overall coordination of the service secured."[17] Clearly the Irish public administration was to be a tighter ship altogether.

The recommendations of the Devlin Group were wholesale and thorough. Perhaps also they were doctrinaire. By the mid-1970s, intellectual doubts were being expressed by a senior officer of the Public Service Department itself: "Some of the recommendations of the report . . . while having much managerial logic and combined wisdom as their basis, could, perhaps, be regarded as too technocratic and neat for their effective and immediate application to the democratic institutions and processes of our State."[18] Reviewing the Devlin Group's report a decade after it was published, Geoffrey MacKechnie saw it as a product of the optimistic 1960s, being based on two aspects of management and organization theory then very much in vogue that were associated with the economic progress of postwar years. The first was the systems concept: "At its zenith the new 'systems approach' was elevated by its proponents to the level of a superior philosophy and a means of integrating the social and physical sciences into a single elegant synthesis."[19] The second was the form of structure then generally reckoned to be appropriate to large-scale organizations, known as the federally decentralized or "General Motors" structure. "Both of these," in MacKechnie's view, "clearly influenced the thinking of the Review Group."[20] But within a decade, as he pointed out, the received wisdom of the 1960s was considerably discredited, particularly the stress on structural answers to organizational problems.[21] In any case, he argued, solutions that would suit large business corporations might not be appropriate for government departments: "The separation of policy making from the actual conduct of the administrative process is far from clear cut" in the public sector.[22]

Many of the major recommendations of the Devlin Group have not been implemented and some only partially. A Department of the Public Service, which was intended to be and in practice became the engine of Devlinesque change and the heart of the organization and personnel functions, was set up in 1973. The Aireacht concept was introduced into a handful of departments in the 1970s, but had little visible impact on their working practices or on the attitudes of the officers concerned. In any case, the concomitant creation of executive offices, which would have required changes in legislation to relieve ministers of responsibility and confer it upon the heads of the executive offices, was not carried out. The main impact of Devlin was in the increasing attention paid to recruitment, training, and executive development; in the introduction of modern management practices and techniques; and in the systematic introduction of the staff support systems. In addition, the Group's proposals for administrative appeals machinery bore fruit in the shape of an ombudsman (provided for by statute in 1980), and proposals for reviewing the effectiveness of public service activities were partly responsible for the creation in 1977 of the Joint Committee on State-Sponsored Bodies.

The failure to implement the core recommendations of the Devlin Group, despite the lip service paid to them by successive governments, was due not so much to intellectual doubts about the soundness of their theoretical foundations, such as those of MacKechnie, as to the lack of political will for reform and the resistance of public servants generally to the changes involved, particularly changes involving any loss of autonomy. In 1975, the Public Service Advisory Council reported that there was little hope of the major Devlin reforms being implemented "unless there is a clear lead from the top, from the individual ministers and the government."[23] Despite further declarations of support for reform by ministers, that lead was never forthcoming.

Even if it had been, it is doubtful how much could have been achieved in the face of the hostility of senior public servants, particularly higher civil servants. Looking back over his period as chairman of the Public Service Advisory Council, Patrick Lynch, himself a distinguished public servant, was quite specific about the cause of failure: "We achieved nothing whatever in promoting reform because of the absolute resistance to change among senior civil servants."[24] Certainly, many resisted the "coordination" inherent in the four staff functions, at least insofar as it seemed to mean more control over individual departments, just as they did in the 1960s during the period of the Second Programme for Economic Expansion.

Scepticism about the viability of a more centralized central administration was increased by the failure of programme budgeting, introduced in a few departments in the early 1970s only to be quietly dropped later. In the state-sponsored bodies, not only scepticism but hostility was aroused by attempts to establish "consistency" between the salaries of senior officers in the various branches of the public service by means of another Devlin committee (the Review Body on Higher Remuneration in the Public Sector) and to control public service salary increases generally by placing them under the surveillance of the Department of the Public Service.

By 1980, attempts to integrate state-sponsored bodies, in particular the public enterprise group, were being strongly resisted and fiercely attacked. A study group with a prestigious membership, appointed by the National Economic and Social Council to examine measures to mobilize more fully enterprise in the public sector, noted that "the concept of the unity of the public sector has begun to be interpreted more rigidly and narrowly than in the past. There is an increasing emphasis on centralised decision-making within the public sector and a tendency towards greater central control of the activities of state-sponsored bodies." The group condemned this tendency: "In our view these efforts to introduce uniformity throughout the whole of the public sector are seriously impeding enterprise in the state-sponsored bodies." In the study group's opinion, "changes are urgently required in some official attitudes within Government Departments towards state-sponsored bodies and how they operate. We are concerned about the danger of an inexorable growth of unnecessary administrative control."[25] Asked to comment on the group's views, a number of government departments returned trenchant replies.[26] It is obvious that there were serious differences of view at the top levels of the public service.

Even though the major reforms proposed by the Devlin committee were not by any means systematically carried through, the 1970s were marked by increasing centralization of administration. As we shall see, the same tendency occurred in local government also. The Devlin Group, it seems, had their disciples as well as their critics, and the influence of their report, for all the failure fully to implement its major recommendations, was considerable. At the beginning of the 1980s, the state of the public service could best be described as unsettled.

THIRTEEN

The Central Administration and the Civil Service

The basic statute governing Irish public administration is the Ministers and Secretaries Act (1924). This act did two important things. First, it provided the legal basis for the structure and organization of the central administration by designating the extent of ministerial authority in respect of the performance of public functions. Second, it established the departments of state and allocated public business between them. Subsequent amending acts and orders have made adjustments without seriously altering the fundamentals of the system then established.

The Irish Free State Constitution provided for cabinet government and required ministers to be responsible to Dáil Éireann. The Ministers and Secretaries Act followed it up by making precise the nature and extent of that responsibility:

Each of the Ministers, heads of the respective Departments of State mentioned in section 1 of this Act, shall be a corporation sole under his style or name aforesaid . . . and shall have perpetual succession and an official seal (which shall be officially and judicially noticed), and may sue and (subject to the fiat of the Attorney General having been in each case first granted) be sued under his style or name aforesaid, and may acquire, hold and dispose of land for the purposes of the functions, powers or duties of the Department of State of which he is the head or of any branch thereof.

In essence, the minister *is* the department and normally all the department's acts are reckoned to be his. In practice, of course, this is not possible and, although he is not empowered by statute to do so, he must delegate. The legal and political responsibility of the minister is, nevertheless, complete. "The official knows that the minister will stand over his action vis-à-vis public and parliament if this action is in conformity with his general views. The Minister knows that the official in taking any action will always be conscious that the Minister may . . . be challenged."[1] Both the manner in which public business is conducted and the whole character of the civil service are governed by the relationships implied in this act.

This concept of ministerial responsibility with the particular minister–civil servant relationships and the basic characteristics of the civil service that flow from it was not new to Ireland by any means. For the former British civil service, which was simply taken over, life went on much as before. The final *Report of the Commission of Enquiry into the Civil Service, 1932–35* describes the impact on the service of the change to independence:

The passing of the State services into the control of a native Government, however revolutionary it may have been as a step in the political development of the nation, entailed, broadly speaking, no immediate disturbance of any fundamental kind in the daily work of the average Civil Servant. Under changed masters the same main tasks of administration continued to be performed by the same staffs on the same general lines of organization and procedure.[2]

The civil service had in fact already prepared for the change, for under the abortive Government of Ireland Act (1920) provision had been made for dividing the personnel of the various Irish offices between Dublin and Belfast, the capital of the new Northern Ireland. During 1921, a committee of civil servants representing the Civil Service Associations (the staff side) and the state (the official side) had been at work on this plan. In the event, men working in the south who had worried whether they would (or would not) be transferred to Belfast under that arrangement found that they could decide for themselves. Those few (a hundred or so) who wished to go north did so and joined the new Northern Ireland administration. Swiftly, something like an iron curtain came down between the two administrations, partly perhaps because many of the Northern Ireland senior officers were not Irish or had no Dublin connections, but also because at the political level the atmosphere was glacial. There had to be some contacts, of course, but they were mainly confined to technical matters and technical men for many years.

Under the Treaty the future tenure and conditions of employment of the officers transferred to the service of the Irish Free State were protected, and generous provision was made for compensation in the event of retirement. It is no wonder, therefore, that the Treaty was welcomed with relief by most civil servants. The number who transferred to the service of the new state was about 21,000 out of a total of 28,000 who were then working in Ireland. Of these 21,000, fewer than 1,000 decided to retire prematurely under favourable conditions in the first few years. To what was thus virtually a complete service were added 131 people who had served in the Dáil administration service and 88 who had formerly been in the civil service but who had resigned or been dismissed because of nationalist sympathies or activities. In addition, 64 officers holding posts in departments in Great Britain were invited to transfer and returned to Ireland in the next year or two.

Naturally, there were unrivalled opportunities for advancement, for each of the new departments had to be provided with a full headquarters organization and top management. In fact, the process was remarkably free from nepotism, and there was no great scramble for place, owing largely to the presence in the Department of Finance, which controlled personnel, of austere senior officers strongly imbued with British civil service traditions, among them officials lent to the new Irish government by its erstwhile foes. An analysis of the careers of the thirty-four secretaries and assistant secretaries or their equivalents in the new departments reveals that twenty-one of them were transferred officers, two from departments in London; five were former members of the Dáil administration; and five, including two more Dáil civil servants, were former civil servants who were reinstated. Only three came from elsewhere, two from the army to the Garda Síochána and one, a barrister, brought in from outside. Thus, twenty-six out of thirty-four of the top men were career civil servants, though a few of them suddenly found themselves considerably higher in the hierarchy than they could otherwise have expected to be. Among those who retired, there might well have been a few who were in effect forced to retire, but there was nothing in the nature of a purge. The smoothness of the operation and the overwhelming sense of continuity led to the central administration's being carried over into the new regime to a great extent unaltered and in working order.

II

The departments in which civil servants found themselves, though new creations, were in most cases composed of existing units transferred *en bloc* as going concerns. The Ministers and Secretaries Act finalized the *ad hoc* reduction and grouping made in 1922 of the forty-seven departments, boards, or other offices that existed before the Treaty and created eleven departments including a Department of the President of the Executive Council (Prime Minister). The circumstances of the time precluded any comprehensive survey of the functions of the state and their allocation to administrative organizations, central or local, on some overall scheme based on administrative principles. Introducing the bill, W. T. Cosgrave, President of the Executive Council, told the Dáil: "As the House well knows, there were during the British administration, quite a multiplicity of Boards and Statutory bodies, and during the last two years it has not been possible to survey the whole field and to see how better we may construct the Government machine."[3] With few exceptions, the existing offices as they stood were accepted and were combined into common-sense groupings. To a large extent, the offices of the previous administration fell into natural enough groups by reason of either proximity of purpose or historic connections. In addition, two departments had to be created, for under the Union there had been no call for them. These were Finance and External Affairs. The latter was essentially a continuation of the Dáil government department that had consisted of a minister and a number of diplomatic representatives, many of whom had been stationed in Paris, where they had sought recognition from the powers negotiating the peace treaty after the First World War.

The allocation of functions made in 1924 was not systematically reviewed until the Devlin Group's enquiry in the late 1960s. Over the years, a few new departments were created, and a few transfers of divisions from one department to another were made. In most cases, the creation of new departments resulted from the increase in state functions: first, the growth of the social services after the Second World War, when the Department of Local Government and Public Health was split up and three separate departments—Local Government, Health, and Social Welfare—emerged; second, the assumption by the state of responsibility for the planning, development, and control of the economy, which led to the hiving off from the Department of Industry and Commerce of Transport and Power (in 1959) and Labour (in 1966). The Devlin Group's proposal to reallocate government functions to fourteen departments (there were sixteen at the time) was not followed, but its influence can be seen in the removal of responsibility for personnel matters from the Department of Finance and the creation of a Department of the Public Service in 1973.

Despite the recommendations of the Devlin Group, subsequent changes were to a great extent governed by considerations of political convenience or advantage. The creation (in 1977) and winding up (in 1979) of the Department of Economic Planning and Development illustrate this well. On the other hand, the creation of Departments of Energy and Fisheries in 1979 probably reflected the growing importance of these matters, as much as it did political convenience. The Public Service Advisory Council was right in remarking in its sixth report that in the

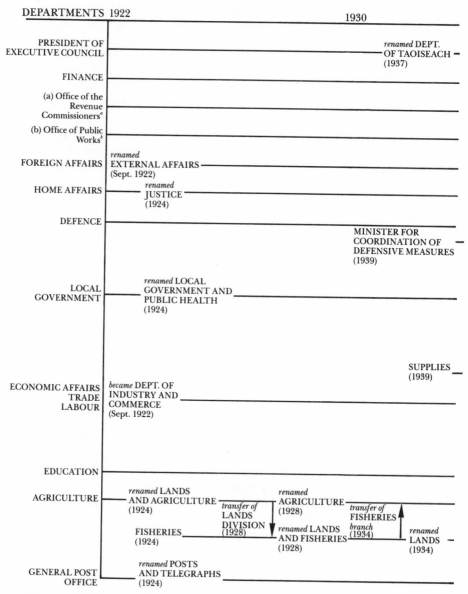

DEPARTMENTS 1922   1930

PRESIDENT OF EXECUTIVE COUNCIL	*renamed* DEPT. OF TAOISEACH (1937)
FINANCE	
(a) Office of the Revenue Commissioners[a]	
(b) Office of Public Works[b]	
FOREIGN AFFAIRS	*renamed* EXTERNAL AFFAIRS (Sept. 1922)
HOME AFFAIRS	*renamed* JUSTICE (1924)
DEFENCE	MINISTER FOR COORDINATION OF DEFENSIVE MEASURES (1939)
LOCAL GOVERNMENT	*renamed* LOCAL GOVERNMENT AND PUBLIC HEALTH (1924)
	SUPPLIES (1939)
ECONOMIC AFFAIRS TRADE LABOUR	*became* DEPT. OF INDUSTRY AND COMMERCE (Sept. 1922)
EDUCATION	
AGRICULTURE	*renamed* LANDS AND AGRICULTURE (1924); *transfer of* LANDS DIVISION (1928); *renamed* AGRICULTURE (1928)
	FISHERIES (1924); *renamed* LANDS AND FISHERIES (1928); *transfer of* FISHERIES branch (1934); *renamed* LANDS (1934)
GENERAL POST OFFICE	*renamed* POSTS AND TELEGRAPHS (1924)

[a]The Revenue Commissioners operate under the general control of the Minister for Finance.
[b]The Parliamentary Secretary to the Minister for Finance acts as a Minister for Public Works.

Fɪɢ. 13.1. Development of the Central Administration in Ireland, 1922–80

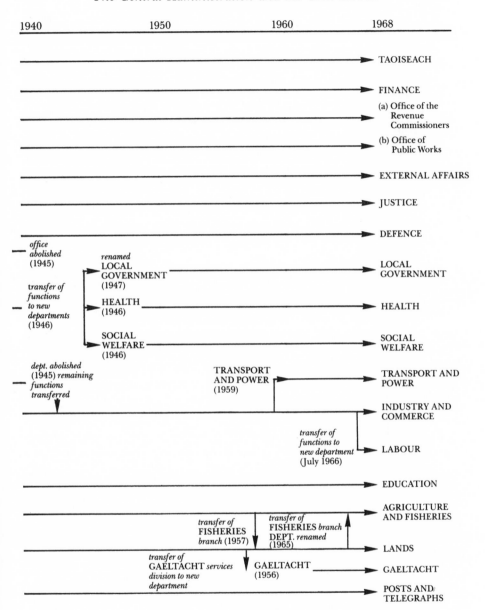

1940   1950   1960   1968

TAOISEACH

FINANCE

(a) Office of the Revenue Commissioners

(b) Office of Public Works

EXTERNAL AFFAIRS

JUSTICE

DEFENCE

office abolished (1945)

transfer of functions to new departments (1946)

renamed LOCAL GOVERNMENT (1947) — LOCAL GOVERNMENT

HEALTH (1946) — HEALTH

SOCIAL WELFARE (1946) — SOCIAL WELFARE

dept. abolished (1945) remaining functions transferred

TRANSPORT AND POWER (1959) — TRANSPORT AND POWER

INDUSTRY AND COMMERCE

transfer of functions to new department (July 1966) — LABOUR

EDUCATION

AGRICULTURE AND FISHERIES

transfer of FISHERIES *branch* (1957)

transfer of FISHERIES *branch* DEPT. *renamed* (1965)

LANDS

transfer of GAELTACHT *services division to new department*

GAELTACHT (1956) — GAELTACHT

POSTS AND TELEGRAPHS

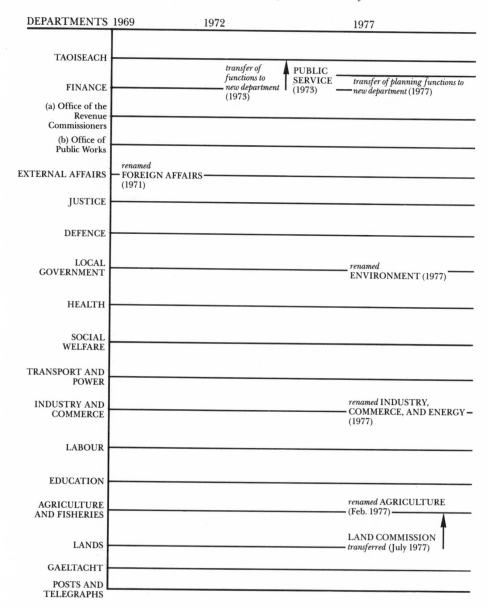

Fɪɢ. 13.1 (*continued*)

	1978	1979	1980

TAOISEACH

PUBLIC SERVICE

FINANCE

ECONOMIC PLANNING AND DEVELOPMENT —— *functions reallocated* (Dec. 1979)

(a) Office of the Revenue Commissioners

(b) Office of Public Works

FOREIGN AFFAIRS

JUSTICE

DEFENCE

ENVIRONMENT

HEALTH

SOCIAL WELFARE

renamed TOURISM AND TRANSPORT (1978) — *renamed* TRANSPORT; *transfer of* TOURISM (Dec. 1979) — TRANSPORT

transfer of ENERGY *to new department* (Dec. 1979) — INDUSTRY, COMMERCE, AND TOURISM

ENERGY

LABOUR

EDUCATION

AGRICULTURE

transfer of FISHERIES *branch* DEPT. *renamed* (July 1977) — *renamed* FISHERIES AND FORESTRY (1978) — FISHERIES AND FORESTRY

GAELTACHT

POSTS AND TELEGRAPHS

matter of distribution of functions to ministers, Ireland is no different from other countries: "functional logic is not the major determining factor." Rather, apart from some basic functional requirements, changes of this sort depend "on political considerations and on the management style of the Prime Minister."[4] (For details of the development of the central administration, see Fig. 13.1.)

III

The assumption of new duties and the creation of new departments as state services expanded inevitably brought an increase in the number of civil servants. In 1980, the size of the civil service was nearly three times what it had been at the inception of the state. Big increases took place in two main phases, as Table 13.1 shows. The number of civil servants did

TABLE 13.1

Number and Percentage of Civil Servants, by Grade, 1922–80

Group	1922	1934	1940	1947
Administrative and executive		1,740 (8.1%)	2,217 (8.7%)	2,303 (8.0%)
Clerical, subclerical, and typing grades		4,596 (21.3)	6,562 (25.9)	7,480 (25.9)
Inspectorate		549 (2.6)	774 (3.0)	1,094 (3.8)
Professional, scientific, and technical		1,026 (4.8)	1,111 (4.4)	1,296 (4.5)
Supervisory, minor, and manipulative[b]		10,337 (48.0)	10,724 (42.3)	11,516 (39.9)
Messengers, cleaners, etc.		1,370 (6.4)	1,657 (6.5)	1,883 (6.6)
Industrial staff		1,904 (8.8)	2,342 (9.2)	3,260 (11.3)
TOTAL	21,035	21,522 (100%)	25,387 (100%)	28,832 (100%)

Group	1953	1968	1980
Administrative and executive	2,715 (8.2%)	3,409 (9.4%)	6,275 (10.4%)
Clerical, subclerical, and typing grades	7,826 (23.5)	8,278 (22.7)	15,119 (25.0)
Inspectorate	758 (2.3)[a]	1,304 (3.6)	3,144 (5.2)
Professional, scientific, and technical	2,076 (6.2)[a]	2,909 (8.0)	5,803 (9.6)
Supervisory, minor, and manipulative[b]	13,186 (39.6)	15,822 (43.5)	20,832 (34.4)
Messengers, cleaners, etc.	2,137 (6.4)	1,967 (5.4)	2,649 (4.4)
Industrial staff	4,601 (13.8)	2,699 (7.4)	6,641 (11.0)
TOTAL	33,299 (100%)	36,388 (100%)	60,463 (100%)

SOURCE: *Return of Staff in Government Departments* (Stationery Office, Dublin, 1924); T. P. Linehan, "Growth of the Civil Service," *Administration*, Vol. 2, No. 2 (Summer 1954), facing p. 72; information supplied by the Central Statistics Office, the Department of Finance, and the Department of the Public Service.

[a] In 1953, all persons with professional qualifications were classed in the professional, scientific, and technical group.

[b] Mainly in the Department of Posts and Telegraphs.

not increase at all in the first decade of the state's existence. That was a period of conservative governments and austere, even parsimonious, senior civil servants. During the next twenty years, there was continuous and steady growth as governments began to play a more active role in development and as the social services developed. By 1953, the number of civil servants had increased by 55 per cent. During the 1950s and 1960s, a period when the state added considerably to its responsibilities, there was only a modest increase (less than 10 per cent by 1968). The succeeding decade was very different. Perhaps as part of its response to the criticisms heard in the 1960s of the inadequacy of the service and the need for more "coordination," there was a rapid growth. Between the late 1960s and the end of the 1970s, the civil service increased in size by two-thirds.

The ever increasing need to coordinate and control a widening range of functions led to the addition of new departments and new divisions in existing departments and necessitated big increases in the numbers of administrators and their support staffs. The number of the very top ranks (assistant secretaries, secretaries, and their equivalents) more than quadrupled in the half-century from the foundation of the state. In the early 1920s, there were rather more than 30; in 1939, about 40; in 1950, about 50; in 1965, about 65; and in the fifteen years between then and 1980, the number doubled to about 130. The size of office staff has also nearly doubled in the same period, as Table 13.1 indicates.

Table 13.2, which shows the numbers and proportions of civil servants in the various activities of government, reveals that in 1980, as at the beginning of the state's existence, the great proportion of civil servants were employed either in the postal and telecommunications services or in providing basic services such as justice, defence, and public works, and in the collection of taxes and customs duties, all services administered directly by the central government. However, these groups have declined as a proportion of the whole as the control and administration of economic and social services have necessitated more manpower. These staffs, it must be remembered, are mostly involved in the oversight and control of economic and social services that are largely provided by the burgeoning staffs of other public authorities—local authorities, health boards, and state-sponsored bodies, as Table 12.1 (see p. 238) shows.

IV

The service that emerged in the 1920s was a British-type civil service in miniature, and in many respects it remains so. This continuity over more than half a century is clearly to be seen in the structure of the service.

TABLE 13.2

Number and Percentage of Civil Servants Engaged in the Provision of State Services, 1922–80

Sector[a]	April 1, 1922[b]	October 1, 1923[c]	1950	1965	1980
Basic services	3,163 (15.0%)	4,666 (21.0%)	5,705 (22.8%)	8,870 (25.8)	14,707 (24.3%)
Postal and telecommunications services	13,518 (64.3)	13,418 (60.2)	10,849 (43.4)	15,225 (44.3)	24,955 (41.3)
Economic services	3,388 (16.1)	3,180 (14.3)	4,652 (18.6)	6,158 (17.9)	12,852 (21.3)
Social services	904 (4.3)	891 (4.0)	3,090 (12.4)	3,278 (9.5)	6,063 (10.0)
Other	62 (0.3)	114 (0.5)	688 (2.8)	830 (2.5)	1,886 (3.1)
TOTAL	21,035 (100%)	22,269 (100%)	24,984 (100%)	34,361 (100%)	60,463 (100%)

SOURCE: For 1922 and 1923, *Return of Staff in Government Departments* (Stationery Office, Dublin, 1924). For 1950, 1965, and 1980, information supplied by the Central Statistics Office, the Department of Finance, and the Department of the Public Service.

[a] Basic services: Justice, Defence, Foreign Affairs, Taoiseach, Public Works, Revenue. Postal and Telecommunications Services: Post and Telegraphs. Economic Services: Finance; Public Service; Industry, Commerce, and Tourism; Transport; Energy; Agriculture; Fisheries and Forestry. Social Services: Education, Health, Environment, Social Welfare, Gaeltacht. Other: President's Establishment, Oireachtas, Comptroller and Auditor General, Central Statistics Office, State Laboratory, Civil Service Commission, Stationery Office, Valuation and Ordinance Survey, Attorney General's Office, Law Reform, Director of Public Prosecutions.

[b] The date of the formal transfer of staff from British to Irish control.

[c] By October 1923, many of the new services necessitated by the establishment of the Irish Free State had been instituted.

At the top of each department there is a "secretary," the civil service head of the department who "is answerable to the Minister for every official action of every officer of his department."[5] He is the minister's chief adviser and, as the Devlin Report delicately put it, "the apex of the machine through which policy questions are formulated for ministerial consideration."[6] (As we observed in our analysis of policy making, the influence of senior civil servants is often likely to be greater than that statement suggests.) The secretary is also "responsible for the overall management of the Department."[7] The secretary's immediate subordinates are deputy secretaries and assistant secretaries, and below them are principal officers and assistant principals.

These top managers are at the head of what, following British terminology, are known as the general service classes, who are "recruited to perform the general duties of Departments from the routine clerical operations to the highest policy advisory and managerial work."[8] They are recruited at appropriate educational levels into what is for most of them a life-time career in one or another of the "classes"—clerical assistant, clerical, executive, and administrative. Fig. 13.2 shows the strong resemblance of the Irish structure to that of the British just after the First World War (and for long after).

This class system had its origins in Victorian Britain. In theory and originally to a great extent in practice also, each class performed work suited to the ability of the people in it; each was recruited directly from school or university; and once in a class an officer progressed up through that class. In Ireland, as in the United Kingdom, the concept of a class system was progressively modified:

There are still promotion groupings related to class and movement from one group to another involves either a competition conducted by the Civil Service Commissioners or acceptance by the Commissioners that the person concerned is qualified for appointment to the new position. However, in the general service, movement from the clerical to the executive class is now relatively unimpeded and all higher administrative posts are open to members of the Executive grades.[9]

Thus, "it is still possible to speak of the general service classes but, in practice, they are merging into a single class."[10]

In addition, in departments with specialized duties such as the Office of the Revenue Commissioners or the Department of Posts and Telegraphs, there are departmental classes, each in turn with many grades. In general, these classes and grades are related to one or another of the general service classes and grades, and promotion from them by competi-

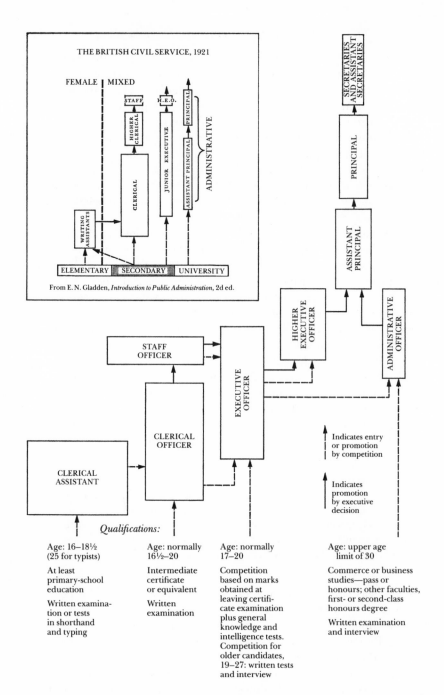

FIG. 13.2. Structure of the Civil Service in Ireland, General Service Grades, 1980

tion into the general service is possible. Thus, there exists the possibility for almost all of promotion from grade to grade and class to class, and there is considerable movement of this sort. In 1980, as the following tabulation shows, over half of the 1,998 executive officers had come into the grade by way of competitions confined to serving civil servants:

Executive Officers recruited from:	No.
School-leavers competition	721
Open adult competition	227
Confined competition	1,050

Likewise, at the top of the service, half of those holding the posts of secretary, deputy secretary, or assistant secretary had advanced through the executive grades (see Table 13.3). Finally, there are other specialist officers recruited to do jobs for which particular professional or technical qualifications are required. These are "professional," "scientific," or "technical" officers. Their numbers doubled in the decade up to 1980.

It will be seen from Fig. 13.2 that the higher posts, those of assistant principal and above, are appointed both from administrative officers (who might in turn have come from the executive officer grade) and from higher executive officers, who are the best of the executive officers, promoted on average after from four to six years in the grade. Administrative officers and higher executive officers thus form a pool from which higher officers are selected, and they perform the same type of duties, being interchangeable with each other.

TABLE 13.3

Mode of Entry to the Civil Service of Officers Holding the Rank of Secretary, Deputy Secretary, and Assistant Secretary in 1980

Mode of Entry	Secretaries[a]	Deputy secretaries	Assistant secretaries	Total
First appointed as administrative officer	1	—	10	11
First appointed in some other grade and advanced through administrative officer	13	6	27	46
Advanced through the executive stream	9	4	50	63
Advanced through other channels	3	1	5	9
TOTAL	26	11	92	129

SOURCE: Information supplied by the Department of the Public Service.

NOTE: The Department of Foreign Affairs has been omitted. In that department, these grades are interchangeable with the grades of ambassador and minister. In fact, most will have entered as third secretaries (that is, as graduates).

[a] Includes 2 posts with secretary status in the Department of the Taoiseach, 4 in the Department of Finance, 3 in the Office of the Revenue Commissioners, and 1 in the Office of Public Works.

This arrangement was one of the few major deviations from the British pattern. It was the result of the belief of the first establishment officers in the Department of Finance that the work in Ireland would continue to need comparatively few "first division" people, as they had been called in the British civil service, a point upon which the Treasury had always stood firm against the pressure of the heads of the Irish departments and offices. It was a mistaken belief, for it ignored the new need for senior management of a now entirely self-governing country, however small. It led to a situation where the top jobs were not only open to people recruited at secondary-school level but largely filled by them. In fact, because of the paucity of graduates coming forward from the universities to compete for administrative officer posts in the past, nine out of ten of posts from assistant principal upward were occupied by people recruited at secondary-school level. That is not to say that their education did in fact end at the secondary level; some of them obtained diplomas, degrees, and professional qualifications by evening study. However, this tendency for higher civil servants to have come into the service from school and not from university was clearly very important in influencing the character of the service and increased its needs in respect of education and training.

Surveying the civil service in the late 1960s, the Devlin Group obviously found its structure complicated and even confusing. One member, T. J. Barrington, had long before dubbed it an "elaborate contrivance," arguing that "the variation in the level of work passing through a Government department is not as great as the number of grades that handle it. Thus each grade tends to overlap the other . . . and indefensible lines of demarcation tend to be drawn between the grades."[11] At that time, indeed, there were no less than one thousand grades in the civil service as a whole, and even the comparatively few people above higher executive officer or its professional equivalent were divided into three hundred grades. Moreover, although the general classes were in theory available to serve in any department, there was not much mobility at higher levels and each department had tended to be a self-contained unit with most promotions made internally.

Because of this and because of the comparative lack of coordination, notwithstanding financial and personnel controls operated by the Department of Finance and later by its offshoot, the Department of the Public Service, the Devlin Group's "first impressions of the civil service tended towards the view that there is not one civil service but sixteen, that each department has its own service."[12] The Group commented on the difficulties in this situation of getting a free flow of talent to where it was most needed. This was, and is, made the more difficult by the protective policies of the service unions. "Barriers between organisations tend to impede the flow of the best talent to where it is most needed. . . . In the civil service, interdepartmental barriers are often as hard to surmount as the barriers between other bodies in the public service."[13] Following recommendations by the Devlin Group, the efforts of the Department of the Public Service to institute schemes of service-wide promotion, each of which involved protracted negotiations with the staff associations, had some impact on movement between departments up to the level of higher executive officer. Above that, there was "little or no headway" throughout the 1970s.[14] Consequently, there was "very little mobility between departments at higher levels."[15]

V

Although the civil service retained many of the structural features that it inherited, it was not to be expected that so Irish an organization would remain unaltered in character and *mores* for long. Some basic characteristics were, it is true, retained. Given the great continuity and the acceptance by politicians and public servants alike of the British cabinet system and the minister–civil servant relationships that went with it, and given also the high level of morality in public affairs in the British Isles, it was only natural that the civil service should remain an incorruptible, nonpartisan, and usually anonymous corps whose members, secure in their employment, considered themselves the servants of the legitimate government, whoever they may be. It was also natural that they should tend to conservative austerity with regard to the functions of the state and to their role in public business.

This was, in Barrington's words, "a formidable asset for the state," but, as he pointed out,

certain weaknesses were also inherited, particularly the lack of overall concern for the performance of the system as a whole, as distinct from the day-to-day operation. One of the maxims of the British civil service was "clear sight over short distances." This became very much the mark of the Irish civil service. Coupled with this was the tradition, reinforced by the bent of the Irish temperament, of being suspicious of any thinking that claimed to be systematic and concerned with the long-term.[16]

Writing in 1980 after a decade of reform, Barrington maintained that "these still remain, overall, significant criticisms that can be made of our civil service."[17]

Although the Irish temperament in this instance underpinned and perpetuated a characteristic of the service inherited from the United Kingdom, in respect of other characteristics it tended to modify the inheritance. Despite the fact that Ireland was to some extent assimilated to Great Britain culturally and enjoyed comparable types and levels of education, the social structure was always different and became more so after the Treaty. It was to be expected that Irish institutions would increasingly reflect Irish rather than British conditions.

To begin with, the British civil service like many European services had a distinctively upper-class tradition in its higher ranks, and its social tone in the early twentieth century was still rather superior. The administrative class was largely filled by graduates of Oxford and Cambridge, which, even after the First World War, continued to be overwhelmingly the preserves of the public schools and of the upper middle and upper classes. By reason of this background, by membership in their gentlemen's clubs, and by the socialization process they underwent in their first years in the civil service, members of the administrative class were well endowed to become part of the "establishment" and as a body to form a well-defined subgroup within it. The tone of the British service, especially its gentlemanly "generalist" tradition, was set by this group and continued to be so until well after the Second World War.

Notwithstanding the distance and differences between Dublin and London, these values had applied in Dublin also. And although higher civil servants in Ireland before the Treaty were by no means so uniform in origin and training, they too could be said to be part of a local "establishment." McDowell's analysis of the forty-eight top officials in 1914 shows them to have been middle and upper middle class, the sons of professional men and lesser landowners; at least forty-three of them had had university—mainly Dublin (Trinity College), Oxford, or Cambridge—or professional education and training.

This situation could hardly continue in the new Ireland. Independence marked formally the end of the dominance of the Anglo-Irish "establishment." Although the independence movement had been inspired and led largely by middle-class people, they were on the whole not people aspiring to higher social position, and they led a movement that cut across the class lines of the lower strata of society. The character of the newly independent community reflected this. It was bourgeois and republican, and although the class lines that developed later are hard to trace, it is clear enough at least that there was no aristocracy and no "establishment." This was bound to be reflected in the civil service, which soon became peopled at the top levels by officers who, though middle class, were often lower—rather than upper—middle class and by no means out of the same mould as their equivalents in the British service. The higher civil service at once ceased to be an upper-class preserve. One of the most obvious results of this was that senior officers had (and continue to have) an understanding of, and affinity with, the *administrés*, which comes from close association and personal knowledge. Thus, one of the necessary changes in the character of the bureaucracy to make it suitable for a modern democratic state was quickly and easily effected.

Because university graduates entered the service in only small numbers and because of the arrangement by which top jobs were (and are) open to higher executive officers, the higher civil service became increasingly composed of people who had entered the service directly from secondary school. An analysis made by A. S. Cohan of the careers of all those who had held the post of secretary of a department between 1923 and 1968 revealed that only a quarter of them had university degrees.[18] The contrast with McDowell's 1914 group is striking. In the late 1960s, perhaps 90 per cent of the posts of assistant principal and above were filled by people recruited from secondary school, and four of the fifteen heads of departments had entered as clerical officers.

What are the results of the higher civil service being largely composed of people who entered from secondary school? Since secondary education was not free before 1967 and since many country people were not close enough to a school for their children to attend daily, the children of the poor, especially poor country people, tended to have a civil service career barred to them. With this important exception, many children of all social classes attended schools run by religious orders, which provided the bulk of Irish secondary education remarkably cheaply, and it is from these that most of the recruits to the service have come. Some were the sons of salaried people or of farmers of some substance, albeit far from rich. At the poorer end of the scale, however, were many whose parents could hardly afford even the small expense of sending their children to these very cheap schools. For them particularly, success at the civil service examinations was more prized than a university scholarship, for it opened up the prospect of immediate self-sufficiency and a good career. With too few job opportunities available, there was a certain inevitability about a career in the civil service for the poor and unconnected secondary-school student of above-average ability. Despite the fact that the situation changed somewhat in the 1970s, the service was still heavily peopled with the products of the earlier situation. By 1980, the service, if not open to all classes, was within wide limits classless.

Inevitably civil servants displayed some dominant characteristics of their schooling. This was to be seen most obviously in the case of the considerable, even preponderant, proportion of them who were educated at schools run by the Christian Brothers. This Catholic order, founded in 1808 to provide education for poor boys, by the early twentieth century was providing secondary education for all classes. Until the 1960s at least, the Christian Brothers gave an education of a particular type and tended to produce men with certain characteristics. The civil service came to reflect these characteristics.

Writing in 1955, S. Ó Mathuna, himself a product of a Christian Brothers school, suggested that the Christian Brothers' necessary concentration on preparing boys for examinations contributed perhaps inevitably to a comparative neglect of nonacademic and extracurricular activities.[19] Moreover, "though the development of character was always in the forefront of their teaching, those who passed through their schools were liable to acquire a slightly over-academic education and to lack in some degree a fully rounded personality."[20] His view was confirmed by another distinguished Christian Brothers' product, Dr. Jeremiah Dempsey, a former chief executive of Aer Lingus, the state airline: "If the education was intensive, it was also narrow. For years after I left, I was unaware of anything around me that didn't belong to the work in hand."[21] In contrast with the British tradition, Ó Mathuna also noted that "there is little solidarity, in the old school tie sense, between ex-pupils of the Christian Brothers."[22] These characteristics, he argued, had an important influence on the character of the service, which was, in his opinion, a very homogeneous group, as was to be expected when one considers the remarkable uniformity of their origins, education, experience, and point of entry.

Many students of Irish public administration, both inside and outside the civil service, agree that in the higher civil service there was indeed a Christian Brothers school stereotype, which dominated the service until at least well into the 1960s and perhaps even beyond and gave it some of its most marked characteristics. Higher civil servants generally perhaps tended to be intellectually able and hard working but rather narrowly practical in their approach and inclined to be concerned with the short-term objective. They were not inclined to speculate broadly or to reflect on long-term ends or cultural values. With rather narrow secondary education in the case of so many, or at best for some others the limited opportunities offered by an evening degree course and no other professional training or outside experience, they may have had restricted horizons. They were, on account of their schooling, likely to accept "the system" with little question, though in this they surely did not differ from civil servants almost everywhere. Also, they tended to share with the public servants of many, perhaps most, countries the belief that the outsider probably had little to contribute. Men of this sort were admirable at "running the machine" and administering the comparatively modest public services that were the feature of the first half of the state's existence, but some thought that they did not measure up to the demands that subsequently were, all of a sudden, made upon them.

Paradoxically, the publication of *Economic Development* in 1958 and the inauguration of the first programme of economic development owed much to the initiative of a handful of civil servants and were the outcome of a fruitful partnership between a few ministers, a few civil servants, and one or two professional economists. However, they did not mark a change in the attitudes of many higher civil servants, who saw no need for reform, particularly if the Department of Finance was behind it. "We are aware," the Devlin Group reported, that "in the late 1950s, proposals for a reorganisation of the civil service were formulated in the Department of Finance but, after consideration by all Departments were, by reason of the statutory autonomy conferred on Departments, whittled down to affect only the lower ranks of the general service leaving the higher levels unchanged."[23] Consequently, the higher civil service was soon being identified as an obstacle to development by the tiny but increasing number of politicians and administrators who were promoting it.

In 1961, the Taoiseach, Seán Lemass, who was by then urging departments to see themselves as "development corporations," voiced his doubts about their ability to act in that capacity:

I think it is true to say that in some government departments there is still a tendency to wait for new ideas to walk in through the door. It is perhaps the normal attitude of an administrative department of government to be passive rather than active, to await proposals from outside, to react mainly to criticism or to pressure of public demand, to avoid the risks of experimentation and innovation and to confine themselves to vetting and improving proposals brought to them by private interests and individuals rather than to generate new ideas themselves.[24]

Lemass said frankly that doubts about the suitability of the civil service to do development and promotional work had led to the widespread use of the state-sponsored body type of organization. He urged the need for departments to think in terms of new opportunities and to provide leadership. The permanent secretary of the Department of Finance, who had been the chief inspiration and author of *Economic Development,* echoed him: "What is needed is a more lively and general appreciation by the Civil Service of the part it can and should play in promoting national development."[25]

Following Lemass, a small but growing number of senior officers and some politicians began to recognize the need for a thorough reappraisal. That reappraisal was conducted by the Public Service Organisation Review Group (the Devlin Group), to which reference has already been made. Following this, in turn, there began a period of reform, much influenced by the Devlin Group report, that extended through the 1970s and was by no means completed by the end of that decade.

The Devlin Group provided a blueprint for change and, although the basic structural reforms that they proposed were not fully implemented—as much because of lack of political will as of administrative hostility—much of what they proposed became in effect a programme for implementation as and when practicable. It was a formidable programme covering recruitment, education, training, staff development, mobility, the introduction of modern management techniques, the development of management services and operations research, the exploitation of the computer, and mechanisms for reviewing cost-effectiveness. The public service in general and the civil service in particular were to be thoroughly modernized in accordance with modern management theory and precepts. A Department of the Public Service was to carry through the programme, and such a department was created and set to work accordingly. The record of its success and failures is to be found in the series of reports issued by the Public Service Advisory Council—another creature of Devlin[26]—which saw itself as "an agent of change" whose "existence can be justified and made meaningful only by the extent to which it stimulates the public service to effective reform."[27] Time and again, it took as its criteria of progress in reform the principles and precepts of the Devlin Group.

There can be little doubt that the Devlin Group and its offspring created a considerable impetus to administrative reform. The Group coincided with, and was part of, a general climate of change that set in in Ireland from the mid-1960s. By that time, too, a marked generational change had occurred in the top ranks of the civil service. Although the generation of those whose experience stretched back to the early days of the state was replaced by men only a little if at all less conservative, *their* successors tended increasingly to be more open to change. Fewer of the recruits coming in from the mid-1960s onwards conformed to the Christian Brothers' stereotype, and in any case, by that time, many of the Christian Brothers schools were changing. The higher civil service was expanding, too, and there were more opportunities for advancement. This lifted morale, as did the relative improvement in salaries as a combined result of the efforts of Lemass to narrow the gap between salaries at the top of the public. sector and the salaries of top executives in the private sector, and growth in the power and effectiveness of the service associations. The civil service also became more outward looking, more willing to engage expert advice and hire consultants and to contemplate their prescriptions. Ireland's accession to the European Communities provided as stiff a test in the 1970s as the demands of economic planning had in the 1960s. The civil service rose to the demands, which were the heavier because of the small size of the Irish administration as compared with public service sectors of most of the nine. The doubts and the strictures of Lemass and others in the 1960s over the ability of the civil service to meet the needs of that decade were not repeated by the commentators of the 1970s as they contemplated the Irish civil service face to face with Brussels.

The fact is that, for all the pessimism of the Public Service Advisory Council and the evident frustration of enthusiasts like T. J. Barrington,[28] the civil service of the late 1970s had adapted or was in the process of adapting to the needs of the time. It was, too, above all more professional, more modern, and more open to change. If, as Barrington argued, it still "does not engage in any significant degree of review of its general effectiveness" and is not self-conscious enough about the need for, and potential of, systematic and continuous administrative development, this is perhaps, as Barrington himself hypothesized, because it "is too well adapted to the prevailing climate of wary anti-intellectualism and of general scepticism about the efficacy of administrative self-consciousness."[29] Nevertheless, the service has come a long way from the time when most of its leaders regarded the administrative sciences and management theory as third-rate witchdoctory.

FOURTEEN

State-Sponsored Bodies

The considerable variety of administrative bodies that was a feature of Irish government before independence was only temporarily reduced to near uniformity when the new state took over. Within a few years, new public authorities in forms other than that of a ministerial department or local authority began to be set up. Since then, with the great growth in the range and volume of state activity, the number and variety of such bodies have increased considerably. They now surround the central administration like satellites, each one to a greater or lesser degree under the surveillance or control of a department. A general term has been coined to refer to most of them, though its connotation is far from precise. They are generally known as "state-sponsored bodies," a term that has to a large extent superseded "semi-state bodies," which was once much used.

There seems to be no legal or other authoritative definition of "state-sponsored body." In 1969, the Public Services Organisation Review Group (the Devlin Group) reported that "there is a certain looseness about the term."[1] In 1976, the Minister for the Public Service told the Dáil that "it is not possible to give a precise definition of the term 'state-sponsored body.' Generally, the term may be taken to include bodies established by or under statute and financed wholly or partly by means of grants or loans made by a Minister of State or the issue of shares taken up by a Minister."[2]

State-sponsored bodies are autonomous public authorities (other than universities, judicial bodies, or purely advisory bodies) endowed with duties and powers by statute or by ministerial authority. Their staffs are not civil servants; the government or individual ministers appoint some or all of the members of their governing boards or councils. The legal form of most state-sponsored bodies is that of a statutory corporation or of a public or private company incorporated under the Companies Acts with a minister or ministers holding some or all of the shares. Some, however, are "statutory companies"; others are set up as corporate bodies under general enabling acts; still others are unincorporated. Some state-sponsored bodies are even not wholly publicly owned but are mixed public and private enterprises.

Just as state-sponsored bodies are autonomous in the sense that each has a legal status and personality, so, too, are they free both from the full rigours of control by the Departments of Finance and the Public Service, to which central departments are subject, and from detailed scrutiny by the Oireachtas, to which in principle at least departments must submit. Each state-sponsored body, however, has a sponsor minister who is ultimately responsible for it. The overall picture, as the Devlin Group saw it, is of "a central core of departments with their associated fringe of agencies reporting to those departments with which they are functionally connected. . . . In essence, each state-sponsored body . . . consists of a Board with a Chairman reporting to the Minister and an executive and/ or operational staff under a chief executive with a more or less informal reporting relationship to the Department."[3]

This type of organization has been used for a wide variety of purposes including the regulation of certain economic and social activities; the provision of certain social services; the operation of a number of infrastructure industries and a wide range of other enterprises producing goods and services for sale; the provision of finance; and the provision of marketing, promotional, and research and development services. There is no definitive list of state-sponsored bodies, but ministerial answers to Dáil questions in 1979 revealed that there were then about a hundred of them, a few of which in turn had subsidiary organizations. (See the list in Appendix D.) In that year, their staffs amounted to 54 per cent of public service employment (not including teachers and Gardaí) and 9 per cent of all employment.

State-sponsored bodies do not constitute a neat or even coherent group of public authorities. On the contrary, a thoroughgoing pragmatism uninfluenced by socialist doctrine or administrative theory was the main feature of their growth and development in Ireland, at least until the Devlin Group reported on them at the end of the 1960s. A general acceptance of the proposition that ministerial departments are suitable for the direct administration of only a comparatively narrow range of state activities was clearly the starting point of a search for the most practicable form of organization when a new problem arose, a new opportunity presented itself, or the need for a new state initiative was realized. However, the search was never a long one and never systematic. Governments and ministers adopted practical solutions *ad hoc,* sometimes paying scant regard to the need on constitutional grounds to provide clear and comprehensive legal instruments or adequate parliamentary control. Individual departments even developed their own particular practices and "house style" in the forms they adopted and the relationships they prescribed.

The situation is the more complicated and confusing because both inside and outside the central administration's penumbra of state-sponsored bodies are organizations of many kinds. They range from bodies that are to all intents and purposes departments, though they do not have ministerial heads, to bodies like the Economic and Social Research Institute and the Institute of Public Administration, which, though they were not set up by the state, carry out functions in which the state has an interest and for which it pays. These and bodies like them, including the universities, are on the outer edge of the public sector and are being inexorably sucked into it.

The essential feature of state-sponsored bodies, it might be thought, is that they have some degree of legal and operational independence of the central administration. For the Devlin Group, their appearance on the administrative stage was significant because

it represented, in the first place, an abandonment, in particular areas, of the concept of the Minister as a corporation sole; there was delegation by law to appointed boards of some executive powers of the State. Secondly, it brought together in the area of government, persons with public and private sector experience to guide and assess the performance of management of public enterprises and, thirdly, it introduced new freedoms in the performance of executive functions of government.[4]

Nevertheless, we should be hesitant to use the word "autonomous" in respect of them. A legal existence separate from their parent departments they do have, and their functions and powers are prescribed in some legal instrument or other; but such endowments by no means ensure operational independence from their sponsor departments. It does not necessarily follow from their having their own boards or their own (non–civil service) staffs or from their not being bound to comply with civil service rules and procedures that they will be independent of their minister and sponsor department. Nor does independence follow from their being free from detailed Oireachtas scrutiny: as we shall see, ministerial control and Oireachtas surveillance are not always co-extensive. In practice, the degree of independence that state-sponsored bodies enjoy varies enormously from one to another and depends in each case on one or more of three main factors: (1) the nature of the function performed and particularly its political significance or sensitivity; (2) the financial position of the body and especially its sources of funds; and (3) the habits of departmental control that have become established and that might perhaps have originated largely in accidents of personality.

II

Although it is not possible to categorize all state-sponsored bodies un-equivocally, most of them seem to fall into one or another of three main groups. First, there are those set up to engage in producing goods and services for sale. These are often referred to as "commercial" bodies or "public enterprises." Second, there are those established to carry out marketing, promotional, or development (including research) activities connected with industry and commerce. Third, there are bodies that ad-minister or regulate some area of social or economic activity or provide a social service.

Surveying the administrative scene in the late 1960s, the Public Ser-vice Organisation Review Group found that "the commercial state-spon-sored bodies form a sector of the public service qualitatively different from the non-commercial bodies and there is an instinctive recognition of this fact in the tendency to refer to them as the 'public enterprises.' "[5] However, even if they are to be thought of as the state in business—and this is certainly the way they have been thought of in the past and by some still today—they owe their origin to a political decision that the state should go into or acquire some productive enterprise in the national interest and not simply to make profits. Sometimes, too, they find them-selves obliged to engage in activities or to pursue policies for social rather than for economic reasons. Governments make such decisions; state-sponsored bodies, however entrepreneurial they might seem to be, are essentially agents of government policy. For example, the rural electrifi-cation programme of the Electricity Supply Board and its use of turf (peat) as a fuel to make electricity were both policies dictated by govern-ments and undertaken "in the national interest."

The public enterprise sector in Ireland is quite large. By the early 1960s it was, in Garret FitzGerald's view, "relatively highly developed . . . bearing in mind the absence of heavy industrial activity which in some other European countries is partly or even largely under the con-trol of the state."[6] In 1979, it comprised twenty-five bodies; in addition a few of these had subsidiary companies as, for example, the Industrial Credit Company with its subsidiaries, Mergers Ltd. and the Shipping

Finance Corporation. As in most countries, the public enterprise sector included most of the infrastructure industries—energy (but only a toe-hold in oil) and transport, which alone account for 80 per cent of all employment provided by this group; banking and the provision of capital; and broadcasting. As in other countries, also, it included a miscellaneous collection of other industries and enterprises whose presence in the public sector owed more to particular circumstances than to general policy.

How did this come about? It owed little to socialist theory. After the eclipse of the left wing of the labour movement during the latter part of the First World War, there were few socialists in Ireland, no socialist movement worth the name, and no developing body of socialist doctrine. The very term "socialism" was anathema to most, the more so because, following the lead of the Catholic Church, most people identified it with communism. The Irish Free State was liberal-democratic and conservative. Its governments and those that followed reflected public opinion generally in showing no lack of confidence in private enterprise. Irish opinion was and still is truly reflected in Article 45.3.1° of Bunreacht na hÉireann (one of the "Directive Principles of Social Policy"), which declares that "the state shall favour and, where necessary, supplement private initiative in industry and commerce." This attitude was echoed in 1961 by the then Taoiseach, Seán Lemass, when he stated: "Even the most conservative among us understands why we cannot rely on private enterprise alone, and state enterprise in fields of activity where private enterprise has failed or has shown itself to be disinterested, has not only been accepted but is expected. . . . Nobody thinks of us as doctrinaire socialists."[7]

It was, however, precisely the considerable need to "supplement private initiative in industry and commerce," and at times to rescue it, together with the inexorable and universal tendency for public utilities to come under public management, that led to the sizeable public enterprise sector. Thus, there was little nationalization of already existing business enterprises. Only some half-dozen businesses were taken over, in every case either as a rescue operation or in response to the need to ensure an adequate public service. On the other hand, there was considerable state initiative in starting enterprises.

It should be remembered that the Irish state started out with considerable economic handicaps. Ireland remained very much part of a larger economic and financial unit that was London oriented; and it was, considered as a unit by itself, in some respects relatively underdeveloped and certainly unbalanced, as was the rural western seaboard of the British

Isles generally. This situation was exacerbated by the exclusion from the Irish state of the only industrial area in the island, Belfast and its environs. Because of this and because of the more attractive prospects for capital on the London market, which was still open to Irish investors, private capital was not available to the extent necessary for development, and private enterprise was distinctly unenterprising.

Conservative in outlook though it was, the first government of the Irish Free State nevertheless inherited the tradition of Sinn Féin and followed a definite line of development leading to state enterprises to provide capital and to exploit the natural resources of the country. In transport, although the exact circumstances under which the state started companies (as in the case of the airlines and Irish Shipping Ltd.) or nationalized them (as in the case of the railways and road services) differed from case to case, their inclusion in the public sector was in line with developments in many other countries. This was so, also, in radio and television and in the nationalization of central banking. The remaining trading enterprises either owed their origin to rescue operations or had a social service origin. Examples of the first were the Irish Life Assurance Co. Ltd. and Irish Steel Holdings Ltd. An example of the second was An Bord Iascaigh Mhara (the Irish Sea Fisheries Board), whose origins are well illustrated by the fact that it was originally registered as a "Friendly Society"—that is, an association registered under the Friendly Societies Act.

Most of the bodies in the second group, the marketing, promotional, and research and development organizations, came into existence as the Irish state, again like most other developed states, assumed responsibility for the development of the economy as a whole. They were created to aid and stimulate Irish enterprise by promoting markets for Irish goods and services as, for example, Bord Fáilte Éireann (the Irish Tourist Board) and Córas Tráchtála (the Irish Export Board); to engage directly in marketing as does the Pigs and Bacon Commission; to encourage and facilitate the setting up of new industries in Ireland, which is the function of the Industrial Development Authority; to carry out training and other developmental activities as do AnCo (the Industrial Training Authority) and the Kilkenny Design Workshops; to engage in and foster research as does An Foras Talúntais (the Agricultural Institute). In 1979, there were twenty-five of them.

The use of the state-sponsored body for these purposes arose, it seems, from ministers' perception that the suitability of the civil service to engage in development work was limited; in general the state-sponsored body reflected a lack of confidence in the ability of departments to cope with some of the new tasks of the modern state. Speaking in 1961, the Taoiseach, Seán Lemass, was quite explicit about this:

It is fair to assume that it was the persistence of doubt about the suitability of Government Departments, as now organized, to operate as development corporations and to perform, in the manner desired, particular functions deemed to be necessary for the nation's progress—functions which required exceptional initiative and innovation—which have led to decisions of the Government from time to time to set up by statute or otherwise a number of more or less independent authorities. I am not referring to the administration of state-owned commercial-type undertakings. . . . I have in mind the administration of activities of another kind, where the purpose is to provide services to promote development generally or to help private concerns to make headway—such as aids to industrial development, export trade, tourism and so forth. In these instances the decision might have been either way—either to administer these schemes directly through the appropriate Departments, or to set up boards and authorities outside the departmental system for the purpose. If Ministers decided to do it one way rather than the other, it was better because they believed that the results would be better.[8]

There were, he conceded, other reasons also: the need to attract the services of people who were not, and would not become, civil servants; the desire to be free of detailed departmental and Oireachtas control; the hope that the public would cooperate more readily. "It may be," Lemass speculated, "that whether by accident or by design, we have in fact devised a better system of administration . . . and that activities which are still direct departmental responsibilities could, with increased efficiency, be passed out to similar extern authorities."[9]

There can be little doubt about the role and position of the bodies in this group. They do not produce goods for sale and do not, therefore, have their own funds, relying instead on state grants. As the Devlin Group pointed out, they "are really agencies with a governmental role . . . more in the nature of service bodies for the producer." In fact, the example the Group gave illustrates the point well: "Bord Bainne [the Milk Marketing Board, now a cooperative] is concerned primarily with the disposal of milk products surplus to home requirements, the production of which is encouraged by the structure of the agricultural subsidies. Neither in primary purpose or in policy is it governed by normal commercial considerations."[10] Nevertheless, since the activities of many of this group are designed to promote business, those who work in them are oriented to the world of trade and commerce and would claim to be as "business-like," even entrepreneurial, as any in the public enterprise sector. The practices, habits, and *mores* of civil service–type administrators would not do in their business.

The administrative, regulatory, and social service group, which in 1979 comprised forty-eight bodies, can be divided into three main subgroups: (1) bodies established for the government of certain professions, (2) bodies set up to control certain economic activities, and (3) bodies set up to provide or administer certain social services, particularly health and environmental services. Little need be said about the first. Although professions are almost by definition self-governing, many need the backing of the state, and in the case of some, the public interest makes, it necessary to define the functions and powers of their governing bodies. In the past, they got powers to regulate entry and govern the profession by charters from the British Crown; in modern times, they are governed by statutes that set up governing bodies endowed with duties and powers.

There can be no doubt about the genesis of most of the second and third subgroups: they were created as executive agencies of government—the term that the Devlin Group in fact proposed should be applied to all the "non-commercial" organizations—a convenient alternative to administration by the civil service. In the view of the Group, this was an easy, even lazy, way out of an organizational problem:

For the "non-commercial" function, the state-sponsored body type of organisation is an attempt to cure, on an ad hoc basis, defects in the traditional organisation of the executive functions of government. Most of the activities of the "non-commercial" state-sponsored bodies are such as are, were or could be carried out within the civil service. . . . every decision to allocate a new function to a state-sponsored body while similar functions are left in the existing civil service structure represents a failure to face the problem of the efficiency of the existing machinery of government, or at least, to think through the roles of the parts of that machinery.[11]

This was, perhaps, a harsh judgement at least so far as it was aimed at areas of activity in which there was a need to associate interested parties with the administration of their own business, or the users or recipients of a service with the administration of that service. Nevertheless, in many cases the increasing propensity, after the Second World War, to devolve segments of public administration to state-sponsored bodies that were sometimes mere extensions of their sponsor departments did reflect simply administrative convenience.

III

The increased use of state-sponsored bodies from the Second World War onwards precipitated major problems of their relationships with ministers and departments, and also problems of the proper extent and appropriate means of Oireachtas control. It is essential to distinguish clearly between the two.

According to the prewar "autonomous corporation" theory, at least the trading bodies were to be free of both ministerial and Oireachtas control except in emergencies. Ministers being responsible for very little, it followed that the Oireachtas could hold them accountable for very little. Today, no one doubts that ministers often have considerable powers, sometimes extending from the most general policy to matters of comparative detail. Until recently, at least, the Oireachtas had neither the information nor the machinery to effect adequate control. Even yet it is handicapped by reason of the fact that it is not clear in some instances either what the objectives of an organization are or who (minister or board) is responsible for what. Ministers might, therefore, wield power without responsibility.

Ministerial (or governmental) power over state-sponsored bodies is of four kinds. First, the sponsor minister (sometimes with the consent of another interested minister) or the government appoints some or all of the members of the governing boards of these bodies and may dismiss them. This power is a potential source of great patronage. When a party is in power for a long time, as Fianna Fáil was, the boards tend to become peopled by party supporters and those who deserved well of it. Certainly, the changes of government from Fianna Fáil to National Coalition and back again in the 1970s were each followed by a spate of appointments very obviously governed by considerations of party or patronage.[12] In many and perhaps even most cases, however, the choice of directors at least until recently was often as explicable in terms of relevant experience, representation of interests, and the preferences of senior civil servants as in terms of party politics or nepotism.

Second, in each case, the appropriate minister sees that the organization's operations are kept in line with government policy. This involves approval for capital projects and other important policy proposals and for matters such as general wage and salary increases. Third, ministers have a general power of surveillance and the right to intervene on behalf of the community since, at the end of the day, they have an overall responsibility for the organizations in the departmental penumbra. The extent and degree of control vary greatly from body to body and perhaps from time to time. Certainly, it is often not possible to rely upon legal instruments to gauge their extent. Ministerial intervention (including under that head the activities of the minister's civil servants) sometimes has no statutory or other basis; a minister might have no explicit legal power to direct a body whose decisions he in fact influences decisively or even dictates. Finally, the minister has powers to govern the presentation and form of reports and accounts and to provide for audit, and he also has the right to be given whatever information he requires. These matters, unlike those mentioned previously, are usually specifically provided for in statutes, orders, or articles of association.

Ministerial supervision and control make it necessary for ministers and chairmen to keep in touch. Each organization ought at all times to know what the policy of its sponsor department is. In fact, it is not uncommon for boards and state-sponsored bodies not to know what a minister's policy is and to be unable to find out.[13] Clearly, also, departments have to have an intimate knowledge of the activities of the bodies within their orbit. The contacts necessary to effect this are made at all levels. They are by no means confined to the boards and senior executives on the one side and the minister and his senior civil servants on the other.

Garret FitzGerald, who had personal experience in one of the trading bodies, describes civil servants as "having frequent routine contact with officials of the state-sponsored bodies at various management and supervisory levels." He notes that "in some of these instances the matters dealt with may well be of such a character as to require clearance by the Minister, or at least to require that he should be informed of what is passing. But in many instances—probably the majority—the contacts are confined to the civil servant/management level." He comments that "these 'second-level' contacts, many of them of a very informal nature, are an essential part of a smooth-running administrative machine that involves the implementation of many aspects of state policy through state-sponsored bodies."[14]

Supervision and control might also be effected by the device of appointing civil servants to boards. This practice is quite common except in the public enterprise group. Obviously, the work of many of these bodies needs to be coordinated with that of their sponsor departments, and the presence of civil servants on boards is a handy coordinating device. Nevertheless, there are some objections to the practice. C. S. Andrews, a former chairman of Córas Iompair Éireann, the state transport authority, cogently condemned the practice when he said, "I cannot see how a civil servant functions properly if he is wearing two hats and if, having participated in the councils of a board, he returns to his Department and sits in judgement on the decisions reached."[15] Obviously, also, the practice could (but should not) be used as a means of effecting departmental control while avoiding detailed parliamentary control. Certainly, unless the circumstances are exceptional, a board composed of, or dominated by, civil servants would seem to be undesirable, for this is in effect departmental administration without the normal parliamentary safeguards. It is equally undesirable for ministers to tell civil service members of boards how they are to vote on issues, for to do so might make it impossible for them properly to discharge their obligations as board members.[16]

Problems of ministerial control are comparatively recent. They hardly arose in the first twenty or thirty years of the state's existence, when there were comparatively few state-sponsored bodies and when most of those few were reckoned to have commercial objectives. It was possible to contend, and in fact it was contended, that such "business enterprises" should be "removed as far as it is possible from political pressure."[17] Postwar developments changed the picture considerably.

After the Second World War, the number of state-sponsored bodies increased enormously, and by the late 1960s there were over seventy of them. The growing propensity to use this form of organization for developmental, regulatory, and social service purposes brought into existence many bodies that were simply executive agencies but "no serious attempt was made . . . to work out a comprehensive system of communication and control within a unified public service."[18] On the contrary, Lemass took the opposite view: "We do not work on the basis of theory. We work always on the basis of the best method of getting a particular job done."[19] As a result, by the 1960s, the area was an administrative jungle made the worse by the casual way in which some bodies were created and the cavalier failure in some cases to draw up adequate legal instruments governing functions and powers or, where necessary, to revise them to reflect the realities of growing state control (for by this time the exigencies of state planning and control of the economy had called into question the concept of the autonomous state enterprise).

Once it was recognized that the government's job was to steer the national economy, the policies of the major public enterprises had to conform to overall government programmes. Surprisingly, the need for such compliance was not at first always accepted. Lemass drew attention to this in 1959: "There develops a tendency in some boards to think of themselves rather as sovereign independent authorities than as integral parts of a larger organization and they are sometimes disposed to resent pressures to keep them in line."[20] In 1965, the *Report on Economic Planning* by the National Industrial Economic Council made a similar complaint.[21] In the next decade, the far-reaching implications of central planning of the economy, as ministers and senior civil servants saw them, were inexorably brought home to the boards and executives of even the most powerful public enterprises, not least in respect of pay policy, including the salaries of their chief executives. By this time, too, many of the more recently spawned administrative agencies were no more than extensions of their parent departments, their activities quietly controlled or guided by civil servants but operating well below the horizon of the Oireachtas.

What was lacking was a set of agreed-upon principles to regulate such bodies and in particular minister-board relationships. The Devlin Group criticized this deficiency in particular and in order to remedy it proposed two systems of uniform relationships and procedures—one for the public enterprises; the other for the remainder, lumped together as "non-commercial" bodies.[22] In their view, departments should become small policy-making and reviewing bodies coordinating the activities of all the units charged with implementing state policy in their functional areas. Looking at the executive branches of departments and the non-commercial state-sponsored bodies, the Group reported that "we have not discovered any universally applicable principles which dictate whether a particular function should be allocated to a non-commercial state-sponsored body or to a Department. . . . We, therefore, recommend that all executive activities (excluding those now carried out by local authorities or commercial state-sponsored bodies) assigned to Ministers should be divided on a functional basis and operated by units of Departments."[23] These units would be of two types. Where an executive function was being exercised by a department, the Devlin Group recommended that it be hived off to a unit called an "executive office." Where the function was being carried out by a state-sponsored body, the board should continue in existence, and the unit should be known as an "executive agency." In both cases, department-unit relationships would be identical.[24]

In the Devlin Group's view, the position of the public enterprises was different, but not all that different. "While we refer to these bodies as commercial, it must be remembered that they are all instruments of public policy and cannot operate with full commercial freedom." The Group recommended unequivocally that "the commercial bodies must be effectively integrated in the public sector. . . . commercial state-sponsored bodies should be linked to the Aireachts to which they are functionally related. . . . the sponsoring Departments should not interfere in viable commercial operations but should actively engage in the definition and review of goals, the appraisal of results and the control of capital expenditure."[25]

The recommendations of the Devlin Group on this subject were never formally accepted or fully implemented. That does not mean that they have not had some influence. On the contrary, there seems to have been a sustained attempt by the Department of the Public Service when making changes to follow Devlin principles whenever and wherever possible. In one area in particular, that of pay and conditions of service, the development in the 1970s of national pay bargaining with a series of National Wages Agreements has created both the necessity and the opportunity to impose uniform wage policies and salary structures and to force state-sponsored bodies to submit to centrally controlled procedures for dealing with claims and disputes.

The trend towards central control and uniformity was fiercely resented by some of the boards and executives of public enterprises. In 1972, there was hostility to the recommendations of the inelegantly titled Review Body on Higher Remuneration in the Public Sector, chaired by the same Liam St. John Devlin who had led the Public Services Organisation Review Group and whose thinking the Review Body reflected in its report:

All employments covered in this reference are integral parts of the public sector and are thus interrelated in role, function and operation with other parts of the public sector and are quite distinct from the private sector in a number of ways. This characteristic in itself, apart from any other consideration, justifies, in our view, a coordinated approach to the determination of remuneration throughout the entire area of reference. . . . Pay in commercial state-sponsored bodies should also reflect pay in the rest of the public sector.[26]

The Review Body's proposals for standardized salaries and scales were accepted by the government and implemented despite protests. A second report on the same subject by the Review Body in 1979 followed the same lines and had a like reception.[27]

By the end of the 1970s, complaints by members of boards and executives in public enterprises were more frequent and wholesale. They were epitomized in the strictures of a study group of the National Economic and Social Council, in its report *Enterprise in the Public Sector*. The study group's report was a fierce attack on the attempt of the central administration to corral public enterprises to the detriment, they thought, of initiative and dynamism:

It has been recognised from the beginning that the practices and procedures which govern the operation of other public agencies were not the most appropriate to state-sponsored bodies. . . . Yet the acceptance of this distinctive nature of state-sponsored bodies is being eroded. The concept of the unity of the public sector has begun to be interpreted more rigidly and narrowly than in the past.

There is an increasing emphasis on centralised decision-making within the public sector and a tendency towards greater central control of the activities of state-sponsored bodies. . . . In our view, these efforts to introduce uniformity throughout the whole of the public sector are seriously impeding enterprise in the state-sponsored bodies. The autonomy and authority which are assigned by Government to these bodies are being increasingly undermined.[28]

The exchange of views between the study group and the central departments, which was published in the report, revealed a deep division of opinion between them, or worse, for the study group reported that "some of the Departmental comments on our recommendations seem to us to result from an implied mistrust of state-sponsored bodies, as if any freedom given to them would be abused."[29] The chairman's accompanying letter is as acidulous and pointed as it is possible to be in published official exchanges:

It is our unanimous view that there is nothing in them [the departmental comments] that causes us to alter our recommendations. On the contrary, we would most strongly urge those concerned to read our report again and to consider precisely what we have said.

Most of the comments from Government Departments exemplify the perspective of the controller as opposed to that of the entrepreneur. These illustrate explicitly the attitudinal problems which we identified as the central crucial issue in our report.[30]

The chairman was right: there is a crucial issue here. It was very clear in 1980 that the problem of the proper relationship between public enterprises and the central administration was unsettled and becoming acute.

IV

Whereas the power of the central administration over state-sponsored bodies increased as their numbers and role grew, the ability of the Oireachtas to scrutinize them remained trivial. The result was a constitutional imbalance that was as obvious as it was undesirable.

The requirements of constitutional propriety seem clear enough. Ministers are responsible to the Dáil not only for the duties laid upon them by the Constitution and the statutes, including their failure to act when they should have acted, but for all their actions as ministers and for those of their departmental officials. There is a political obligation upon them to explain and defend, and the Dáil (with the Seanad as a potentially useful auxiliary) ought to be in a position to make this responsibility a reality. Surprisingly, when it came to state-sponsored bodies, such a view was not universally held.

Seán Lemass, who as Minister for Industry and Commerce was responsible for the creation of a number of these bodies and whose views on them were rightly influential, took a different line: "There has arisen . . . in recent times, in Dáil Éireann, and perhaps even more surprisingly, in Seanad Éireann, a tendency towards endeavouring to make the decisions of some statutory boards, taken within the powers given to them by law, subject to review and even to veto in the legislature."[31] Lemass deplored this. Correctly, he saw a danger: "These bodies were set up with the deliberate intention of avoiding close state control."[32] But "it is probable that when any semi-state board becomes the centre of controversy—as is not unlikely at some period of its existence—its independence is likely to be in serious jeopardy, because Ministers, realizing the folly of accepting responsibility without effective power, will be disposed to bring their operations under closer supervision, which could reduce if not eliminate their special utility as an administrative device."[33]

However, Lemass' contention that "additional parliamentary control is unnecessary having regard to the wide ministerial powers in relation to state-sponsored bodies" was surely mistaken.[34] It is, indeed, exactly the reverse. Additional parliamentary control is necessary precisely when ministers acquire additional powers. Ministerial control is not sufficient: the Oireachtas must be in a position to scrutinize ministers' exercise of (or their failure to exercise) their powers. Above all, it must be crystal clear what those powers are and what are the relationships between ministers and boards and between departments and executives of state-sponsored bodies.

The problem of Oireachtas control is not just one of principle. The Oireachtas suffered from serious practical handicaps that until recently made its control of this sector little more than cursory. First, there was—and still is—the basic handicap that the precise objectives of some state-sponsored bodies are not clearly stated and, more generally, that the statutes and legal instruments constituting and regulating them are sometimes inadequate or anomalous, particularly in defining the respective functions and powers of ministers and the relationship between them. Ministers might and do wield considerable powers without specific authority. Second, until the late 1970s, there were no adequate procedures and facilities for acquiring information or for the systematic scrutiny of the performance of state-sponsored bodies. The inadequacies of question time and debates as procedures for scrutinizing performance are manifest (see pp. 214–16). Furthermore, in the past, most members of the Oireachtas did not seem to care very much. It was generally believed that the state-sponsored bodies were doing a good job; debates were both few and far between; those who participated in them, except for the minister, were poorly informed and in many cases concerned only with parochial matters.

From the late 1940s, desultory requests for a select committee, which British and continental European experience had shown was the best device for systematic scrutiny, were made from time to time by members of parties out of power. Lemass himself, when in opposition briefly, had moved a motion for a select committee "akin to the Committee of Public Accounts to which these [state-owned] company accounts and reports would be submitted,"[35] only to reject the idea when in power, as we have seen. Eventually, a growing awareness among parliamentarians of the inadequacies of Oireachtas control led in 1976 to the government's moving to set up a Joint Committee on State-Sponsored Bodies "to examine the Reports and Accounts and overall operational results of state-sponsored bodies engaged in trading or commercial activities." Introducing the motion, the Minister for the Public Service justified confining the committee to twenty-six of the commercial bodies on the grounds that

there is a significant difference between the commercial and non-commercial state-sponsored bodies. The latter are in many ways similar to the executive branches of Government Departments, except that they have a larger degree of operating freedom. There is a problem in relation to their responsibility to the Oireachtas but, at this stage, it seems that a solution may well be in a redefinition of their relationship to Ministers.[36]

That statement seemed to presage a change in their status following the Devlin Group's recommendations, but this did not occur. In March 1980, an opposition motion for a Joint Committee on Autonomous Non-Commercial Bodies was rejected by the Dáil, the minister arguing that it was necessary to have more time to evaluate the experience of the existing committee dealing with public enterprises before venturing on another.[37]

From 1978, the Joint Committee on State-Sponsored Bodies, which takes evidence in public and was the first select committee to have professional help made available to it, began to produce reports that have immeasurably improved the quantity and quality of information made available to the Oireachtas and published. Up to 1980, however, it was still far from certain that the Oireachtas would make full use of such information.

FIFTEEN

Local Government

In all countries, the administration of public services involves not only the central departments, but also some combination of functional and areal dispersion of duties and powers. In Chapter 14, we examined functional devolution to state-sponsored bodies. In this chapter, we turn to areal dispersion.

In Ireland the areal dispersion of government functions and powers has taken two forms: one has its roots deep in history and is bound up with the development of democracy; the other is an *ad hoc* and piecemeal creation of politicians and bureaucrats in recent times for administrative convenience. The first is local government, the devolution of functions and powers to locally elected representative authorities—principally the councils of counties, county boroughs, boroughs, urban districts, and "towns." Although subject to the supremacy and supervision of the national government, these local authorities have been endowed with jurisdiction over the provision of certain services subject to the approval of their electors. The second is regional government, a term used imprecisely to cover a number of arrangements for devolving and deconcentrating business to authorities whose jurisdiction embraces areas larger than those of the local authorities.

As it is used at present, the term "regional government" covers several types of organization. First, there are authorities having the administration of some service devolved upon them, whose governing bodies consist of representatives of local authorities and interested associations or groups in the region—for example, the eight Area Health Boards and the eight Regional Tourism Organizations. Second, in the provision of some services, the central authorities concerned have decentralized business to regional organizations or offices for administrative, managerial, or, occasionally, customer convenience. "These represent the deconcentration of significant powers to the appropriate managers."[1] For example, state-sponsored bodies like Córas Iompair Éireann and the Electricity Supply Board have regional organizations and the Industrial Development Authority has "regional offices." Likewise, some government departments with branch offices or field services divide the country up into administratively convenient units whose managers have some discretionary powers.

All—both the authorities with devolved powers and the organizations set up for deconcentration of administration—have boundaries to suit their own convenience; the regional areas thus created do not coincide.[2] Since there is also an underlying network of local authorities, the result is a jungle of administrative areas that is both impenetrable to the ordinary citizen and frequently inconvenient for any kind of business that involves more than one authority or regional organization. Many of these arrangements have come into existence in the last quarter of a century or less. In the words of the Institute of Public Administration's study group in 1971, there has been "rapid and uncoordinated growth both of regional authorities and systems of regional administration."[3] This "rather haphazard tangle of regional boundaries"[4] badly needs reducing to order.

The creation of regional bodies seems to represent an effort on the one hand to push business away from the centre or, conversely, on the other hand, to coordinate the activities of areally smaller authorities. For, notwithstanding the growth of regional organizations, the main foci of government and politics are, as they always have been, (1) central (national-level) government, whose services are administered by central departments or the state-sponsored bodies in their penumbra, and (2) local government, which is the main subject of this chapter.

II

Viewed as part of a national system of public *administration,* local government can be seen as one of a trio of groups of authorities, the others being the central departments and the state-sponsored bodies. However, local authorities are not to be regarded *simply* as administrative organs allocated functions by the central authorities as convenience dictates, though this is to a large extent what they have become. The system of local government developed in Great Britain and Ireland in the nineteenth century was one of two systems of government (central and local) to cope with virtually all public business. It was intended to be local *self-*government—democracy carried down to the smallest community unit practicable and, by the device of committee administration of all services, to the most intimate details of their application. The great growth of the state-sponsored bodies may be seen simply as the development of devolved or decentralized administration of central government functions, for state-sponsored bodies answer to the cabinet and the Oireachtas. Local government should not be similarly viewed. To do so is to ignore both its history and its rationale.

It cannot be denied, of course, that local government is subordinate government, since local authorities, having no inherent authority of their own, derive their functions and powers from the Oireachtas. Nevertheless, local authorities are different in kind from state-sponsored bodies, for they are in themselves representative. Local government embodies the concept of local democracy as an integral feature. Services are administered under the supervision of locally elected persons who have some discretion in their conduct of affairs and who can be called to account. No doubt, in the twentieth century, the exigencies of the welfare state have pressed inexorably in upon the body of local self-government, crushing it almost to death. Nevertheless, local government will not be understood unless it is remembered that originally the citizens who paid local taxes (for local government has a source of funds of its own, the "rates"—now much attenuated) were intended to have considerable autonomy in the provision of local services.

In this tradition, there is a generally accepted belief in Ireland in the value of local government as a *democratic* institution, perhaps even as an essential part of democracy. This legacy of Victorian liberalism was expressed in 1971 in a government white paper on the reform of local government:

The real argument . . . for the provision of local services by local authorities . . . is that a system of local self-government is one of the essential elements of democracy. Under such a system, local affairs can be settled by the local citizens themselves or their representatives, local services can be locally controlled and local communities can participate in the process and responsibilities of government. Local government exists, therefore, for democratic as well as practical reasons.[5]

Paradoxically, Irish local government is, in T. J. Barrington's opinion, "one of the most centrally controlled of local government systems."[6] In addition, local authorities are more bureaucratic than they were when the system was inherited from the British. Ireland has a council-manager system of local government, having largely abandoned the British principle of direct committee administration of services in favour of the conduct of all services under the direction of a single individual, the city or county manager, who answers to his council but yet has a statutory position and statutory powers. Since managers are appointed and local government committees in the British tradition consist of elected councillors, there is obviously a greater willingness in Ireland to forfeit participation in order to achieve efficiency. Perhaps, also, Irish people do not feel very strongly about local self-government. When in the 1960s and 1970s local elections were postponed to suit the convenience of the national political timetable, hardly a voice was raised in protest. When councils were suspended or abolished for nonperformance of their duties, they went out of existence with scarcely a whimper or cry of alarm. Even the suspension of the Dublin City Council in 1969 for failure to strike an adequate rate did not arouse much public hostility. If the public does not care all that much, neither do all but a few politicians: indeed, the present national-local relationships and the bureaucratic administration of services suit many of them quite well, as we shall see.

The equivocal attitudes of public and politicians reflect the fact that there is a fundamental problem in local government: how are democratic procedures and local autonomy to survive in the face of the evident trend of modern welfare states toward uniform and ever rising standards and levels of service that people demand but that seem to require bigger and bigger catchment areas? The importance of the problem can be gauged by measuring the size and range of the services provided by local authorities.

Table 15.1 shows that in the forty years up to the late 1970s, local authorities were responsible for a third (more or less) of the total expenditure of public authorities. As a percentage of the gross national product, their expenditure had risen in this period from under 10 to nearly 17 per cent. Furthermore, the objects of this considerable expenditure include the provision of basic environmental services such as roads, water, sewerage, refuse collection, burial grounds, and fire protection. Although the removal of responsibility for personal health and public assistance services in the 1970s was a major piece of administrative surgery, this was to some extent compensated for by the extension of local authorities' control over physical planning and development and building.

Local authorities, it seems, have reverted to what they were in the past—the providers of environmental services and the protectors of the environment. This fact is well illustrated by the headings of the "programme groups" of local authorities' functions listed in official documents: "housing and building"; "road transportation and safety"; "water supply and sewerage"; "development incentives and controls"; "environmental protection"; "recreation and amenity"; and two ragbags of residual or peripheral functions, namely, "agriculture, education, health and welfare" and "miscellaneous services." (For a detailed list of local gov-

TABLE 15.1

Total Expenditure of All Local Authorities as a Percentage of the Total Public Sector Budget and Gross National Product, 1939–78

| | Year ending March 31 | | | | Calendar |
Expenditure	1939	1949	1959	1965	year 1978
Total expenditure of local authorities (IR£ million)	16.0	30.2	65.6	106.0	1,041.8
Total public sector budget (IR£ million)	47.7[a]	97.2	182.8	332.8	3,587.8
Local authorities' expenditure as percentage of total public sector budget	33.5%	31.1%	35.9%	31.9%	29.0%
GNP at factor cost (IR£ million)	161.6	333.7	517.8	826.0	6,245.0
Local authorities' expenditure as percentage of GNP	9.9%	9.1%	12.7%	12.8%	16.7%

SOURCE: Compiled from *Irish Statistical Survey* and *National Income and Expenditure,* both published annually by the Stationery Office, Dublin.

[a] Excludes a special payment of IR£10 million to the British government under a Treaty agreement.

TABLE 15.2

Expenditure of Local Authorities, 1977

| | Expenditure (IR£m) | |
Programme group	Current	Capital
Housing and building	93.6	103.4
Road transportation and safety	86.9	2.4
Water supply and sewerage	40.3	26.5
Development incentives and controls	6.1	4.4
Environmental protection	25.6	1.3
Recreation and amenity	17.1	2.5
Agriculture, education, health, and welfare	24.2	0.8
Miscellaneous services	23.3	4.1

SOURCE: Derived from *Returns of Local Taxation, 1977* (Stationery Office, Dublin, 1980).

NOTE: "Local authorities" are county councils, county borough corporations, borough corporations, urban district councils, town commissioners, and a number of joint bodies. Vocational Educational Committees, County Committees of Agriculture, health boards, and harbour authorities are not included.

ernment functions by class of authority, see Appendix E.) As Table 15.2 shows, in terms of spending, the big business of local government lies in the first three of the programme groups—housing and building, roads, and water and sewerage. These are the heart of local government and mark its essentially environmental character. This reversion of local authorities to being principally environmental authorities was symbolized in 1977 by the alteration of the title of their principal sponsor minister from Minister for Local Government to Minister for the Environment.

Although Irish local authorities are the providers of important services and, in particular, essential environmental services, it should be noticed that their range of responsibilities is quite restricted. In the other countries of the European Communities, local authorities are involved in police and court functions, in education, in the provision and promotion of cultural services to a far greater extent than the meagre library and museum services provided in Ireland, and in a wide range of health and welfare services.[7] Even in respect of physical planning and industrial development, where with the enactment of the Local Government (Planning and Development) Act (1963) it seemed that local authorities might be expected to play a leading role as developers of their areas, in Barrington's judgement, "the real action was to lie elsewhere."[8]

III

The institutions of local government derive, on the one hand, from the British tradition of civic autonomy dating from medieval times and symbolized by the royal charters granted to towns by monarchs. On the other hand their origins may be traced to the practice of placing the onus for law and order in the countryside on the local gentry, who were also expected to administer on an amateur and unpaid basis such state regulations as applied in their neighbourhood and such public services as were absolutely essential, like the relief of destitution and the provision of roads. From the 1830s, a new and unified system was created in stages to deal with the social problems of the industrial revolution when and as they were perceived in Great Britain. It was completed by the end of the nineteenth century.

The authorities then created were representative and were progressively democratized. The system was extended to Ireland stage by stage in line with developments in Great Britain with as few modifications as were essential, though conditions in Ireland were often different from those "across the water." Thus, to understand Irish local government, it is necessary to begin with British experience and British solutions applied in an Irish setting. However, in the twenty years from independence to the Second World War, modifications and additions of such magnitude were made by the first indigenous governments that the resultant pattern was by no means merely a variation of the British model.

The reforms and developments of the nineteenth century centred principally on three units: (1) the counties, (2) the boroughs and other towns, and (3) the poor-law "unions" created in 1838 each with its "boards of guardians" to administer the relief of destitution. (In Great Britain, the poor-law unions were literally unions of parishes; in Ireland, the unit was an area of ten miles radius around each of 130 market towns.) It was to these three groups of authorities that the state turned from the 1830s on for the administration of a growing range of services, particularly public health and other environmental services designed to protect the community and to relieve the worst hardships of its poorest members. In particular, the efficient poor-law guardians were loaded with the administration of public and personal health services and the provision of housing that went far beyond the relief of destitution. These three sets of authorities were reorganized and reformed when rising standards of efficiency and a growing acceptance of the principle of democracy so demanded. To a great extent, reforming legislation enacted by Westminster for Ireland was very similar to that devised for Great Britain and followed it closely in time.

By 1880, two types of representative urban authority had been created. The councils of sizeable towns including the boroughs—the "urban district councils" as they came to be called—were developing as major multipurpose authorities. The representative bodies of the smaller towns, called "town commissioners," were endowed with a narrower range of responsibilities that did not extend to public health services, for the provision of which they relied on the appropriate union and later on the county council. With the reshaping of county government in Great Britain in 1888 and 1896, the administration of services in the countryside in Ireland was clearly due for reform: the contrast between the oligarchic and increasingly anachronistic grand jury system by which local persons of consequence performed both administrative and judicial functions and the representative and increasingly democratic urban government was becoming ever sharper. Under the Local Government (Ireland) Act (1898), the functions of the grand juries were transferred to democratically elected county councils. Since the franchise was wide, extending as it did to male householders or occupiers, a considerable measure of democracy came to the Irish countryside with dramatic suddenness and was immediately turned to account in the developing national struggle for independence.

Besides providing democratic government at the county level, the 1898 act arranged for the transfer of the public health functions of the poor-law guardians to county district authorities called "rural district councils," thus setting up a two-tier system in the countryside as in the towns. However, the largest boroughs (Dublin, Cork, Limerick, and Waterford) were created counties (termed "county boroughs"), as the largest British towns had been in 1888, and were completely divorced for local government purposes from the adjoining county areas. The county borough councils thus became almost all-purpose local authorities.

By the end of the century, then, a more or less coherent pattern of authorities had been established to replace the confusing mass of over-lapping bodies that had been created *ad hoc* earlier in the century, and a simplified taxation system in the form of the rates, a tax on housing and other fixed property, provided an autonomous source of funds. Yet not all "local government" had been subsumed in this set of authorities. Apart from services such as police and education—which, in contrast to Great Britain, had been nationalized and were administered bureaucrat-ically by central government departments—there still existed local public bodies such as harbour boards and port sanitary authorities, and the boards of guardians, which were, however, fully democratized and partly assimilated to the main system, being composed of members of the ap-propriate urban and rural authorities. On paper at least, this system resembled very closely the British pattern, lacking only the parish coun-cils that in Britain formed a third or bottom tier of local authorities in the rural areas and were the culmination of Victorian grassroots democ-racy.

Between 1898 and independence, local government was dominated by national political issues and movements. The new franchise brought about a great change in the composition of the councils. The county councils in particular became centres of nationalism. In 1906, a French writer, L. Paul-Dubois, pointed out that the 1898 act was "revolutioniz-ing the antiquated local government system. . . . By providing the popu-lar movement with a lever against the Castle and at the same time a permanent local focus, it gave Ireland a new weapon to advance its claims."[9] Thus, as J. J. Horgan put it, "the Local Government Act of 1898, although indeed its authors knew it not, was the legislative father of the Irish Free State."[10]

After the Dáil government was established in 1919, the large majority of local councils, in the words of the *First Report of the Department of Local Government,* "challenged the authority of the Imperial Parliament by refusing to recognize the control of the Local Government Board and by making declarations of allegiance to Dáil Éireann."[11] Of all the Dáil government departments, Local Government was the most successful and least shadowy. In this heady atmosphere, the administration of local services suffered somewhat, a decline that was hastened by the financial disabilities placed by the British on recalcitrant authorities, by the breakdown in the collection of rates, and by the fact that civil war fol-lowed immediately after the Treaty. The combined effect of all this on a local government system that was not in any case working well in the cities and in which committee administration, the democratic powerhouse of the British system, was patently inefficient in Irish conditions and conducive to nepotism, was to force the new government to suspend some authorities for incompetence or neglect and to consider the whole question of the machinery and procedures of local government. Two decades of reform followed. The result was that, whereas the pattern of Irish local authorities today is largely a late-nineteenth-century creation, the machinery and processes of local government are products of the first generation of independent rule.

IV

The first rulers of the Irish Free State approached local government with the view that as the elected representatives of the Irish people, now come into their own, they had a duty to organize an honest and efficient governmental system and to do so quickly and with no nonsense. Local authorities, for all their displays of national fervour, were in many cases not particularly efficient. Their administration was often sloppy and tainted with nepotism and jobbery, which were anathema to many of the austere and high-minded ministers and their even more austere civil servants. Imbued with the ideals of Sinn Féin and supported by middle-class and influential business interests in Cork and Dublin who clamoured for efficient and economical city administration, they began at once to think in terms of structures and procedures that were less democratic and more bureaucratic to effect these ends. From 1922 on, a second phase of reforms took place. It was not completed for twenty years. Between 1922 and 1942, the machinery and procedures of Irish local government were transformed from a close and apparently unsatisfactory imitation of those of Britain to a unique system of managerial government and central supervision that is undoubtedly more bureaucratic in its operation than what went before.

Although the general trend of local government development after independence was away from the Victorian democratic ideal of the greatest possible devolution of appropriate functions to elected representatives, democracy in one respect was quickly achieved. The restrictions on full adult franchise in the 1898 act and plural voting by reason of ownership of property were removed by 1935. Since that date, the qualifications for registration as a local elector have been only adult status (that is, age 21 or over until 1973 and thereafter age 18 or over) and residence. There is not even a necessity to be an Irish citizen or national, as there is to have a vote in general elections.

The Victorian concept of local democracy, which in Great Britain resulted in a two- or three-tier system of authorities everywhere except in the largest cities, was never fully implemented in Ireland, for parish councils were never set up. Indeed, after independence, the trend towards grassroots authorities was reversed, a process that has continued ever since. The poor-law guardians were abolished in 1923, the rural district councils in 1925; in both cases their functions were transferred to the county councils. The smaller urban authorities came under increasing strain and tended to lose or give up their functions and powers. During the interwar period, there were always at any one time a handful of town authorities suspended by ministerial order for nonperformance of their duties, and by 1940 the councils of a few of the smaller towns had ceased to exist altogether.

This trend continued: by 1960 six town commissions had disappeared. Besides this, a few of the councils of urban districts (the larger town authorities) gave up their urban district status in favour of the lowlier "town" status. Increasingly, also, town councils were permitted to hand over the actual performance of duties—for example, house building, paving, lighting, and cleaning—to the councils of the counties in which they were situated and did so. After the introduction in the counties of the manager system, with the county manager being manager for all the local authorities in his county areas, there was virtually a single administration in each county, and it was thus easier for the smaller authorities to give up functions.

This trend reflected the increasing technical, administrative, and financial inadequacy of small units faced with the growing range and rising level of public services. One result was that the county units, including the county boroughs (the major cities, which have county status), came more and more to dominate local government. Local government in Ireland became and is now primarily county council government. Another result is that because there are so few small district authorities, the total number of local councils is small. According to Barrington, "By the standards of other small democracies, we have very few directly elected authorities, and if we accept that, in practice, we have only thirty-one with a significant range of functions, extremely few by the standards of any other country."[12] Nevertheless, the structure of authorities is still recognizably based on the British system that obtained before independence and indeed survived in Britain until the great reforms after the Second World War (see Fig. 15.1).

The counties and county boroughs have in turn come under strain. Even in 1898, the decision to make the counties as they stood the major units of local government was open to question. However, the counties were there and, although their boundaries were in origin largely the

IN ENGLAND AND WALES

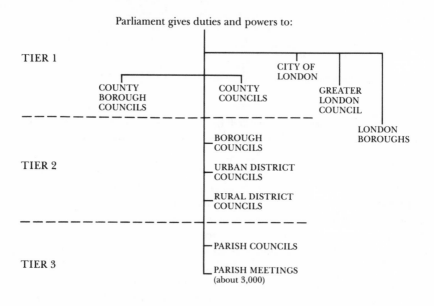

Parliament gives duties and powers to:

TIER 1

COUNTY BOROUGH COUNCILS

COUNTY COUNCILS

CITY OF LONDON

GREATER LONDON COUNCIL

LONDON BOROUGHS

TIER 2

BOROUGH COUNCILS

URBAN DISTRICT COUNCILS

RURAL DISTRICT COUNCILS

TIER 3

PARISH COUNCILS

PARISH MEETINGS (about 3,000)

IN THE REPUBLIC OF IRELAND

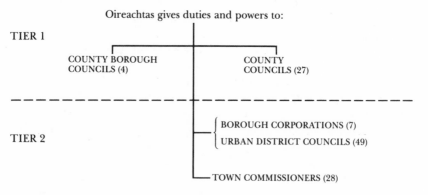

Oireachtas gives duties and powers to:

TIER 1

COUNTY BOROUGH COUNCILS (4)

COUNTY COUNCILS (27)

TIER 2

BOROUGH CORPORATIONS (7)

URBAN DISTRICT COUNCILS (49)

TOWN COMMISSIONERS (28)

FIG. 15.1. Major Local Authorities in England and Wales (Until 1973) and in the Republic of Ireland

product of accidents, they were accepted without question and without reference to the large differences among them in area, wealth, and population. Population changes, the increase in public services, and scientific and technical advances exacerbated these differences while putting strain upon all, big and small.

For example, by the third quarter of the twentieth century, even comparatively strong county authorities were patently not big enough units for hospital services, and the same was being asserted in relation to other services also. In 1970, the administration of health services generally was removed from the direct control of local authorities and was assigned to Area (that is, regional) Health Boards. Physical planning was also placed on a regional basis and indeed, as the Institute of Public Administration's report *More Local Government* pointed out, by 1971, regional authorities and administrative units of one sort or another had proliferated. In that same year, the government white paper *Local Government Reorganisation* conceded that the county was less suitable than the region for the planning of many services and for the delivery and administration of some.[13] However, sentiment, both patriotic and sporting, had attached itself to the county units. In the face of this, the government in 1971—and succeeding governments—shelved the problem. By 1980, it was serious, not least in the Dublin area and its immediate hinterland, where there seemed to be a crying need for a new arrangement of authorities for what had become a burgeoning conurbation.

The democratic element in local government was lessened not only by the concentration of functions in fewer authorities; local government also became markedly more bureaucratic—and more efficient. Bureaucratization took three forms: (1) increasing central government control; (2) the creation of a single local government service, centrally selected by open competition and controlled in many respects by the central administration; and (3) most important in its consequences, the institution of the manager system. These trends, Barrington thought, "all arose from the assumption by central government of responsibility for raising the level of efficiency of local government according to the conceptions of efficiency in the 1920s and 1930s. . . . The other side of this coin was the subjection of a great part of the day-to-day operations of local authorities to the most intense subordination and control."[14]

Central control by ministerial departments increased steadily from the 1920s until by 1950 it was ubiquitous, though unsystematic and uneven in its incidence. Increasingly, the older conception of local government as a separate governmental system was displaced by the idea of local authorities as agents of central government. Not only did central control increase in volume, but the number of departments involved in supervision grew as local authorities came increasingly to be viewed as handy field agencies for the administration under supervision of new services. Although the principal reporting relationship of local authorities was to the Department of Local Government (later Environment), by the late 1960s they were reporting also to the Departments of Health, Agriculture and Fisheries, Education, Justice, Social Welfare, Transport and Power, and Defence.[15]

Sometimes, new services occasioned the creation of new single-purpose statutory authorities separate from the local authorities proper, though linked to them by representation. The most important of these were the County Committees of Agriculture and the Vocational Education Committees, each operating under their own statutes and under the supervision of their own sponsor minister. Such arrangements tended to remove the services concerned from direct control by local authorities and to insulate them somewhat. Likewise, in the 1970s, the regional and county development organizations were closely "coordinated" by a Central Development Committee under the aegis of the Department of Finance.

Local authorities had of course been objects of central government surveillance and supervision from mid-Victorian times, when a reformed and efficient central bureaucracy was expected by parsimonious politicians to keep a close watch over the poor performance and lax standards of unreformed local administrations. By the time local authorities had become more professional and able to achieve high standards unaided, the tradition of control had hardened. Moreover, a pattern of ever increasing financial dependence on central funds had been established and led inevitably to central control to protect the taxpayers' interest. (See Table 15.3 for the sources of local authorities' revenue.) Control was the

TABLE 15.3
Sources of Local Authorities' Revenue in 1939, 1959, and 1979

	1939		1959		1979 (estimates)	
Source	IR£m	Pct.	IR£m	Pct.	IR£m	Pct.
Rates	6.3	50%	20.6	40%	89.7	21%
State grants	4.7	37	22.2	43	266.4	61
Other (mainly rents and repayments for housing)	1.7	13	8.8	17	80.1	18
TOTAL[a]	12.6	100%	51.5	100%	436.2	100%

SOURCE: For 1939 and 1959, *Returns of Local Taxation* (annual, Stationery Office, Dublin). For 1979, *Local Authority Estimates, 1979* (Stationery Office, Dublin, 1980), p. 20.
  [a] Some amounts have been rounded.

more detailed because grants were often allocated for prescribed purposes and hedged about with stringent conditions, ranging from the need to get prior approval of plans in detail, to payments after inspection or on proof of attaining set standards. In addition, there was stringent audit.

This type of detailed control evidently became a permanent feature of local government, for in 1969 the Public Services Organisation Review Group (the Devlin Group) reported about local authorities' engineering, construction, and planning schemes that

projects must be approved by the Department of Local Government. There is extremely close financial and technical control over county and city engineers through inspection and financial sanction. Although overall approval is obtained from the Department of Local Government for the annual programme of schemes, each individual scheme requires separate approval at various stages. Financial sanction for each project must be obtained from the relevant Department. The amount of reference back involved is considerable. Checking may be carried out at the outline scheme stage, at detailed design stage, at contract drafting stage and at the final tender acceptance stage. There is considerable duplication and delay.[16]

The financial dependence of local authorities on central government was greatly increased as a result of the decision—to honour an election promise—to abolish rates on domestic property in 1977. Between 1977 and 1978, local authorities' revenue from rates dropped by 25 per cent and state grants increased by nearly 60 per cent.[17] As Table 15.3 shows, whereas in 1959 40 per cent of local authorities' revenue came from rates, in 1979 it was only half that proportion. The consequences of the abolition of rates were immediate and marked. The central government's moves to determine the maximum increases in rates on the types of property that were still liable deprived local authorities of almost the last room they had for manoeuvre in determining expenditure. There were, no doubt, strong pressures on the government in the interests of the national economy to curb the spending of local authorities, which now had less and less incentive to economize, but the results were clear: "The centre has virtually taken over local taxation."[18]

The control of central government extends to supervision not only of performance but of personnel. This takes two forms: (1) selection on a national basis of administrative and professional officers and (2) control by the Department of Local Government of personnel matters generally.

Even before independence, Sinn Féin had indicated its intention of reforming the local government system, which was, in truth, not a single service at all. Local officials were chosen and appointed by the local authorities themselves, and, "as might be expected in such circumstances, recruitment on considerations other than merit was only too frequent."[19] Moreover, authorities being separate jurisdictions, many very small, promotion opportunities were inadequate, and consequently morale and incentive were low. Condemning these weaknesses, Sinn Féin promised a national service, appointment by open competition, and mobility.

Such a system was duly instituted, notably by the creation in 1926 of an independent Local Appointments Commission to select and nominate to all administrative and professional posts, and in the creation of a local service code administered by the Department of Local Government. In its annual report for 1950–51, the Department of Local Government could point out that "over a long period the law has vested in the central authority a tight control over local authorities in staff matters. The purpose of this was to ensure that staffs are properly recruited and fairly treated. Generally that position has been reached." Once again, however, efficiency had been achieved at the cost of local autonomy, a cost that in this instance few would regard as heavy. A single and efficient local service with adequate career opportunities is of particular importance in a small country with small local administrations. In addition, the experience over the years of the filling of those few appointments that still remain in the hands of elected representatives and in the employment of manual staff where the employing officers are subject to continuous pressure by public representatives bears witness to the undesirability of leaving any door at all open for nepotism, jobbery, or "representations."[20]

The tight hold of the central administration over local authorities often evoked critical comment. The impact of detailed, complicated, and confusing controls at times inevitably frustrated councillors and officials alike. In 1963, J. L. Garvin, then Secretary of the Department of Local Government, frankly admitted to "the ever-present tendency in supervising authorities to concentrate on controls as being easier to operate than to curtail, involving no fresh thinking." He spoke of a change in his department "in the direction of cutting out particular controls, of generalizing sanctions and of freeing local authorities to operate within reasonably wide limits of autonomy." In the future, the relationship "will not be of leader and led, still less of controller and controlled, but a partnership."[21] In fact, there were no major or fundamental changes. The verdict of the Devlin Group in 1969 was unequivocal: "The striking feature of the Irish system of local government, whether it is compared with local government systems abroad or with other administrative systems within the country, is the degree and extent of the controls exercised over it."[22]

Although, in respect of some activities of local authorities, the control of detail and the need to refer minutiae might have lessened since then, the overall tendency has been towards more not less control in an era of centrally inspired development planning. In particular, there has been an ever tightening hold on salaries and industrial relations matters by the Local Government Staff Negotiations Board, set up in 1971, and the Department of the Public Service. The abolition of domestic rates, though welcome to the public as taxpayers, was in the eyes of many councillors a final nail in the coffin of local self-government. Writing in 1980, Barrington echoed the Devlin Group's verdict: "Ours remains one of the most centrally controlled of local government systems." In particular, it has no opportunity to exercise discretion or take initiatives: "Our local government system remains shackled with archaic legal and administrative impediments to the displaying of such qualities. Unless the central authority sanctions, supports and legislates for a new initiative, little or nothing can be done."[23]

V

Whereas central control has diminished the discretion of both local councillors and local officials, the creation of a managerial system has increased the local official's role at the local councillor's expense. The manager was intended to replace committee administration; thus, in intention and result, the arrangement was an important modification of the British inheritance. It was the outcome of a combination of growing dissatisfaction with the operation of local government before independence, the austere idealism of Sinn Féin in the persons of the first rulers (politicians and civil servants) of the Irish Free State, and the influence of urban businessmen who wanted to see business methods and procedures applied to city administration, as they thought had been the case in the United States. Governmental commissions and departmental enquiries alike reported in favour of a managerial system "so that there could be brought to the solution of many urgent local problems an absolute impartiality and an understanding of modern developments in city management."[24]

Because the most insistent pressure came from Cork, where a group of professional men and businessmen calling themselves "The Progressives" drafted proposals for a scheme, and because Cork posed a less complicated problem than the much larger Dublin, it was in the Cork City Management Act (1929) that management was first introduced to Ireland. The Cork pattern was followed with minor variations when it was extended to Dublin in 1930, to Limerick in 1934, to Waterford in

1939, and, finally, to the counties in 1942. As county managers also became managers for each urban authority in their county, all the major local authorities operate under this system.

The basic principle of the management system, as it was expressed in the Management Acts of 1929 to 1940, is "a legal dichotomy of reserved powers of councils and executive functions of managers."[25] That legislation prescribes the functions of the council (the "reserved functions") and the functions of the manager (the "executive functions"). Elected members are to concern themselves with two main types of business: first, general policy matters such as the adoption of the budget, the striking of the rate, borrowing, the disposal of council property, the making of local laws (called "bylaws") and important planning decisions; and, second, what might be called representational matters, such as the control of elections, the selection of persons to be members of other bodies, the appointment of committees, and the salary of the mayor (in towns and cities).

All the functions and duties of the council that are not specified as reserved functions are executive or managerial functions. These managerial functions explicitly include the appointment and control of staff, insofar as these matters are not centrally controlled, and the making of contracts including the letting of houses. Until the removal of responsibility for health and welfare services, they included also the administration of health services and the determination of entitlement to health and other social benefits. Thus, functions that involved decisions open to personal and political influence and that increasingly, as the welfare state developed, required a mass of detailed administration and decisions unsuited to committee procedures were removed from the elected representatives and from committee decision. Since there was no longer any need for a full-blown committee system, councils were made smaller in size.

The manager is an officer of the council or councils that he serves; he is required to keep members informed about business and to aid and advise them in the performance of their duties. He must attend council meetings, and as the chief executive officer he is responsible for the work necessary to implement council decisions. In his own sphere, he must act by formal "Order" in matters that, had they been council decisions, would have required a resolution of the council. A register of these orders must be available for council inspection.

Though an officer of the council, the manager is not chosen by the council, being nominated to it by the Local Appointments Commission. Nor can he be dismissed by his council, which has the power (never so far used) only to suspend him and to request the Minister for Local

Government to remove him. Thus, clearly, the manager, who has statutory functions and powers and who is neither hired nor fired by his employers, is far removed in conception from the managers of the typical United States system, "where the manager is so clearly the servant of the elected council."[26]

The principle of a rigid division of functions and powers as envisaged in the Management Acts up to 1940 was, however, as little likely to operate in practice as the principle of the dichotomy of politics and administration propounded by the contemporary public administration theorists, to whom the concept perhaps owed something. Inevitably, in the words of a former Dublin City manager:

The original intention of the legislators to draw a clear line, both in law and in practice, between the Council's reserved functions and the Manager's executive functions has been lost sight of in some degree in the evolution of the system. Managers find themselves involved in business reserved to the Councils. . . . On the other hand Councillors have gained over the years considerable influence in relation to the Manager's functions.[27]

The blurring in practice of the legal distinction between reserved and executive functions was hastened by tensions that arose with the coming of county management in the early 1940s. County councillors, accustomed to administering their own services, which on the whole they did badly, resented the new system. Furthermore, many saw the new managers as agents of the Department of Local Government. Perhaps, also, some of the first county managers were rigid and pedantic in interpreting their powers according to the letter of the Management Act. A series of circulars were issued from the Department through the 1940s pointing out that although there was a legal distinction between reserved and executive functions, this did not imply that managers should carry out their duties independently of the councils; the circulars exhorted closer collaboration. Under the pressure of public opinion, the Department increasingly insisted on "the predominant position of the elected body," as one circular put it.

Subsequent legislation, and particularly the City and County Management (Amendment) Act (1955), formally invested the elected representatives with more power. Under that act, the manager is required to inform his council before he undertakes new works, other than maintenance and repair work. The council may, if it chooses, prohibit these works, provided that they are not required by law to be done. Also, members may by resolution require the manager to do any action that is lawful and for which money has been provided, notwithstanding that the action is within the area of the manager's discretion. Thus, for example, although the letting of houses is a managerial function, a council may require a manager to let a house to a particular person. This power, the so-called section 4 resolution, has been much used—and abused—particularly by councillors in some counties who have interested themselves in planning permissions.

The 1955 act also provided that, although the control of staff is a managerial function, council sanction is needed to vary the number and rates of remuneration of staff. Likewise, although the making of contracts rests with the manager, elected members have the power to prescribe the procedures to be followed in seeking and processing tenders. Finally, the act gave councils the right, if they wish, to set up estimates committees to take over, formally at least, the preparation of the annual budget; some of the larger councils do appoint such committees.

Despite the conscious attempt to turn back the tide of managerial bureaucracy and to give the elected members the last say even in the manager's own area of competence, the growth of public services and the need to plan and organize complex schemes led to the manager's increasingly becoming the major source of initiative in a local authority. Although the council must approve the estimates and vote the rates, the manager, sometimes with committee help, prepares the budget and it is to him that councillors look to propose and prepare schemes of all sorts. Even the use of estimates committees has not affected the initiating role of the manager, but it does at least give a few members of the council some part in planning future activity.

If the managers have become the main source of initiative in local government, the councillors have considerable opportunities to influence the managers' decisions, big and small, within the narrow limits for manoeuvre that the central government has left local authorities. Managers are likely to consult councillors about matters involving their own districts or their own constituents (for example, in formulating their road programmes or when letting houses), and councillors expect them to receive representations on matters within their executive powers. Managers even promote the setting up of advisory groups of the council to give them advice on matters within their managerial competence. Thus the roles of councillor and manager have evolved differently from those that were at first envisaged and that the original statutes spelled out. These roles are well understood and accepted.

VI

The role of the councillor as it has developed in the Irish system is a long way from the Victorian ideal of local representatives who decide and administer neighbourhood affairs in the workshops of local government, the committees of the council. As is the case at national level with TDs, the elected member is a consumer representative and more of a factor in the administration of services than a policy maker or legislator. Of course, local government as a whole is to a large extent administration in any case, in the sense that it is concerned with the provision of services decided upon elsewhere; but even within the area of a local authority's discretion, the manager tends to be the architect of community services.

As is the case at national level also, councillors to a great extent accept this role. Most councillors are far more conscious of being frustrated by some action or lack of action in a central department than by the manager or the managerial system. Yet again, as at the national level, councillors are quite well suited to their role. In any case, they are bound to play it. Their chances of reelection depend upon doing so, and for many this is the first step in a political career, the only route to national office, and the only way to make sure of retaining that office once it is attained. To a great extent, local government and national government are, from the viewpoint of the politicians and party activists, virtually one system and not two.

Local representatives, who are overwhelmingly male, are of course people who belong in the districts they represent. The counties are divided for local government purposes into county electoral areas. A very strong local patriotism, reinforced by a firm—and well-founded—belief that it pays to have a councillor in one's own district, ensures that only people belonging to an area will represent it. Even in the cities, which are divided into wards for local electoral purposes, the neighbourhood appeal is a strong one.

In Chapter 5, we noticed that county councils are largely composed of farmers, professional people, especially teachers, and shopkeepers, publicans, and other family businessmen. The last-named group in particular is grossly overrepresented in relation to their numbers in the community, as it is also, together with the professional group, in the cities and towns, where the nonmanual working class is also well represented. (For details, see Table 5.4, p. 87.) On the other hand, few people in the manual working class get elected. On the county councils, farm labourers are not represented in the districts where they are to be found in some numbers—that is, in the east and southeast—and the same is true of manual workers generally. Nor are there many of these on the city councils. Only in the smaller urban authorities are they present in some numbers; there, the working class is strongly represented: in 1967 and 1974 people in manual occupations took almost 30 per cent of the seats. Only in the small towns, then, is politics other than a middle-class or prosperous-farmer activity. But these are the minor authorities. In the major authorities, as in national politics, the better-off predominate.

From the point of view of most citizens, however, the predominance of certain occupational groups on local councils probably does not seem important and certainly is not seen as a threat to the proper consideration of citizens' interests. To the citizen, the councillor is a neighbourhood contact man whose duties are to render help with problems such as housing, planning permission, and getting grants of one sort or another, and to secure a good share of new amenities for the district. From the citizen's point of view, it is as well that the councillor should be a person of some social standing and active as a local notable. Such an individual is thought more likely to have influence than a less well placed one. What is more, citizens are in a position to impose this role, for their votes are at issue here. "Service" is an important *quid pro quo* for political support in local as in national politics. The TD is as concerned as the councillor—and at the same level of public business, for it is primarily local authority services that most often and most intimately concern the ordinary person.

This constraint upon representatives has important consequences. It forces the councillor to concentrate upon relative trivia, and it establishes between the representatives and the manager and his staff a relationship that is rather more that of importunate—though important—clients seeking favours than that of a board of directors and their top management. In the council chamber things are different, but many of the matters with which councillors are most concerned, being details, are not effected there. It is possible also for an element of deception to enter into this activity. Sometimes—too often, say some local officials—councillors make requests that they know are impossible to grant, merely in order to appear to be doing a service for a constituent. Similar electoral considerations can also colour their speeches in public debate in the council chamber. Local newspapers give much space and prominence to the monthly meetings of the councils, and councillors sometimes strike public attitudes that are unrealistic and even two-faced, but newsworthy and, they hope, vote catching.

Most councillors, however, are not only local contact men but party representatives, and, as at national level, the public undoubtedly sees them in both roles. Local government is in fact dominated by the national political parties on the electoral plane and to a considerable extent also in the council chamber. This has been the case ever since the state came into existence. From the democratization of local government in

1898, councils were involved in national issues and became foci of nationalism. Subsequently, the civil war split and the deep political divisions that ensued were carried into local government. The tradition established in those days still lingers on in the propensity that councils have to pass resolutions on matters in which they have no competence. Such resolutions are often nationalistic in content and largely ritualistic.

Because the cleavage in the community over the civil war was so deep, local elections were from the beginning fought on national party lines. Nevertheless, the fact that the election system is the single transferable vote in multimember constituencies has always meant that, for most, a choice of candidates within one's party is available. Thus it is possible to give weight to local and other considerations without going outside the party. Nor has the domination of national parties at the local level meant that genuinely independent candidates have been totally absent or that councillors have invariably followed the party line. Some councils have prided themselves on sinking party differences, and it has been common to find working arrangements for filling the post of chairman or mayor, or in electing to other bodies, that have ignored party affiliations.

The strong party hold on local government and the single transferable vote system of election have usually produced a high turnout at local elections—high at least compared with turnouts in the United Kingdom, where low polls and, in the past, large numbers of uncontested seats afforded a poor example of local democracy in practice. Table 15.4 shows the turnout at elections since 1950. (In interpreting this and the following table, it should be remembered that electors in the four county boroughs and in the countryside vote to fill seats on a single authority, the city or county council, but those who live in towns with "urban district" or "town" status have two votes, one for the county council and one for the town authority.)

The table reveals, first, a marked contrast in turnout between Dublin, the only big city, and the rest of the country, whether urban or rural. Comparatively, the towns of Ireland other than Dublin are small and have a considerable community spirit; the rural population is likewise strongly oriented to local communities. It is probably the sense of community together with a perceived obligation for social reasons in small communities to be seen to vote that explains the higher turnout there. Indeed, as the table also suggests, there is some correspondence between size of town and turnout: the smaller the town, the higher is the proportion who vote.

The support given to the political parties at local elections confirms the strong party orientation of Irish people to which reference was made

TABLE 15.4

*Voting at Local Elections, 1950–79: Total Valid Poll
as a Percentage of the Electorate Entitled to Vote*

Authority	Election					
	1950	1955	1960	1967[a]	1974[a]	1979
County councils	62%	65%	60%	70%	67%	66%
Urban authorities:						
Dublin County Borough Council	39	39	29	51	40	47
Other county borough councils	57	65	55	66	57	58
Urban district councils						
(including boroughs)	62	62	59	67	64	63
Town commissioners	67	68	60	71	69	69
Average total valid poll	58	60	54	67	61	63

SOURCE: For 1950–67, derived from information made available by the Department of Local Government. For 1974, derived from *Local Elections, 1974: Results and Statistics* (Department of Local Government, Dublin, 1975). For 1979, derived from *Local Elections, 1979: Results and Statistics* (Department of the Environment, Dublin, 1980).

NOTE: The proportion of spoiled votes is, on average, between 1 and 2 per cent.

[a] Elections for local authorities are usually held every five years. The elections held in 1967 and 1974 had been delayed because of the incidence of other elections and referenda.

TABLE 15.5

*Party Support at the Central and Local Government Levels, 1960–79:
Percentage of First-Preference Votes Won by Each Party*

Election	Fianna Fáil	Fine Gael	Labour	Independents and others
Local elections, 1960[a]	*38.4%*	*26.5%*	*10.2%*	*24.9%*
General election, 1961	43.8	32.0	11.6	12.6
General election, 1965	47.8	33.9	15.4	2.9
Local elections, 1967[b]	*38.8*	*31.8*	*14.9*	*14.5*
General election, 1969	45.7	34.1	17.0	3.2
General election, 1973	46.2	35.1	13.7	5.0
Local elections, 1974[b]	*38.7*	*32.6*	*13.5*	*15.2*
General election, 1977	50.6	30.5	11.6	7.3
Local elections, 1979[b]	*38.2*	*34.0*	*12.3*	*15.5*

SOURCE: For 1960 and 1967 local elections, derived from information made available by the Department of Local Government. For all other elections, derived from official returns.

[a] Counties and county boroughs only.

[b] All local authorities.

in earlier chapters. Table 15.5 shows in a rough way the correspondence between the support a party gets at general elections and that at local elections. As at national elections, so, too, at local, the volume of support for the major parties places them in three different leagues, and this support has remained remarkably stable over time. The table shows also that candidates of small parties and independent candidates attract more support at the local than at the national level.

TABLE 15.6

Percentage of First-Preference Votes Won by
Each Party at Local Elections in 1967, 1974, and 1979

Party	County councils	County borough councils	Urban district councils[a]	Towns
Fianna Fáil:				
1967	41.3%	34.2%	29.2%	34.6%
1974	41.6	33.0	29.4	35.0
1979	41.1	30.1	31.9	34.7
Fine Gael:				
1967	35.4	23.6	25.3	29.9
1974	34.9	27.9	25.4	30.9
1979	36.2	30.1	26.8	30.8
Labour:				
1967	12.3	23.6	17.4	12.4
1974	11.5	18.9	17.8	14.4
1979	10.5	17.9	16.2	10.9
Independents and others:				
1967	11.0	18.6	28.1	23.1
1974	12.0	20.2	27.4	19.7
1979	12.2	21.9	25.1	23.6

SOURCE: For 1967, derived from information made available by the Department of Local Government. For 1974, *Local Elections, 1974: Results and Statistics* (Department of Local Government, Dublin, 1975). For 1979, *Local Elections, 1979: Results and Statistics* (Department of the Environment, Dublin, 1980).

[a] Including boroughs.

The appeal of independents and small-party candidates is notably stronger in the towns than in rural areas and stronger in the smaller towns than in the larger, as Table 15.6 shows. This is almost certainly due in part to the fact that it is less difficult for an urban candidate on his own to reach the electors and to the fact that the quotas necessary for election are lower in the small towns. It might also be that small-town voters are particularly susceptible to the appeal of a neighbour, are more aware of local issues, and feel more immediately concerned with them than are the voters of the cities or of the comparatively large county electoral areas.

VII

Most Irish people almost certainly approve of the idea of local democracy, although to judge by the lack of concern about its emasculation they do not feel strongly about it. Only in the context of a campaign in support of some local demand or a defence of some local institution do politicians spring to the defence of local autonomy; but this they can often do very effectively. Yet the trend towards bigger units, the stranglehold of the central departments over local administration, and considerable bureaucratization all suggest that local government is in practice not much more than the decentralized administration of centrally ordained and controlled services.

Governments in the 1960s and 1970s recognized the malaise in local government. In contemplating reform, they spoke of the need to succour local autonomy and democracy. The movement for reform, however, came to nothing. It needed a more radical and vigorous approach than governments and their advisers were prepared to adopt. In the face of the fierce antagonism evoked by suggestions for change of any kind, governments simply abdicated their responsibilities. The 1970s were punctuated only by declarations of successive governments that they were "considering" or "reviewing."[28] The truth is that the system as it is both suits the central administration, which has it in thrall, and answers the needs of most politicians, who are able to manipulate it to the extent necessary to supply a satisfactory service to their constituents and therefore block any proposal for reform that does emerge.

By 1980, the reform of local government was long overdue. The fact that the standards of some services in Ireland and particularly in Dublin were falling and that cities and towns were becoming increasingly tatty, the removal of functions from local authorities, and the *ad hoc* proliferation of regional arrangements all bore witness to the need. Some national leaders and a few younger TDs and senators readily conceded it. Unfortunately, given the symbiotic relationship of national and local government that the Irish political tradition has forged and the election system has underpinned, the chances of major reforms were probably poor. In Barrington's words, "local government [was] like any other historical ruin, something that we are perhaps reluctant to see removed wholly, but which we are prepared to see moulder away."[29]

SIXTEEN

Controlling the Administration

Public authorities, as T. J. Barrington observed, "exist basically to serve the people, not only The People, but individual people."[1] In considering the surveillance and control of the administration, this is an important distinction to make. The interests of "The People" require that there exist effective procedures for finding out whether the solutions devised by governments for the problems the community faces have been effective, and whether the administration has operated efficiently in applying them. From the point of view of the individual, however, it is the openness, accessibility, responsiveness, and sensitivity of government agencies when dealing with his or her particular problem that matter: the existence of effective procedures to ensure each of these contributes as much as elections, independent and alert representatives, and adequate consultation to the citizen's belief that he or she lives in a free and just community.

Important though this distinction is, we should notice that not very much is made of it in the institutions and procedures that were developed for controlling the administration. The two sets of institutions and procedures traditionally used tend to be dual-purpose and to obscure it.

Surveillance and control of the administration are effected, first, by parliamentary procedures, such as they are, which TDs and senators can use to question or criticize at both a macro level (the conduct of business in general) and a micro level (queries and appeals on individual cases). Surveillance and control are effected, second, through the courts and quasi-judicial officials attached to the administration itself—namely, administrative tribunals, ministers acting in an appellate capacity rather than as political decision makers, and designated civil servants endowed with specific statutory duties and powers. These deal with disputes between individual parties, both persons and institutions. If the plaintiff is an individual person, he or she will most likely be contending that a wrong has been done to him or her personally. Thus, as a controller of the administration, the courts and other officials are mostly called upon to act in the interests of "individual people" and not "The People," though sometimes an individual citizen goes to the courts on behalf of his or her fellow citizens, usually to question a general policy or administrative practice. Dr. John O'Donovan did this in 1961 when he successfully challenged the constitutionality of the Electoral (Amendment) Act (1959); so, too, did the Murphys, whose contention that it was unconstitutional to tax them as a married couple in such a way that they were charged more tax than two single people with the same incomes was upheld in the Supreme Court in 1980.[2]

Essential to the successful operation of these processes are the mass media. They not only provide information and comment on the major items of public policy and on the government's conduct of business, but they have the ability to throw light into dark corners and to bring to attention in a compelling way matters that, once noticed, call for investigation and remedy. In Chapter 4, we considered the mass media as part of the context within which politics is carried on. In this chapter, we shall be concerned only with their ability to publicize and comment on the actions of public authorities.

II

The forms of control over administrative action in Ireland derive from the British tradition, involving principles and practices dating from the seventeenth century. Their pattern and the way in which they have operated reveal a wholesale acceptance of British constitutional and legal theory and practice as these existed in the early part of the present century, and to a considerable extent continue to exist today.

From the seventeenth century on, it was thought that the legality of government actions could and should be controlled by the courts, which were then emerging to considerable independence, and the political acceptability of government actions would be determined by parliament. As J. D. B. Mitchell points out, it is essential to realize that the basic shape and limits of each of these forms of control, legal and political, were established and settled by the latter years of the nineteenth century, *before* the great increase in state functions resulted in a mass of detailed administration and the creation of a myriad of small individual rights and obligations.[3]

Legal control was effected through the ordinary courts, whose main concern was the enforcement of legal rights and obligations, not the fulfillment of public policy. Political control operated through the machinery of ministerial responsibility to parliament. Belief in this system can be seen in "the steady rise in the popularity of Parliamentary Questions, a rise which reflects both this reliance on parliamentary controls, and the need for a mechanism for dealing with individual grievances."[4] The operations of the emerging welfare state brought the system into difficulties. Its deficiencies as a check on administrative action and for securing redress became increasingly obvious as social and economic legislation began to pour out of parliament.

By this time, however, strong and seemingly almost unbreakable traditions had been established. On the one hand, the doctrine of ministerial responsibility commanded great respect. This respect continued to be accorded in spite of the failure of parliamentary practice to deal effectively with the emergence of strong rule by party leaders that followed the coming of the mass parties and machine politics. In the form assiduously fostered by party leaders, especially those in power, ministerial responsibility came down to two propositions: first, that ministers had to have considerable power and discretion to act and to protect their servants and their sources of information and advice; and, second, that they were answerable only in the House of Commons and, more narrowly, "on the floor of the House" (that is, in full session) and by the traditional (though increasingly archaic) procedure of the debating hall (which the House of Commons essentially was, and is). Even wide-ranging parliamentary committee investigation and discussion were, and are, held to derogate from "the principle of ministerial responsibility."

On the other hand, for their part, the legal profession had developed an unshakable belief in the efficiency of private law procedures and nursed an insular and myopic suspicion of the development in France and elsewhere of "administrative law"—that is, the branch of public law "relating to the organization and working of the public services and the relations of those services with private persons."[5] At the same time, the courts in their judgements showed a great respect for political controls and a consequent reluctance to interfere with administrative action. This extended to "the refusal of courts to examine the realities of parliamentary life and, hence, their inevitable tendency to build the law upon the fictions rather than the realities of that life."[6] Although legislation grew in volume and complexity and ministers acquired rule-making powers to an increasing degree (both without corresponding developments in parliamentary procedures to effect adequate scrutiny), the courts continued to give decisions based on the fiction that parliament did in fact control.

Likewise, as the volume of administration increased, a similar myth continued to be accepted in relation to the growing number of disputes in which ministers assumed the role of arbitrators or judges. A judge in an important case decided during the First World War put it thus: "My Lords, how can the judiciary be blind to the well known facts applicable not only to the Constitution but to the working of such branches of the executive. The department is represented in Parliament by its responsible head."[7] It followed from this, went the argument, that "the individual was not entitled to know or see the individual official who decided (this being, it was considered, immaterial, since the Minister was responsible) and that decisions need not be reasoned."[8]

The Irish state adopted *in toto* these constitutional and legal principles, myths and all, and the procedures and inhibitions to which they gave rise. However, within these confines, institutions and procedures have been developed to improve the ability of the Oireachtas both to enquire into the conduct of business generally and to review individual cases. Also, to an increasing extent in recent years, the decisions of the administration have been made subject to review and appeal, and the courts have become more and more inclined to question administrative action and to exploit the resources of the Constitution to protect individuals from the state.

III

The surveillance and control of the government's implementation of policies already decided upon are obviously to a great extent matters for the Oireachtas representing "The People." Equally obviously, they are inextricably linked with the Oireachtas' role in the *making* of policy (the subject of Part 3 of this book). Both when criticizing proposed policies and when urging remedial action, reforms, or new departures upon a government, parliamentary representatives are quite likely to start by commenting upon policies already being implemented and to draw conclusions from the existing situation. These provide them with much of their ammunition and many of their arguments.

In practice, also, the procedures of the Oireachtas tend not to draw much distinction between making policy and making the government behave (to use K. C. Wheare's phrase). Debates on legislative or policy proposals and on the estimates are opportunities to criticize current administration; parliamentary questions may be asked about the government's policy intentions and about administrative action, though most questions are in fact directed to the latter. If Oireachtas committees are largely confined to enquiring into the administration's performance in carrying out policy, it is sometimes but a short step thence to raising policy issues, a step that the Joint Committee on State-Sponsored Bodies, for example, was more and more often taking by 1980.

Likewise, as was made clear in Chapter 11, the handicaps from which the Oireachtas suffers by reason of the deficiencies of these procedures apply equally to making the government behave and to making the laws. Save in one area, the operations of public enterprises—and that only recently—the Dáil, much less the Seanad, does not subject the administration of policy to a searching and systematic appraisal, nor does either of them measure achievement against objectives in any precise or regular fashion. The remedies canvassed in Chapter 11—namely, the development of an effective committee system and the provision of adequate services and assistance—would improve the Oireachtas' ability to vet administrative action as much as it would improve its potential to take part in the formation of public policy. Above all, as was also argued in Chapter 11, the members' own perception of their role as representatives has led to their poor performance. Their domination by the government is a result of their failure to see themselves as a powerful corporate institution of state with the right and duty as an institution to call the government to account on behalf of the people and to insist on making that right effective.

In theory, the political responsibility of ministers brings them to account in the Dáil. However, as we have observed, the operation of the system under conditions of strict party loyalty and discipline leads to "responsibility" meaning something different in practice from what constitutional theory suggests. In practice, responsibility comes down to an obligation on ministers to answer questions asked by representatives and to deal with matters raised in debate. Both for maintaining public confidence in the honesty and efficiency of the public service and for securing to the individual citizen an opportunity to get a review of administrative decisions and perhaps redress, this obligation, as it is honoured and carried out in practice, is of the greatest importance. The practice of responsibility—that is, the obligation to answer—helps to maintain an environment of questioning and criticism that is accepted as normal and legitimate. Again, even if it is not likely to involve the removal of a minister from office, it does at least emphasize the subordination of the civil service. Both an environment of questioning and criticism and the subordination of the civil service are important ingredients of democracy. In states where they do not exist, the quality of public life is very different indeed.

IV

From the point of view of the individual citizen, the obligation of ministers to answer in the Dáil or Seanad is a valuable procedure in its own right and, more significantly perhaps, is important because of what it leads to. Because of it, deputies and senators can communicate directly with officials in departments and obtain information about individual cases and transactions; following on, in some cases, they can get action or quicker action, force a review, secure the mitigation of a penalty, or perhaps obtain redress for harm done. (As we shall see, they might also influence an administrative decision in favour of their client: this is a constitutionally much more questionable outcome.) Much the same procedure operates at the local government level, where councillors and officials are in something like the same relationship. Very occasionally, this type of activity uncovers a serious injustice or an administrative mess.

Because the public expects such a service from its representatives and because the operation of the election system obliges representatives to perform it, the volume of such transactions is very large and their range enormous. Because Ireland is a country with a small population and a comparatively large number of public representatives—one member of the Oireachtas for every 16,000 and one local councillor for every 2,200—and because most of these live among their constituents, who expect them to "do a turn" if asked and act accordingly, this service is in practice fairly accessible to the public generally and is comparatively effective. Individuals can in fact get information, action, and a review of their cases. No doubt the accessibility of representatives and the effectiveness of their interventions vary between individuals and perhaps from area to area. The procedure is universal enough, however, for a minister to be able to declare with justice, in 1966, that "there is hardly anyone without a direct personal link with someone, be he Minister, T.D., clergyman, county or borough councillor or trade union official, who will interest himself in helping a citizen to have a grievance examined and, if possible, remedied."[9] In 1974, TDs and senators alone received about 140,000 representations.[10]

Among the matters most frequently dealt with by this procedure are housing and housing grants; entitlement to health and other social services, benefits, and facilities; getting telephone service; roads, drainage, and flood control; land redistribution and compulsory purchase. Help might also be sought and given in matters such as children's allowances and old-age pensions despite the fact that the decisions are routine and a representative's intervention is not needed except perhaps when a delay occurs. Nevertheless, whether the representative can help or not, he or she has to take action and to be seen to be doing so.

The ability of public representatives to intervene in the administration directly has its effects upon administrative procedures and decision making. To take a minor matter, in order to facilitate members, "most of the departments send out their replies [to the deputies' representations] with carbon copies. The deputy sends the carbon reply to the constituent."[11] In recent years some ministers and ministers of state have ordered their departmental officials to give them an advance copy of their replies to deputies' representations so that it can be quickly sent to the ministers' party colleagues in the locality, thus forestalling the diligent deputy who has done the work. Some deputies say that efforts by the party in power to exploit their ministers' positions in this way have increased in recent years. When a by-election is pending in a constituency, the number of items of constituency business that are suddenly decided in favour of those in the district is surprising.

There can be no doubt either that representatives' activities extend to trying to influence appointments, though the scope for jobbery is mercifully small. Mention has already been made of jobbery at the local government level (see p. 300), and there is some evidence of representations and perhaps even attempted interference in appointments made centrally. Two cases mentioned by a civil servant in his memoirs even involved ministers.[12] In 1980, the Dáil heard allegations that representations were made in respect of appointments by the Civil Service Commission (which were certainly not going to have any effect whatsoever) and that ministers were requesting information about the progress and results of civil service competitions.[13] The *Irish Times'* political correspondent commented that "there is, it seems, an acceptable level of jobbery (if you want to call it that) in Irish politics." Opposition members were claiming, he added, that that level had been exceeded by the government then in office.[14]

The extension of the activities of parliamentary representatives to this kind of matter and to attempting to influence decisions before they are made goes beyond what is necessary or proper to enable the Oireachtas to oversee the conduct of the administration in order to further the legitimate interests of individual constituents. For a deputy or senator to use parliamentary position in this way is, on the contrary, an abuse of the procedures. Nowhere is this more obvious than in efforts to influence members of the Garda Síochána and the customs service to get prosecutions dropped or quashed. Yet in April 1980 the president of the Association of Garda Sergeants and Inspectors complained that politicians, including ministers, were trying to influence promotions and to have prosecutions quashed.[15] In June 1980 the general secretary of the Association of Customs and Excise Officers revealed that he had correspondence "on file" giving names, dates, and times when interference in the work of customs officers had taken place. If the minister wanted substantiation of the Association's charges, he said when the charges were denied, "we will have a queue outside his office next Tuesday or Wednesday."[16] The representative's right to intervene inevitably gives the deputy or senator a role in the administrative process; the danger of interventions of this sort is that the role will be malevolent.

It should not be supposed that this could not happen, for certainly pressure is exerted upon representatives to engage in this type of activity. Requests for help and favours are part of the daily life of all of them, and the role of contact man is one they readily accept (see pp. 227–28). Raven and Whelan, in their enquiry into the political culture of the Irish, found that among those who said that they could do something about an unjust or harmful law or regulation—half of their respondents took this view—the preferred strategy for doing so was to contact an elected representative. About one-half of them selected this course of action.[17] Nevertheless, as Barrington observed, "to an increasing extent the old recourse to parliament as a means of remedying grievances is felt to be inadequate."[18] People are more and more looking elsewhere and in particular to the courts, the other major road along which to pursue redress of grievances.

V

Judicial control over government derives from Bunreacht na hÉireann, which provides for courts, including courts empowered with jurisdiction extending "to the question of the validity of any law having regard to the Constitution." The Constitution also ensures, so far as it can, that the judges shall be independent. Since, in addition, it contains statements of the fundamental rights of the citizen and of the functions and powers of the various organs of government, Ireland is formally at least provided with a reference point for judging governmental action and establishing authoritatively both the rights and duties of the citizens and the procedures by which such judgements may be made.

Bunreacht na hÉireann is not sacrosanct: it can be amended. To do so, however, requires the approval of both the Oireachtas and a majority at a referendum—provisions that have the effect of giving a final say to the political rather than to the legal authority. Nor, of course, at bottom, does a citizen's protection from the state or the rights he or she actually enjoys depend merely upon their being written down in a constitution. The foundations of legal control over the government lie in a widespread belief—a belief shared with many Western peoples—that the law should be obeyed, not least by public officials; that it is the duty of courts fearlessly to say what the law is, even if this involves restraining the government itself; and that the courts should be independent in their performance of this duty and for this purpose need to be insulated from politics and political pressure. Bunreacht na hÉireann provides for justice normally to be dispensed in public, in courts established by law, by judges who "shall be independent in the exercise of their judicial functions and subject only to this Constitution and the law." Their independence is ensured by a judge's not being subject to dismissal "except for stated misbehaviour or incapacity and then only upon resolutions passed by Dáil Éireann and by Seanad Éireann calling for his removal" and by the safeguard that a judge's remuneration "shall not be reduced during his continuance in office."[19]

It might be thought surprising, therefore, that the appointment of judges is in the hands of the government and that by custom the Attorney General, a political appointee, who is the government's legal adviser and state prosecutor, is always offered any vacancy to the High Court that occurs during his term of office. (Places on the Supreme Court are usually filled by promotion by seniority from the High Court.) The results are not surprising. P. C. Bartholomew found that on appointment about three-quarters of the judges were supporters of Fianna Fáil, the party that was in office for all but six years from 1932 up to 1971, the year he made his enquiries. The same proportion had been politically active prior to appointment. Bartholomew commented that, "with rare exceptions, a person named as judge will be one who is favourably regarded by the Government. . . . Even in the rare instance where an adherent of the opposition party is named this may well be for indirect advantage of the Government party in that such a 'nonpartisan' appointment projects an image of objectivity."[20]

It does not follow, of course, that judges appointed by politicians, even judges with overt political affiliations, are politically biased in their professional activities; in fact, there are few in Ireland and none in the law profession who think for one moment that they are. Nevertheless, the practice seems inappropriate to a system that is otherwise insulated from contact with party politics.

Given a politically independent judiciary, what matters to the citizen facing the government is, first, the accessibility of the courts and, second, the extent of the courts' powers to review the actions of public authorities. To be accessible, courts must be physically near at hand; they must be expeditious in their handling of cases; they must not be so expensive that the poor are at a handicap; and they must not be barred to the citizen by laws that give immunity to any person or, particularly, to the state.

The Irish courts are geographically reasonably convenient, and although there are delays in the hearing of some types of cases, they are much less common than in many countries. On the other hand, the expenses of litigation can be heavy; a system of free or subsidized legal aid is essential if the courts are to be available to all equally. Not until 1962, however, was a general provision made, in the Criminal Justice (Legal Aid) Act (1962), for free legal aid at criminal proceedings. Help in civil actions was not given until much later. Only after Ireland had been found in breach of Article 6 of the European Convention on Human Rights (an Irish plaintiff, Mrs. Airey, did not enjoy an effective right of access to the courts by reason of the absence of a scheme of legal aid) were more adequate arrangements made.[21] In 1980, a Legal Aid Board was set up to provide free or assisted legal advice and aid in civil matters (with some exceptions) on a means test where "a reasonably prudent person . . . would be likely to seek such services . . . and a competent lawyer would be likely to advise him to obtain such services."[22]

Until the 1960s, access to the courts was somewhat hampered by the remaining vestiges of the British principle of the immunity of the Crown (that is, the government), which had been carried over into the new state at independence. However, since then, in a period when the courts began to take a much broader approach to interpreting the Constitution and to cast a more critical eye upon the activities of the administration, decisions in a number of important cases have considerably broadened the right of access.[23]

Since Ireland is endowed with a constitution and courts that have the power to examine and pronounce upon the constitutionality of any measures or actions, and Irish citizens have ready access to those courts, they ought to be able to get disputed administrative actions checked and redress if appropriate. Are the courts effective in practice?

An examination of the record of the Irish courts in respect of issues of constitutionality shows that between 1938, when Bunreacht na hÉireann was enacted, and the late 1970s, there were two distinct phases (the transition from the one to the other occurred in the mid-1960s). In the first phase, the courts were cautious and took a narrow approach to constitutional interpretation. They were, in Edward McWhinney's judgement, "rarely innovatory."[24] Nevertheless, during that period there were twenty-three decisions of unconstitutionality in a total of sixty-nine cases, and these touched upon many of the most vital areas of citizens' rights (see Table 16.1).

By 1967, a leading constitutional lawyer, John Kelly, could already discern a change: "Judicial interpretation of the Constitution has been

TABLE 16.1
Court Decisions of Unconstitutionality, 1938–66

Cases involving	No. of cases
Freedom of the person	3
Right of association	1
Property rights	3
Rights of the family, parents, marriage, divorce	7
Exercise of judicial functions by bodies other than courts	3
Right of access to courts	3
Other	3

SOURCE: Compiled from data in L. P. Beth, *The Development of Judicial Review in Ireland, 1937–66* (Dublin, 1967), Appendix, Table 2.

becoming increasingly bold."[25] Some judges began to take a broader approach to interpreting the Constitution and to be more creative in identifying the rights in the Constitution or rights that could be inferred from it. The section of Bunreacht na hÉireann most substantially developed was the fundamental rights section (Articles 40–44), in particular Article 40.3. Basing their decisions on a concept of "undisclosed human rights," the courts markedly improved the position of the citizen in a decade or so. It appeared that the Constitution offered more scope than was earlier thought possible for the judges to increase and enlarge the rights of the citizen and protect him or her (some important cases concerned women's rights) against the state.

In the view of another distinguished constitutional lawyer, R. F. V. Heuston, some of the courts' decisions "have been exceedingly inconvenient from an administrative point of view."[26] Nor must the international courts be forgotten. In particular, the Court of Justice of the European Communities (usually known as the European Court) stands alongside and in some circumstances stands above the domestic courts. Its powers to check the activities of the Irish government and public authorities were amply demonstrated in the late 1970s and are likely to be more used in the future as more recourse is had to it.[27]

The principal limitations of the Irish courts in respect of the activities of public authorities are two, and they both arise from the absence of a system of administrative law and courts. First, as the United Kingdom (including Ireland) became a modern welfare state, the increasing need for appellate machinery was met, not by developments in the judicial system proper, but by providing for appeals to ministers, to designated civil servants acting on their own personal responsibility and not under ministerial instruction, or to independent tribunals. In some but by no means all cases, further appeals lie thence to the courts. Second, when it comes to administrative action carried on inside the powers given by the law, the courts' powers are limited: "Provided an authority entrusted with administrative discretion keeps inside its *vires* and (where appropriate) commits no open breach of natural justice, it may act as foolishly, unreasonably or even unfairly as it likes, and the courts cannot (or at least will not) interfere."[28] There exist no procedures such as, for example, those in France, where there are courts to review administrative action from the point of *détournement de pouvoir* (the abuse of discretion).

What this means in practice is that in dealing with the claims of citizens, administrators are not bound to follow any given procedures unless the law specifically requires them to, provided that, where appropriate, they act judicially and in accordance with the principles of natural justice. It means also that the development of administrative adjudication by ministers, civil servants, or tribunals has been unsystematic and patchy. The All-Party Informal Committee [of the Oireachtas] on Administrative Justice reported in 1977 that, "despite the provision of special facilities in the Social Welfare and Revenue areas, the greater part of the public service, including areas with a high incidence of direct dealings with the public, remains unprovided for."[29] In some of the areas where they do exist, the number of cases is very large (as Table 16.2 shows). It is quite likely that if appeals procedures were available throughout the administration, they would be heavily used.

The subject of administrative justice and appellate systems was taken

TABLE 16.2
Appeals Against Administrative Decisions, 1973

Type of appeal	No. of appeals
Income-tax appeals to Commissioners	18,041
Trademark appeals to Minister for Industry and Commerce	0
Appeals under higher education grants scheme to Minister for Education	2
Appeals to Redundancy Appeals Tribunal	1,035
Appeals to Levy Appeals Tribunal	218
Rating appeals to Commissioner for Valuation	9,664
Appeals against refusal of bull licenses	60
Social welfare appeals	11,980

SOURCE: *Report of the All-Party Informal Committee on Administrative Justice* (Dublin, May 1977), p. 12.

up by the Public Services Organisation Review Group (the Devlin Group) in the late 1960s. Adopting the report of a study group under the chairmanship of the Chief Justice, which it sponsored, the Devlin Group recommended a systematic scheme for reviews and appeals from the decisions of public authorities:

It should be an accepted principle that an appeal may be taken to an appeal tribunal from any decision of a deciding officer. This is a principle generally acknowledged elsewhere.... Appeal tribunals should, therefore, be set up in every major executive agency. Where the volume of work would not justify a separate tribunal for each agency, a tribunal for a group of small agencies might be attached to the parent ministry.

The whole system should be subject to review by a "Commissioner for Administrative Justice," who would in addition "perform the functions of an ombudsman in following up complaints from the public in cases where no tribunal exists or administrative remedies have been exhausted."[30] This recommendation was far-reaching in its implications, for it would have required major changes in the procedures for making administrative decisions.

Like so many of the recommendations of the Devlin Group, this proposal was not implemented. The All-Party Committee of the Oireachtas in 1975 found "great difficulties in its application." Looking at the needs of the situation from the point of view of the Oireachtas, it thought that "the institution required is one to review, through the examination of complaints, the operation and execution of the legislative provisions enacted by the Oireachtas and to guard against, eliminate or demonstrate the non-existence of, maladministration in any form." The All-Party Committee proposed an ombudsman, "an institution which has operated increasingly in other jurisdictions over the past decades." In doing so, it recognized frankly that it had "not dealt with the question of the extension of appellate facilities to areas of the public service where they are deficient at present."[31]

What the All-Party Committee had done, however, was to suggest some provision for a considerable grey area that fell outside the existing system of review. Although some ministers and deputies had previously taken the view that "the basic reason . . . why we do not need an ombudsman is because we have so many unofficial but nevertheless effective ones,"[32] the need for some institution to fill the gap between the Oireachtas and the legal system was increasingly recognized by members of the Oireachtas. The Ombudsman Act of 1980 (no. 26) provided for the appointment of such an officer appointed by, and dismissible only by, themselves.

Under that act, the ombudsman's remit extends only to the activities of the central departments, though a commitment was given by the government that it would be extended to cover local authorities and Health Boards quite soon after appointment. Within his area of jurisdiction, the ombudsman may investigate any action when it appears to him "that the action was or may have been (i) taken without proper authority, (ii) taken on irrelevant grounds, (iii) the result of negligence or carelessness, (iv) based on erroneous or incomplete information, (v) improperly discriminatory, (vi) based on an undesirable administrative practice, or (vii) otherwise contrary to fair or sound administration."[33] Unlike the case in the United Kingdom and France, where complaints must be submitted through parliamentary representatives, people in Ireland may invoke the ombudsman's help directly, and he can, if he thinks fit, initiate investigations himself. He has considerable powers to get information and to require the attendance of "any person." When he finds that the action he has investigated adversely affected a person, he may recommend to the department concerned that the matter be further considered or that measures including specified measures be taken to remedy the adverse effect of the action. If the response is in his view unsatisfactory, he may report accordingly to the Oireachtas and, as a matter of routine, he is required to report annually.

With the institution of the ombudsman and with more active courts—in particular, as Barrington pointed out, the fact that "they are increasingly reluctant to accept the attempts by the administration to preserve secrecy on the grounds of ministerial privilege—"[34] the position of the individual attempting to challenge the administration is slowly being improved. Nevertheless, the area of administrative discretion is still frighteningly large. In addition to discretionary powers in respect of matters such as aliens, passports, telephone tapping, and opening mail, which all states seem to require, the Irish state has always had a battery of emergency and security powers.

These powers are the legacy of the war of independence and the civil war, both of which cast inordinately long shadows. In these shadows, there have always been subversive organizations, notably the IRA, and occasional eruptions of violence. More recently, the Republic has experienced the spill-over effects of more than a decade of civil strife in Northern Ireland. In Ireland in 1980 there existed laws empowering the government to arrest without warrant, to detail without trial, and to try accused persons in special courts that do not have to follow normal judicial processes. In 1980, Special Criminal Courts, which sit without a jury, were operating just as they had been in 1940. Likewise, a "state of emergency" existed as it had since 1939, thus enabling the Oireachtas to enact any law it wished, however repugnant to the Constitution, provided that such law is said to be for the purpose of securing the public safety. The courts, though, are increasingly prone to question such powers. The Supreme Court in 1976 "expressly [reserved] for future consideration whether the courts have jurisdiction to review such [state of emergency] resolutions."[35] It is far from certain what would be their attitude to legislation enacted under them.

VI

One theme has recurred throughout this chapter, as also elsewhere in this book—the disadvantages the public suffers through lack of information, a deficiency that neither public representatives nor the courts have as yet wholly remedied, though they have made some inroads in the last decade. Undoubtedly, discussion and criticism of general policy and the systematic appraisal of the administration of general policy suffer most from this comparative lack of openness. Sometimes an individual with a wrong to be righted might have been handicapped in the past, though the presence of the ombudsman and legal aid centres should make this less likely in the future. The citizen looking for a house or the district for a new health centre is hardly handicapped at all.

To some extent, lack of official information is compensated for by the fact that the country is small and homogeneous. The numbers of politicians, administrators, journalists, and judges are small enough for them to be known to each other and for "horizontal" communications to be easy. Furthermore, journalists are both responsible and alert, although radio and television have been to some extent inhibited from exposing the shortcomings of public authorities or seeking out public scandals (see pp. 75–76)[36]

What they do not have access to, however, is the type of material that an efficient parliamentary system would cause to be produced and published. In Barrington's opinion, "There has been a great falling off, as compared with the practice of last century, in the information conveyed in the annual reports of government departments, where they still continue to produce them at all. . . . the operations within government departments and within state-sponsored bodies are almost entirely closed to public scrutiny."[37] Above all, Ireland badly needs a freedom of information act, which would give members of the public and journalists the right to see official files. Such a legal provision for access to administrative documents was established long ago in Scandinavian countries and has existed in the United States since 1966.

Although there are some signs of improvement—notably in the success of the Joint Committee on State-Sponsored Bodies in extracting information and in a greater willingness in some departments to make information available to journalists—public servants and in particular civil servants are not accustomed to giving information freely, much less engaging in open discussion of matters of public concern. In fact, not only are civil servants and some other public servants not accustomed to engage in it, they are not permitted to do so. In respect of public affairs, civil servants have to seek permission to publish or appear on radio or television and, in practice, have often found it quite hard to get it, even for innocuous material. Such activities have not been encouraged, to say the least. Nearly twenty years ago, Desmond Roche explained why: "The traditional attitude has been to present as narrow a front as possible towards the public, since from that direction there is little to be expected except mud and brickbats. Consequently information is strictly controlled or channelled—sometimes to the point of ceasing to flow at all. It requires an effort to change so well established a position, which has on the whole been advantageous to the defenders."[38] Most civil servants would think that this is as true today as it was then.

Of course, there must be some limits to the disclosure and discussion of public business, but the limits that obtain in any country owe almost as much to the development of a particular environment and the acceptance of certain practices—which, strictly, need not have been accepted—as they do to constitutional rules or the law. The Irish environment is, comparatively, one of considerable reticence, even secrecy.

VII

This review of the surveillance and control of the administration confirms the deficiencies of the Oireachtas. It suggests also that people seeking redress might be handicapped by the absence of a developed system of administrative law, though this has become less likely recently. However, most people will never suffer in practice from these limitations and are unaware of them because they have little or no business with public authorities that is not of a purely routine nature. The handicaps, real or imagined, of the individual facing the administration must not be overestimated. What little evidence there is of the perceptions of Irish people suggests that they have a quite favourable picture of public servants. Raven and Whelan concluded from their survey of attitudes in the early 1970s that Irish people, like those in the United States and the United Kingdom, felt that Ireland was "a *just* society."[39]

Most citizens, thus, may well be content enough with the situation.

The public representatives busying themselves with their "contact man" activities, the bolder and more creative attitudes of the judges, and (one hopes) the mediation of the ombudsman all contribute to softening the administration of public services and lubricating the abrasive edge of government where it bears upon the *administré*. If, as seems to be the case, it is at the macro level (the surveillance of the conduct of business in general) that Irish institutions do not work well, this might not matter much to average men and women with their own jobs to do and their own lives to lead.

Sovereignty and Democracy on a Small Island

"Ireland is a sovereign, independent, democratic state"; so says the Constitution. Independence and sovereignty imply autonomous powers of decision over domestic and foreign policies: democracy can be measured by the extent to which decision-making processes allow for the participation of the public and are sensitive to their wishes and feelings. It is with these topics, sovereignty and democracy, in the context of a country with a small population that this final chapter is concerned.

II

In respect of both sovereignty and democracy, the British connection has been the critical factor. British influence has been a persistent theme of this book. The British influence on Ireland stemmed from the demographic fact of the unequal numbers of inhabitants, the geographical fact of nearness, the historical fact of political dominion and social and economic dominance, and the intellectual context of similarity of language and cultural blanketing. Given the small population of the Republic, its geographical position, and its history, it might have been expected in an age of mass production, mass markets, and mass communications that, for all its formal sovereignty, Ireland would have developed as not much more than a detached province of the United Kingdom. This might have seemed the more likely since the Irish state was for a long time after independence partly dependent economically upon the United Kingdom and wholly dependent strategically.

It is true that, during the Second World War, Ireland was neutral and remained inviolate, but only because on balance it suited the Anglo-American alliance to have it so and on condition that it was a benevolent neutrality from the British and American point of view. Until the accession of Great Britain and Ireland to the European Communities in

1972, Ireland's dependence was from time to time brought home by the inability of its government to prevent the British government from making decisions that directly affected Ireland adversely—for example, the imposition of import restrictions in 1964 and again in 1968.

Moreover, Great Britain not only influenced Ireland but insulated it from continental Europe, effectively blocking off the social, cultural, and economic influences that might otherwise have affected the life of the country and the policy of the Irish state. Even as a sovereign state, the Republic remained for long comparatively isolated not only from the European continent but from the world in general. Evidence of the effects of insulation could be seen not merely in the public's ignorance about Europe and the rest of the world generally, but in unconcern. Until well after the Second World War, Ireland was simply not involved with what was going on in Europe. Because of the communications filter interposed by the barrier of language and the dominance of British publishing, even continental Catholic currents of thought and speculation did not permeate to any extent until after the Second Vatican Council.

Strong British influence and insulation from the rest of the world, it could be argued, were to be expected on geopolitical grounds alone. They were the more marked because the inability of the Irish independence movement to win a complete victory in 1921 led to an obsession with the border and constitutional issues, and with the United Kingdom as the supposed author and possible righter of a number of wrongs that Irish people believed they had suffered.

Since Britain filled the new Ireland's horizon, Irish people had no European perspectives and the Irish government practically no foreign policy. Only a few of the original leaders had European horizons, and when they were gone, Ireland virtually lost sight of Europe. De Valera made a mark in the League of Nations in the 1930s, but this had little effect on the country; no more than had Seán MacBride's activities as Minister for External Affairs from 1948 to 1951. In the Second World War, hostility to Britain and preoccupation with the border—*the* problem as politicians and people alike saw it—led to neutrality, which in turn led to exclusion from the new international groupings of postwar years or unwillingness to join them. This isolation—political, social, economic, and cultural—meant that the great changes in postwar Europe made little impact upon Ireland. Not until the late 1950s were there signs of a change. In 1956, Ireland was admitted to the UN, where its participation in peacekeeping operations and its position as an ex-colonial and impeccably noncolonial country that was equally impeccably anti-Communist made it *persona grata* with Western and emerging countries alike and gave it some scope for diplomatic activity.

If the ability to scan all one's neighbours and not to be oriented on one alone is a sign of a truly independent people, and if the recognition and pursuit of a wide range of international interests is the mark of a truly sovereign state, there are some grounds for speculating about whether, for all her formal sovereignty, Ireland was in practice any more than a detached province of the United Kingdom. Some in the world outside and, indeed, some in Ireland did see her thus. It would be a mistake, however, to conclude that this was the reality. The Irish state was not simply the most advanced stage of decentralization achieved by the communities peripheral to England, the most distant stop on a line whose intermediate halts were Wales, Scotland, and Northern Ireland. Ireland was a smaller European democracy and not a larger British province because, unlike the peoples of the other peripheral areas of the British Isles, her people were not culturally absorbed to the extent necessary to bank down the fires of national self-consciousness and, hence, were not successfully subsumed into the British political system.

Political independence not only reflected the need to recognize differences but, once granted, bred them. First, and obviously, the political significance of independence was vast. However inevitable political decisions may be for a small country, it makes a very great difference if the country makes them itself. Ireland's ability to decide to remain neutral in the Second World War—however much the inviolability of the country depended on the grace of the United Kingdom and the United States—convinced more Irish men and women that their country was really independent than almost any other single decision from 1921 on. To have different tax rates, to operate a customs barrier, to make a consular agreement, to receive a foreign head of state, to abstain in a vote at the UN when Britain is committed—to be able to do these things and more like them, however limited the elbowroom for manoeuvre, is to greatly increase the range of decisions that a community has to make for itself and can feel responsible for. That a state is very small does make it more vulnerable to decisions made by a larger state without considering or consulting its neighbour; does narrow the range of options in many matters, sometimes to one; does mean that certain policies that a larger state could consider must be laid aside; and, conversely, does make the presence of some items on the national agenda otiose. What small size does not affect is the importance to a people of the range of decisions that may be considered at home.

Autonomy was important not only politically in greatly extending the range of political questions for domestic decision, but also because it increased the number and range of matters dealt with within the community exclusively. A state boundary, however permeable, produced discontinuities of a different order from other boundaries. The contrast between the equivocal provincialism of Wales, Scotland, and even Northern Ireland and the sense of national identity of the Republic became more and more marked. Dublin was not just a southern Belfast, let alone a western Cardiff. Just as the comparative stability of some states of Western Europe from medieval times led to the growth of separate nations within their borders, so independence in the case of the Republic and control by Westminster in the case of Northern Ireland created different foci of interest and decision. The Republic was Dublin oriented; Northern Ireland was, and is, London oriented. Because the full range of public affairs in the Republic was dealt with in Dublin, those who wished to influence their course had to pursue their activities there. After 1921, finance and industry, trade associations, unions (with a few exceptions), and the professions all reoriented themselves at varying speeds, but inevitably, upon Dublin.

Paradoxically, one might think, accession to the European Communities, a matter on which it was widely believed that Ireland had no option but to follow the United Kingdom, at once widened Ireland's international horizon and thus made her sovereignty the more obvious and at the same time began the process of inevitably eroding that sovereignty. One of the arguments put forward by some politicians for joining the Communities was that membership would weaken the strong orientation to the United Kingdom in trade and other matters and would loosen the ties that seemed to bind the two countries together in a special relationship. In a Community setting, the United Kingdom would cease to loom so large, for the Republic would have wider horizons and its voice would, formally at least, count as much as that of the United Kingdom. Also, in that setting, the United Kingdom, it was thought (wrongly), could not continue to treat Northern Ireland, that most important and permanent item on the British-Irish agenda, as if it were a domestic family matter.

In the debates preceding the referendum on joining the Communities in 1972, the question of Irish sovereignty was an issue, albeit a minor one. The government argued that although "all international cooperation involves some limitation on sovereignty," the key issues, foreign policy and defence, were untouched because the Communities' activities under the Treaties of accession did not extend to them.[1] On the contrary:

Such limitations on national freedom of action which membership of the Communities will involve for us will be more than counterbalanced by the influence which we will be able to bring to bear on the formulation of Community policies affecting our interests. We must contrast this with our present position as a very small country, independent but with little or no capacity to influence events abroad that significantly affect us.[2]

In fact, the issue of sovereignty did not arise in any serious fashion in the years after accession. Nevertheless, the impact and inhibiting effects of Community policy and law were beginning to be experienced by Irish public authorities in the late 1970s. Increasingly, people were coming to recognize that in some matters power resided in Brussels and not in Dublin. By 1980, Ireland was a member of the European Monetary System. By then, too, Community prime ministers and foreign ministers had got into the habit of meeting to discuss foreign affairs and to coordinate their national stances as far as possible. Slow though the movement to European union is—and it is going to get slower as more countries join—the evolution of the European Communities will eventually erode the sovereignty of individual member states. As it does, it is quite likely that, from the public's point of view, the issue of sovereignty, which seemed so vital when the Irish state was set up and immediately thereafter, will not be considered of much importance.

III

The United Kingdom was a large exporter of democracy. Like the older Commonwealth countries, Ireland absorbed a great deal of the British democratic tradition and acquired political institutions of the British pattern. Throughout this study, we have noted many similarities not only of formal political and administrative organizations but of procedures, conventions, standards, and style. Cabinet government, parliamentary processes, minister–civil servant relationships, the civil service, local government, the courts, and the law—all have a British stamp upon them. The continuing influence that arises from the propensity, by reason of convenience and narrow horizons, to look for models to British ways of handling public issues and problems tends to mean that changes both in the form of political institutions and in the content of policies have flowed in the same direction. Wider horizons and accession to the European Communities had not had very much impact in this respect by 1980.

For all the similarity between the United Kingdom and the Republic so far as political institutions are concerned, there is one obvious contrast that, one might think, could and perhaps should lead to striking differences in practice. When it comes to participation in politics and getting consensus, or to the likelihood of citizens identifying with their government or being alienated from it, a country with 3.4 million inhabitants and an electorate of a little over 2 million, as the Republic is, seems to offer greater possibilities for the practice of democracy than a country of 56 million with an electorate of 41 million. The smaller the number in the unit, the more directly should citizens be able to communicate with leaders and the less should be the leaders' dependence on intermediary subleaders for information about public demands and reactions. If so, Ireland enjoys conditions more favourable to the generation of mutual understanding and hence genuine and higher quality democracy. What has been the Irish experience in fact?

Ireland has a ratio of 1 deputy to 20,000 inhabitants; if one counts senators, the ratio of national representatives to people is 1 to 16,000. (In the United Kingdom it is 1 to 88,000.) In Ireland, also, there is 1 local councillor to 2,200 persons; and, because of the small total numbers involved, this ratio is possible without the difficulties and loss of contact that arise from having too many layers of authorities from bottom to top or too many units of government. The connection between local and national government is close, and there is overlap. The linkage is remarkably close in fact—from citizen to local councillor or party activist (often a personal and certainly a local connection) and in turn thence to TD or senator and onwards to minister or department. Where the local councillor is a parliamentary representative, the connection between local and national government is direct. Thus the channels of communication are short and have few intermediary links.

It would be wrong, however, to conclude that this state of affairs leads Irish citizens to participate more positively in policy making or to have a greater influence than the citizens of a larger democracy. Clearly, a ratio of 1 to 20,000 is as impossibly large for the consideration of individual views on national policy as a ratio of 1 to 200,000 or, for that matter, 1 to 2,000 would be. In any case, the vast majority of citizens do not desire a more active role in government, nor are they equipped for it. Irish public representatives do not do much to educate even those who would be educated politically. On the contrary, they are poor communicators of general political information to their constituents. Parties are no better: they conform rather to Richard Rose's "top-down" model, which sees local party organizations and personnel as existing to fight elections in order to get party leaders into office.[3] Policies in parties like these are generated not at the grassroots level but by a small group of national leaders who look to the party to sell them.

Most politicians do not desire to change this state of affairs, which, indeed, suits them well. The hostile reaction of public representatives in 1971 to a proposal made by the Institute of Public Administration to integrate local community organizations with the local government system and to include their officers on local councils was typical of this attitude.[4] Most public representatives do not want to share power. On the contrary, they regard other activists as potential rivals, threatening their position, which depends on their ability to monopolize the opportunities for patronage and service and use them to their electoral advantage.

The truth is that small numbers permit, and the election system requires, representatives to construct and work political brokerage machines as described by Mart Bax in Cork and Paul Sacks in Donegal.[5] They busy themselves with these machines, which process homely but, to the ordinary person, important matters like houses and welfare benefits, rather than policy issues. There is communication certainly, but it is not concerned with general policy. For that the Irish citizen relies, as do citizens of all countries, mainly on the mass media, where small scale has no particular advantage.

This concentration by the representative on his or her role as a "contact man"—and indeed the intimacy that small numbers in general allow—tends also to produce too many representatives who are parochial in their interests and outlook and who, for all their virtues, do not seem themselves as national legislators. They do regard themselves, by reason of their "contact man" activities, as being especially well placed to know the opinions and feelings of their constituents. However, they see themselves as reacting to policy proposals rather than as architects of policy.

It is clear, nevertheless, that this modest showing of parliamentary representatives when it comes to policy does not arise solely or even mainly from small scale and a concentration upon brokerage activities. Rather, it has to do with the development and continuation of a tradition of strong cabinet government and puny parliaments. What this study has attempted to show is how, in such a system, the general election is the decisive political battleground; how victory there gives the government its dominating role and hegemonic position; and how attenuated the role of the Oireachtas tends to be as compared with systems where parliament makes the laws. That is not to say that unexploited opportunities do not exist under the present system or that the Oireachtas could not be a more effective critic of policy and a more constructive force in government than it is. Doubtless small size and parochial attitudes contribute to this state of affairs, but it should be remembered that this system developed in the United Kingdom (whence it was imported to Ireland)

and has remained the major feature of that country's government and politics. There, too, cabinets dominate and parliaments are relatively weak. What British and Irish experience taken together suggests is that the decline of parliament has occurred for reasons that have little to do with size. There is much evidence of the same development in other countries too.

If cabinet government (British style) belittles the role of the elected representative, so, more generally, does the general acceptance by Western democracies of what Theodore Lowi called the ideology of "interest-group liberalism."[6] As this study has revealed, much policy is made and many public issues are decided by ministers and their civil service advisers after consultation with the spokesmen of the organized pressure groups. These all-important meetings take place in the minister's room, the civil servant's office, the department's conference room; at this or that council, committee, and advisory or consultative body meeting. In some policy areas in recent years, this style of policy making has developed into "tripartism"—a system in which governments and pressure groups accept mutually binding undertakings and governments seem to lose the final say. Those involved are no doubt in some senses representative, but all this is a long way from the people's elected representatives and from the representative assembly. In this system, the contribution of the elected representative to the crucial stages of decision making may well be, at best, an expression of the symptoms of unease (where the shoe pinches) or negative influence based on an instinct for political survival (what *they* won't put up with "down the country"); at worst, it is peripheral.

The whole drift of Irish government might indeed be, as it seems to be in many Western countries, toward Robert Dahl's "democratic Leviathan":

By the democratic Leviathan I mean the kind of political system which is a product of long evolution and hard struggle, welfare-oriented, centralized, bureaucratic, tamed and controlled by competition among highly organized elites, and, in the perspectives of the ordinary citizen, somewhat remote, distant and impersonal even in small countries like Norway and Sweden. The politics of this new democratic Leviathan are above all the politics of compromise, adjustment, negotiation, bargaining; a politics carried on among professional and quasi-professional leaders who constitute only a small part of the total citizen body; a politics that reflects a commitment to the virtues of pragmatism, moderation and incremental change; a politics that is un-ideological and even anti-ideological.[7]

If this is the general trend, then the effects of small scale and a rural setting are but marginal either way. The locally oriented rural deputy might be slightly less well fitted to play an inevitably small part; on the other hand, small scale and a rural setting help to counter the citizen's feeling of remoteness.

On the whole, these most prominent tendencies in Irish government and politics seem to be related more to the system, procedures, and functions of government than to numbers; small size may only exacerbate them or soften them. In at least two respects, however, scale does seem to be more obviously influential. First, as we have seen, small numbers and the consequential high ratio of representatives to people and direct local-central linkage make possible administrative procedures that could hardly operate in a large system except for a favoured few. The business of individual citizens and local interests can be the subject of direct representations to the appropriate administrator, local or central; a review of a decision already made can be more easily obtained and the righting of a wrong more easily effected. For ordinary people these are valuable assets of the system. Our study of representatives shows that this possibility has been exploited to the full and, perhaps, beyond what is desirable.

Again, insofar as the shortcomings of representatives arise from a shortage in their ranks of people who are by training, by profession, and by inclination fitted to consider and appraise large-scale public business, this is part of a more general danger of smallness—the danger of a lack of sufficient talent to man governmental and political posts. It would be difficult to quantify the amounts or specify the kinds of talents and expertise needed to staff a political system and to measure their availability in Ireland today. The Committee on the Constitution (1967) reported that one of the arguments it had heard in favour of increasing the number of deputies was to provide an adequate pool from which to select enough ministers:

On the basis of present Dáil membership, the Deputies supporting the Government are likely to number 70 or so. As many of these would, for one good reason or another, be unable to take up Ministerial office, the Taoiseach is, in effect, left with some 35–40 Deputies out of whom he must find about 20 Ministers and Parliamentary Secretaries. This imbalance ought to be rectified, and there is a strong case for an immediate increase in the total membership of the Dáil.[8]

Industry and commerce, the trade associations, the unions and interest organizations generally, the public services, the parties—all are short of the right kinds of experts and, perhaps, of enough talent. In all too many of the places where government comes into contact with the spokesmen of the community or appoints a chairman for a commission, a board member, or a nominee, a few names recur again and again. Politicians and civil servants claim that it is not easy to find well-qualified people to serve or to employ for this or that job; conversely, leading businessmen say that there are all too few really able people in politics or the public service. Both may be exaggerating, and the same is said in communities far larger than Ireland.

Reference Matter

Demographic, Social, and Economic Statistics

TABLE A.1
Population of Ireland, 1821–1979

Year	Republic of Ireland (26 counties)	Northern Ireland (6 counties)	Total All Ireland (32 counties)
1821	5,421,376	1,380,451	6,801,827
1841	6,528,799	1,648,945	8,177,744
1861	4,402,111	1,396,453	5,798,564
1881	3,870,020	1,304,816	5,174,836
1901	3,221,823	1,236,952	4,458,775
1926	2,971,992	1,256,561	4,228,553
1946	2,955,107	—	—
1966	2,884,002	1,484,775	4,368,777
1971	2,978,248	1,536,065	4,514,313
1979	3,364,881	—	—

SOURCE: For Republic of Ireland, 1821–61, Saorstát Éireann, *Census of Population, 1926,* Vol. 1; for 1871–1966, *Census of Population of Ireland, 1966,* Vol. 1; for 1971, *Census of Population, 1971,* Vol. 1; for 1979, *Census of Population of Ireland, 1979, Preliminary Report.* For Northern Ireland, 1821–1966, *Census of Population, 1966;* for 1971, *Census of Population, 1971.*

TABLE A.2
Population Density of Ireland and Other Countries of the European Communities, 1978

Country	People per sq. km.
Belgium	323
Denmark	118
France	98
Germany (F.D.R.)	247
Ireland	47
Luxembourg	138
Netherlands	338
United Kingdom	229

SOURCE: *Basic Statistics of the Community,* 18th ed. (Eurostat, Luxembourg, 1980), Table 1.

TABLE A.3
Regional Variations in Population, 1971

Region	Percentage of total population in state	Percentage of population of region classified as rural[a]
Dublin: total county	28.6%	3.5%
East: Kildare, Louth, Meath, Wicklow	9.6	59.2
South: Cork, Waterford, Limerick, South Tipperary	21.5	49.1
Southeast: Carlow, Kilkenny, Wexford	6.1	69.2
Midlands: Laois, Offaly, Westmeath, North Tipperary	6.9	66.7
Southwest: Kerry, Clare, Galway	11.3	73.8
North: Sligo, Cavan, Donegal, Monaghan	8.6	81.6
Northwest: Mayo, Leitrim, Roscommon, Longford	7.4	85.9
TOTAL	100.0%	47.8%

SOURCE: P. Commins, P. G. Cox, and J. Curry, *Rural Areas: Change and Development*, National Economic and Social Council Report No. 41 (Dublin, 1978), p. 15.

[a]The "rural" population is defined as all those persons living in places with a population of less than 1,500.

TABLE A.4
Population in Towns and Rural Areas, 1841–1971

Population	1841	1861	1881	1901	1926	1946	1966	1971
Town population (thousands)[a]	1,100	986	932	911	959	1,161	1,419	1,556
Rural population (thousands)	5,429	3,416	2,938	2,311	2,013	1,794	1,465	1,423
TOTAL (thousands)	6,529	4,402	3,870	3,222	2,972	2,955	2,884	2,979
Percentage of total:								
In towns	16.8%	22.4%	24.1%	28.3%	32.3%	39.3%	49.2%	52.1%
In rural areas	83.2	77.6	75.9	71.7	67.7	60.7	50.8	47.9
Percentage of total:								
In Dublin	4.1%	7.2%	8.4%	11.1%	13.6%	18.0%	22.5%	22.8%
In Dún Laoghaire	0.3	0.7	0.9	1.0	1.2	1.8	2.9	3.3
In Cork	1.2	1.8	2.1	2.4	2.6	3.7	4.3	4.5
In Limerick	0.7	1.0	1.0	1.2	1.3	1.5	2.0	2.1
In Waterford	0.4	0.6	0.7	0.8	0.9	1.0	1.0	1.1
TOTAL	6.7%	11.3%	13.1%	16.5%	19.6%	26.0%	32.7%	33.8%

SOURCE: For 1841, Census of Population of Ireland, 1946, General Reports, Tables 1 and 4. For 1861, Statistical Abstract of Ireland, 1939, Table 9. For 1881–1946, Statistical Abstract of Ireland, 1964, Table 9. For 1966, Census of Population of Ireland, 1966, Vol. 1. For 1971, Census of Population, 1971, Vol. 1.

[a] The "town" population is defined as all those persons living in towns with a population of 1,500 or more.

TABLE A.5

Civilian Employment by Main Sectors of Economic Activity in Ireland and Other Countries of the European Communities, 1979

Country	Agriculture	Industry	Services
Belgium (1978)	3.2%	36.7%	60.7%
Denmark	8.3	30.2	61.5
France	8.8	36.3	54.9
Germany (F.D.R.)	6.2	44.9	48.9
Ireland	21.0	31.9	47.1
Italy	14.8	37.7	47.5
Luxembourg	6.1	44.7	49.2
Netherlands	4.8	32.7	62.4
United Kingdom	2.6	39.0	58.4
EUR 9	7.6	39.9	53.5

SOURCE: *Basic Statistics of the Community*, 18th ed. (Eurostat, Luxembourg, 1980), Table 9.

TABLE A.6

Occupational Structure, 1926–77

Sector	1926	1946	1966	1971	1977
Agriculture, forestry, and fishing	53.4%	46.8%	31.3%	25.9%	20.8%
Mining, manufacturing, etc.	13.0	17.0	27.6	30.6	31.2
Services	33.6	36.2	41.2	43.5	48.0

SOURCE: For 1926–46, calculated from *Census of Population of Ireland, 1926*, Vol. 2; and *Census of Population of Ireland, 1946*, Vol. 2. For 1966, *Census of Population of Ireland, 1966*, Vol. 3. For 1971, *Census of Population of Ireland, 1971*, Vol. 3. For 1977, *Labour Force Survey, 1977* (Stationery Office, Dublin, 1978).

TABLE A.7

Changes in Tenure of Agricultural Land, 1870–1929

Year	Owners	Tenants	
1870	3.0%	97.0%	(landholders)
1906	29.2	70.8	(landholders)
1916	63.9	36.1	(landholders)
1929	97.4	2.6	(land area)

SOURCE: E. Rumpf and A. C. Hepburn, *Nationalism and Socialism in Twentieth-Century Ireland* (Liverpool, 1977), p. 227.

TABLE A.8

Size of Farms, 1975

Area	Percentage of total
Up to 15 acres	23.5%
15–50 acres	44.3
51–100 acres	21.0
More than 100 acres	11.1

SOURCE: Statistical Abstract of Ireland, 1976.

TABLE A.9

Estimated Gross Domestic Product per Capita of Ireland and Other Countries of the European Communities, 1980

Country	GDP per head (ECUs)[a]
Belgium	8,462
Denmark	9,229
France	8,735
Germany (F.D.R.)	9,674
Ireland	3,713
Italy	4,923
Luxembourg	8,791
Netherlands	8,259
United Kingdom	6,445
EUR 9	7,538

SOURCE: Derived from *European Economy, November 1980, Annex,* Table 6 (Directorate General for Economic and Financial Affairs of the Commission of the European Communities, Brussels).
[a] The ECU is a "basket" unit, based on a certain quantity of each Community currency, weighted on the basis of the average gross national product (GNP) over five years (1969–73) and of the intra-Community trade of each member state.

TABLE A.10

Estimated Net Migration, 1926–79

(Annual average rate per 1,000 of population)

Period	Ireland	Leinster	Munster	Connacht	Ulster (part)
1926–36	−5.6	−0.4	−8.1	−10.2	−10.3
1936–46	−6.3	−2.9	−7.7	−10.3	−9.7
1946–51	−8.2	−2.1	−11.7	−15.1	−14.6
1951–56	−13.4	−11.4	−12.8	−17.4	−19.6
1956–61	−14.8	−13.1	−14.2	−18.3	−20.7
1961–66	−5.7	−1.5	−6.4	−13.6	−14.2
1966–71	−3.7	−1.7	−3.5	−10.0	−6.6
1971–79	+4.2	+5.3	+3.2	+2.4	+3.6

SOURCE: For 1926–46, *Commission on Emigration Report, 1948–54,* p. 326. For 1946–71, *Statistical Abstract of Ireland, 1976,* Table 10. For 1971–79, *Census of Ireland, 1979, Preliminary Report.*
NOTE: A minus sign (−) denotes emigration; a plus sign (+) denotes immigration.

TABLE A.11
Percentage of Irish Speakers, 1851–1971

Area	1851	1871	1891	1911	1926	1946	1961	1971
Ireland	29.1%	19.8%	19.2%	17.6%	19.3%	21.2%	27.2%	28.3%
Dublin City and County	1.2	0.4	0.8	3.7	8.3	15.5	21.1	24.5
Rest of Leinster	4.3	1.6	1.3	3.3	10.2	17.2	23.4	24.4
Munster	43.9	27.7	26.2	22.1	21.6	22.0	28.7	30.6
Connacht	50.8	39.0	37.9	35.5	33.3	33.2	37.6	37.2
Ulster (part)	17.0	15.1	17.8	20.4	23.9	26.0	31.4	29.5

SOURCE: For 1851–1926, Saorstát Éireann, *Census of Population, 1936,* Vol. 8. For 1946, *Census of Population of Ireland, 1946,* Vol. 8. For 1961, *Census of Population of Ireland, 1961,* Vol. 9. For 1971, *Census of Population of Ireland, 1971,* Vol. 8.

NOTE: The category "Irish speakers" includes all those who speak Irish only or who can speak Irish and English. It excludes those who can read, but cannot speak, Irish. The number of "Irish speakers" is far less susceptible of exact measurement than any of the other matters in the census.

TABLE A.12
Ireland's Imports from and Exports to the United Kingdom as a Percentage of Ireland's Total Imports or Exports, 1938–79

	1938	1948	1958	1968	1977	1979[a]
Imports	50.5%	53.9%	56.3%	51.0%	48.2%	48.7%
Exports	92.7	87.3	76.9	69.4	47.0	46.2

SOURCE: For 1938, *Trade and Shipping Statistics, 1938* (Stationery Office, Dublin). For 1948, *Trade Statistics of Ireland, December 1948* (Stationery Office, Dublin). For 1958–, *Statistical Abstract of Ireland* (annual, Stationery Office, Dublin).

[a] From January to August.

Representation of the Federated Union of Employers and the Irish Congress of Trade Unions on Public Authorities

Organizations on Which the Federated Union of Employers Was Represented in 1978

Regional and National Levels

Advisory Committee of the Limerick, Clare, and Tipperary (N.R.) Region

AnCo (The Industrial Training Authority)
 Board
 Industrial Training Committees (7)

Cork Advisory Committee

Employer-Labour Conference

Employment-Appeals Tribunal

Employment-Equality Agency

Irish Productivity Centre

Joint Industrial Councils (10)

Joint Labour Committees (20)

Labour Court

Mines and Quarries Advisory Council

National Economic and Social Council

National Industrial Safety Organization

Office Premises Advisory Council

Regional Development Organization

Retirement Planning Council of Ireland

Training Levy Appeals Tribunal

Women's Representative Committee

International Level

European Communities

Advisory Committees (4)

European Social Fund Committee

Standing Committee on Employment

Union of Industries of the European Community

Other

Business and Industry Advisory Committee to OECD

International Labour Organization

SOURCE: Federated Union of Employers, *Annual Report, 1978;* and information supplied by the Irish Congress of Trade Unions.

*Organizations on Which the Irish Congress of Trade Unions Had
Representatives or to Which It Made Nominations in 1980*

Regional and National Levels

Advisory Council on Development
Cooperation

An Bord Altranais

AnCo (The Industrial Training
Authority)

Board

Industrial Training Committees (7)

An Foras Forbartha

City of Dublin Vocational Education
Advisory Committee

Comhairle na nOspidéal

Commission on Industrial Relations

Commission on Safety, Health, and
Welfare at Work

Commission on Taxation

Committee on Educational
Broadcasting

Committee on Emigrants' Services

Dangerous Substances Advisory
Council

Employer-Labour Conference

Employment Appeals Tribunal

Employment Equality Agency

Factories Advisory Council

Fire Prevention Council

Government-ICTU Working Party
on Taxation

Harbour Commissioners (25)

Institute for Industrial Research and
Standards (advisory committees)

Irish Goods Council

Irish Productivity Centre

Joint Labour Committees (20)

Labour Court

Limerick (Cooperative Education
Committee)

Manpower Consultative Committee

Mines and Quarries Advisory
Council

National Board of Science and
Technology (Subcommittee on New
Technologies)

National Consumer Advisory Council

National Economic and Social
Council

National Health Council

National Industrial Safety
Organisation

National Institute for Higher
Education

National Prices Commission

National Rehabilitation Board—
Advisory Committee on
Rehabilitation of the Blind

National Road Safety Association

National Savings Committee

National Social Service Council

Office Premises Advisory Council

Post Office Users' Council

Regional Manpower Committees (5)

Regional Technical Colleges—Boards
of Management and College
Councils (9)

Retirement Planning Council

Taxi Services Council

Transport Consultative Commission

Tripartite Committee on Employment

Working Party on Child Care
Services and Facilities for Working
Parents

Working Party on Import
Substitution

Working Party on Local Authority
Superannuation

International Level

European Communities

Advisory Committee on Freedom of
Movement of Workers

Advisory Committee on Safety, Hygiene, and Health Protection at Work

Advisory Committee on Social Security for Migrant Workers

Advisory Committee on Vocational Training

Commission of Producers and Workers on Industrial Safety and Medicine

Consultative Committee of the European Coal and Steel Community

Economic and Social Committee

European Centre for Vocational Training

European Foundation for the Improvement of Living and Working Conditions

European Social Fund Committee

European Trade Union Confederation and its various committees

General Commission for Safety and Health in the Iron and Steel Industry

Joint Committee on Social Problems of Agricultural Workers

Mines Safety and Health Commission

Standing Committee on Employment

Other

International Labour Conference

OECD—Trade Union Advisory Committee

The Dáil Electoral System as It Stood in 1980

For general elections, the Republic of Ireland is divided into forty-one constituencies. Fifteen of them return five members each; thirteen return four members each; and thirteen return three members each.

All citizen's who have reached the age of 18 and are not placed under a legal disability have the right to vote. To do so, however, they must be registered as a Dáil elector, which means they must fill in a form. Registers are prepared annually by county councils and county borough corporations, and to be registered in a constituency a person must be at least 18, a citizen of Ireland, and ordinarily resident in the constituency.

Similarly, every citizen who has reached the age of 21 and is not placed under a disability or incapacity by Bunreacht na hÉireann or by the law is eligible for membership in the Dáil (or the Seanad). The following are barred by the Constitution or statute from being elected to or sitting in either House: the President of Ireland, the Comptroller and Auditor General (the parliamentary auditor of the public accounts), the judges, any person undergoing a prison sentence of six months or more of "hard labour" or of any period of "penal servitude," people of unsound mind, undischarged bankrupts, persons found guilty of corrupt practices or other election offences, members of the defence forces and of the Garda Síochána (police), civil servants, and members of the boards of state-owned companies or corporations.

A candidate for election is not by law required to reside in the constituency he or she is contesting, though almost all do. Any eligible person may nominate himself or herself or may consent to be nominated by another person, who must be registered in the constituency as a Dáil elector. The nominee must deposit IR£100, which is returned "provided that the number of votes credited to him at any time during the counting of the votes exceeds one-third of the quota." In 1974, 101 out of the 334 candidates (30 per cent) lost their deposits; in 1977, 122 out of 375 (32 per cent).

The conduct of elections in each constituency is in the hands of a returning officer, who is a local government official on whom statutory duties are placed. The returning officer accepts nominations, arranges polling places, election machinery, and personnel, presides over the poll, and conducts the count. Polling takes place on a day fixed by the Minister for the Environment between two dates fixed by statute by reference to the dissolution of the previous Dáil. Polling must take place on the same day in every constituency, except in the case of islands, where, because of the possibility of delay due to the weather, the returning officer may fix a day before the general polling day. Voters cast their ballots in polling places, often national schoolhouses, near their homes; they may vote only in the polling places prescribed for them and of which they are notified by post. Only in the case of members of the defence forces and the Garda Síochána is postal voting permitted.

The ballot paper lists the names of the candidates in alphabetical order. The surname of each candidate and the name of his or her political party, if any, are printed in a large typeface, the candidate's full name, address, and occupation in a small typeface. All or part of this may be in Irish or English.

Candidates do not have complete freedom to designate their own party affiliations. The law provides for the establishment and maintenance of a register of political parties. To be registered, a party must be a genuine political party and must be organized to contest elections. Certain criteria to establish these facts are laid down by law. The Clerk of Dáil Éireann is designated registrar. Appeals from his decisions may be made to a judicial tribunal. The name of a party will not be registered if it is identical with the name of any party already registered or may be confused with one such. Some organizations have in fact been refused registration. A candidate is entitled to have the name of his or her party included on the ballot paper if the party is registered and if he or she has been accepted officially as a party candidate by the party officers. A candidate who is not a party candidate is entitled to have the term "Non-party" inserted after his or her name on the paper.

To vote, the elector enters the polling place, identifies himself or herself, and is checked on the register by the presiding officer and the personation agents appointed by the parties. The elector casts a single transferable vote—a vote that, in the words of the statute, is "capable of being given so as to indicate the voter's preference for the candidates in order" and "capable of being transferred to the next choice when the vote is not required to give a prior choice the necessary quota of votes or when, owing to the deficiency in the number of votes given for a prior choice, that choice is eliminated from the list of candidates." Voting machines are not used. Voters must put the figure 1 opposite the name of their first choice. They may then put the figure 2 opposite the name of their second choice, 3 opposite their third choice, and so on. A ballot paper that does not contain the figure 1 opposite the name of a candidate is invalid. If the voter omits a choice—for example numbering the choices 1, 2, 4, 5—the paper becomes invalid when the gap occurs (in this case after the second choice). Voters are not obliged to indicate more than one choice and may indicate as many choices as they please.

The procedures for counting the votes and ascertaining who has been elected are laid down in a precise and detailed way in the legislation. Ballot papers are not machine readable, and no use is made of computers. All ballot boxes in a constituency are brought to an appointed place. The returning officer and staff inspect them, open them, count the number of ballot papers, and verify the ballot paper account accompanying each box. They then mix all the papers from the various boxes together.

The first stage in the count is to scrutinize all papers and to reject invalid votes. A vote is invalid if it does not bear the official mark, if it does not bear the figure 1 standing alone when only one choice is made (though some returning officers do in practice accept an X), if it contains the figure 1 more than once, or if the voter has written anything on the paper by which he or she may be identified. The valid papers are sorted into "parcels" according to the first preferences recorded for each candidate, and the parcels are counted. Each candidate is credited with the number of votes in his or her parcel, and the total of the valid votes is ascertained. At this point the returning officer is able to calculate and declare the "quota." The quota is the number of votes necessary to secure the election of a candidate. The quota used in Irish elections is the Droop quota, the smallest number of votes that suffices to elect the requisite number of candidates while being just big enough to prevent any more from being elected. It is expressed in this formula:

$$\text{Quota} = \frac{\text{No. of valid votes}}{\text{No. of seats} + 1} + 1$$

Any candidate who obtains a quota or more is now declared elected. In 1977, most quotas were between 7,000 and 8,000.

If the number elected is less than the number of places to be filled, the counters begin to transfer votes from first to later preferences according to detailed rules. First, any "surplus" votes of the candidates declared elected at the first count are transferred to other candidates, the biggest "surplus" first, and so on. A "surplus" is "the number of votes by which the total number of votes credited to a candidate exceeds the quota." To distribute the surplus of an elected candidate, all his or her votes are resorted and arranged in parcels in order of the next available preferences, if any, shown on them—"available preferences" because a preference for a candidate already elected is ignored and account is taken of the next preference. Candidates who receive such preferences have transferred to them a proportionate number of the appropriate parcel. The number is calculated by using this formula:

$$\begin{matrix} \text{No. of Candidate A's} \\ \text{votes to be transferred} \\ \text{to Candidate B} \end{matrix} = \frac{\begin{matrix}\text{No. of Candidate A's} \\ \text{surplus votes}\end{matrix}}{\begin{matrix}\text{No. of votes transferable} \\ \text{from Candidate A to all} \\ \text{other candidates}\end{matrix}} \times \begin{matrix}\text{No. of papers in} \\ \text{Candidate B's parcel} \\ \text{of votes transferable} \\ \text{from Candidate A}\end{matrix}$$

The transfer is made by physically removing voting papers from the top of the elected candidate's parcel and putting them with the other candidates' parcels. Thus, the elected candidate is left with his or her quota, and the other candidates have passed on to them appropriate additions to their parcels of votes. Whenever, in the later stages of the count, a candidate is elected with more than the bare quota, this process is repeated, except that, instead of all the votes credited to the elected candidate throughout the count being resorted, only the last parcel he or she received is taken and resorted.

When, in the course of a count, there are no surpluses to be transferred and seats still remain to be filled, the candidate with the lowest number of votes is declared eliminated from the contest and his or her votes are transferred to the next available preferences shown on the ballot papers. When there is no indication on a ballot paper of the voter's next preference, the vote is declared "non-transferable" and is put on one side and not used. This process of transferring surpluses and the votes of eliminated candidates goes on until either the necessary number of seats is filled or only two candidates are left, neither with a quota. In the latter case, the candidate with the highest number of votes is declared elected "without reaching the quota." In practice, a number of candidates are so elected: in 1977, 31 (21 per cent of the total).

The number of counts necessary to carry out this process can run into double figures in constituencies where there are a lot of candidates. In the 1977 election there were twelve counts in the three-member constituency of Dublin Artane, where the candidates numbered thirteen, and in five other constituencies there were ten counts. In the same election only three counts were required to fill the three seats in South Kerry.

In the case of a by-election, the single seat is filled in the same way. The election is thus by the single transferable vote in a single-member constituency, and the quota needed by a candidate to win a seat is an absolute majority.

State-Sponsored Bodies in 1979

Commercial (25)

Aer Lingus Teo.
Aer Linte Éireann Teo.
Aer Rianta Teo.
Agricultural Credit Corporation Ltd.
Arramara Teo.
B and I Shipping Ltd.
Bord Gais Éireann
Bord na Mona
Ceimici Teo.
Central Bank
Comhlucht Siuicre Éireann
Córas Iompair Éireann
Electricity Supply Board

Foir Teoranta
Gaeltarra Éireann
Industrial Credit Co. Ltd.
Irish Life Assurance Co. Ltd.
Irish Shipping Ltd.
Irish Steel Holdings
Min Fheir Teo.
National Building Agency
National Film Studios of Ireland Ltd.
Nitrigin Éireann Teo.
Radio Telefís Éireann
Voluntary Health Insurance Board

Marketing, Promotional, Developmental, Research (25)

An Bord Iascaigh Mhara
An Chomhairle Oiliúna (AnCo)
An Chomhairle Olla
An Foras Forbartha Teo.
An Foras Talúntais
Bord Fáilte Éireann
Bord na gCapall
Córas Beostoic agus Feola
Córas Tráchtála
Cork District Milk Board
Council for Education, Recruitment,

and Training for the Hotel,
Catering, and Tourism Industries
(CERT)
Dublin District Milk Board
Industrial Development Authority
Inland Fisheries Trust Incorporated
Institute for Industrial Research and
Standards
Irish Goods Council
Irish National Stud Co. Ltd.
Irish Potato Marketing Co. Ltd.

SOURCE: Compiled from written answers to Dáil questions published in *Dáil Debates,* Vol. 311, Cols. 868–86 (February 8, 1979).

Kilkenny Design Workshops
National Agricultural Authority (sub-
   sequently named An Chomhairle
   Oiliúna Talmhaíochta [ACOT])
National Board for Science and
   Technology

Nuclear Energy Board
Pigs and Bacon Commission
Racing Board
Shannon Free Airport Development
   Co. Ltd.

Administrative, Regulatory, Social Service

The Government of Professions (6)
An Bord Altranais
Bord na Radharcmhastoirí
Council for Postgraduate Medical
   and Dental Education
Dental Board
Medical Registration Council
Pharmaceutical Society of Ireland

*The Regulation of Economic
   Activities* (3)
An Bord Pleanála
Bord na gCon
Local Government Staff Negotiations
   Board

The Provision or Administration of Health or Environmental Services (39)

An Chomhairle Leabharlanna
Beaumont Hospital Board
Blood Transfusion Service Board
Board for the Employment of the
   Blind
Comhairle na Nimheanna
Comhairle na nOspidéal
Dublin Dental Hospital Board
Dublin Rheumatism Clinic
Fire Prevention Council
General Medical Services (Payments)
   Board
Health Boards (8)
Health Education Bureau
Hospitals Joint Services Board
Hospitals Trust Board
Irish Water Safety Association

James Connolly Memorial Hospital
   Board
Local Government Computer Services
   Board
Medical Bureau of Road Safety
Medico-Social Research Board
National Committee on Pilot Schemes
   to Combat Poverty
National Drugs Advisory Board
National Health Council
National Rehabilitation Board
National Road Safety Association
National Social Service Council
Regional Hospital Boards (3)
St James's Hospital Board
St Laurence's Hospital Board
St Luke's Hospital
Water Pollution Advisory Council

Others (2)

Agency for Personal Service Overseas   Bord na Gaeilge

The Functions of Major Local Authorities

The functions of county councils, county borough corporations, borough corporations, and urban district councils may be classified into eight programme groups as follows:

1. *Housing and Building:* management and provision of local authority housing; assistance to persons housing themselves or improving their houses; itinerant rehabilitation; enforcement of certain housing standards and controls; etc.

2. *Road Transportation and Safety:* road upkeep and improvement; public lighting; traffic management facilities; safety education and propaganda; registration and taxation of vehicles; licensing of drivers; etc.

3. *Water Supply and Sewerage:* public water supply and sewerage schemes; assistance towards the provision in existing dwellings of a piped water supply and/or sewerage facilities; public conveniences; etc.

4. *Development Incentives and Controls:* physical planning policy; control of new development and building; promotion of industrial and other development; etc.

5. *Environmental Protection:* waste collection and disposal; burial grounds; safety of structures and places; fire protection; pollution control; etc.

6. *Recreation and Amenity:* swimming pools; libraries; parks; open spaces; recreation centres; art galleries; museums; theatres; conservation and improvement of amenities; etc.

7. *Agriculture, Education, Health, and Welfare:* contributions to County Committees of Agriculture, Vocational Education Committees, Joint Drainage Committees; the Unemployment Assistance Fund and the scheme of Supplementary Welfare Allowances; rates waiver schemes; other services of an agricultural, educational, or welfare nature; etc.

8. *Miscellaneous Services:* financial management and rate collection; elections; courthouses; coroners and inquests; consumer protection measures; markets; fairs; abattoirs; gas works; corporate estate; malicious injuries; etc.

SOURCE: *Local Authority Estimates, 1979* (Stationery Office, Dublin, 1979), pp. 8–9.

The functions of town commissioners are of a more limited nature—management of local authority houses, allotments, fairs and markets, etc., other than those of maintenance or repair. The local authority may prohibit the undertaking of any works so brought to their notice, unless the authority is required by law to execute them. The manager must obtain the consent of the elected council to proposals to change the number of permanent staff or the rate of remuneration of officers or employees.

Notes

1. Basic Influences

1. Bunreacht na hÉireann (the Constitution of Ireland), Article 4. The Republic of Ireland Act (1948), Article 2, declares that "the description of the State shall be the 'Republic' of Ireland."
2. J. G. A. Pocock, "The Case of Ireland Truly Stated: Revolutionary Politics in the Context of Increasing Stabilisation" (Unpublished paper, Department of History, Washington University, St. Louis, Mo., 1966).
3. B. Farrell, *The Founding of Dáil Éireann: Parliament and Nation-Building* (Dublin, 1971), p. xv.
4. *Ibid.*, p. 78. See also B. Farrell, "The Legislation of a 'Revolutionary' Assembly: Dáil Decrees, 1919–1922," *Irish Jurist,* 10 n.s. (1975), 112–27.
5. F. Munger, *The Legitimacy of Opposition: The Change of Government in Ireland in 1932* (London, 1975), p. 6.
6. J. Blanchard, *Le droit ecclésiastique contemporain d'Irlande* (Paris, 1958), p. 11.
7. A. W. Orridge, "Explanations of Irish Nationalism: A Review and Some Suggestions," *Journal of the Conflict Research Society,* 1 (1977), 49.
8. See A. S. Cohan, *The Irish Political Elite* (Dublin, 1972).
9. P. A. Pfretzschner and D. M. Borock, "Political Socialisation of the Irish Secondary School Student," in J. Raven *et al., Political Culture in Ireland: The Views of Two Generations* (Dublin, 1976), p. 113; see also Tables 50–55.
10. See Oliver McDonagh, *Ireland: The Union and Its Aftermath* (London, 1977), pp. 73–74.
11. *Ibid.*
12. See E. Rumpf, *Nationalismus und Sozialismus in Irland* (Meisenheim am Glan, 1959).
13. Pfretzschner and Borock, "Political Socialisation of the Irish Secondary School Student," p. 132.
14. E. E. Davis and R. Sinnott, *Attitudes in the Republic of Ireland Relevant to*

the Northern Problem (Economic and Social Research Institute, Dublin, 1979), p. 149. Their findings were strongly challenged by politicians and some of their professional colleagues.

15. Rumpf, *Nationalismus und Sozialismus in Irland,* p. 67.
16. See, for example, D. O'Connell, "The Rural-Urban Dichotomy and Irish Politics" (Paper read to the conference of the Sociological Association of Ireland, April 1979).
17. T. Shanin, "The Peasantry as a Political Factor," *Sociological Review,* 14 (1966), 7.
18. *Ibid.,* pp. 10 and 17.
19. A. J. Humphreys, *New Dubliners: Urbanization and the Irish Family* (London, 1966), p. 12.
20. D. Schmitt, *The Irony of Irish Democracy* (Lexington, 1973), p. 55.
21. *Ibid.*
22. For a brief sketch of changes in rural life, see T. P. Coogan, *The Irish: A Personal View* (London, 1975), ch. 12.
23. P. M. Sacks, *The Donegal Mafia: An Irish Political Machine* (New Haven and London, 1976), p. 28.
24. E. Larkin, "Church, State and Nation in Modern Ireland," *American Historical Review,* 80 (1975), 1267 and 1276.
25. T. Inglis, "How Religious Are Irish University Students?" *Doctrine and Life,* 30 (1978), 404. Detailed results of the survey are given in Marie Nic Ghiolla Phadraig, "Religion in Ireland—Preliminary Analysis," *Social Studies,* 5 (1976), 113–80.
26. Rev. Patrick J. Brophy, Professor of Dogmatic Theology at Carlow Theological Seminary, quoted in *Sunday Independent,* October 29, 1967.
27. Larkin, "Church, State and Nation in Modern Ireland," p. 1244.
28. J. Whyte, *Church and State in Modern Ireland, 1923–1979,* 2nd ed. (London and Dublin, 1980), p. 370.
29. Humphreys, *New Dubliners,* p. 26.
30. Schmitt, *The Irony of Irish Democracy,* p. 44.
31. C. McCarthy, *The Distasteful Challenge* (Dublin, 1968), p. 109.
32. Schmitt, *The Irony of Irish Democracy,* p. 3.
33. Sacks, *The Donegal Mafia,* p. 48.
34. Blanchard, *Le droit ecclésiastique contemporain d'Irlande,* p. 86.
35. Quoted in *Irish Times,* February 6, 1967.

2. The Changing Face (and Mind?) of Ireland

1. See G. Almond and S. Verba, *The Civic Culture* (Princeton, 1963), pp. 31–32.
2. B. Farrell, "The Mass Media and the 1977 Campaign," in *Ireland at the Polls: The Dáil Elections of 1977,* ed. H. R. Penniman (Washington, D.C., 1978), p. 106.
3. *Ibid.*
4. *Ibid.,* p. 154.

5. *Ibid.*, p. 156.
6. *Ibid.*
7. G. FitzGerald, *Towards a New Ireland* (Dublin, 1973), p. viii.
8. T. P. O'Mahony, *The Politics of Dishonour* (Dublin, 1977), p. 113.
9. Reported in *Irish Times*, September 23, 1969.
10. *McGee* v. *The Attorney General*, [1974] I. R. 284.
11. Reported in *Irish Times*, April 11, 1975.
12. Reported in *Irish Times*, January 5, 1977.
13. Micheál MacGréil, *Prejudice and Tolerance in Ireland* (Dublin, 1977), pp. 411 and 412.
14. See *Irish Times*, December 14, 1978.
15. T. Hamilton, "The Upholding of Values in a Pluralist Society," *Studies*, 67 (1978), 7 and 8.
16. O'Mahony, *The Politics of Dishonour*, p. 115.
17. T. Inglis, "How Religious Are Irish University Students?" *Doctrine and Life*, 30 (1978), 419. See also his "Dimensions of Irish Students' Religiosity," *Economic and Social Review*, 11 (1980), 237–55.
18. Interview on Radio Telefís Éireann reported in *Irish Times*, March 31, 1976.
19. See O'Mahony, *The Politics of Dishonour*, pp. 104–5.
20. In J. Whyte, "Introduction," to J. Raven *et al.*, *Political Culture in Ireland: The Views of Two Generations* (Dublin, 1976), pp. 2–3.
21. *Ibid.*, p. 4.
22. *Ibid.*, p. 3.
23. J. Raven and C. T. Whelan, "Irish Adults' Perceptions of Their Civic Institutions and Their Own Role in Relation to Them," *ibid.*, p. 25.
24. P. A. Pfretzschner and D. M. Borock, "Political Socialisation of the Irish Secondary School Student," *ibid.*, pp. 89 and 118.
25. Whyte, "Introduction," p. 2.
26. Raven and Whelan, "Irish Adults' Perceptions of Their Civic Institutions," p. 26.
27. *Ibid.*, p. 29.
28. Ian Hart, "Public Opinion on Civil Servants and the Role and Power of the Individual in the Local Community," *Administration*, 18 (1970), 386.
29. Raven and Whelan, "Irish Adults' Perceptions of Their Civic Institutions," p. 50.
30. MacGréil, *Prejudice and Tolerance in Ireland*, pp. 413–14.
31. *Ibid.*, p. 525.

3. The Framework of Limited Government

1. K. C. Wheare, *Modern Constitutions* (London, 1966), p. 2.
2. J. Temple Lang, *The Common Market and Common Law* (Chicago and London, 1966), p. xi.
3. The definitive text of the Constitution of Dáil Éireann is in Irish and is

published in *Dáil Éireann: Minutes of the Proceedings of the First Parliament of the Republic of Ireland, 1919–21,* p. 13. An English version published in the press on January 22, 1919, is reproduced in D. Macardle, *The Irish Republic,* 4th ed. (Dublin, 1951), pp. 923–24.

4. B. Farrell, *The Founding of Dáil Éireann: Parliament and Nation-Building* (Dublin, 1971), pp. 83 and xviii.

5. B. Farrell, "The Legislation of a 'Revolutionary' Assembly: Dáil Decrees, 1919–1922," *Irish Jurist,* 10 n.s. (1975), 116.

6. P. Béaslai, *Michael Collins and the Making of a New Ireland,* Vol. 1 (London, 1926), p. 259.

7. The Constitution as enacted is published in *The Constitution of the Irish Free State (Saorstát Éireann) Act, No. 1 of 1922 and the Public General Acts Passed by the Oireachtas of Saorstát Éireann During the Year 1922* (Stationery Office, Dublin, 1923).

8. N. Mansergh, *Survey of British Commonwealth Affairs: Problems of External Policy, 1931–39* (London, 1952), p. 289.

9. *Bunreacht na hÉireann* (Government Publications Office, Dublin).

10. *Dáil Debates,* Vol. 68, Col. 430 (June 14, 1937).

11. C. O'Leary, *Irish Elections, 1918–77: Parties, Voters, and Proportional Representation* (Dublin, 1979), p. 29.

12. J. Whyte, *Church and State in Modern Ireland, 1923–1979,* 2nd ed. (London and Dublin, 1980), p. 50.

13. *Ryan v. Attorney General,* [1965] I.R. 294.

14. For a discussion of this point, see B. Chubb, *The Constitution and Constitutional Change in Ireland* (Dublin, 1978), pp. 42–46.

15. De Valera's work on this article and his difficulties with it are described by the Earl of Longford and T. P. O'Neill in *Eamon de Valera* (Dublin, 1970), pp. 295–98.

16. See *Report of the Committee on the Constitution, December 1967,* PR9817 (Dublin, 1967), pars. 135–38. Cardinal Conway's declaration is reported in *Irish Times,* September 23, 1969.

17. R. F. V. Heuston, "Personal Rights Under the Irish Constitution," *Irish Jurist,* 11 n.s. (1976), 211. Heuston cites cases.

18. K. Loewenstein, "Reflections on the Value of Constitutions in Our Revolutionary Age," in *Comparative Politics,* ed. H. Eckstein and D. E. Apter (Glencoe, 1963), p. 154.

19. J. Kelly, *Fundamental Rights in the Irish Law and Constitution,* 2nd ed. (Dublin, 1967), p. 25. For a discussion of judicial interpretation of Bunreacht na hÉireann, see Chubb, *The Constitution and Constitutional Change in Ireland,* ch. 8.

20. *State (Healy) v. Donoghue,* [1967] I.R. 347.

21. [1965] I.R. 294.

22. See Chubb, *The Constitution and Constitutional Change in Ireland,* pp. 62–63. For a survey of the amendments made in 1972, see *ibid.,* ch. 7.

23. C. Cruise O'Brien, *States of Ireland* (St. Albans, 1974), p. 116.

24. Jack Lynch, then Taoiseach, in an interview in *Irish Times,* December 29, 1977.

25. For a more detailed discussion of the impact and implications of Ireland's membership in the Communities, see Chubb, *The Constitution and Constitutional Change in Ireland,* ch. 9.

4. *Political Communications and the Mass Media*

1. J. Whale, *The Politics of the Media* (London, 1977), p. 114.

2. L. Pye, *Communications and Political Development* (Princeton, 1963), p. 26.

3. J. G. Blumler and J. Madge, *Citizenship and Television* (London, 1967), p. 7.

4. B. Farrell, "The Mass Media and the 1977 Campaign," in *Ireland at the Polls: The Dáil Elections of 1977,* ed. H. R. Penniman (Washington, D.C., 1978), p. 99.

5. H. Reynolds, "The De Valera Divine Right to Rule the Irish Press," *Magill,* August 1978, p. 45.

6. D. Helme, "The Press in a TV Age," *Management,* March 1976, p. 35.

7. A. Smith, *The Politics of Information* (London, 1978), p. 158.

8. T. P. Coogan, "Can the Media Survive the Growing Challenge?" *Irish Broadcasting Review,* No. 4 (Spring 1979), 53.

9. Quoted by A. Whitaker in *The Development of the Irish Newspaper Industry* (Dublin, 1978).

10. *Joint National Media Research, 1979–80,* 2 vols., prepared by Irish Marketing Surveys Ltd. and made available to the author by Irish Marketing Surveys Ltd.

11. Figures for 1968 derived from *National Readership Survey in Ireland, 1968,* carried out by the British Market Research Bureau and Social Surveys (Gallup Poll) Ltd.

12. M. Tracey, *The Production of Political Television* (London, 1977), p. 24.

13. A. Smith in *Irish Broadcasting Review,* No. 2 (Summer 1978), 44.

14. Quoted in *Irish Times,* November 1, 1967.

15. Broadcasting Authority (Amendment) Act (1976), s. 13.

16. *Ibid.,* s. 3.

17. *Ibid.*

18. Broadcasting Authority Act (1960), s. 31.

19. Broadcasting Authority (Amendment) Act (1976), s. 16.

20. Farrell, "The Mass Media and the 1977 Campaign," p. 120.

21. Broadcasting Authority (Amendment) Act (1976), s. 3.

22. For the controversy in the 1970s over whether to use a second Irish channel to carry BBC 1 Northern Ireland, see D. Fisher, *Broadcasting in Ireland* (London, 1978), pp. 39–40.

23. Farrell, "The Mass Media and the 1977 Campaign," p. 127.

24. *Ibid.,* p. 106.

25. Fisher, *Broadcasting in Ireland,* p. 29.
26. *Ibid.,* p. 31.
27. A. Smith, ed., *Television and Political Life: Studies in Six European Countries* (London, 1979), pp. 232–33.
28. Farrell, "The Mass Media and the 1977 Campaign," p. 106.
29. Fisher, *Broadcasting in Ireland,* p. 32.
30. Farrell, "The Mass Media and the 1977 Campaign," p. 106.
31. *Dáil Debates,* Vol. 224, Cols. 1045–46 (October 12, 1966).
32. Quoted in *Irish Times,* March 29, 1979.
33. Tracey, *The Production of Political Television,* pp. 230–31.
34. P. McInerney, "How Bad Is Good?" *Irish Broadcasting Review,* No. 3 (Autumn–Winter 1978), 25.
35. "Guidance" for RTE staff in interpreting broadcasting legislation and "Revised Guidelines" in relation to the ministerial direction in force at the time are published in *R.T.E. Handbook* (1978).
36. Smith, *Irish Broadcasting Review,* p. 45.
37. *Report on Censorship in R.T.E.* was published by the Standards Committee of the Dublin Broadcasting Branch of the National Union of Journalists. See Dublin newspapers, July 1, 1977.
38. Smith, *Television and Political Life,* p. 233.
39. Tracey, *The Production of Political Television,* p. 231.
40. Rudolf Klein, *The Observer,* April 7, 1968.

5. Patterns of Participation and Representation

1. See, for example, R. Rose, *Politics in England Today* (London, 1974), pp. 179 and 185; L. W. Milbrath and M. L. Goel, *Political Participation: How and Why Do People Get Involved in Politics?* (Chicago, 1977), pp. 22–23; G. Di Palma, *Apathy and Participation: Mass Politics in Western Societies* (New York, 1970), ch. 1.
2. J. Raven and C. T. Whelan, "Irish Adults' Perceptions of Their Civic Institutions and Their Own Role in Relation to Them," in J. Raven *et al., Political Culture in Ireland: The Views of Two Generations* (Dublin, 1976), pp. 26 and 30.
3. See B. Chubb, *The Government and Politics of Ireland* (Stanford and London, 1970), p. 94.
4. T. Nealon, *Guide to the 21st Dáil and Seanad* (Blackrock, 1977), p. 135, gives a figure of seventy-five full-time politicians in the Dáil.
5. See Institute of Public Administration, *More Local Government: A Programme for Development* (Dublin, 1971), p. 18.
6. See *ibid.,* pp. 16–20.
7. For discussions of the socioeconomic and psychological factors that influence a person's propensity to participate in politics, see H. McClosky, "Political Participation," *International Encyclopedia of the Social Sciences,* Vol. 12 (New York, 1968), pp. 252–65; R. E. Dowse and J. Hughes, *Political Soci-*

ology (London, 1972), pp. 292 ff; and Milbrath and Goel, *Political Participation*.

8. Dowse and Hughes, *Political Sociology,* p. 317.
9. Milbrath and Goel, *Political Participation,* p. 74.
10. Nealon, *Guide to the 21st Dáil and Seanad,* p. 134.
11. A. S. Cohan, *The Irish Political Elite* (Dublin, 1972), p. 57.
12. Hans Daalder, "Parties, Elites and Political Developments in Western Europe," in *Political Parties and Political Development,* ed. J. LaPalombara and M. Weiner (Princeton, 1966), pp. 70–71.

6. Political Parties

1. See T. Garvin, "The Prehistory of a Party System: Irish Secret Societies and Mass Political Mobilisation" (Paper presented at the European Consortium for Political Research Workshop on Nationalism and Territorial Identity, Strathclyde, January 1978).
2. *Ibid.,* p. 24.
3. T. Garvin, "Nationalist Elites, Irish Voters and Irish Political Development: A Comparative Perspective," *Economic and Social Review,* 8 (1977), 169.
4. P. Mair, "Labour and the Irish Party System Revisited: Party Competition in the 1920s," *Economic and Social Review,* 9 (1977), 62.
5. P. A. Pfretzschner and D. M. Borock, "Political Socialisation of the Irish Secondary School Student," in J. Raven *et al., Political Culture in Ireland: The Views of Two Generations* (Dublin, 1976), p. 132.
6. Mair, "Labour and the Irish Party System Revisited," p. 64.
7. S. M. Lipset and S. Rokkan, eds., *Party Systems and Voter Alignments* New York, 1967), p. 52.
8. T. Garvin, "Political Cleavages, Party Politics and Urbanisation in Ireland: The Case of the Periphery-dominated Centre," *European Journal of Political Research,* 2 (1974), 310.
9. G. Sartori, *Parties and Party Systems: A Framework for Analysis,* Vol. 1 (Cambridge, 1976), p. 179.
10. *Ibid.*
11. O. Kirchheimer, "The Transformation of the Western European Party Systems," in *Political Parties and Political Development,* ed. J. LaPalombara and M. Weiner (Princeton, 1966), p. 186.
12. J. Whyte, "Ireland: Politics Without Social Bases," *Comparative Electoral Behavior,* ed. R. Rose (New York and London, 1974), p. 645.
13. See Garvin, "Political Cleavages, Party Politics and Urbanisation in Ireland," pp. 307–28.
14. See M. Gallagher, *Electoral Support for Irish Political Parties, 1927–1973* (London and Beverly Hills, 1973); and T. Garvin, "Nationalist Elites, Irish Voters and the Formation of the Irish Party System: A Comparative Perspective," *Economic and Social Review,* 8 (1977), 161–86.

15. See the party allegiance profiles in *Political Opinion* (June 1977), an unpublished report prepared by Irish Marketing Surveys Ltd.

16. Whyte, "Ireland," pp. 619–51.

17. *Ibid.,* p. 642.

18. Gallagher, *Electoral Support for Irish Political Parties, 1927–1973,* p. 25 and Table 1.

19. Pfretzschner and Borock, "Political Socialisation of the Irish Secondary School Student," p. 107; see also tables 44 and 45.

20. Information from an unpublished survey made available by Economic and Social Research Institute, Dublin.

21. See Irish Marketing Surveys Ltd., *Political Opinion.*

22. See Table 6.3. See also Whyte, "Ireland," pp. 632–33.

23. Irish Marketing Surveys Ltd., *RTE "Survey"—Politics* (Report prepared for Radio Telefís Éireann, September 1976), p. 6.

24. D. Borock and P. A. Pfretzschner, "Irish Students and the Political Parties" (Paper delivered at the Southwestern Political Science Association Meeting in Dallas, Texas, April 1976), pp. 7 ff.

25. *Ibid.,* p. 7; see also Irish Marketing Surveys Ltd., *RTE "Survey"—Politics.*

26. W. Moss, *Political Parties in the Irish Free State* (New York, 1933), p. 99.

27. Seamus Brennan, General Secretary of Fianna Fáil, in a letter to the author.

28. Information supplied by the Irish Congress of Trade Unions.

29. T. Garvin, "Local Party Activists in Dublin: Socialization, Recruitment and Incentives," *British Journal of Political Science,* 6 (1976), 376.

30. R. Rose, *The Problem of Party Government* (Harmondsworth, 1976), p. 144.

31. See P. M. Sacks, *The Donegal Mafia: An Irish Political Machine* (New Haven and London, 1976); and M. Bax, *Harpstrings and Confessions: Machine Style Politics in the Irish Republic* (Assen and Amsterdam, 1976).

32. Cited in Garvin, "Local Party Activists in Dublin," pp. 377–79.

33. *Ibid.,* p. 378.

34. *Irish Times,* July 19, 1978.

35. *Labour '79: The Labour Party Annual Report, 1979* (Dublin, 1979), p. 41.

7. *Pressure Groups*

1. R. Rose, *Politics in England* (London, 1965), p. 130.

2. F. G. Castles, "Towards a Theoretical Analysis of Pressure Politics," *Political Studies,* 14 (1966), 347.

3. For the concept of "segmented pluralism" see V. R. Lorwin, "Segmented Pluralism: Ideological and Political Cohesion in the Smaller European Democracies," *Comparative Politics,* 3 (1971), 141–75.

4. M. Maguire, "Pressure Groups in Ireland," *Administration,* 25 (1977), 349–64.

5. *Ibid.,* p. 349.

6. *Ibid.,* pp. 349–50.

7. *Ibid.,* p. 352.

8. *Social Indicators, 1960–75* (Eurostat, Brussels, 1977), Table 111/3.

9. Brian Trench, "Stormy Weather and Divided Ranks," *Magill,* October 1979, p. 29.

10. Maguire, "Pressure Groups in Ireland," p. 354.

11. G. A. Almond and J. S. Coleman, *The Politics of the Developing Areas* (Princeton, 1960), pp. 34 and 35.

12. T. P. Coogan, *Ireland Since the Rising* (London, 1966), p. 211.

13. J. Blanchard, *The Church in Contemporary Ireland* (Dublin, 1963), pp. 18–19. This book is a translation of Blanchard's *Le droit ecclésiastique contemporain d'Irlande* (Paris, 1958).

14. J. Whyte, "Church, State and Society, 1950–70," in *Ireland, 1945–70,* ed. J. J. Lee (Dublin, 1979), p. 78.

15. See, for example, *Irish Times,* September 5, 1978; *Roscommon Herald,* September 8, 1978; *Irish Medical Times,* March 2, 1979, and September 14, 1979.

16. Coogan, *Ireland Since the Rising,* p. 239.

17. See J. Whyte, *Church and State in Modern Ireland, 1923–1979,* 2nd ed. (Dublin, 1980), chs. 5–8.

18. *Ibid.,* p. 376.   19. *Ibid.,* p. 365.

20. *Ibid.,* p. 374.   21. *Ibid.*

22. *Ibid.,* p. 368.   23. *Irish Times,* December 6, 1979.

24. Whyte, *Church and State in Modern Ireland,* p. 369.

25. T. McNamara, "Pressure Groups and the Public Service," *Administration,* 25 (1977), 368–69.

26. R. A. Dahl, *Preface to Democratic Theory* (Chicago, 1956), p. 146.

27. Trench, "Stormy Weather and Divided Ranks," p. 26.

28. *Ibid.*

29. Quoted in "The IFA: An *Irish Times* Special Report," *Irish Times,* February 10, 1977.

30. *Report of the Commission on Vocational Organization* (Dublin, 1944), par. 474.

31. McNamara, "Pressure Groups and the Public Service," p. 369.

32. T. Smith, *The Politics of the Corporate Economy* (Oxford, 1979), p. xiii.

33. P. Schmitter quoted in J. J. Richardson and A. G. Jordan, *Governing Under Pressure: The Policy Process in a Post-Parliamentary Democracy* (Oxford, 1979), p. 163.

34. In D. Kavanagh and R. Rose, *New Trends in British Politics: Issues for Research* (London and Beverly Hills, 1977), p. 172.

35. G. Ionescu, *Centripetal Politics: Government and the New Centres of Power* (London, 1975), p. 4.

36. Lee, *Ireland, 1945–70,* p. 20.

37. S. Lemass, statement made at the inaugural meeting of the National Industrial Economic Council, October 9, 1963.

38. Lee, *Ireland, 1945–70,* p. 20.
39. C. McCarthy, *Decade of Upheaval: Irish Trade Unions in the Sixties* (Dublin, 1973), p. 197.
40. D. J. McAuley, "New Relations Between Government and Management" (Paper presented at the International Management Seminar on Collective Bargaining and Inflation, OECD, Paris, 1976), p. 20.
41. L. Panitch, "The Development of Corporatism in Liberal Democracies," *Comparative Political Studies,* 10 (1977), 66.
42. S. E. Finer, *Anonymous Empire,* 2nd ed. (London, 1966), p. 113.
43. *Ibid.,* p. 114.

8. Elections

1. Bunreacht na hÉireann provides another possible opportunity for citizen participation. Article 27 provides that "a majority of the members of Seanad Éireann and not less than one-third of the members of Dáil Éireann may by a joint petition . . . request the President to decline to sign and promulgate as a law any Bill to which this Article applies on the ground that the Bill contains a proposal of such national importance that the will of the people thereon ought to be ascertained." The President has it in his discretion to grant such a request and, if he does, he delays signing the bill "until the proposal shall have been approved either (i) by the people at a referendum . . . or (ii) by a resolution of Dáil Éireann passed . . . after a dissolution and reassembly." This provision has never been operated.
2. R. A. Dahl, ed., *Political Oppositions in Western Democracies* (New Haven and London, 1966), pp. 338–41.
3. *Ibid.,* p. 339.
4. D. W. Rae, *The Political Consequences of Electoral Laws* (New Haven and London, 1971), pp. 169 and 167.
5. M. Gallagher, "Disproportionality in a Proportional Representation System: The Irish System," *Political Studies,* 23 (1975), 503.
6. *Ibid.,* p. 507.
7. Rae, *The Political Consequences of Electoral Laws,* p. 111.
8. C. O'Leary, *Irish Elections, 1918–77: Parties, Voters and Proportional Representation* (Dublin, 1979), pp. 112–13.
9. Rae, *The Political Consequences of Electoral Laws,* pp. 42–43.
10. M. Gallagher, "Party Solidarity, Exclusivity and Inter-party Relationships, 1922–1977: The Evidence of Transfers," *Economic and Social Review,* 10 (1978), 1–22. See his Table 1, p. 4, for figures.
11. See J. Knight and N. Baxter-Moore, *Republic of Ireland: The General Elections of 1969 and 1973* (London, 1973), pp. 25 and 45 ff; and T. Nealon, *Ireland: A Parliamentary Directory, 1973–74* (Dublin, 1974), pp. 113–15.
12. M. Gallagher, "Party Solidarity," pp. 9–10.
13. J. Whyte, "Ireland: Politics Without Social Bases," in *Electoral Behavior,*

ed. R. Rose (New York and London, 1974), pp. 629–30. See P. M. Sacks, "Bailiwicks, Locality and Religion: Three Elements in an Irish Dáil Constituency Election," *Economic and Social Review*, 1 (1969–70), 531–54; and P. M. Sacks, *The Donegal Mafia: An Irish Political Machine* (New Haven and London, 1976), ch. 7.

14. Knight and Baxter-Moore, *Republic of Ireland*, p. 23.
15. M. Gallagher, "The Impact of Lower Preference Votes on Irish Parliamentary Elections, 1922–77," *Economic and Social Review*, 11 (1979), 21–23.
16. Rae, *The Political Consequences of Electoral Laws*, p. 111.
17. *Ibid.*, p. 96; Gallagher, "Disproportionality," p. 503.
18. O'Leary has also calculated indexes of proportionality for each election. See *Irish Elections, 1918–1977*, pp. 100–107.
19. See Gallagher, "Disproportionality," pp. 504–8; and O'Leary, *Irish Elections, 1918–77*, pp. 107–11.
20. *Dáil Debates*, Vol. 108, Col. 924 (October 23, 1947); see also *ibid.*, Vol. 51, Col. 1283 (March 23, 1934).
21. Whyte, "Ireland: Politics Without Social Bases," p. 627.
22. *Ibid.;* Gallagher, "Disproportionality," p. 509.
23. Gallagher, *ibid.*, p. 510.
24. For details, see B. Chubb, "Analysis of Results, Dáil General Election 1977," in T. Nealon, *Guide to the 21st Dáil and Seanad* (Blackrock, 1977), pp. 130–31.
25. *Ibid.* See also *RTE "Survey"—Politics* (September 1976) and *Political Opinion* (June 1977), both prepared by Irish Marketing Surveys Ltd. On the electorate generally see R. Sinnott, "The Electorate," in *Ireland at the Polls: The Dáil Elections of 1977*, ed. H. R. Penniman (Washington, D.C., 1978), ch. 3.
26. Sinnott, "The Electorate," p. 58.
27. B. Farrell and M. Manning, "The Election," in *Ireland at the Polls*, p. 157.
28. For a possible example, see Knight and Baxter-Moore, *Republic of Ireland*, p. 45.
29. C. Robson and B. Walsh, "The Importance of Positional Voting Bias in the Irish General Election of 1973," *Political Studies*, 22 (1974), 203.
30. *Dáil Debates*, Vol. 171, Cols. 993–98, quoted in G. FitzGerald, "PR—The Great Debate," *Studies*, 48 (1959), 2.5.
31. Reported in *Irish Times*, August 28, 1968.

9. *The Policy Makers*

1. C. E. Lindblom, *The Policy-Making Process* (Englewood Cliffs, 1968), p. 29.
2. *Ibid.*, p. 30.
3. K. C. Wheare, *Legislatures* (London, 1963), p. 119.
4. W. I. Jenkins, *Policy Analysis: A Political and Organizational Perspective* (London, 1978), p. 15.

5. Lindblom, *The Policy-Making Process,* p. 30.
6. *Seanad Debates,* Vol. 75, Col. 486 (July 11, 1973).
7. P. Self, *Administrative Theories and Politics,* 2nd ed. (London, 1977), p. 153.
8. For an account of the impact of the changes in 1932 and 1948 see R. Fanning, *The Irish Department of Finance, 1922–58* (Dublin, 1978), chs. 6 and 10.
9. N. Johnson, "Who Are the Policy Makers?" *Public Administration,* 43 (1965), 283.
10. *Reform of the Dáil: Fine Gael Policy on Reform of the Dáil, January 1980* (Dublin, 1980), p. 3.
11. *Ibid.*
12. Wheare, *Legislatures,* p. 163.
13. Self, *Administrative Theories and Politics,* p. 68.
14. J. G. March and H. A. Simon, *Organizations* (New York, 1958), pp. 165–66.
15. Lord Windlesham, "Can Public Opinion Influence Government?" *The Listener,* August 22, 1963.
16. J. Temple Lang, *The Common Market and Common Law* (Chicago and London, 1966), p. 10.
17. J. P. Mackintosh, *The Government and Politics of Britain* (London, 1970), p. 123.

10. *The Government and the Dáil*

1. W. Bagehot, *The English Constitution* (London, 1963), pp. 65–66.
2. Joseph Connolly combined a ministerial post with the party leadership of the Seanad from 1932 to 1936. Seán Moylan, a senior minister, was defeated at the 1957 general election, and he was nominated to the Seanad by the Taoiseach to enable him to continue in office.
3. A. S. Cohan, *The Irish Political Elite* (Dublin, 1972), p. 5.
4. A. S. Cohan, "Career Patterns in the Irish Political Elite," *British Journal of Political Science,* 3 (1973), 218–21.
5. Máire Geoghegan-Quinn was a teacher. She succeeded to her father's Dáil seat in 1975 at the age of 25.
6. Cohan, *The Irish Political Elite,* p. 58.
7. There have only been three—Noel Browne, appointed Minister for Health in 1948; Kevin Boland, appointed Minister for Defence in 1957 when his father Gerard Boland was retired from office by his old comrade De Valera (see B. Farrell, *Chairman or Chief? The Role of the Taoiseach in Irish Government* [Dublin, 1971], pp. 38–49); and Martin O'Donoghue, appointed Minister for Economic Planning and Development in 1977. O'Donoghue had been economic adviser in the Department of the Taoiseach from 1970 to 1973.
8. G. Moodie, *The Government of Great Britain* (London, 1964), p. 88.

9. W. Moss, *Political Parties in the Irish Free State* (New York, 1933), p. 29.

10. For Lemass' decisive, even curt, handling of this affair, see Farrell, *Chairman or Chief?* pp. 65–67.

11. It should be noticed, however, that the issue of collective responsibility was not stressed in the Dáil debates on the resignations and dismissals. The reason given by the Taoiseach was the allegations of secret transshipments of arms. *See Dáil Debates,* May 8 and 9, 1970.

12. Including an issue concerning health, for which he was the responsible minister. See, for example, *Irish Medical Times,* May 11, May 18, and June 29, 1979.

13. *Dáil Debates,* Vol. 110, Col. 77 (February 18, 1948).

14. Deputy P. McGilligan, *Dáil Debates,* Vol. 119, Col. 2521 (March 23, 1950).

15. For a discussion of the constitutional implications of Cosgrave's action, see Senator Mary Robinson's article in *Irish Times,* July 24, 1974.

16. In 1936, Senator Connolly resigned on the abolition of the Seanad of which he was the majority leader.

17. A parliamentary secretary was forced to resign in 1946 after a judicial enquiry into the affairs of a firm with which he was connected.

18. See *Dáil Debates,* Vol. 294, Cols. 429–31 (November 23, 1976), and *ibid.,* Vol. 325, Cols. 563–65 (December 9, 1980).

19. *Ibid.,* Vol. 67, Col. 51 (May 11, 1937).

20. The Offences Against the State (Amendment) Bill (1940), the School Attendance Bill (1942), the Electoral Amendment Bill (1961), the Criminal Law (Jurisdiction) Bill (1975), and the Emergency Powers Bill (1976).

21. See, for example, Childers' nomination acceptance speech reported in *Irish Times,* April 7, 1973, and the reaction to his appearance on an American television programme, reported in *Irish Independent,* July 18, 1973.

22. For an account of this incident and the crisis it precipitated, see B. Chubb, *The Constitution and Constitutional Change in Ireland* (Dublin, 1978), pp. 29–31.

23. *Dáil Debates,* Vol. 293, Col. 188 (October 21, 1976).

24. M. Gallagher, "The Presidency of the Republic of Ireland: Implications of the 'Donegan Affair,' " *Parliamentary Affairs,* 30 (1977), 382. This article contains a full discussion of the matter. See also J. Kelly, "The Garden Party Is Over," *Irish Times,* October 25, 1976.

25. M. Ó Muimhneachain, "The Functions of the Department of the Taoiseach," *Administration,* 7 (1959–60), 293.

26. "Lemass on Government," interview quoted in *Léargas,* No. 12 (January–February 1968), 3.

27. B. E. Carter, *The Office of Prime Minister* (London, 1956), p. 200.

28. *Dáil Debates,* Vol. 68, Col. 348 (June 14, 1937).

29. Farrell, *Chairman or Chief?* p. 27.

30. *Irish Press,* February 3, 1969.

11. The Oireachtas

1. K. C. Wheare, *Legislatures* (London, 1963).
2. J. McG. Smyth, *The Houses of the Oireachtas*, 4th ed. (Dublin, 1979), p. 40.
3. A. J. Ward, "Parliamentary Procedures and the Machinery of Government in Ireland," *Irish University Review*, 4 (1974), 229.
4. The Constitution (Election of Members of Seanad Éireann by Institutions of Higher Education) Bill (1979), approved by referendum in July 1979, amended Bunreacht na hÉireann by providing for the election by universities and other institutions of higher education specified by law of up to six senators as prescribed by law.
5. Smyth, *The Houses of the Oireachtas*, p. 52
6. B. Desmond, *The Houses of the Oireachtas: A Plea for Reform, a Memorandum to the Government* (Dublin, 1975), p. 4.
7. *Reform of the Dáil: Fine Gael Policy on Reform of the Dáil, January 1980* (Dublin, 1980), p. 3.
8. T. Troy, "Some Aspects of Parliamentary Questions," *Administration*, 7 (1959), 252.
9. P. Keatinge, *A Place Among the Nations* (Dublin, 1978), pp. 220–21.
10. *Reform of the Dáil*, p. 4.
11. Desmond, *The Houses of the Oireachtas*, p. 11.
12. *Reform of the Dáil*, p. 4.
13. Ward, "Parliamentary Procedures and the Machinery of Government in Ireland," pp. 234–35.
14. *Ibid.*, p. 234.
15. Wheare, *Legislatures*, p. 119.
16. *Reform of the Dáil*, p. 6.
17. *Dáil Debates*, Vol. 229, Col. 1133–34 (July 4, 1967). The consideration of foreign affairs by the Oireachtas is dealt with in P. Keatinge, *The Formulation of Irish Foreign Policy* (Dublin, 1973), ch. 7.
18. T. Garvin, "Continuity and Change in Irish Electoral Politics," *Economic and Social Review*, 3 (1972), 361.
19. *Ibid.*
20. P. M. Sacks, "Bailiwicks, Locality and Religion: Three Elements in an Irish Dáil Constituency Election," *Economic and Social Review*, 1 (1969–70), 531–54.
21. T. Nealon, *Ireland: A Parliamentary Directory, 1973–74* (Dublin, 1974), p. 121.
22. See T. Nealon, *Guide to the 21st Dáil and Seanad* (Brackrock, 1977), p. 134. See also Nealon, *Ireland: A Parliamentary Directory, 1973–74*, p. 119.
23. See T. Garvin, *The Irish Senate* (Dublin, 1969), p. 65.
24. *Ibid.*, p. 63.
25. Garvin, "Continuity and Change in Irish Electoral Politics," p. 360.

26. Léo Hamon, "Members of the French Parliament," *International Social Science Journal*, 13 (1961), 557.

27. Senator M. Hayes, *Seanad Debates*, Vol. 55, Col. 1686 (December 19, 1962).

28. Deputy M. Hilliard, quoted in D. E. Butler, ed., *Elections Abroad* (London, 1959), p. 202.

29. The case was extensively reported in the press. See *Irish Times*, January 12–26, 1961.

30. Information supplied by Deputy John Horgan in answer to a query by the author.

31. *Official Journal of the European Communities*, February 11, 1980 (Office for Official Publications of the European Communities, Luxembourg).

32. Desmond, *The House of the Oireachtas*, p. 6.

33. *O'Donovan* v. *Attorney General*, [1961] I.R. 114 at p. 136.

34. J. D. B. Miller, *Australian Government and Politics*, 2nd ed. (London, 1959), p. 116.

12. The Pattern of Public Administration

1. R. B. McDowell, *The Irish Administration, 1801–1914* (London, 1964), p. 27.

2. Quoted *ibid.*, p. 31.

3. See *ibid.*, p. 27.

4. *Ibid.*, pp. 47–48.

5. T. J. Barrington, "Public Administration, 1927–36," *Administration*, 13 (1965), 316.

6. T. J. Barrington, *The Irish Administrative System* (Dublin, 1980), p. 59.

7. Deputy P. McGilligan, Minister for Industry and Commerce, *Dáil Debates*, Vol. 18, Col. 1907 (March 15, 1927).

8. C. Brady, *Guardians of the Peace* (Dublin, 1974), p. 197.

9. *Ibid.*, p. 2.

10. *Ibid.*, pp. 224–25.

11. See R. Fanning, *The Irish Department of Finance, 1922–58* (Dublin, 1978), ch. 3.

12. *Report of the Public Services Organisation Review Group, 1966–1969* (Dublin, 1969), p. 150 (hereafter cited as Devlin Report).

13. National Industrial Economic Council, *Report on Economic Planning*, Report No. 8 (Dublin, 1965), p. 14.

14. Public Service Advisory Council, *Report for Year Ended 31 October 1976* (Dublin, 1977), par. 3.11.

15. *Devlin Report*, p. 144.

16. *Ibid.*, p. 163.

17. *Ibid.*, p. 145.

18. N. Whelan, "Reform (or Change) in the Irish Public Service, 1969–75,"

Administration, 23 (1975), 110. Dr. Whelan was the deputy secretary of the Department of the Public Service. On the other hand, see D. Kelly, "The Public Service Reform Programme," *Administration,* 27 (1979), 399–407, for a reasoned defence of Devlin by an officer of the same department.

19. G. MacKechnie, "Devlin Revisited," *Administration,* 25 (1977), 14.
20. *Ibid.*
21. *Ibid.,* pp. 16–17.
22. G. MacKechnie, "Progress in Public Service Reform," *Management,* November 1978, p. 36.
23. Public Service Advisory Council, *Report for Year Ended 31 October 1975,* Report No. 2 (Dublin, 1976), p. 23.
24. Quoted in *Irish Times,* January 24, 1980.
25. National Economic and Social Council, *Enterprise in the Public Sector,* Report No. 49 (Dublin, 1979), pp. 16–17, 32.
26. See *ibid.,* pp. 47–67.

13. The Central Administration and the Civil Service

1. *Report of the Public Services Organisation Review Group, 1966–1969* (Dublin, 1969), p. 61 (hereafter cited as Devlin Report).
2. *Report of the Commission of Enquiry into the Civil Service, 1932–35* (Dublin, 1935), par. 8.
3. *Dáil Debates,* Vol. 5, Cols. 917–18 (November 16, 1923).
4. Public Service Advisory Council, *Report for Year Ended 31 October 1979,* Report No. 6 (Dublin, 1980), p. 13.
5. Devlin Report, p. 63. 6. *Ibid.*
7. *Ibid.* 8. *Ibid.,* p. 65.
9. *Ibid.* 10. *Ibid.*
11. T. J. Barrington, "Elaborate Contrivance," *Administration,* 3 (1955), 97.
12. Devlin Report, p. 52.
13. *Ibid.,* p. 141.
14. Public Service Advisory Council, *Report for Year Ended 31 October 1979,* p. 2.
15. Public Service Advisory Council, *Report for Year Ended 31 October 1977,* Report No. 4 (Dublin, 1978), p. 11.
16. T. J. Barrington, *The Irish Administrative System* (Dublin, 1980), p. 31. For a discussion of the role and characteristics of higher civil servants, see P. Pyne, *The Irish Bureaucracy: Its Political Role and the Environmental Factors Influencing This Role* (Londonderry, 1973).
17. Barrington, *The Irish Administrative System,* p. 31.
18. See A. S. Cohan, *The Irish Political Elite* (Dublin, 1972), p. 25.
19. S. Ó Mathuna, "The Christian Brothers and the Civil Service," *Administration,* Vol. 3, Nos. 2–3 (1955), 69–74.
20. *Ibid.,* pp. 71–72.

21. Quoted in M. Viney, "The Christian Brothers," *Irish Times,* November 17, 1967.
22. Ó Mathuna, *The Christian Brothers and the Civil Service,* p. 73.
23. Devlin Report, p. 150.
24. S. Lemass, "The Organization Behind the Economic Programme," *Administration,* 9 (1961), 5.
25. T. K. Whitaker, "The Civil Service and Development," *Administration,* 9 (1961), 84.
26. See Devlin Report, pp. 166–67.
27. Public Service Advisory Council, *Report for Year Ended 31 October 1976,* Report No. 3 (Dublin, 1977), pp. 9–10.
28. Barrington's frustration is evident in *The Irish Administrative System;* see especially ch. 8.
29. *Ibid.,* pp. 209 and 221.

14. State-Sponsored Bodies

1. *Report of the Public Services Organisation Review Group, 1966–1969* (Dublin, 1969), p. 29 (hereafter cited as Devlin Report).
2. *Dáil Debates,* Vol. 293, Col. 1407 (November 10, 1976).
3. Devlin Report, p. 30.
4. *Ibid.,* p. 14.　　　　　5. *Ibid.,* p. 31.
6. G. FitzGerald, *State-Sponsored Bodies,* 2nd ed. (Dublin, 1964), p. 1.
7. S. Lemass, "The Organization Behind the Economic Programme," *Administration,* 9 (1961), 3.
8. *Ibid.,* pp. 5–6.　　　　　9. *Ibid.,* p. 8.
10. Devlin Report, p. 31.　　　　　11. *Ibid.,* pp. 43–44.
12. The journal *Hibernia* monitored appointments for a number of years. See, for example, *Hibernia,* March 1, 1974; September 13, 1974; January 21, 1977; July 27, 1978; and August 2, 1979.
13. See, for example, the evidence about the relationships between Erin Foods Ltd. and the Department of Finance revealed in the report of management consultants published in *Irish Times,* October 14, 1966; the complaints of the general manager of Córas Iompair Éireann in *Management,* May 1967, 29–37; and the first and second reports of Comhairle na nOspidéal (*First Report, September 1972–December 1975,* pp. 1 and 31–32; *Second Report, January 1976–December 1978,* p. 24).
14. FitzGerald, *State-Sponsored Bodies,* pp. 49–50.
15. *Administration,* 6 (1958–59), 298.
16. For an example and for a clear exposition of a minister's view of the role of a civil service member, see *Dáil Debates,* Vol. 308, Cols. 492–93 (October 17, 1978).
17. P. M. McGilligan, Minister for Industry and Commerce, *Dáil Debates,* Vol. 18, Col. 1919 (March 15, 1927).

18. Devlin Report, p. 14.
19. *Seanad Debates,* Vol. 33, Col. 1583 (April 16, 1947).
20. S. Lemass, *Role of the State-Sponsored Bodies* (Dublin, 1959), p. 9.
21. See National Industrial Economic Council, *Report on Economic Planning,* Report No. 8 (Dublin, 1965), p. 14.
22. The Devlin Group's recommendations are in Devlin Report, pp. 157–64.
23. *Ibid.,* p. 157.
24. See *ibid.,* pp. 157–58.
25. *Ibid.,* pp. 163–64.
26. Review Body on Higher Remuneration in the Public Sector, *Second Report to Minister for Finance,* July 11, 1972 (Dublin, 1972), pp. 87–88.
27. See Review Body on Higher Remuneration in the Public Sector, *Report No. 20 to Minister for the Public Service on the Levels of Remuneration Appropriate to Higher Posts in the Public Sector,* October 30, 1979 (Dublin, 1979), chs. 1 and 10.
28. National Economic and Social Council, *Enterprise in the Public Sector,* Report No. 49 (Dublin, 1979), p. 16.
29. *Ibid.,* p. 33.
30. *Ibid.,* p. 29.
31. Lemass, "The Organization Behind the Economic Programme," p. 7.
32. *Ibid.,* p. 11.
33. *Ibid.,* p. 7.
34. *Ibid.,* p. 11.
35. *Dáil Debates,* Vol. 119, Col. 367 (February 21, 1950).
36. *Ibid.,* Vol. 293, Col. 1406 (November 10, 1976).
37. See *ibid.,* Vol. 319, Cols. 169–202 (March 19, 1980).

15. Local Government

1. T. J. Barrington, *The Irish Administrative System* (Dublin, 1980), p. 49. For descriptions and discussions of regional organizations, see *ibid.,* pp. 49–56, and *More Local Government: A Programme for Development,* the report of a study group set up by the Institute of Public Administration (Dublin, 1971), pp. 27–32 and Appendixes 4, 5, and 6.
2. For maps of the regional organization of the various services in 1971, see *More Local Government,* Appendix 5.
3. *Ibid.,* p. 28.
4. *Ibid.*
5. *Local Government Reorganisation,* Government White Paper (Stationery Office, Dublin, 1971), p. 9.
6. Barrington, *The Irish Administrative System,* p. 47.
7. See *ibid.,* p. 46.
8. *Ibid.,* p. 44.
9. L. Paul-Dubois, *L'Irlande contemporaine et la question irlandaise* (Paris, 1907), pp. 183, 186; my translation.

10. J. J. Horgan, "Local Government Developments at Home and Abroad," *Studies*, 15 (1926), p. 535.

11. *First Report of the Department of Local Government and Public Health, 1922–25* (Dublin, 1927), p. 11.

12. Barrington, *The Irish Administrative System*, p. 43.

13. See *Local Government Reorganisation*, chs. 5–7.

14. Barrington, *The Irish Administrative System*, pp. 43–44.

15. *Report of Public Services Organisation Review Group, 1966–1969* (Dublin, 1969), pp. 48–49 (hereafter cited as Devlin Report).

16. *Ibid.*, p. 271.

17. See *Local Authority Estimates, 1979* (Stationery Office, Dublin, 1979), p. 20.

18. C. A. Collins, "Local Political Leadership in England and Ireland," *Administration*, 28 (1980), 79.

19. D. Turpin, "The Local Government Service," *Administration*, Vol. 2, No. 4 (Winter 1954–55), 83.

20. For a brief description and discussion of the allocation of jobs in one rural local authority area, see P. M. Sacks, *The Donegal Mafia: An Irish Political Machine* (New Haven and London, 1976), pp. 83–88.

21. J. L. Garvin, "Local Government and Its Problems," *Administration*, 11 (1963), 226.

22. Devlin Report, p. 48.

23. Barrington, *The Irish Administrative System*, pp. 46–47.

24. *Fourth Report of the Department of Local Government and Public Health, 1928–29* (Dublin, 1930), p. 17.

25. A. W. Bromage, "Irish Councilmen at Work," *Administration*, Vol. 2, No. 1 (Spring 1954), 93.

26. *Ibid.*, p. 94.

27. M. Macken, "City and County Management and Planning Administration," *Léargas*, No. 10 (June–July 1967), 2–3.

28. See, for example, *Local Government Reorganisation* (Stationery Office, Dublin, 1971); *Local Government Reorganisation, Discussion Document* (issued by Department Information Bureau, May 26, 1977); and *Dáil Debates*, Vol. 317, Cols. 10–11 (November 27, 1979).

29. Barrington, *The Irish Administrative System*, p. 40.

16. Controlling the Administration

1. T. J. Barrington, *The Irish Administrative System* (Dublin, 1980), p. 171.

2. *O'Donovan* v. *Attorney General*, [1961] I.R. 114. *Murphy* v. *Attorney General*, unreported, Supreme Court, January 25, 1980.

3. See J. D. B. Mitchell, "The Causes and Effects of the Absence of a System of Public Law in the United Kingdom," *Public Law* (1965), 95–118.

4. *Ibid.*, p. 99.

5. L. Rolland, *Précis de droit administratif*, 11th ed. (Paris, 1957), p. 1; my translation.

6. Mitchell, "The Causes and Effects of the Absence of a System of Public Law in the United Kingdom, p. 101.

7. Lord Shaw of Dunfermline in *Local Government Board* v. *Arlidge,* [1915] A.C. 120 at p. 136, quoted *ibid.*

8. Mitchell, "The Causes and Effects of the Absence of a System of Public Law in the United Kingdom," p. 102.

9. Deputy C. J. Haughey, then Minister for Finance, quoted in *Irish Times,* November 12, 1966.

10. D. P. Murray quoted in Barrington, *The Irish Administrative System,* p. 177. See also B. Chubb, "Going About Persecuting Civil Servants: The Role of the Irish Parliamentary Representative," *Political Studies,* 11 (1963), 272–86.

11. Senator M. Hayes, *Seanad Debates,* Vol. 55, Col. 1687 (December 19, 1962).

12. See "The Peter Berry Papers," *Magill,* June 1980, p. 46. Mr. Berry had been Secretary of the Department of Justice. The memoirs were published after his death.

13. *Dáil Debates,* Vol. 320, Cols. 41–51 (April 29, 1980).

14. *Irish Times,* May 1, 1980.

15. See *Irish Independent,* April 29, 1980.

16. Mr. T. O'Sullivan, interviewed on Radio Telefís Éireann on June 22, 1980, reported in *Irish Times,* June 23, 1980.

17. J. Raven and C. T. Whelan, "Irish Adults' Perceptions of Their Civic Institutions and Their Own Role in Relation to Them," in J. Raven *et al., Political Culture in Ireland: The Views of Two Generations* (Dublin, 1976), pp. 26–32 and especially p. 32.

18. Barrington, *The Irish Administrative System,* p. 172.

19. Bunreacht na hÉireann, Article 35.

20. P. C. Bartholomew, *The Irish Judiciary* (Dublin and Notre Dame, 1971), pp. 33 and 48–49.

21. See European Court of Human Rights, *Airey Case, Judgement* (Strasbourg, October 9, 1979).

22. *Scheme of Civil Legal Aid and Advice,* laid by the Minister for Justice before each house of the Oireachtas in December 1979 (Dublin, 1979), p. 6.

23. For a brief summary, see B. Chubb, *The Constitution and Constitutional Change in Ireland* (Dublin, 1978), p. 78. For a discussion of the major cases, see J. M. Kelly, *The Irish Constitution* (Dublin, 1980), pp. 426–28 and 560–69.

24. E. McWhinney, *Judicial Review in the English-speaking World* (Toronto, 1969), p. 172.

25. J. Kelly, *Fundamental Rights in the Irish Law and Constitution,* 2nd ed. (Dublin, 1967), p. 25.

26. R. F. V. Heuston, "Personal Rights Under the Irish Constitution," *Irish Jurist,* 11 n.s. (1976), 211. For a brief survey of the main developments, see Chubb, *The Constitution and Constitutional Change in Ireland,* pp. 76–79.

27. The most important cases were *Minister for Fisheries* v. *Schonenberg* (88/77), 1978, E.C.R. 473; *Pigs and Bacon Commission* v. *McCarren and Company* Ltd. (177/78) 1979, E.C.R. 2161; and *Commission of the European Communities* v. *Ireland* (55/79) 1980, E.C.R. 481.
28. J. Kelly, "Administrative Discretion," *Irish Jurist*, 1 n.s. (1966), 210.
29. *Report of the All-Party Informal Committee on Administrative Justice* (Dublin, May 1977), p. 13.
30. *Report of Public Services Organisation Review Group, 1966–1969* (Dublin, 1969), pp. 451 and 453.
31. *Report of the All-Party Informal Committee on Administrative Justice*, pp. 17–19.
32. C. J. Haughey, then Minister for Finance, quoted in *Irish Times*, November 12, 1966.
33. Ombudsman Act, 1980 (No. 26), s. 4.
34. Barrington, *The Irish Administrative System*, p. 176.
35. *In re Article 26 of the Constitution and the Emergency Powers Bill, 1976* [1977] I.R. 159. On the Special Criminal Court, see M. T. W. Robinson, *The Special Criminal Court* (Dublin, 1974). For a discussion of emergency and discretionary powers, see Chubb, *The Constitution and Constitutional Change in Ireland*, pp. 42–46.
36. See D. Fisher, *Broadcasting in Ireland* (London, 1978), pp. 31–35.
37. Barrington, *The Irish Administrative System*, pp. 190 and 191. See also the remarks of Deputy Michael Keating, Fine Gael spokesman on human rights and law reform, reprinted in *Irish Times*, December 6, 1981. He spoke of "the often almost paranoid refusal by public agencies to divulge even the minimum information about projects or concerns of public interest."
38. D. Roche, "The Civil Servant and Public Relations," *Administration*, 11 (1963), 108.
39. Raven and Whelan, "Irish Adults' Perceptions of Their Civic Institutions," p. 46. Notice, however, that the perceptions of secondary-school students, as revealed in the enquiries of Pfretzschner and Borock, are not so favourable. See P. A. Pfretzschner and D. M. Borock, "Political Socialisation of the Irish Secondary School Student," in Raven *et al.*, *Political Culture in Ireland*, pp. 145–53.

Conclusion: Sovereignty and Democracy on a Small Island

1. *Membership of the European Communities: Implications for Ireland* (Stationery Office, Dublin, 1970), p. 5.
2. *The Accession of Ireland to the European Communities* (Stationery Office, Dublin, 1972), p. 59.
3. See R. Rose, *The Problem of Party Government* (Harmondsworth, 1976), p. 144.
4. See T. J. Barrington, *The Irish Administrative System* (Dublin, 1980), p. 195.

5. See M. Bax, *Harpstrings and Confessions: Machine Style Politics in the Irish Republic* (Assen and Amsterdam, 1976), especially Part 2; and P. M. Sacks, *The Donegal Mafia: An Irish Political Machine* (New Haven and London, 1976), especially chs. 1–6.

6. T. Lowi, "The Public Philosophy: Interest-Group Liberalism," *American Political Science Review,* 61 (1967), 5–24.

7. R. A. Dahl, "Reflections on Opposition in Western Democracies," *Government and Opposition,* 1 (1965), 19–20.

8. *Report of the Committee on the Constitution, December 1967* (Dublin, 1968), par. 48.

Further Reading

General Works

Ayearst, M. The Republic of Ireland: Its Government and Politics. New York and London, 1970.
Langrod, G., and M. Clifford Vaughan. *L'Irlande,* Tome 16 in the "Comment ils sont gouvernés" series. Paris, 1968.
O'Donnell, J. How Ireland Is Governed. 6th ed. Dublin, 1979.

Works of Reference

Administration Yearbook and Diary. Annual. Institute of Public Administration, Dublin.
Chubb, B., ed. A Source Book of Irish Government. Dublin, 1964.
Statistical Abstract of Ireland. Annual. Stationery Office, Dublin.

Historical Background

Beckett, J. C. The Making of Modern Ireland, 1603–1923. London, 1966.
Coogan, T. P. Ireland Since the Rising. London, 1966.
Cruise O'Brien, C. States of Ireland. St. Albans, 1974.
Cullen, L. M. An Economic History of Ireland Since 1660. London, 1972.
Dudley Edwards, O., ed. Conor Cruise O'Brien Introduces Ireland. London and Dublin, 1969.
Hancock, W. K. Survey of British Commonwealth Affairs. Vol. 1: Problems of Nationality, 1918–1936. London, 1937, chs. 3, 6.
Harkness, D. W. The Restless Dominion: The Irish Free State and the British Commonwealth of Nations, 1921–31. London and Dublin, 1969.
Lee, J. J., ed. Ireland, 1945–70. Dublin, 1979.
The Earl of Longford and T. P. O'Neill. Eamon de Valera. Dublin, 1970.
Lyons, F. S. L. Ireland Since the Famine. 2nd ed. London, 1973.
———. Culture and Anarchy in Ireland, 1890–1939. Oxford, 1979.
Macardle, D. The Irish Republic. 4th ed. Dublin, 1951.

McDowell, R. B. The Irish Administration, 1801–1914. London, 1964.

McManus, F., ed. The Years of the Great Test, 1926–39. Cork, 1967.

Mansergh, N. The Irish Free State: Its Government and Politics. London, 1934.

Meenan, J. The Irish Economy Since 1922. Liverpool, 1970.

Murphy, J. A. Ireland in the Twentieth Century. Dublin, 1975.

Nowlan, K. B., and T. D. Williams, eds. Ireland in the War Years and After, 1939–51. Dublin, 1969.

O'Mahony, T. P. The Politics of Dishonour: Ireland, 1916–1977. Dublin, 1977.

O'Sullivan, D. The Irish Free State and Its Senate. London, 1940.

Rumpf, E., and A. C. Hepburn. Nationalism and Socialism in Twentieth Century Ireland. Liverpool, 1977.

Tierney, M. Modern Ireland, 1850–1950. Dublin, 1972.

Williams, T. D., ed. The Irish Struggle, 1916–1926. London, 1966.

Social Structure and Political Culture

Arensberg, C. M. The Irish Countryman. London, 1937.

Arensberg, C. M., and S. T. Kimball. Family and Community in Ireland. 2nd ed. Cambridge, Mass., 1968.

Connery, D. S. The Irish. London, 1968.

Coogan, T. P. The Irish: A Personal View. London, 1975.

Darby, J. Conflict in Northern Ireland: The Development of a Polarised Community. Dublin and New York, 1976.

Davis, E. E., and R. Sinnott. Attitudes in the Republic of Ireland Relevant to the Northern Problem. Vol. 1: Descriptive Analysis and Some Comparisons with Attitudes in Northern Ireland and Great Britain. E.S.R.I. Paper No. 97. Dublin, 1979.

Farrell, B. The Founding of Dáil Éireann: Parliament and Nation-Building. Dublin, 1971.

Fennell, D., ed. The Changing Face of Catholic Ireland. London, 1968.

Freeman, T. W. Ireland: A General and Regional Geography. 4th ed. London, 1969.

Gray, T. The Irish Answer: An Anatomy of Ireland. London, 1966.

Heslinga, M. W. The Irish Border as a Cultural Divide: A Contribution to the Study of Regionalism in the British Isles. 2nd ed. Assen, 1971.

Humphreys, A. J. New Dubliners: Urbanization and the Irish Family. London, 1966.

MacGréil, M. Prejudice and Tolerance in Ireland. Dublin, 1977.

Moody, T. W. Nationality and the Pursuit of National Independence. Belfast, 1978.

Munger, F. The Legitimacy of Opposition: The Change of Government in Ireland in 1932. London and Beverly Hills, 1975.

O'Faolain, S. The Irish. Rev. ed. Harmondsworth, 1969.

O'Hanlon, T. J. The Irish: Portrait of a People. London, 1975.

"Pluralism in Ireland," articles in Studies, 67 (Spring–Summer 1978), 1–99.

Raven, J., C. T. Whelan, P. A. Pfretzschner, and D. M. Borock. Political Culture in Ireland: The Views of Two Generations. Dublin, 1976.

Rose, R. Governing Without Consensus: An Irish Perspective. London, 1971.

———. Northern Ireland: A Time of Choice. London, 1976.

Schmitt, D. E. The Irony of Irish Democracy: The Impact of Political Culture on Administrative and Democratic Political Development in Ireland. Lexington, 1973.

Sheehy, M. Is Ireland Dying? Culture and the Church in Modern Ireland. London, 1968.

Ussher, A. The Face and Mind of Ireland. London, 1949.

Viney, M. The Five Per Cent: A Survey of Protestants in the Republic. Dublin, 1965.

White, J. Minority Report: The Anatomy of the Southern Irish Protestant. Dublin, 1975.

Constitution

Chubb, B. The Constitution and Constitutional Change in Ireland. Dublin, 1978.

FitzGerald, G. Towards a New Ireland. Dublin and London, 1973.

Kelly, J. M. Fundamental Rights in the Irish Law and Constitution. 2nd ed. Dublin, 1967.

———. The Irish Constitution. Dublin, 1980.

Kohn, L. The Constitution of the Irish Free State. London, 1932.

Report of the Committee on the Constitution, December 1967. Stationery Office, Dublin, 1967.

The Mass Media

Fisher, D. Broadcasting in Ireland. London, 1978.

Kelly, J. "Are Our Broadcasting Structures Out of Date?" Irish Broadcasting Review, No. 2 (Summer 1978), pp. 5–8.

O Briain, C. "Broadcasting Today: A Status Report," Irish Broadcasting Review, No. 1 (Spring 1978), pp. 5–9.

Report of the Broadcasting Review Committee. Stationery Office, Dublin, 1974.

Stapleton, J. Communication Policies in Ireland. UNESCO, Paris, 1974.

Thornley, D. A. "Television and Politics," Administration, 15 (1967), 217–25.

Whitaker, A. The Development of the Irish Newspaper Industry. Dublin, 1978.

Participation, Parties, Pressure Groups, and Elections

Bax, M. Harpstrings and Confessions: Machine Style Politics in the Irish Republic. Assen and Amsterdam, 1976.

Cohan, A. S. The Irish Political Elite. Dublin, 1972.

Gallagher, M. "Disproportionality in a Proportional Representation System: The Irish Experience," *Political Studies,* 23 (1975), 501–13.

———. Electoral Support for Irish Political Parties, 1927–1973. London and Beverly Hills, 1976.

Garvin, T. "Continuity and Change in Irish Electoral Politics," *Economic and Social Review,* 3 (1972), 359–72.

———. "Nationalist Elites, Irish Voters and Irish Political Development: A Comparative Perspective," *Economic and Social Review,* 8 (1977), 161–86.

———. "Political Cleavages, Party Politics and Urbanisation in Ireland: The Case of the Periphery-Dominated Centre," *European Journal of Political Research,* 2 (1974), 307–27.

Lagoni, R. Die Politischen Parteien im Verfassungssystem der Republik Irland. Frankfurt am Main, 1973.

Lawless, M. "The Dáil Electoral System," *Administration,* 5 (1957), 57–74.

Maguire, M. "Pressure Groups in Ireland," *Administration,* 25 (1977), 349–64.

Mair, P., and M. Laver. "Proportionality, PR and STV in Ireland," *Political Studies,* 23 (1975), 491–500.

Manning, M. Irish Political Parties: An Introduction. Dublin, 1972.

Moss, W. Political Parties in the Irish Free State. New York, 1933.

O'Leary, C. Irish Elections, 1918–77: Parties, Voters and Proportional Representation. Dublin, 1979.

Penniman, H. R., ed. Ireland at the Polls: The Dáil Elections of 1977. Washington, D.C., 1978.

Rose, R., ed. Electoral Behavior. London, 1974, ch. 4 by J. Whyte entitled "Ireland: Politics Without Social Bases."

Ross, J. F. S. The Irish Election System: What It Is and How It Works. London, 1959.

Sacks, P. M. The Donegal Mafia: An Irish Political Machine. New Haven and London, 1976.

Whyte, J. Church and State in Modern Ireland, 1923–79. 2nd ed. Dublin, 1980.

Policy Formation, the Government, and the Oireachtas

Chubb, B. Cabinet Government in Ireland. Dublin, 1974.

Chubb, B., and P. Lynch, eds. Economic Development and Planning. Dublin, 1969.

Farrell, B. Chairman or Chief? The Role of Taoiseach in Irish Government. Dublin, 1971.

Garvin, T. The Irish Senate. Dublin, 1969.

Harvey, B. Cosgrave's Coalition: Irish Politics in the 1970s. London, 1978.

Keatinge, P. A Place Among the Nations. Dublin, 1978.

———. The Formulation of Irish Foreign Policy. Dublin, 1973.

McCracken, J. L. Representative Government in Ireland: A Study of Dáil Éireann, 1919–48. London, 1957.

Smyth, J. McG. The Houses of the Oireachtas. 4th ed. Dublin, 1979.

———. The Theory and Practice of the Irish Senate. Dublin, 1972.

Whyte, J. Dáil Deputies: Their Work, Its Difficulties, Possible Remedies. Dublin, 1966.

In addition, *The Economic and Social Review* contains many articles on public policy issues. So, too, do the reports of the National Industrial Economic Council (1963–70) and the reports of the National Economic and Social Council (1973–).

The Administration of Public Services

Barrington, T. J. From Big Government to Local Government. Dublin, 1975.

———. The Irish Administrative System. Dublin, 1980.

Chubb, B. "Going About Persecuting Civil Servants: The Role of the Irish Parliamentary Representative," *Political Studies,* 11 (1963), 272–86.

Collins, J. Local Government. 2nd ed. by D. Roche. Dublin, 1963.

Coyle, P. "Public Enterprise in Ireland," in Public Enterprise in the Community. Centre européen de l'entreprise publique, Brussels, 1975.

Dooney, S. The Irish Civil Service. Dublin, 1976.

Fanning, R. The Irish Department of Finance, 1922–58. Dublin, 1978.

FitzGerald, G. Planning in Ireland. Dublin, 1968.

———. State-Sponsored Bodies. 2nd ed. Dublin, 1963.

Lemass, S. F. The Role of the State-Sponsored Bodies in the Economy. Dublin, 1959.

Local Government Reorganisation: Proposals for the Reorganisation of the Existing Structure of Local Government and for Modifications and Improvements in the Operation of the System (Government White Paper). Stationery Office, Dublin, 1971.

Marshall, A. H. Section on local government in Ireland in *Local Government Administration Abroad,* Vol. 4 of the *Report of the Committee on the Management of Local Government in England and Wales.* Her Majesty's Stationery Office, London, 1967.

Meghen, P. J. Local Government in Ireland. 5th rev. ed. by D. Roche. Dublin, 1975.

More Local Government: A Programme for Development, the report of a study group set up by the Institute of Public Administration. Dublin, 1971.

Pyne, P. The Irish Bureaucracy: Its Political Role and the Environmental Factors Influencing This Role. Londonderry, 1973.

"Regionalism," five articles in *Administration,* 18 (1970), 199–255.

Report of the All-Party Informal Committee [of Dáil Éireann] on Administrative Justice. Dublin, 1977.

Report of the Public Services Organisation Review Group, 1966–69. Dublin, 1969.

In addition, the Institute of Public Administration has published works on various public services and on the organization and working of public authorities. The Institute's journal, *Administration,* contains many articles on these subjects.

The Courts and the Legal System

Beth, L. P. The Development of Judicial Review in Ireland, 1937–1966. Dublin, 1967.

Bartholomew, P. C. The Irish Judiciary. Dublin and Notre Dame, 1971.

Delany, V. T. H. The Administration of Justice in Ireland. 4th rev. ed. by C. Lysaght. Dublin, 1975.

Robinson, M. T. W. The Special Criminal Court. Dublin, 1974.

Index